LEFT OUT

From the late 1930s through the mid-1950s, the Congress of Industrial Organizations (CIO) brought together America's working men and women under a united class banner. Of the thirty-eight CIO unions, eighteen were "left-wing" or "Communist-dominated." Yet the political struggle between the CIO's "Communist-dominated" and right-wing unions was divisive and self-destructive. How did the Communists win, hold, and wield power in the CIO unions? Did they subordinate the needs of workers to those of the Soviet regime? The authors provide testable answers to these questions with historically specific, quantitative analyses of data on the CIO's origins, internal struggles, and political relations. They find that the CIO's Communist-led unions were among the most egalitarian and progressive on class, race, and gender issues, and fought to enlarge the freedom and enhance the human dignity of America's workers.

Judith Stepan-Norris is Professor of Sociology at the University of California, Irvine, and the author (with Maurice Zeitlin) of *Talking Union* (1996).

Maurice Zeitlin is Professor of Sociology at the University of California, Los Angeles. Among his books are *Cuba: An American Tragedy* (with Robert Scheer, 1964), *Revolutionary Politics and the Cuban Working Class* (1967), *The Civil Wars in Chile* (1984), *Landlords and Capitalists* (with Richard E. Ratcliff, 1988), *The Large Corporation and Contemporary Classes* (1989), and *Talking Union* (with Judith Stepan-Norris). this edited volumes include *Latin America: Reform or Revolution?* (with James Petras, 1968), *American Society, Inc.* (1970), and *Classes, Class Conflict, and the State* (1980).

"Finally someone has engaged the old and new anti-Communist scholarship, treated it seriously, and having put its assertions to the test of thorough empirical research, finds this literature to be radically wrong. Finally someone gives the Communists their due without soft pedaling their apologetic stance toward the former Soviet Union. This book will replace Lipset's classic on the ITU as the last word on trade union democracy and its relationship to anti-communism. The book will also put to rest the various functionalist accounts that assume the inevitability of trade union class collaboration."

> – David Wellman, author of *The Union Makes Us Strong: Radical Unionism on the San Francisco Waterfront*

"In their latest *tour de force* Judith Stepan-Norris and Maurice Zeitlin return to the union radicalism of the 1930s and 40s. They peel away the veil of anti-communism and organizational pessimism to reveal an insurgent communism that was no Stalinist front for 'infiltrating' or 'colonizing' unions, but was instead the backbone of popular struggles for decent working conditions, racial equality, women's rights, and participatory democracy. Culling and compiling data from many sources, they discover a broad, grassroots support for the Communist Party and its organizing initiatives. The postwar decline of labor is, then, tied to the aggressive purge of communism on the one side, and the failure of communist unions to forge their own Labor Federation on the other. Going against the shibboleths of our time, Stepan-Norris and Zeitlin question the inevitability of American labor's self-destructive accommodation to corporate capitalism. Courageous, clear and compelling, this is counterfactual history at its best – history returned to the actors who make it."

> – Michael Burawoy, *University of California, Berkeley, and President-Elect of the American Sociological Association*

LEFT OUT
Reds and America's Industrial Unions

JUDITH STEPAN-NORRIS

University of California, Irvine

MAURICE ZEITLIN

University of California, Los Angeles

CAMBRIDGE
UNIVERSITY PRESS

PUBLISHED BY THE PRESS SYNDICATE OF THE UNIVERSITY OF CAMBRIDGE
The Pitt Building, Trumpington Street, Cambridge, United Kingdom

CAMBRIDGE UNIVERSITY PRESS
The Edinburgh Building, Cambridge CB2 2RU, UK
40 West 20th Street, New York, NY 10011-4211, USA
477 Williamstown Road, Port Melbourne, VIC 3207, Australia
Ruiz de Alarcón 13, 28014 Madrid, Spain
Dock House, The Waterfront, Cape Town 8001, South Africa

http://www.cambridge.org

First published 2003

Printed in the United States of America

Typeface Garamond #3 11/12 pt.   *System* LATEX 2ε [TB]

A catalog record for this book is available from the British Library.

Library of Congress Cataloging in Publication Data
Stepan-Norris, Judith, 1957–
Left out : reds and America's industrial unions / Judith Stepan-Norris,
Maurice Zeitlin.
p.   cm.
Includes bibliographical references and index.
ISBN 0-521-79212-6 – ISBN 0-521-79840-X (pbk.)
1. Labor unions and communism – United States – History.   2. Labor union –
United States – Political activity.   3. United States – Politics and government.
I. Zeitlin, Maurice, 1935–   II. Title.
HX544 .S76   2002
331.88′33′097309041–dc21   2001037655

ISBN 0 521 79212 6 hardback
ISBN 0 521 79840 x paperback

for Rick
and
for Marilyn

CONTENTS

FIGURES AND TABLES

Figures

Tables

PREFATORY NOTE

We wrote this book so that it can be understood by every literate reader – of whom we demand only intelligence and memory but no specialized knowledge of statistics. Any reader who wants to skip over the statistical tables and technical notes – which are included for the benefit of specialists – can do so without loss. All of the crucial findings of the quantitative analysis, as well as explanations of occasional technical terms used (e.g., "regression" or "logit"), are presented in plain English.

ACKNOWLEDGMENTS

This is a joint work in the fullest sense; authors are listed alphabetically.

Funding for this project was generously provided by the John Simon Guggenheim Memorial Foundation, the Academic Senates of the University of California, Los Angeles and Irvine, the UCI School of Social Sciences, and by the UCLA Institute of Industrial Relations (IIR). We are grateful to Daniel J. B. Mitchell, then IIR Director, and Archie Kleingartner, then Associate Director, for helpful counsel. We also want to thank Mitchell for discovering and helping us obtain the batch of collective bargaining contracts at California Institute of Technology.

Our research led us to several archives. These include the California Institute of Technology's Industrial Relations Library; the Ford Industrial Archives; the Henry Ford Museum and Greenfield Village Research Center, Dearborn, Michigan; the Southern California Library for Social Studies and Research; the U.S. Department of Labor Library; the Wayne State University Archives of Labor History and Urban Affairs; and the microfilmed papers of the National Association for the Advancement of Colored People (NAACP). We are grateful to these organizations for allowing us the opportunity to utilize their collections.

No research effort is done in isolation, and this one is no exception. We received cogent and incisive comments and suggestions on various parts of this book from the following individuals: Perry Anderson, Stanley Aronowitz, Jeremy Brecher, Michael Burawoy, Sam Cohn, Daniel Cornfield, Lewis Coser, Theodore Draper, William Form, Walter Galenson, the late Supreme Court Justice and United Nations Ambassador Arthur Goldberg, Michael Goldfield, Larry Griffin, Larry Isaac, Howard Kimeldorf, John H. M. Laslett, Harvey Levenstein, Robert K. Merton, Ruth Milkman, George Strauss, Julia Wrigley, and Robert Zieger. Herbert Hill generously provided documents on discrimination in UE's Philco and Allen-Bradley locals and gave provocative comments on drafts of Chapters 8 and 9. Richard Berk, Phillip Bonacich, Wang Feng, and Kazuo Yamaguchi generously advised us about logit and log-linear modeling, and Berk, especially, carefully guided us through their pitfalls. Jody Borrelli coded the constitutional data; Jan Bitar supervised the transcriptions of the oral history interviews; and Cheryl Larsson kindly assisted with the manuscript preparation.

Earlier versions of some parts of this book appeared in the *American Journal of Sociology*, *American Sociological Review*, and *Social Forces*.

Finally, we are each indebted to our families for their patience and support. Stepan-Norris has found a constant source of inspiration in Rick, her husband, who helped with the data collection in the early years of this project. Her sons, Brandon, Devin, and Austin, have enriched her life in immeasurable ways and provided a welcome diversion from the long hours of research and writing that went into this book. Zeitlin thanks his friends and family for tolerating his long days and hard nights ignoring them (except for the newest member of the clan, Devin Alyssa, who always enticed him out to play a little) while he was writing the final draft of this book.

ABBREVIATIONS

ACA	American Communications Association (CIO)
ACTU	Association of Catholic Trade Unionists
ACW	Amalgamated Clothing Workers of America (CIO)
AECT	Architects, Engineers, Chemists and Technicians (CIO)
AFL	American Federation of Labor
AFL-CIO	American Federation of Labor–Congress of Industrial Organizations
ANG	American Newspaper Guild (CIO)
AWU	Auto Workers Union (TUUL)
BBC	Barbers and Beauty Culturists (CIO)
CARD	Committee to Abolish Racial Discrimination
CIO	Congress of Industrial Organizations
CP	Communist Party, USA
CRC	Civil Rights Committee
DPOW	Distributive, Processing and Office Workers (Ind.)
FBI	Federal Bureau of Investigation
FE	United Farm Equipment and Metal Workers of America (CIO)
FEPC	Fair Employment Practice Committee
FTA	Food, Tobacco, Agricultural and Allied Workers (CIO)
GCC	Gas, Coke and Chemical Workers (CIO)
GE	General Electric
GM	General Motors
HUAC	House Un-American Activities Committee (U.S. Congress)
IAM	International Association of Machinists (AFL)
IB	Inland Boatmen's International Union (CIO)
IBEW	International Brotherhood of Electrical Workers (AFL)
IEB	International Executive Board

IFLWU	International Fur and Leather Workers Union (CIO)
ILA	International Longshoremen's Association (AFL)
ILGWU	International Ladies Garment Workers Union (AFL)
ILWU	International Longshoremen's and Warehousemen's Union (CIO)
IPP	Independent Progressive Party
IRC	Industrial Relations Center (at Cal Tech)
ITU	International Typographical Union (AFL)
IUE	International Union of Electrical, Radio and Machine Workers (CIO)
IUMSBW	International Union of Marine and Shipbuilding Workers (CIO)
IWA	International Woodworkers of America (CIO)
IWO	International Workers Order
IWW	Industrial Workers of the World
MCS	Marine Cooks and Stewards (CIO)
MM	International Union of Mine, Mill and Smelter Workers (CIO)
MOWM	March on Washington Movement
MWIU	Metal Workers International Union (TUUL)
NAACP	National Association for the Advancement of Colored People
NAM	National Association of Manufacturers
NLRB	National Labor Relations Board
NMU	National Maritime Union (CIO)
NWLB	National War Labor Board
OLS	ordinary least squares
OWIU	Oil Workers International Union (CIO)
RIA	Research Institute of America
RILU	Red International of Labor Unions
RWDSU	Retail, Wholesale and Department Store Union (CIO)
SACB	Subversive Activities Control Board
SCM	State, County and Municipal Employees (CIO)
SOC	Southern Organizing Campaign
SUM	Save the Union Movement
SWOC	Steel Workers Organizing Committee (CIO)
SWP	Socialist Workers Party
TUEL	Trade Union Educational League
TUUL	Trade Union Unity League
TWOC	Textile Workers Organizing Committee (CIO)
TWU	Transport Workers Union (CIO)

Abbreviations

TWUA	United Textile Workers Union of America (CIO)
UAW	United Automobile Workers (CIO)
UE	United Electrical, Radio and Machine Workers Union (CIO)
UMW	United Mine Workers (AFL, CIO, Independent)
UOPW	United Office and Professional Workers (CIO)
UPW	United Public Workers (CIO)
UPWA	United Packinghouse Workers of America
URW	United Rubber, Cork, Linoleum and Plastic Workers of America (CIO)
USS	United States Steel
USWA	United Steel Workers of America (CIO)
UTSE	United Transport Service Employees (CIO) (Red Caps)
UTW	United Textile Workers (AFL)
WPR	Walter P. Reuther
WSUA	Wayne State University Archives of Labor and Urban Affairs

1

THE CONGRESS OF INDUSTRIAL
ORGANIZATIONS:
LEFT, RIGHT, AND CENTER

Communism is now only a memory, but its specter still haunts America, obscuring and distorting our nation's recent past. The time has come to rid ourselves of its dead hand, and to try, in E. H. Carr's phrase, "to master and understand [the past] as the key to the understanding of the present." We aim, therefore, to dispel certain coercive illusions about the long "Red Decade," from the early 1930s through the late 1940s, when American capitalism was challenged by a "powerful and pervasive radical movement," built and led by Communists.[1] "It is unfortunate, though very natural" – if we may borrow Thomas Carlyle's fitting comment on the French Revolution – "that the history of this period has so generally been written in hysterics. Exaggeration abounds, execration, wailing; and, on the whole, darkness . . . so that the true shape of many things is lost for us."[2]

We have tried in this work, though a series of interrelated systematic empirical analyses, to illuminate the "darkness" that still envelops the reality of Communist-led industrial unionism in America. For, despite the supine and craven obedience of the Communist Party's (CP) officials and functionaries to the dictates of the Soviet regime through every tortuous twist in its line, Communist unionism during the Congress of Industrial Organizations (CIO) era was "the main expression of native, working class radicalism in the United States."[3]

The CIO was the Communists' "greatest source of institutional power," as a book on the "Red Menace" in America avers: "[U]nions with Communist-aligned leaders represented about 1,370,000 unionists, a quarter of the CIO's total. Their power within the labor movement gave Communists entree into mainstream politics." In turn, it "was the shift of the CIO to an aggressively

---

[1] Starobin (1972, p. ix); also see Cochran (1977, pp. 98–99).

[2] Carlyle ([1837] 1906, Part III, Book I, Ch. 1, Vol. 2, p. 131).

[3] Laslett (1981, p. 115).

anti-Communist stance" in the late 1940s that was "one of the decisive events in the victory of anti-Communist liberalism."[4]

The CIO was born in the midst of an upheaval that "ripped the cloak of civilized decorum from society, leaving exposed naked class conflict." The CIO incarnated the spirit of the unparalleled workers' insurgency of the 1930s against the overlordship of capital, and embodied the most "sustained surge of worker organization in American history." The CIO united the country's working men and women, of all creeds, colors, and nationalities, under a single banner – a broad banner, not of "trade" or "craft" but of "class." In sum, the CIO "transformed American politics" by reconfiguring the nexus among the working class, civil society, and the state.[5]

From the beginning, the CIO sought to nourish "a new conception of [workers'] class duty...and class identity."[6] At all levels, CIO organizers and leaders – many of whom were veterans of years of earlier industrial battles, ranging from "run-of-the-mill" unionists to radicals of all stripes, anarcho-syndicalists, "Wobblies," socialists, and Communists – were committed to "industrial unionism" and "class solidarity."[7]

The CIO originated as a "Committee for Industrial Organization" within the American Federation of Labor (AFL), which was then the nation's major labor federation. The CIO was first convened by United Mine Workers (UMW) president John L. Lewis in late October 1935. This was just three weeks after the AFL's annual convention at which Lewis threw his famous punch decking an AFL official who had opposed his appeal – echoing the cause of his radical predecessors – to "organize the unorganized" in the industrial heartland. On November 9, 1935, the CIO established itself formally, and made the fulfillment of Lewis's appeal its primary objective. A year later, the AFL "suspended" the committee's ten international unions on charges of "fomenting insurrection" and "dual unionism." Soon after, other unions also broke with the AFL to join the committee. In November 1938, the CIO, under its new name, Congress of Industrial Organizations, officially became an independent labor organization. By then, the CIO already consisted of forty-one affiliated unions and "CIO organizing committees." The CIO's

---

[4] Haynes (1996, pp. 36, 131). Similarly: "The CPUSA's role in the CIO, helped the party transform itself from a vocal but marginal group into a significant force in American life" (Haynes and Klehr 1998, p. 54).

[5] Bernstein (1970, p. 217); Foner (1976, p. 227); Zieger (1995, p. 1).

[6] CIO (1936).

[7] Kampelman (1957, xiv). On the "Wobblies," a nickname (origins unknown) for the members of the Industrial Workers of the World, see Foner (1965); Dubovsky (1988); Kimeldorf (1998, 1999).

constitution declared that it aimed "to bring about the effective organization of the working men and women of America regardless of race, creed, color
or nationality, and to unite them for common action into labor unions for their
mutual aid and protection."[8]

"The CIO," its organizers declared, "is a people's movement, for security,
for jobs, for civil rights and freedom. It speaks for all the working men and
women of America, Negro and white ... [and] fights to bring the benefits
of industrial organization to all working people ... in the only way it can be
done – by organizing all the workers, excluding none, discriminating against
none." In fact, the CIO organized so many workers so quickly that less than a
decade later, in 1947, its constituent international unions already represented
roughly 80 percent of the country's industrial workers.[9]

At the CIO's first postwar convention in 1946, 39 "international unions"
sent delegates, 38 of which are included in our analysis.[10] Of the 38, according to anti-Communist sources, 18 were "left-wing" or "Communist-
dominated."[11] Communists also had significant pockets of workers' support
in another ten – although these internationals were said by one observer to be

---

[8] Bernstein (1970, pp. 217, 422–23); Zieger (1995, pp. 2, 22–24); Foner (1976, p. 228);
Matles and Higgins (1974, p. 41).

[9] CIO (1942, pp. 4, 10); Bell (1960, p. 91).

[10] CIO unions were referred to as "internationals" or "international unions" because they also
had locals in Canada, as well as in Hawaii and Alaska (which at the time were still U.S. colonial
territories). We use the descriptive terms *international* and *international union* interchangeably
throughout this book. This study includes all but one of the CIO internationals listed in
Peterson's *Handbook of Labor Unions* (1944), namely, the Aluminum Workers of America,
which merged with the Steel Workers. The United Railroad Workers, also represented at
the 1946 convention, lasted only a year (Kampelman 1957, pp. 45, 46, 59n2). The Optical
and Instrument Workers Organizing Committee was also represented at that convention,
but we could find no relevant data on it, and it is not listed in Peterson's *Handbook*. Leo
Troy (1965, pp. A20–A23) lists eleven short-lived CIO unions, founded sometime during
the CIO era, only four of which lasted more than three years, and none of these eleven are
on Kampelman's list of forty. All thirty-six internationals listed in "a special report" on *The
Communists in Labor Relations Today* by the Research Institute of America (RIA) are included
in this study (RIA 1946, pp. 17–18).

[11] Kampelman (1957, pp. 45–47, 121–40, 167–224); also see Avery (1946); Research Institute
of America (1946, pp. 17–18). Of the eighteen internationals in Kampelman's "Communist
camp," seventeen are on the RIA's list of "left-wing unions." The remaining one is classified
by the RIA as "probably left-wing." For other more or less contemporary estimates of
Communist strength in the CIO, see Mills (1948, p. 195); Moore (1945, p. 37); Seidman
(1950). According to Kampelman (1957, p. 249), "Communist-led unions in 1949 claimed
a membership of more than two million." He gives no source for this estimate; it is almost
certainly inflated.

merely "troubled by, but not under the threat of . . . [Communist] control." In short, as Irving Howe and Lewis Coser observe, "The Communists were the best-organized political group within the CIO."[12]

No twentieth-century political struggle among organized workers in America was more chronic and divisive and ultimately self-destructive than the one between the "right" and the "left," especially as it unfolded within the CIO. Nor is any question in the writings about "the CIO era" as contentious, and the conventional answers given as tendentious and less substantiated by systematic evidence, as the legacy of the Communists and their radical allies in the CIO.

The empirical analyses in this book focus on the *consequences* of the political struggles and political relations within the CIO. So we do not attempt to examine the origins or assess the validity, let alone the morality, of the stances taken by the left, right, and center on the political issues – ideological, programmatic, or strategic – that divided and eventually tore the CIO asunder, and all but put an end to radical, class-conscious unionism in America.

Yet these issues and the effects of the struggles over them cannot be dissevered historically. On the eve of the CIO's pseudotrials and purges of its "Communist-dominated" affiliates, the "primary charges" made by "liberal and left wing opponents" against the Communists in the CIO were summed up as follows by a young anti-Communist radical and sociologist named C. Wright Mills:

> First, the turns of these U.S. Stalinists from leftward to rightward, and back again, have been determined not by their judgment of the changing needs of the working people, or by pressures from these people, but by the changing needs of the ruling group in Russia. Second, the ways for maintaining power which are habitual with the U.S. Stalinists include personal defamation and intrigue, carried, if need be, to the point of wrecking a man or a labor union. . . . Third, Communist rule within the U.S. unions they control is dictatorial; although they talk the language of democracy they do not believe or practice democratic principles. . . . Fourth, the existence of Communist factions, and their lack of independence, is a strong deterrent to . . . any genuine leftward tendencies of labor in America.[13]

Implicit in these "left-wing charges," then, is a critical historical question: How did the Communists win and hold power in the CIO's international

---

[12] Mills (1948, p. 195); Howe and Coser (1957, p. 375).
[13] Mills (1948, pp. 199–200).

4

unions, and what did they do with it, once they had it? More specifically, What were their political practices and concrete achievements? Was Communist "rule" in fact "dictatorial"? Did Communist unionists subordinate the "needs" of the workers they represented to the "needs" of the Soviet regime? What impact did they have on the shop-floor conditions and broader life experiences and commitments of the workers they represented, as compared with their rivals on the center and right? We try in the following chapters to provide replicable, testable, and refutable answers to these questions, by means of historically specific quantitative analyses of data on the CIO's origins, internal struggles, and political relations. We also examine the aftermath of the purge and follow the organizing activities of the expelled unions into the 1950s. And finally, we assess the relevance of the purge for subsequent developments in the American labor movement.

The CIO's "Political Camps"

Classifying any union in the United States politically during these years, as none had any formal political affiliations or party alignments, is both inherently problematic and controversial, especially when it comes to designating a union, in the standard Cold War terminology, as "Communist-dominated." "Redbaiting," or charging someone with being a "Red" or "Communist," was a stock political tactic in the United States used by capitalists resisting unionization long before the Bolsheviks took power in Russia.[14] Militant unionists of all political hues suffered at the hands of company security forces and freelance goons during the long hard years preceding the birth of the CIO. But the most brutal terror by employers was reserved for the Communists and their "Red unions." What's more, officials of the AFL and its affiliates also freely denounced their opponents in labor as Communists, and it was long common

---

[14] As John Brophy, a Mine Workers veteran who had become director of the "committee for industrial organization," said in 1938: "Redbaiting, lies, slanders, raising the cry of 'Communist' against militant and progressive union leaders, is nothing more than a smokescreen for the real objective . . . [which] is to kill the CIO, destroy collective bargaining, destroy the unity of the organized and unorganized that the CIO is building through the nation." Walter Reuther, then still a young auto worker organizer, also said: "Now the bosses are raising a scare – the Red Scare. They pay stools to go around whispering that so-and-so, usually a militant union leader, is a Red. What the bosses actually mean, however, is not that he is really a Red. They mean they do not like him because he is a loyal, dependable union man, a fighter who helps his brothers and sisters and is not afraid of the boss. So let us all be careful that we do not play the bosses' game by falling for the Red Scare" (Matles and Higgins 1974, pp. 117–18).

5

for AFL officials and affiliates to prohibit Communists from holding union office or even from being members.

From 1922 through 1929, Reds, socialists, anarchists, syndicalists, and other radicals, including "many of the most active and influential militants in the American trade union movement," were allied under the umbrella of the Trade Union Educational League (TUEL). The league was "a system of informal committees throughout the entire union movement," as its organizing pamphlet *Amalgamation* declared, " . . . working for the closer affiliation and solidification of our existing craft unions until they have developed into industrial unions." The league rejected "dual unionism" and welcomed members of every political party or political tendency; it called upon the AFL to recognize, in the words of the TUEL's founder, William Z. Foster, that "the organization of the unorganized is the supreme problem of our times. Upon its solution depends the welfare if not the actual life of the whole labor movement."[15]

Any TUEL adherent who openly advocated the TUEL's program in an AFL affiliate was subjected to "drastic punitive measures. . . . Many unions insisted on loyalty pledges. TUEL members were removed from union offices and others were expelled."[16] And if the affiliate failed to purge and expel them, the affiliate itself was thrown out of the AFL altogether.

These repressive measures against "Reds" and other radicals by the AFL intensified during the next decade. So, for example, on the eve of the CIO's formation within the AFL, the "president's page" of an AFL affiliate featured this notice in July 1935:

WARNING FROM AMERICAN FEDERATION OF LABOR – WAR ON REDS – The *united front* plan of the Communists for taking over labor leadership in the United States was effectively scotched this week by AFL President [William] Green, when . . . he warned that any local unions affiliated with the [AFL] . . . that admit Communists *will not be recognized* and they may expect to have their *charters withdrawn.*

Such warnings against "Communist maneuvers" and advocacy of a "war on Reds" in AFL publications were frequent during the "turbulent years" of workers' uprisings that brought the CIO to birth.[17]

---

[15] Written by the anarchosyndicalist Jay Fox, *Amalgamation* was distributed to a quarter million unionists during the summer and fall of 1922 (Foner 1991, pp. 127, 133, 152, 158; also see Foner 1994).

[16] Saposs (1959, p. 84).

[17] Kampelman (1957, p. 9); Saposs (1959, p. 84, bold caps and italics in original).

Even in the CIO's halcyon years, when unionists on the left, right, and center were still allies, many CIO internationals prohibited Communists from holding union office or even from being members.[18] So if Communist unionists rarely "avowed" their membership in the party, it was not a mere Leninist reflex, but a matter of both principle ("don't let Red-baiting break you up") and political – even physical – survival. By denying their membership while hewing to the "party line," however, they made their motives suspect and opened themselves up to charges of "masquerading" their true political identities.[19]

Yet everywhere in the CIO (and even in the unions labeled "Communist-controlled") many so-called Communists were not party members and never had been: Some were men (and a few women) who, in pursuing and holding on to union office, willingly accepted Communist support. Conspicuous examples were George Addes, secretary-treasurer of the United Automobile Workers (UAW), until his defeat in 1947 by Emil Mazey, a Reuther ally, and Joe Curran, president of the National Maritime Union (NMU), who split with his Communist allies early in the Cold War. Some were independent radicals or even otherwise "nonpolitical" labor activists who considered Communists legitimate aspirants to working-class leadership and regularly allied with them in intraunion politics. Notable among them were Albert Fitzgerald, president of the United Electrical, Radio and Machine Workers (UE), and Shelton Tappes, recording secretary of the megalocal at the Ford Rouge plant, UAW Local 600.

Even some union leaders who are commonly assumed to have been Communists apparently were not members of the party. The Australian-born "Red 'arry" Bridges of the International Longshoremen's and Warehousemen's Union (ILWU) was "the most celebrated or notorious pro-Communist trade unionist in America," as David Caute puts it, in part because of the government's twenty-one-year long battle to deport him. Bridges was repeatedly hauled before committee investigators and congressional committees, who

---

[18] Saposs (1959, p. 121); Taft (1953, p. 23). For instance, the constitution of the Utility Workers, which was still a CIO Utility Workers Organizing Committee as late as 1944, provided that "[a]ny member accepting membership in the Communist, Fascist, or Nazi party shall be expelled from the Utility Workers' Union of America and is permanently barred from holding office" (Kampelman 1957, pp. 46–47; Peterson 1944, pp. 400–401).

[19] The risks and dangers were magnified, of course, for those who were not only Red but black, especially in the South, where CIO leaders themselves usually "were still far more conservative compared with the rest of the country, particularly on issues related to racial equality. . . . [So] black Communists had to hide their political affiliations, [but] they . . . remained outspoken rebels on racial issues." Nor, except rarely, could black Communists in the South become regular union officers "in the way their comrades had in Northern and Western CIO unions" (Kelley 1990, p. 147).

sought to prove his membership in the party at the time of his arrival and use such proof to denaturalize and deport him. He readily declared to them and anyone else who cared that he was a Marxist and that he sought advice from Communists, worked closely with them, and counted on their support; and the positions he took in his speeches and editorials in the union's newspaper, *The Dispatcher*, dovetailed closely with the party line.[20] But he consistently denied that he was then or ever had been a member of the party himself. And the government, despite two decades of spying and trying, never was able to prove the contrary.[21]

Or take James J. Matles, director of organization of UE, the CIO's "Red fortress." *Fortune* featured him in November 1946 as one of America's ten most outstanding labor leaders: He gives "no impression of big union bossism," said *Fortune*, "– though he is the driving power and a large part of the brains of the CIO's biggest Communist-line union."[22] With UE under intensifying raiding by rival CIO and AFL unions, Matles and UE's other officers found themselves "compelled to take the distasteful but necessary defensive

[20] The government's effort to deport him began at the time of the 1934 San Francisco general strike under his leadership and ended only in July 1955 when a court's ruling against the government finally put an end to this unremitting deportation drive (Caute 1979, pp. 237–38). After the Taft–Hartley Act went into effect, 94 percent of ILWU's rank-and-file longshore and warehouse members voted in a 1948 election that Bridges and other elected ILWU officers should not comply with the requirement to sign on oath a non-Communist affidavit (McWilliams 1999).

[21] Joseph Starobin, a former senior party official and longtime foreign editor of the *Daily Worker*, characterizes Bridges's relationship to the party as follows: "[A]lthough he was close to anarcho-syndicalism and never a Communist, [Bridges] enjoyed intimate ties with the party, *usually on his own terms*" (1972, p. 258n51, emphasis added). Robert Cherny's research in the newly accessible Comintern files in Moscow on the CP of the United States through the late 1930s confirms that Bridges did, in fact, consult often with party officials during the 1930s, but that, as earlier historical studies had already concluded, Bridges "never relinquished control of union policy to the party" (Schwartz 1980, p. 76; also see Kutler 1982, pp. 150–51). Cherny says that nothing in the files he examined contradicts the conclusions of these studies about Bridges as a union leader: After consulting with the party's representatives, Bridges often did not do what the party wanted him to do, and when he went his own way – for instance, in taking the Pacific Coast ILA locals out of the AFL into the CIO – they promptly decided he was right and made his views or actions, or both, into party policy (Cherny 1998, pp. 7, 11–13, 16). Other researchers in Soviet archives dealing with Communist activities in the United States promise that a "subsequent volume in this series will reproduce documents definitely establishing Bridges's membership in the CPUSA" (Haynes, Klehr, and Firsov 1995, p. 104n24), but no such document is referenced or reproduced in the next volume in that series (Klehr, Haynes, and Anderson 1998).

[22] "Ten Who Deliver," p. 147.

measure of qualifying for appearance on the ballot in elections conducted under Taft–Hartley auspices."[23]

[23] UE alone suffered "more than 500" raids by CIO rivals – as well as by the IAM and the Teamsters – between August 1947 when the Taft–Hartley Act (Labor–Management Relations Act) became effective and UE's October 1949 convention. UE's main CIO predators were the UAW under Walter Reuther and, crucially, after USWA officers signed the Taft–Hartley affidavits in July 1949, Murray's own USWA (Zieger 1995, p. 284; Emspak 1972, pp. 317–18; Levenstein 1981, pp. 269–78, 289–93; Matles and Higgins 1974, pp. 192–94, 249). The Taft–Hartley Act's section 9(h), requiring a "non-Communist affidavit" of responsible union officials, triggered the sudden escalation of raiding on the membership of the Communist-led unions. Every union official had to sign on oath an annual affidavit that "he is not a member of the Communist Party nor affiliated with such party, and that he does not believe in, and is not a member of or supports any organization that believes in or teaches, the overthrow of the United States Government by force or by any illegal or unconstitutional means." A union whose officers refused to comply with the non-Communist affidavit could not be certified as a bargaining agent with the NLRB, could not participate in NLRB elections, and could not insert a union-shop clause in any renewed or subsequent contract nor apply for redress to the NLRB against an employer engaged in unfair labor practices. This severely restricted a union's ability to hold on to the workers it already represented and made it harder still, if nearly impossible, to gain bargaining rights in unorganized workplaces (Caute 1979, pp. 354–58). The 1935 Wagner Act (National Labor Relations Act) had set up the National Labor Relations Board (NLRB) with broad powers to oversee union certification and to penalize employers that did not recognize the rights of employees to organize and join unions or failed to "bargain in good faith" with their union representatives. The Taft–Hartley Act all but gutted the Wagner Act's protection of workers' right to "self-organization" and broadened employers' rights. It outlawed "secondary boycotts" and other so-called unfair labor practices by unions; authorized the President to enjoin strikes for a "cooling off period"; allowed employers on their own to call for a bargaining election and to include a company union on the ballot, as a way of trying to "decertify" an existing union, that is, deprive it of representation before the NLRB; and made union-management agreements into legally enforceable contracts in federal courts, allowing either party to sue the other for breach of contract. The act also limited union political contributions. Nearly all the main provisions of the act had been on the legislative agenda of the National Association of Manufacturers (NAM) and other conservative groups since the CIO's founding in 1938, and was virtually written by NAM's staff (Slichter 1951; Tomlins 1985; Lichtenstein 1991; Ginger and Christiano 1987, p. 243). "In effect," as David Montgomery observes, "the only union activity which remained legal under Taft–Hartley was that involved in direct bargaining between a certified 'bargaining agent' and the employers of the workers it represented. Both actions of class solidarity and rank-and-file activity outside of the contractual framework were placed beyond the pale of the law" (1979, p. 166). UAW's Walter Reuther called the act "a vicious piece of fascist legislation" and then used the affidavit as a weapon against his left, proceeding almost immediately after it went into effect to sign the non-Communist affidavit and demand that

9

On November 25, 1953, Matles appeared before Senator Joseph McCarthy's committee, in "executive session."[24] McCarthy opened with his customary

all UAW officers sign one. At the CIO's convention in October 1947, Murray, president of both the CIO and USWA, denounced the affidavit requirement as "a diabolical piece of work, extremely discriminatory in nature and revolting to a citizen who believes in decency and in justice and in freedom." But he and the CIO executive board chose to leave the decision on compliance with the affidavit to its constituent unions – which, of course, exposed the Communist-led unions, without CIO unity and support, to attack (Lichtenstein 1995, p. 266; Starobin 1972, p. 169). (At the AFL's convention that same month, its officials also decided – over the strenuous opposition of John L. Lewis, who condemned the act as "the first ugly, savage thrust of Fascism in America" – to leave compliance up to its affiliates, many of whose officers already had signed it. "On this particular issue," Lewis thundered, "I don't think the Federation has a head. I think its neck has just grown up and haired over." Lewis then promptly, and once again, took the UMW out of the AFL (Ginger and Christiano 1987, p. 246; Cochran 1977, p. 316).) Responding to the CIO executive board's decision to allow the unions to decide for themselves whether to comply, Matles said: "I cannot predict what we are going to do next year. . . . If we are ever found in . . . [the Taft–Hartley lineup] we will be found in the rear . . . squawking like hell; we will tell our people we are there because we were compelled to be, because there were too many ahead of us." Murray, whose USWA was still among the CIO holdouts refusing to sign the affidavit, spoke after Matles, saying: "I'm like Jimmy Matles, I do not know [what we'll do]." By July 1949, He knew: He and other USWA officers signed the affidavit. And at the CIO convention a few months later, he supported the resolution that denounced the union led by his erstwhile friend "Jimmy Matles" as "the Communist Party masquerading as a trade union" and expelled it from the CIO. (Lichtenstein 1995, p. 309, says that Walter Reuther was "the principal author" of this resolution.) This was the same Murray who, three years earlier, at the CIO's 1946 Convention, had lauded the UE's officers for their postwar "organizing activities" and noted that, despite initial losses resulting from the war's end, UE's "membership has steadily grown, and continues to grow." Months earlier, in an address to the UE convention, Murray also had told UE's delegates themselves: "In the course of the past eleven years, you have made many magnificent contributions toward the well-being of the people you represent." He also had thanked the UE for "splendid support" of the CIO, and pointedly declared: "So let no enemy of the CIO glibly get by with the argument that they are ever going to be able to destroy a movement like this. It's not in them. It can't be done" (Matles and Higgins 1974, pp. 170, 164, 158).

[24] Matles actually had to work hard to get called by McCarthy, whose committee had come to Lynn, Massachusetts, to hold "hearings" on "Communist infiltration" of the GE "defense" plant there. McCarthy's "investigation" coincided, not incidentally, with a hard-fought NLRB election, petitioned by UE. UE was campaigning to replace the International Union of Electrical, Radio and Machine Workers Union (IUE) as the local bargaining agent, and seemed likely to win. (IUE, the anti-Communist International chartered in 1949 by the CIO in UE's jurisdiction, had won the local in 1950.) McCarthy was calling GE workers active in the campaign for UE, and GE was then firing them if they proved to be "unfriendly

gambit, "Are you a Communist?" Matles shot back:

> My [Taft–Hartley] affidavit answers that. It shows I signed five non-Communist affidavits in the last five years and these affidavits carry a five-year jail sentence and ten thousand dollar fine if falsely signed. . . . You have had a lot to say about spying and espionage. When you accuse us of that you are lying, Senator McCarthy. You are a liar. You are doing a dirty thing, going to Lynn and Schenectady [where UE locals were on strike and under attack] for the General Electric Company, terrorizing and browbeating decent working people. I tell you to stop it.

By now, as Matles tells it, McCarthy had gotten up and come within a couple of feet of Matles and was "glowering over him." Matles stood up and looked at McCarthy "eyeball to eyeball." McCarthy told Matles to sit down. Matles said he'd sit down when McCarthy did.

> McCarthy (back in his seat):
> I want to set you straight on the purpose of this executive session. We've got a lot on you. We wanted to give you a chance to clear yourself.
> Matles:
> You've got nothing on me, not a damn thing. You've been trying to frame me on my non-communist affidavits for three years, the pair of you, and you haven't done it. Let me ask you a question: Are you a spy? The question is as good coming from me to you as coming from you to me.[25]

witnesses." But McCarthy had not called a single UE international officer. So Matles and his fellow officers decided to demand that McCarthy confront one of them, rather than let the rank and file bear the brunt of McCarthy's committee. They sent McCarthy a telegram demanding that he subpoena Matles. "Nothing happened. No reply." So UE's attorney got on the phone with McCarthy's chief counsel, Roy Cohn, and told him that if the committee didn't issue the subpoena, he would tell the press that McCarthy had refused. "That did the trick" (Matles and Higgins 1974, p. 214).

[25] Matles and Higgins (1974, pp. 215–16). Another "well-known Communist" at the head of a major CIO international was *TWU* president Michael J. Quill, known to one and all as "Red Mike." Yet he repeatedly denied, even under oath, that he had ever been a member of the CP. Quill split with the party in 1948, after fifteen years of being closely identified with it, both because of the party's decision to form the new Progressive Party and run Henry Wallace for President (see note 37 below and Chapter 10) and its opposition to raising the "5 cent fare" in New York City to allow a wage increase for his union's members. After the split, he said in an October 1948 interview: "I was kind of careful where my signature went

Some CIO unionists, of course, proudly identified themselves publicly as members of the CP. One of the most prominent was William Sentner, head of UE's district 8 centered in St. Louis. In a feature article on him in *Fortune*, he's quoted as saying: "When I joined [the party], I told everybody in town." Hiding his party membership, he said, would promote the "lie" of a Communist conspiracy in the CIO. Sentner's public credo was: If it strengthens the working class, then it "paves the way for an ultimate transition to an industrial democracy that is complete – some form of socialism." Sentner's union policies often went against the party line. "The C.P. never ran Bill Sentner," he told *Fortune*. "No one fools around with what I believe ... and I don't fool around with what they believe." When the party's head in St. Louis chastised him for his "deviations," Sentner retorted, "You run your organization and I'll run mine."[26]

So, in general, designating a union as being in the "Communist political camp" unavoidably involves some distortion of political reality. The Research Institute of America (RIA) was explicit that, in designating a union as "left wing," it had not made "any attempt to distinguish here between those unions whose action is caused by the fact that the officers are Communist and those unions whose policy is set by the fact of their having either a majority Communist membership or a small but active group of Communist members." Rather, the RIA labeled a union as "left-wing" if it had espoused causes or taken positions similar to the CP positions as revealed by the *Daily Worker*. "Whether this is coincidence or is the result of Communists within the union can best be determined by one who deals with them over a period of time."[27]

In our quantitative analyses, we simply adopt Max Kampelman's classification of the CIO's international unions into rival "political camps." In 1946, according to his lineup, the "Communist camp" consisted of eighteen

---

in certain matters." Earl Browder, the CP's top official until his expulsion in 1945, supported Quill's claim that he had never been a party member (Freeman 1989, p. 254n96).

[26] "A Yaleman and a Communist," p. 148; Filippelli and McColloch (1995, p. 7); Feurer (1992, pp. 111, 103). In early 1947, the Alsop brothers, in an article pointedly titled, "Will the CIO Shake the Communists Loose?," also focused on Sentner. "Sentner was recently re-elected to the presidency of an important district of the United Electrical Workers after a fierce and bitter contest in which Sentner's communism was the main issue. One of the leaders of the opposition [explained]: ... 'The Communist issue wasn't enough all by itself. Sentner brings home the bacon for the men, and you can't take that away from him.' Sentner," concluded the Alsops," ... retains his position entirely on his merits as a union officer" (Alsop and Alsop 1947, p. 106).

[27] RIA (1946, p. 16). The chairman of the RIA's Board of Editors in 1946 was William J. Casey, who was destined to serve as President Ronald Reagan's CIA Director. In an article under his name, Casey repeats virtually verbatim the major conclusions of the RIA's Report (Casey 1946, pp. 15, 31).

internationals, and the "uncertain and shifting" and the "anti-Communist" camp both had ten internationals.[28] Kampelman's criteria for putting a union in one or another of these so-called camps (like the criteria of the RIA and his other anti-Communist predecessors) were the political issues raised, causes advocated, and positions taken – mainly on foreign policy – by its officers over many years. Kampelman, who had been a "congressional aide . . . who helped orchestrate the [CIO] purge," relies heavily for his "evidence" on the CIO's "indictments" in the 1950 pseudotrials of the international unions' officials accused of being "Communist-controlled."[29]

---

[28] Here is a list of the CIO Internationals included in this study, by "political camp" (Kampelman 1957, pp. 45–46): In the "Communist" camp: International Federation of Architects, Engineers, Chemists and Technicians (AECT) (earlier in 1946, the Office and Professional Workers absorbed the AECT, but both were still represented separately at the CIO's 1946 convention); American Communications Association (ACA); UE; United Farm Equipment and Metal Workers of America (FE); United Federal Workers of America (earlier in 1946, the State, County and Municipal Employees (SCM) and the Federal Workers merged to form the United Public Workers (UPW), but both were represented separately at the CIO's 1946 convention); International Union of Fishermen and Allied Workers of America; Food, Tobacco, Agricultural and Allied Workers (FTA, formerly United Cannery, Agricultural, Packing and Allied Workers of America); International Fur and Leather Workers Union (IFLWU), United Furniture Workers of America; Inland Boatmen's International Union (IB); International Longshoremen's and Warehousemen's Union (ILWU); Marine Cooks and Stewards Association of the Pacific Coast (MCS); International Union of Mine, Mill and Smelter Workers (MM); National Maritime Union (NMU), United Office and Professional Workers of America (UOPW); United Shoe Workers of America; State, County and Municipal Workers (SCM); and Transport Workers Union of America (TWU). In the "uncertain and shifting" camp: United Automobile, Aircraft, Agricultural Implement Workers of America (UAW); Barbers and Beauty Culturists' Union of America (BBC); Amalgamated Clothing Workers of America (ACW); United Gas, Coke, and Chemical Workers of America (GCC); National Marine Engineers Beneficial Association; Oil Workers International Union (OWIU); United Packinghouse Workers of America (UPWA); United Retail, Wholesale, and Department Store Employees of America (RWDSU); United Stone and Allied Products Workers of America; and International Woodworkers of America (IWA). In the "anti-Communist" camp: Federation of Glass, Ceramic, and Silica Sand Workers of America; Industrial Union of Marine and Shipbuilding Workers of America (IUMSBW); American Newspaper Guild (ANG) (Kampelman says that the "New York and Los Angeles chapters [are] controlled by [the] Communist Party" (1957, p. 46)); United Paper Workers of America; International Union of Playthings, Jewelry, and Novelty Workers of America; United Rubber, Cork, Linoleum, and Plastic Workers of America (URW); USWA; United Textile Workers Union of America (TWUA); United Transport Service Employees of America (UTSE); and Utility Workers Union.

[29] Kimeldorf (1988, p. 12) reports Kampelman's role as a congressional aide. A salient illustration of the reigning method of identifying "Communist-controlled unions" was given

So the classification of the CIO's internationals into these rival camps originated as a product of what CIO historian Robert Zieger calls the CIO's "own
dispiriting version of the red scare that dominated American politics in the
early 1950s." The CIO's "trials" were based on elaborate pseudolegal "cases."
The "evidence" against them consisted of the record of dissenting foreign
policy positions taken by their officers, who often "parroted the pro-Soviet
line." Anyone with a dissenting reputation soon came under suspicion. "Many
[anti-Communist radicals who] supported at least the original efforts to dis-
credit the pro-Soviet elements, found themselves ... frozen out of union politics, and often hounded out of the labor movement because of their alleged
'subversiveness.'"[30]

Among the stalwarts of the "Communist camp" were UE, the International
Longshoremen's and Warehousemen's Union (ILWU), and the International
Union of Mine, Mill and Smelter Workers (MM). MM, heir to the legacy of
the radical Western Federation of Miners, was alone among Communist-led
international unions in declaring its socialist objectives.[31] Its constitution's
preamble declared:

> We hold that there is a class struggle in Society, ... that the pro-
> ducer ... is exploited of the wealth which he produces, ... that the class

by Father Charles Owen Rice, who listed some on the back page of his 1948 pamphlet,
How to Decontrol Your Union of Communists. The ILWU's Bridges wrote him, on July 17,
1948, inquiring as to why his international was on Rice's list. Rice replied, on July 22,
1948: "My chief reason for listing the ILWU as a Communist-controlled union is that you
control it" (Levenstein 1981, pp. 241, 251n46). Despite the analytical tendentiousness of
Kampelman's classification, we consider it consistent with our own study of the historical
materials and an adequate empirical reflection of the common understandings of activists
of all kinds during the CIO era – with one crucial exception. Kampelman puts the United
Packinghouse Workers of America (UPWA) in the "uncertain and shifting" camp, although
by his own criteria, it surely belonged in the Communist camp. Three years after the anti-
Communist expulsions and purges, James Carey, CIO secretary-general; John V. Riffe, CIO
executive vice president; and other important CIO leaders were still convinced that UPWA
was "Communist dominated" (Zieger 1995, pp. 346–47, 470), and in 1959, David Saposs
(1959, pp. 202–3) was still writing about the "flagrant case of continuing Communist influence in a strong CIO union ... the United Packinghouse Workers of America." Historian
Edward P. Johanningsmeier simply refers to the UPWA as one of the CIO's internationals
that was "controlled" by "Communists or close Communist sympathizers" (1994, p. 314).
The outstanding prolabor record of the CIO's Communist camp revealed in this study would
have stood out even more, compared with the records of the shifting and anti-Communist
camps, if Kampelman had put the UPWA in the Communist rather than the shifting camp.

[30] Zieger (1986, pp. 131–32).
[31] A cursory review of some of the publications of these unions, however, suggests that socialist
ideas were omnipresent, if usually implicit, in their interpretations of issues.

struggle will continue until the producer is recognized as the sole master of his product . . . [and] that the working class, and it alone, can and must achieve its own emancipation.[32]

In the CIO's "uncertain and shifting" camp were internationals in whose ruling coalition Communists were said to be influential, but not in "control." Among this camp's major unions were the UAW, the Amalgamated Clothing Workers (ACW), and the UPWA. The UAW, the CIO's biggest union, had radicals of many stripes among its rival factions. The UAW's 1947 constitution committed the union to "prepar[ing] the ground for the wider and richer economic democracy which our combined efforts will win for our children," but also affirmed that "[t]he worker does not seek to usurp management's functions . . . through his Union [but] merely asks for his rights."[33]

The unions classified in the anti-Communist camp were led by officials of whom few considered Communists a legitimate presence in the CIO. The United Steel Workers of America (USWA), the Textile Workers Union (TWUA), and the United Rubber Workers (URW) were among the most important unions in the anti-Communist camp. Officials of USWA, this camp's most powerful union, were influenced by Catholic labor doctrines emphasizing social harmony and the achievement of "Christian justice" through class collaboration. They stood, as *Steel Labor* declared, for "the right of private property, for a free choice of action under a system of private competitive capitalism."[34]

We have adopted Kampelman's term "political camp" as a convenient label for the CIO's internal political alignments, and, as we show below, the internationals classified in the rival camps did, in fact, differ sharply in how they conducted themselves. But these "camps" were not in any way internally organized or even minimally cohesive, and this also applies, we want to emphasize, to the so-called Communist camp.

---

[32] Mine, Mill (1947, p. 2).

[33] UAW (1947, pp. 1, 4).

[34] Levenstein (1981, pp. 111–13); *Steel Labor*, July 1945, p. 4, as cited in Emspak (1972, p. 52). Murray, president of both the CIO (after John L. Lewis stepped down) and USWA, was "a devout and profoundly antisecular Catholic" who believed, as he told a "labor priest" (an activist in the Association of Catholic Trade Unionists, or ACTU) in 1946, that "[w]hat the CIO is trying to do is basically in the social encyclicals of the Church" (Rosswurm 1990, p. 130). But, just to confuse matters, although he headed the USWA, the major union in the anti-Communist camp, Murray was universally regarded – until his turnaround, in response to the Communists' support of Henry Wallace's third-party ticket – as the *primus inter pares* between "left" and "right" and a representative of the "center."

At critical junctures during the CIO era, from its inception, Communist unionists (or those who were widely thought to be Communists) could sometimes be found on opposing sides in crucial intraunion struggles. David Milton (who had been an activist in the Communist-led NMU and later a shop steward in UE) insists that "[w]hen one speaks of Communists in the CIO, it is necessary to ask, which Communists?" The strategic vision of working-class political action and radical unionism often set the "left-syndicalists" among them at odds with the party and pitted them against fellow unionists who readily accepted the party's dictates.[35] What a member of the party exclaimed in horror about William Sentner, UE district 8's director in St. Louis, and another UE comrade there, applies to many "Communists in the CIO," whether or not they were really party members: "They are not true Communists. . . . They try to follow their own minds instead of the teachings of the great leaders of the Party." In the course of the CIO's internecine strife and again in the wake of the purge, these differences over the question of what it meant to be "true Communists" would erupt into the open.[36]

The internationals in the "Communist camp" displayed little cohesion and less coordination from 1947 on in the face of the mounting attacks on them that erupted within the CIO, provoked by their dissent from the CIO's endorsement of the Truman Doctrine and Marshall Plan and intensified by their support (although unevenly) of Henry Wallace's Progressive Party presidential campaign during 1948. Nor did they appear to have a common, consistent strategy of self-defense in the year following Wallace's dismal showing, as raiding of their membership and the anti-Communist drive against them escalated.[37] Not even the three major Communist-led unions, UE, MM,

---

[35] Milton (1984, p. 268; 1982, pp. 106–7) refers to UE's Matles and Julius Emspak, ILWU's Harry Bridges, the UAW's Wyndham Mortimer, and NMU's Frederick "Blackie" Myers as "left syndicalists." Among others who fit this bill were Harold Christoffel and Robert Buse, the two top leaders of Milwaukee's UAW Local 248, the biggest union in Wisconsin, at the Allis–Chalmers plant; UE's Sentner; and TWU's Quill.

[36] Starobin (1972); Feurer (1992, p. 103). Or take the comment of UAW Local 248's Buse on how he and fellow officer Christoffel dealt with CP officials in Wisconsin: "Oh sure, I got acquainted with them . . . Almost everybody knew Fred Blair [the party head]. He was around like horseshit. But as far as the Communist Party having anything to say, they didn't have nothing to say as to what we were going to do or did." Both Christoffel and Buse signed a Taft–Hartley Act non-Communist affidavit; Buse was never indicted on charges of perjury; but Christoffel was convicted of falsely signing it and was imprisoned for three years (Meyer 1992, pp. 12, 227).

[37] Wallace had been in FDR's cabinet as Secretary of Agriculture for seven years before becoming his vice-president during FDR's third term. In 1944, FDR dropped him from the ticket and replaced him with Harry S Truman, in whose cabinet Wallace then served

and the ILWU, were agreed on a common stance against the onslaught of their enemies. UE's officers decided on their own to withdraw from the CIO. For months before the CIO's 1949 convention, they had been trying to convince CIO head Philip Murray to put an end to raiding of UE by other CIO affiliates, including Murray's own USWA, and reassert the CIO's principle that every union was free to formulate and follow its own policies on all political issues. As the convention began, Murray again rebuffed their last-minute attempt to obtain such a commitment, and UE withdrew from the CIO's Political Action Committee (PAC), withheld UE's per capita dues, and did not send delegates to the convention. The other internationals in the "Communist camp" (except the United Farm Equipment and Metal Workers of America (FE), which had merged only days earlier with UE) attended the CIO convention. Harry Bridges, who considered the UE's withdrawal ill-advised and vowed that his own union, the ILWU, would stay in the CIO until expelled, wryly pointed out the disarray among the Communist camp's delegates to reporters: "This," he said, "should torpedo all that crap about us forming a bloc and the organization of a third labor movement."[38]

How many workers did the Communist-led international unions represent? One anti-Communist analyst, as we noted earlier, estimates that at the height of the CIO era, 1.37 million CIO unionists were led by Communists. In 1949–50, when the CIO expelled eleven "Communist-dominated" international unions, this resulted, according to Zieger, in "the loss of over one million members."[39] Our own estimates for selected years are based on the precise number of "full-time dues paying members" of each international

---

briefly as Secretary of Commerce. In 1946, Truman fired Wallace for sounding off in favor of cooperation with Stalin and friendship with the Soviet Union at just the point when Truman and the Democrats had begun to see the Soviet Union not only as an ideological enemy but as a serious threat to peace whose expected global expansion had to be contained by the West. Wallace continued to oppose Truman and his new Truman Doctrine from within the Democratic Party, but then shifted and ran for the presidency in 1948 as the candidate of the new Progressive Party, in which Communists were conspicuously active.

[38] Levenstein (1981, pp. 281, 291, 301–2).

[39] Haynes (1996, p. 36); Zieger (1995, p. 374). CIO president Murray stated at the 1950 convention that the expulsion of the eleven Communist-led internationals had "resulted in the removal from membership in our various international unions of a total of about 850,000 to 900,000 members" (Saposs 1959, p. 211). This figure does not, of course, nor does Zieger's figure, include five Communist-led internationals (the Fishermen and Allied Workers, Furniture Workers, NMU, Shoe Workers, and TWU) that remained in the CIO, because their dominant officers turned on their erstwhile Communist allies before the CIO's "trials."

union.[40] At the height of the CIO era in 1948, using these figures, the sixteen internationals in the "Communist camp" had a combined total of 1,123,000, or 26.1 percent of the CIO's total full-time membership of 4,298,000. In 1949, after more than a year of intensified, nearly all-out "raiding" of their membership by other CIO unions as well as some AFL unions, these sixteen Red-led unions still had 963,900 full-time members, or 23.7 percent of the CIO's total. A decade earlier, in 1939, the combined membership of eighteen Communist-led internationals had amounted to 25.5 percent of the CIO's total. The Communist camp's share of the CIO's total membership peaked in the immediate postwar years; in 1946, the eighteen original Communist-led internationals (newly reduced to sixteen by mergers) comprised 27.4 percent of the CIO's total full-time membership (Table 1.1). None of these figures takes into account the members of the many Communist-led locals in the internationals in the "uncertain and shifting" camp, and even a few in the anti-Communist camp.

Theoretical Parenthesis

Put in theoretical terms, our analyses address the problem of the "relative autonomy of politics." By this, we mean not merely the possible autonomy (or originative potential) of the "state," but rather, comprehensively, the *relatively independent effects of political phenomena in the shaping and transformation of basic social relations* – especially class and intraclass relations. The effects are "relative" in the sense that they are both limited and made possible by specific "objective conditions" or "structures." But they are never pregiven.[41]

---

[40] The membership figures of each international are given in Troy (1965, table A2); they are based on a union's "per capita receipts," from "full-time dues paying members" and, consequently, considerably understate actual union membership. Part-time dues-paying members, members who were on strike, laid off, and unemployed or in good standing but holding withdrawal cards at the time of the membership survey were not counted. A comparison of Troy's union membership estimates and the estimates of the Bureau of Labor Statistics during the CIO era (1935–55) reveals that Troy's estimates are consistently much lower than the BLS's. In 1954, for example, Troy's estimate was only 71 percent of the BLS's for the MM, 70 percent of the BLS's for the ACW, and 83 percent of the BLS's for the USWA (1965, pp. 17, 19).

[41] As in the "structuralist" theory of Nicos Poulantzas (1973, esp. pp. 85–98), in which a political "practice" in this theory is the expression of its "specific place and function . . . which are its objective" (1973, p. 42). So the consequences of a "practice" are known a priori, even though the theory rhetorically affirms the "relative autonomy of the political." In this remarkable Marxian variant of functionalism, whose progenitor is Louis Althusser, history

Table 1.1. *The "Communist camp" in the CIO: The combined membership of the Communist-led international unions and their share of the total CIO membership in selected years*[a]

Year	Membership of Red-led internationals and percentage of total CIO membership	Number of Red-led internationals	Total CIO membership	Total number of CIO internationals
1939	322,900	18	1,267.700[b]	34
	25.47%			
1946	1,015,900	16	3,709,700	36[c]
	27.38%			
1948	1,123,000	16	4,298,000	36
	26.13%			
1949	963,900	16	4,071,100	36
	23.685%			

[a] The membership figures for all international unions, 1939–49, are from Troy (1965, Table A2), and refer only to "full time dues paying members"; part-time members, laid off or unemployed members, and members in good standing (holding withdrawal cards) are not counted.

[b] Because the United Mine Workers seceded from the CIO in 1942, it is not included here, so that the membership figures in all years are comparable.

[c] Thirty-eight internationals were represented at the 1946 convention; although two of the 38 had merged earlier in the year, they still sent their own representatives to that convention.

Rather, men and women are "both the authors and actors of their own drama." They make their own history, although not just as they please nor under circumstances they choose, but "under circumstances directly found, given and transmitted from the past." And these "circumstances," Marx forgot to add, have also been shaped by the effects both of earlier political struggles by these same men and women and the attempts of previous generations to be the authors and actors of their own history.[42]

The critical question – which can be answered only by men and women through their own practical activity – is, What is within the realm of

"proceeds," as Adam Przeworski (1977, p. 368) remarks, "from relations to effects without any human agency."

[42] Marx (1976, vol. 6, p. 170; 1963, p. 15).

possibility? What are the real options available – what alternatives do they have? And what kind of concrete political struggles, against whom, will they have to wage, if they choose one option rather than another?[43] In turn, and as a result, what sort of political relations will they end up creating, whether wittingly or not, which react back upon and now alter the realm of possibility? In sum, as these questions imply, we argue that "contention has its own historical memory," or, more prosaically, that political struggles shape the political terrain on which subsequent struggles are waged.[44]

The guiding thread of the following analyses, then, is what we call the relative autonomy of "*the intraclass struggle within the class struggle.*" As Max Weber remarks, no "class is infallible about its interests."[45] Nor does any class simply organize itself. Rather, it is organized by the contending parties and factions of a class, in and through struggles to give their own, often opposing, "answers" to the following, recurrent questions: What are the "real" interests of the class? What has to be done to protect and advance them? What is the class struggle "really" about? Indeed, is there a *class* struggle?

The "self-organization" of any class, then, is inherently an intraclass struggle over who – with what consciousness, commitments, and alliances – should organize and lead it, in accord with what strategy, and aiming at what objectives.[46] All this enters in turn into determining the way the class, to the extent that it is organized or cohesive, engages in the class struggle.[47]

Reds and America's Industrial Unions

This is the general theoretical argument whose empirical implications, stated as sociohistorical questions about the comparative achievements of the internationals in the CIO's rival political camps, we analyze in the following chapters.

---

[43] cf. Przeworski (1977, p. 377).   [44] Tilly (1986, p. 6).   [45] Weber (1968, p. 930).

[46] As Frederick Engels remarked about a split in the French left, in a letter to German Socialist leader August Bebel, on October 28, 1882: "*The development of the working-class is everywhere the result of internal struggles*, and France, where a workers' party is organized for the first time, is no exception" (in Lozovsky 1935, p. 85, emphasis in original).

[47] We do not argue, however, that intraclass struggles among workers and efforts to organize them are equivalent to, or have the same sorts of determinants and effects as, those among capitalists. For, unlike workers, capitalists do not have to be organized to act as a class. Capitalists as individuals, outside of any "peak association," have the power that capital-ownership gives them over individual workers and the "right," in exchange for wages, to dispose of their labor time. But workers can organize themselves as a class only if they are already organized by capitalists, as employees of capitalist enterprises (see Brady 1943; Offe and Wiesenthal 1980, pp. 70–72). For an analysis of intraclass struggles in another time and another place, in the making of capitalism and democracy, see Zeitlin (1984).

What, in particular, did Communists and their radical allies in the CIO win (or lose) for workers during that ephemeral but decisive historical moment when they stood at the helm of so many industrial unions?

Is it true, as the Supreme Court of the United States ruled in 1950, in response to a challenge to the constitutionality of the Taft–Hartley Act's non-Communist affidavit, "that Congress had a great mass of material before it which tended to show that Communists . . . had infiltrated labor organizations not to support and further trade union objectives . . . but to make them a device by which commerce and industry might be disrupted when the dictates of political policy require such action"? Was the claim by the House Un-American Activities Committee (HUAC) in 1954 correct, that "Many results beneficial to the workers resulted from expulsion of the Communist-dominated unions from the CIO"?

Walter Reuther, UAW president, charged at the CIO's epochal 1949 convention that "the record is clear" that the CIO's Communists were "not a trade union group" and had "failed to carry out the kind of a program geared to the needs of American workers." Was he right? Or, rather, was Monsignor Charles Owen Rice, who as a young priest had been one of the Communist unionists' most vociferous and effective enemies, right? Nearly twenty years after the CIO purge, Rice acknowledged "that the Communists . . . [built] some of the best unions in the United States."[48]

Such questions, to put it mildly, still arouse passions nearly half a century after the CIO's return to the bosom of its AFL progenitor, and a decade after the Soviet Union's collapse and dissolution.[49] The answers we give and the evidence

---

[48] Caute (1979, p. 356); Saposs (1959, pp. 171, 207); Rice (oral history memoir, October 18, 1967, Pennsylvania State University), as cited in Prickett (1975, p. 329).

[49] Witness, for instance, the debate between Theodore Draper (1985a–d) and several "new historians" of American Communism whom he charges with "political partisanship" and "historical bias." See also the spate of neo–Cold War books published since the disappearance of the Soviet nemesis and the opening of the Kremlin's secret files. As a headline on a *New York Times Magazine* story says, "the battle over moles and spies and Redbaiting rages on – even without Communism" (Weisberg 1999). The common theme of this new/old genre of post-Soviet books, as the author of one of them sounds it, is the following: American Communists, wherever they were found – "among immigrant groups, in the civil rights movement, on college campuses, and in Hollywood," as well as in the labor movement – were collectively bent on "the destruction of American society and its replacement by a state modeled on Soviet Russia" and constituted "the internal ally of America's most dangerous foreign enemy" (Haynes 1996, pp. 198–99). With all the digging by historians such as John Earl Haynes and Harvey Klehr (Haynes, Klehr, and Firsov 1995; Haynes, Klehr, and Anderson 1988) and others doing the same sort of research in the Kremlin's files, and all the long lists they've compiled of alleged moles and spies, they have not found a single

we present throughout this work contradict and confute the chief charges made against the CIO's Communists by assorted activists, pundits, politicians, and Cold War (and neo–Cold War) scholars across a broad band of political colors. But our answers concur with and lend further evidentiary support for the main conclusions of the recent outpouring of serious, probing, and revelatory historical works on American labor and Communism. These works, as Zieger remarks, have "helped sweep aside much of the anti-Communist hysterics that used to pass for scholarship on the general subject."[50] Their interpretive thrust is that Communist unionists, men and women of radical conviction and egalitarian passion, were willing, able, and determined, in practice, to put workers' interests ahead of the zig-zags and momentary "party line" of the CP's officialdom. The unions created and sustained by Communists and their allies, as Zieger concludes in his probing and comprehensive history of the CIO, "were among the most egalitarian, the most honest and well-administered, the most racially progressive, and the most class conscious."

This is the considered judgment of "even some of the pro-Soviet left's fiercest critics" – among whom Zieger counts himself. For, in his view, despite the achievements of the "Communist-influenced unions," their purge or expulsion from the CIO was necessary to cut out "the practical and moral incubus" of Stalinism. "To be a Communist, or even to be a consistent ally and defender of Communists, was to link yourself to Stalinism. It meant that you either denied Soviet crimes that killed and imprisoned millions or you justified them."[51]

This was the tragedy – and historical dialectic – of the CIO's Communists. Their identification with the Soviet tyranny bequeathed them "a legacy both ambiguous and shady." Even at the height of Stalin's terror, however, most of them were ignorant of it (sometimes willfully).[52] How little they really knew or understood of the nightmarish side of Soviet reality is shown by the way those who had stayed in the CP, "even after the full weight of public and private hostility came down on [it] . . . in the early 1950s," responded to Khrushchev's "secret" speech in 1956. Khrushchev's confirmation of Stalin's record of murderous rule "nearly wiped out the party," for it "so shattered Communist morale," as John Earl Haynes notes, "that the CPUSA lost three-quarters of its members in [the next] two years."[53]

Communist who was active in the leadership of a CIO union, at any level, whom they could even insinuate to have acted in any way to endanger "national security."

[50] Zieger (1980, p. 132).   [51] Zieger (1995, pp. 374, 376).

[52] Cochran (1977, p. 333); Healey (1993, pp. 152–58).

[53] Haynes (1996, p. 192). Elsewhere, Haynes and his coauthor Klehr observe: "The totalitarian nature of the Soviet state prevented much of the news of Stalin's oppression from reaching America. And the information about the purges was often not believed or was rationalized by

Their denials of Stalin's terror or apologies (usually unwitting) for the crimes of the Soviet regime should not be allowed to distort or obscure Communist unionists' real, radical and democratic, achievements – whether these unionists were officers of CIO internationals, local officers, or worker activists in the shops. For they were the leading fighters in exemplary struggles, which, as our analyses show below, enlarged the freedom and enhanced the human dignity of America's workers.

American Communists and their sympathizers" (1995, p. 10). Yet although Haynes not only admits this but also reports the mass abandonment of party membership after Khrushchev's disclosures and the Soviet invasion of Hungary months later, he seems not to recognize that this shows in a flash how pernicious and misleading is his pseudohistorical syllogism that, because "all American Communists were Stalinists," they knowingly approved of "Stalin's Great Terror... that murdered millions," and that their real "goal was the destruction of American society and its replacement by a state modeled on Stalin's Russia" (1996, p. 198).

2

"WHO GETS THE BIRD?"

Capitalism in America is "presided over by a class with an 'effective will to power,'" as Selig Perlman put it on the eve of the Great Depression in a neglected passage in his celebrated *Theory of the Labor Movement*. The men of this class defend "its power against all comers," said Perlman, in the conviction that "they alone, the capitalists, know how to operate the complex economic apparatus of modern society upon which the material welfare of all depends."[1]

In fact, the nation's capitalists, singly and collectively, had been waging, as a U.S. Senate Committee put it, a "long and implacable fight" – with a ferocity unparalleled elsewhere in the West – "against the recognition of labor's democratic rights." Once the cause of industrial unionism caught flame among millions of workers in the 1930s, America's capitalists exerted their "will to power" and tried to extinguish that flame with every weapon at their command. They hired their own "undercover operatives" and ran their own secret services to spy on their workers, and they deployed their own private armies (of thugs, ex-cons, and mobsters); they also had the active assistance of federal agents, local police, deputy sheriffs, state troopers, the national guard, and, occasionally, the U.S. military itself, in smashing strikes and repressing workers' attempts to unionize.[2]

Out at Ford's Rouge megaplant, for instance, which was the last great citadel of capital to fall (in the spring of 1941) to the CIO's organizing drive, the thugs in Ford's "service department" had long intimidated, beaten, and sometimes crippled, blinded, or killed suspected union men and women or their

---

[1] Perlman ([1928] 1949, pp. 4–8).

[2] U.S. Congress (1937–38, Part 3, p. 5). On chronic employer "violations of free speech and assembly and interference with the right of labor to organize and bargain collectively," see U.S. Congress (1937, 1937–38). Taft and Ross (1969, p. 289); Goldstein (1978). On the surveillance and infiltration of the TUEL by agents of the then "Bureau of Investigation," at the direct behest of America's major industrialists (and some leading AFL officials), see Johanningsmeier (1994, pp. 180, 183, 214).

sympathizers.[3] The company's "private underworld terrorize[d] the workers. . . . The fear in the plant," as reporter Benjamin Stolberg wrote in 1938, "is indescribable."

A year earlier, a group of Rouge workers and organizers laden with union leaflets were beaten into "a broken bloody mass" by Ford's goons, armed with billies and brass knuckles. One of the young organizers they worked over, slamming him on the concrete, kicking him in the head and groin, and throwing him down the stairs, was Walter Reuther. He had led the group onto the overpass toward the plant, despite the advice of another, veteran organizer, a Scotsman named Bill McKie, who already had been trying to organize a union there for a decade. "Look Walter," McKie had warned him, "stay off the bridge at Gate 4. You're likely to get beat up . . . and thrown off the bridge to the street below."[4]

McKie, who had been a leader of the Red Auto Workers Union (AWU), was already sixty-one on that day of "the battle of the overpass."[5] The embodiment of Communist industrial organizing, he was soon to be elected the first president of the Rouge Local. When Ford finally capitulated and recognized the union in 1941, McKie was elected to the United Automobile Workers' (UAW) first National Negotiating Committee. Across the table sat the company's negotiating team, headed by an ex-FBI man named John Bugas. "As a Communist," he said to McKie, "you take your orders from Moscow." McKie went on to be reelected twice to successive three-year terms as an officer of the new UAW–CIO Ford Local 600.

Walter, half McKie's age, had worked for two years, 1933–35, in a Soviet tool and die shop with his younger brother Victor, and had written home about the "proletarian industrial democracy" they had witnessed there and its "inspiring contrast to what we know as Ford wage slaves in Detroit." In Detroit, after returning from the USSR, Walter had a close working relationship and an apprenticeship in organizing with McKie, Wyndham Mortimer, Nat Ganley, and other Communist auto unionists for nearly three years; and at that time he and Victor were "still enthusiastic about the achievements

---

[3] Sward (1948, part 5).

[4] Lichtenstein (1995, p. 84); Bonosky (1953, pp. 156–58); Stepan-Norris and Zeitlin (1996, pp. 12, 18, 60).

[5] AWU had been founded by Socialists in 1918 and had grown rapidly until 1920, when it was smashed by the Palmer Raids, as a result of which many of its leaders and cadre were deported. Communists joined the AWU in Detroit in 1922, and soon were among its core organizers and leaders. It had nuclei in nearly twenty auto plants, including Ford's, and was to be one of the rival unions that amalgamated to form the UAW in 1937 (Stepan-Norris and Zeitlin 1996b, pp. 9, 10, 70–74; Foner 1994, pp. 121–38).

of the Soviet regime and the character of the new society it was building."[6] Yet by the spring of 1939, Walter would be clashing regularly in factional infighting with McKie and his erstwhile Communist comrades, would get McKie fired as a UAW organizer, and would begin to coalesce the anti-Communist elements in the union under his leadership.[7]

So the events at the "battle of the overpass" were in their own way emblematic of a deeper political struggle under way among the CIO's rival workers' factions and parties over who would win power in its new international unions and – in accord with their own sharply opposed conceptions – define the interests and shape the cohesion and self-consciousness of this newly organized, industrial segment of the working class.[8]

How, then, did their distinctive political strategies and actual practices matter in determining who won union power? How, in particular, did Communists take power in eighteen of the CIO's thirty-eight international unions?

The pat answer, according to Cold War scholars, is that the Communists, who possessed "indisputable organizational adroitness," seized power as "an organized, conspiratorial, disguised movement." "Always military minded," they engaged in "studious and sinister planning and procedure for infiltrating American unions"; then, having "disguised themselves as liberals or as American radicals," they "deploy[ed] their forces" so as to make "effective use of disciplined units of the combat party." Wielding the "organizational weapons" of "colonization," "incursion," "infiltration," and "covert penetration," they "invaded the forces of labor" and "establish[ed] a beachhead" so swiftly that, already by 1938, they "had obtained . . . complete or partial control in at least 40 percent of the CIO unions." They then kept "control" and assured their "domination," as Max Kampelman says, through "their mastery of the techniques of group organization and manipulation."[9]

---

[6] Nelson Lichtenstein says that although Walter and Victor were soon to become "vocal critics of the Soviet regime, . . . Walter certainly did not adopt this stance during the first two and a half years he spent back on American soil" (1995, pp. 44–45).

[7] Bonosky (1953, pp. 135–36, 157); Lichtenstein (1995, pp. 55, 127–31).

[8] That these early struggles had enduring formative political effects is illustrated, for instance, by incidents during Zeitlin's field research among unemployed copper miners in Butte, Montana, in August 1983. He found an old framed news clip from 1934 hanging on the wall in the local union hall of MM there ("Butte Miners Union No. 1"); it listed the men who were scabs in that epochal strike. And when Zeitlin asked the aged men or their wives or children for referrals to still living active opponents of the local's Communist leadership during the CIO era, they'd often refer to them in such terms as "talk to old scab John" or even "talk to old scab John's son, he's still around."

[9] The quoted phrases are taken verbatim from the following: Barbash (1948, p. 217); Saposs (1959, pp. 125, ix, vii–viii, 122); Kampelman (1957, pp. 6, 16, 17 (citing John Dewey),

Remarkably, sociologist Philip Selznick, the leading proponent of this "model" of the Communists' "practices that facilitate penetration and control" of "target unions" in America as elsewhere, has this to say concerning what he terms "the observational standpoint" of his "inquiry": "Although historical materials were studied, . . . the main problem has been *not* so much to discover *what the communists have in fact done*, but what they would like to do and upon what principles they operate."[10]

18, 251); Selznick (1952, pp. 148, 318, 182, also see 175–207 passim). See also, in the same vein, Epstein and Goldfinger (1950, p. 36); Pelling (1960, p. 162).

[10] Selznick (1960, p. xv; 1952, pp. 184, 13; emphasis added). That Selznick had no need to "discover what communists have in fact done" follows from his "methodology of interpretation": "We are interested in constructing a model that will effectively expose a central pattern of motivation and action, *applicable* in its basic features to the bolshevik movement *in all countries and throughout its history*." Given this ahistorical "methodology," any facts about what Communist unionists in America or any other country in any other period actually have done that contradict his "model" become what he calls mere "deviations in detail." In short, as he himself recognizes, "it is not always easy to state the conditions under which it [the model] might be considered false" (1952, p. 12; 1960, p. xv, emphasis added). It is no wonder, then, that the "evidence" presented in the Cold War caricatures of Communist unionists often verge on unintentional self-parody. Take these examples of the Communists' "studious and sinister procedures" for organizing a union: One important organizing "technique" of the Communists, says Selznick, was that they were "highly conscious of the need to *deploy their forces* in the most effective way possible. For example, the [Communists'] 1935 manual on organization . . . states: 'Since the most effective work of the party is inside the factory, it is necessary to find ways and means whereby developed Party members can get a job in a given factory. . . . '" This, Selznick says, is an example of the "organizational practice" of "colonization." Another crucial technique for "penetration" of an existing union and gaining "legitimacy" in it, says Selznick, was " . . . one of the simplest: the moral authority of hard work. In every organization which they seek to capture, the communists are the readiest volunteers, the most devoted committee workers, the most alert and active participants. In many groups, this is in itself sufficient to gain the leadership; it is almost always enough to justify candidacy" (1952, pp. 182, 250; emphasis in original). We are told too that Communists "inject themselves" where – of all things – workers face "unemployment, low wages, poor working conditions, . . . and similar unsettled conditions." Still another nefarious practice by Trade Union Unity League radicals was that they "penetrated" some existing AFL unions, as they had "in the New York area," by "play[ing] an important role in cleaning out the racketeers" (Saposs 1959, pp. 109, 113). The way the Communists "infiltrated" the CIO, says Kampelman (1957, pp. 15–16), was that CIO head "John L. Lewis, faced with the problems of leading a movement whose rapid growth he had not anticipated, . . . accepted the proferred aid of the Stalinists." In fact, documents found in the Comintern's now accessible archives reveal that the CIO's employment of paid, as well as volunteer, Communist organizers was based on active negotiation and mutual agreement in several meetings between CIO leaders Lewis and Sidney Hillman and members of the CP's highest councils in the fall

Our own "main problem," in contrast, is precisely, by carefully and systematically studying the "historical materials," to try to discover what Communists *did in fact do* to win power in America's industrial unions. Our analytical starting point, therefore, is the simple historical fact that Communists won "positions of power and trust," in C. Wright Mills's words, "by the standard method of gaining power in U.S. labor unions: by being the organizers." Or as Irving Howe and Lewis Coser emphasize:

> The main . . . source of CP strength in the CIO, was the participation of thousands of its members in the organizing drives of the late thirties. If there was dirty work to do, they were ready. If leaflets had to be handed out on cold winter mornings before an Akron rubber plant or a New York subway station, the party could always find a few volunteers. If someone had to stick his neck out within the plants, a Communist was available. . . . Never were the Communists more than a minority among the CIO organizers. . . . Plenty of other people, ranging from run-of-the-mill unionists to left-wing Socialists, worked hard and took chances. But the Communists were the best-organized political group within the CIO. . . . The devotion, heroism, and selflessness of many Communist unionists during these years can hardly be overestimated.

Robert Ozanne (like Mills, Howe, and Coser, a devout anti-Communist) makes plain, too, that

> Communists were more willing than the average worker to face gross employer discrimination and even violence. In the labor relations climate of

of 1936. As a result of their negotiations, Lewis hired some fifty full-time paid organizers for the steel workers' organizing drive in "all steel industry centers," as Earl Browder said in a cable to the Comintern in mid-August 1936. These organizers came from a list submitted to Lewis by Clarence Hathaway, representing the party. In the major Chicago district, according to Browder, half the CIO's paid steel organizers were Communists. In Hathaway's report to the Comintern, he noted that Lewis and Hillman had "not only shown a readiness to cooperate in discussions and words, but [had] . . . brought our people in everywhere," including allowing free elections "in a whole series of miners' locals" (that is, in Lewis's own United Mine Workers), " . . . and in these elections, Communists have been elected into the leadership, and this in no sense without his [Lewis's] knowledge" (Haynes, Klehr, and Anderson 1998, pp. 57, 68; Hathaway's entire report is presented verbatim, pp. 58–68; also see Haynes and Klehr 1995, pp. 105–6n26). So much, then, for the Communists' alleged "infiltration" and "covert penetration" of CIO unions.

employer espionage, discrimination and violence . . . such qualities as indifference to being fired, willingness to work night and day and courage to face threats of physical violence were prerequisites for successful organizers. These qualities the Communists possessed.[11]

"Courage," "selflessness," and even "heroism": These qualities, attributed to Communists by their own harshest critics and enemies, unquestionably entered into the process of determination that won Communists the workers' trust. Many were, in a phrase, "charismatic leaders," and, perhaps precisely because we cannot provide an empirical assessment of the importance of these qualities per se in Communists' winning union leadership, the point deserves emphasis.

Take UE's James J. Matles, for example. In June 1947, HUAC called a witness named Michael Berescic from a major anti-Communist UE local, Bridgeport Local 203, to testify about "Communist infiltration" of the UE. And what did Berescic say?

So far as Jim Matles is concerned . . . I will say that if I was to give credit to any one man in the UE for building up the UE to its present position, I would give it to him. He is second to none in any group in this country when it comes to organizational matters. . . . Jim built the UE where it is.

So much for "infiltration."

In 1949, the author of an article about the "biggest Communist union" and the "hardened Stalinists" in its leadership remarks that Matles and Julius Emspak, UE's secretary-treasurer, "are regarded with some awe even by their opponents in the union. 'Matles is a genius,' one of the UE anti-Communists conceded privately. 'He is the sort of man that can go cold into a room with a hundred strangers in it and take complete charge in a couple of minutes. Nobody can stand up to him in a rough and tumble debate.' . . . Politics aside," the author concluded, "Jim Matles is certainly one of the greatest organizers in the American labor movement today."[12]

---

[11] Mills (1948, p. 196); Howe and Coser (1957, p. 375); Ozanne (1954, pp. 103–4, emphasis added); cf. Moore (1945, p. 37).

[12] Filippelli and McColloch (1995, pp. 102–3); Seligman (1949, pp. 38–39).

"More Accident than Pattern"?

Generally, historians of American labor deny that any pattern existed from union to union in which faction or party won the leadership. Harvey A. Levenstein argues, for instance, that "[a]s for patterns in the response to Communist overtures among American workers, the most striking feature is a lack of apparent pattern." Where the "CP was strong" in a union, he suggests, it was "mainly because a few leaders . . . happened to be in the right place at the right time, creating a following for themselves and their factions through their determined leadership under fire. . . . There is *more accident than pattern in CP strength in the . . . CIO unions.*" David Saposs argues that "[w]hoever reaches . . . unorganized masses first, generally holds their confidence permanently." Nathan Glazer makes a similar observation, and concludes: "In the light of the various histories of many unions, large generalizations appear to be crude and clumsy, scarcely helpful in explaining any single outcome. . . . In the end it would seem to be the organizational factors that predominate: the skill and training and luck of Communists and their opponents."[13]

Although these observations are correct, they are also incomplete. For if historical "accidents" such as being "in the right place at the right time" or contingent "organizational factors" such as the "luck" of getting there "first" count in the making of history, the question remains, Why? If "accidents" or "contingencies" matter in history, what makes one rather than another matter? We try to show that this issue – *the social determination of historical contingency* – is closely involved with the issue of the relative autonomy of politics.[14] Our analysis below reveals *an indelible pattern of connections among*

[13] Saposs (1926, p. 185); Levenstein (1981, pp. 71, 55, emphasis added); Glazer (1961, p. 120). We want to emphasize, however, that many suggestive insights relevant to answering this question are contained in the narratives of specific struggles by Levenstein and other labor historians on whose yeoman work we rely for our "historical materials." We have reformulated some of these particularizing and unsystematic observations as explicit hypotheses.

[14] Some of the confusion among historians in the debate about the relevance of "accidents" or "contingencies" in explaining events (cf. Carr 1961, pp. 128–36) stems from not making a crucial conceptual distinction between these terms. Take the famous example of Cleopatra's nose and how the allure it held for Marc Anthony and his infatuation with her in turn affected Egypt's destiny. This, we agree, was an "accident." But the famous Athenian defeat of the Persian expeditionary army at the battle of Marathon and its role in the preservation of "freedom" in the "West" was a "contingency." The conceptual distinction between them is that although both an *accident* and a *contingency* have observable historical effects, a contingency (e.g., Persia's defeat), unlike an accident (e.g., Antony's love for Cleopatra's nose), is also historically determined and can, therefore, be explained by analysis of historical data. The substantive relevance here of this conceptual distinction is, as we see below, that who won "power and trust" in America's industrial unions was no "accident." To the contrary, which of

earlier political practices, emergent political relations, and subsequent political align-ments in the international unions of the CIO.[15]

the rival factions and parties involved in the organizing won was contingent on their distinct types of political practices.

[15] We abstract here from the sorts of "objective conditions," "social bases," or "structural fac-tors" (e.g., unemployment rates, plant size, city size, economic instability, work satisfaction, social mobility, social origins, skill level, status barriers) usually invoked in explanations of workers' political consciousness and action. Certainly, objective conditions matter in de-termining the types of unions and parties that emerge and gain workers' adherence in the course of their struggles. But they do not determine *how* these struggles are waged nor who wins and who loses. In this analysis, we assume that such objective conditions remain con-stant, and we explore how the objective political relations resulting from concrete struggles, whether intended or not, themselves become integral components of the emergent objective conditions for subsequent struggles.

Still, we did also try to assess the relatively independent political effects on the unions of some of the objective conditions and some of the characteristics of the workers in the indus-tries the unions organized. Since union-specific data do not exist for the "objective economic conditions" and demographic characteristics of industries in the 1930s or 1940s, we had to use U.S. Census industry-level Standard Industrial Classification (SIC) data (four digit). But many unions lack such data. Moreover, we doubt that measures based on industry-level data are reliable and valid measures of union attributes. First, the jurisdictions and mem-berships of CIO unions often cut across the boundaries of several SIC categories. Many of the unions had to be categorized, on the basis of our best estimates, into several different ones. We assigned very rough estimates of industry weights in the absence of union-specific data. We examined the relationships with and without these weights and found no substan-tively important differences. Second, unless an industry is quite homogeneous on a given variable, it may not be correct to infer from an industry characteristic to the union. For example, a union in an industry with a high proportion of women may have few women members. Similarly, the industry may contain a high proportion of small shops, but the union may have organized only the largest ones, and so on. Third, we have many miss-ing cases for the economic and demographic variables; the number of international unions for which we have adequate industry-level data on these variables ranges from twenty to twenty-nine.

Withal, we examined the bivariate relationships between each of the following industry-level economic and demographic variables and the union's political camp: (1.1) the industry's "sensitivity to depression" (relation of employment level to gross consumer income, 1936 dollars, $N = 26$); (1.2) the industry's level of unemployment (men only, $N = 29$); (1.3) the size distribution of the industry's establishments (percent large establishments; percent of workers in large establishments, $N = 20$); (1.4) the industry's level of concentration (four-firm, manufacturing only, $N = 22$); (2.1) the industry's skill composition (percent skilled craftsmen, men only, $N = 28$); (2.2) the industry's sexual composition (percent women, $N = 31$); (2.3) the industry's racial composition (percent "nonwhite," men only, $N = 28$); (2.4) the industry's age composition (percent under twenty-five, men only, $N = 28$).

The CIO was itself the proximate historical product of an intraclass political struggle that took place in two phases. The first phase, from the early 1920s on, was the fight for the cause of industrial unionism by "Reds" in opposition to AFL officials' dogged insistence on organizing along only trade or craft lines. The second phase was the radical response to the labor insurgency of the early 1930s, when both AFL officials and AFL affiliates split over the issue of whether and how to organize the unorganized in mass production industries. Then, with the birth of the CIO, rival factions and parties vied with each other for power in the fledgling organization and its constituent unions.

These formative battles and the unions' resultant internal political relations can be seen as constituting and being constituted by four constellations of events involved in organizing them: (1) whether or not, in the pre-CIO era,

We found no theoretically relevant bivariate relationship between any independent variable and the union's political camp, with one exception. Unions in industries with a high proportion (25 percent or more) of skilled craftsmen were less likely than low ones (under 10 percent) to be in the Communist political camp, but the relationship is curvilinear. Unions in industries with "medium" proportions (10 to 24.9 percent) skilled craftsmen were by far the least likely to be led by Communists. That Communist-led unions were less likely to be in high-skilled than low-skilled industries – given the AFL's preeminence among craftsmen – is what we would expect. But it could be misleading because, for instance, a CIO union in an industry with a high proportion of skilled craftsmen might, nonetheless, have few skilled members. These craftsmen could be members of one or more long-standing AFL unions. (This was true of MM and the AFL unions in nonferrous mining.)

But the question remains: Did the strategy of class organization and the consequent political practices of the organizers have different political consequences, depending on variations in the economic conditions in an industry or in its internal social composition or both? That is, was there interaction (or specification) among the variables, such that the "economic" or "social" conditions in an industry determined the measurable effects of the political practices? Alas, we can have no confidence in the results of our efforts in this regard because these variables are at best crude and at worst misleading indicators of the actual conditions in the industry that union organizers encountered. Further, not only do we have many missing cases, but the number of cases with adequate data varies considerably from one variable to another. Moreover, the sparsity of cases varies at different values of these variables. Such unavoidable flaws in the data make an analysis of interaction effects worthless.

Yet for variables with enough cases, we did examine several theoretically relevant "logit models" that also include economic and demographic variables. (See text, p. 47, and note 52 below on "logit analysis.") We found that, controlling for these variables, the direct effects of the political variables did not meaningfully differ from the original logit model. The percent of skilled craftsmen has a small negative effect on the odds of Communist union leadership, but it does not remain significant in a reduced model, that is, one omitting control variables lacking significant effects. Unexpectedly, the percent nonwhite has a small significant negative effect. These logit tables are available from the authors.

earlier Red organizing had planted any roots in the industry in which the CIO union was later established; (2) whether the union seceded from the AFL "from below," as the result of a workers' insurgency, or "from above," through a revolt of its top officers; (3) whether the union was organized independently, that is, by its own organizers, or under the aegis of a CIO organizing committee; and (4) whether the union was formed through amalgamation or as a unitary organization.

These four constellations also represent crucial types of political *practices* and clusters of internal *relationships* among rival political tendencies. We refer to earlier Red organizing, secession via a workers' insurgency, independent organizing, and amalgamation as *insurgent political practices.*[16]

Earlier Red Organizing

If being in the "right place at the right time" with the "skill and training" is what matters in making history, it was neither mere "luck" nor an "accident" that thousands of skilled and trained Communists were in the right place (in the thick of organizing struggles), at the right time (during the workers' uprisings of the 1930s), when others were not. On the contrary, "Red unionism" and the cause of "industrial unionism" (organizing workers by industry, across trade or craft lines) had been almost synonymous for many years before the CIO took up the call. After the repression and demise of the "Wobblies," the Communists "took over as the chief radical element operating within the American labor movement" and were the main carriers of the ideas of militant action and industrial unionism. So in the early days of the CIO's split with the AFL, the Communists were skeptical or even hostile toward CIO efforts. "In a way, the Communists looked upon the CIO as a rival that was capitalizing on some of its issues, particularly that of industrial unionism."[17]

From 1922 on, when the TUEL's first national conference called for industrial unionism and "the organization of the unorganized," radicals of all sorts – or so-called Reds (and *not* only or even mainly members of the CP) – had been trying to organize some of the same industries and plants that the CIO later targeted for organizing. Their aim was to rally the members of AFL affiliates "around burning everyday issues in the class struggle" and shunt aside their

---

[16] We would guess that other, even earlier formative struggles over working-class organization entered into determining who won leadership in the CIO, for instance, the Wobblies' organizing efforts in the decade or so before World War I and the subsequent postwar spawning of "employee representation plans" or "company unions" by employers.

[17] Saposs (1959, pp. 7, 123).

existing reactionary leadership. AFL president Samuel Gompers denounced the TUEL as "a new scheme of destroying the American Federation of Labor and its constituent unions," which "was devised in Moscow."[18]

TUEL cadre sought to "bore from within" the AFL, to "infuse the mass with revolutionary understanding and spirit," push the AFL toward industrial unionism, through "amalgamation" of its craft unions within the same industry, and get them to organize the unorganized in their industry. But where "existing unions are hopelessly decrepit," or no unions exist, the TUEL's militants were to take the lead in organizing new unions.[19] For workers in a variety of unions, the TUEL became the most influential voice for the cause of industrial unionism: its "amalgamation movement . . . gained the endorsements of hundreds of labor groups across the nation, including sixteen state federations, fourteen national unions, dozens of central labor bodies, and thousands of miscellaneous locals."[20] Eugene Victor Debs, the country's most eminent Socialist leader, declared in the spring of 1923 that the TUEL, "under the direction of William Z. Foster, is in my opinion the one rightly directed movement for the industrial unification of the American workers. I thoroughly believe in its

---

[18] In an exchange with Gompers, TUEL founder and head William Z. Foster reminded him that he, Foster, had founded and led the Syndicalist League of North America in 1912 and that its program had been virtually the same as the TUEL's: "Instead of such a movement being a new thing for me, I have been working constantly along these lines for the last ten years. During the packing house and steel industry movements [which Foster, hired by Gompers in 1919, had led as a "free-lance radical"], I had exactly the same thing in mind as I have now" (Foner 1991, pp. 77, 136).

[19] From the 1922 pamphlet *Amalgamation* (Foner 1991, p. 152). The unfortunate phrase "boring from within" was coined by the TUEL's Foster to describe the tactic he advocated of working within existing AFL unions, rather than organizing independent "revolutionary unions" like the Industrial Workers of the World (IWW); it had been the central tactic of his Syndicalist League as early as 1912. During the interwar years, Foster – who had led "the great steel strike" of 1919, which was "one of the great organizing feats in American labor history" (Taft 1957, p. 386; Foster 1920) – was widely considered, as an April 23, 1923, article in the *New York Times* said, "the outstanding radical labor leader in America." That same year, Saposs, then still a friend of Foster, "meditated on the role of the 'free-lance' radical within the labor movement. These 'borers from within' had come to appreciate, through their experiences, that 'aggression leads to isolation,' and that an essentially pragmatic attitude was the soundest way to further their goals. . . . Free lancers thus 'keep their [social] aspirations and ultimate ideals under cover.'" By then, however, Foster was, in fact, no longer a freelance radical, but had joined the CP (then known as the Workers Party) and was embroiled in inner-party struggle over his strategy for labor (Johanningsmeier 1994, pp. 188, 151; also see Barrett 1999).

[20] Johanningsmeier (1994, p. 186).

plan and in its methods and I feel very confident of its steady progress and the ultimate achievements of its ends."[21]

TUEL meetings were repeatedly subjected to government raids and its local leagues infiltrated; its adherents were spied on, intimidated, and arrested by

[21] Ibid., p. 193. Although, through the person of Foster, the TUEL and the Workers Party were identified with each other after he announced his membership in April 1923, the party's other leaders Charles Ruthenberg, Jay Lovestone, and Benjamin Gitlow were vehemently opposed to Foster's labor strategy, the TUEL, and Foster's conception of "boring from within" the existing AFL unions. Inner-party conflict over "Fosterism" remained chronic through the decade. Foster denounced the "dual unionism" of the IWW and opposed the Ruthenberg/Lovestone line of organizing "revolutionary unions." They, in turn, "openly accused Foster of being a syndicalist without coherent Communist principles." In a debate with Comintern representatives, Foster argued "that the TUEL has to be a separate organization," not subject to the Workers Party's authority, keeping "high politics" out of the TUEL, and insisting that "substance and mass strength shall be given preference over ideological clarity." The TUEL program, he said, "must be simplified and concentrated around burning everyday issues in the class struggle." Foster and his allies were denounced by a Comintern representative in Chicago for "double accounting," paying lip service to the Comintern line while "following a political policy against the Comintern." With Comintern backing, Ruthenberg took control of the Workers Party, and he and Lovestone purged its TUEL adherents. In 1926, "Ruthenberg fired TUEL cadres from their positions, and many trade unionists were expelled as a result of the new purge of the 'Fosterites'. Other union cadres who had been recruited to the party through the TUEL, 'almost completely absented themselves and stopped paying dues,' [as Earl] Browder recalled." Foster was at best a recalcitrant adherent of the Red International of Labor Unions (RILU, or "Profintern") during these years; for instance, when he and John Brophy were actively leading the Save the Union Movement (SUM) inside the UMW, Foster ignored the party line to try to turn SUM into "the basis of a new union," and he pointedly refused an invitation in 1928 to attend the RILU's fourth congress in Moscow. Foster did attend a meeting in Moscow with Stalin the next year, at which Lovestone tried to convince Stalin to support him against Foster in the party. "Stalin excoriated him [Foster] for having consorted with 'hidden Trotskyists'" and called him "a speculator in the affairs of the Comintern, a maneuverer and opportunist." Earlier, but to no avail, RILU's head, Solomon Lozovsky, had supported Foster and agreed that the TUEL had to operate independently both of the party and of RILU, and could not take the "precise character" of RILU or Comintern resolutions. In a prescient comment on the United States, in December 1922, Lovosky said that Communist "influence in the working-class movement is secured neither by resolutions nor by certain successful *decisions of the Central Executive Committee {in Moscow}*, but by work done by Communists in their respective labor organizations" (emphasis added). Lozovsky rejected attempts at "mechanical control" or "at mechanical interference in work [of the TUEL] which by its very nature the party can neither carry on nor accomplish" (Johanningsmeier 1994, pp. 207, 388, 225, 240, 246, 189). This was a lesson that, at the height of Communist power in American labor in 1946–47, the party's officialdom had still not learned and Foster, now chairman, had forgotten.

35

government agents and police "Red squads"; and its militants were hounded and expelled from AFL affiliates.[22] By 1929, despite the radiation of its influence among labor militants, the TUEL was not at all making the "steady progress" Debs had expected. The league's emphasis now shifted from "boring from within" to organizing new "Red unions." The TUEL, this time in accord with the line of the CP, transformed itself into the Trade Union Unity League (TUUL), whose primary objective was organizing new independent industrial unions, outside the AFL, in a struggle of "class against class."[23] In fact, as Theodore Draper emphasizes, "The AFL made so little effort to organize the unorganized, that there was plenty of room for a 'dual union,' even if the AFL wasn't destroyed in the process."[24]

So, on the eve of the CIO's birth, several thousand "Reds" already had fought for years trying to organize independent unions and had won a reputation in several industries as militant partisans of industrial unionism and workers' rights. As a result, they won *some* supporters (historians differ on the numbers) among the workers in these industries. They also prepared many others for the coming wave of industrial unionism. In the auto industry, for instance, Reds in the TUEL had started agitating for an industrial union in 1925, and soon were printing shop papers and distributing them to a dozen of Detroit's major auto plants. "These little four-page sheets, sold for a penny or given away by Communist distributors at plant gates . . . provided the only news of conditions and grievances inside the plants available to workers."[25]

TUUL unions led some heroic, fiercely fought, and bloodily suppressed strikes. "All unions were fought bitterly in those days," as Draper says. "But

---

[22] For instance, after a raid in the spring of 1924 on a TUEL meeting by the Los Angeles Police Department's "Wobbly squad," in cooperation with the Justice Department, the *Los Angeles Times* claimed that the raid had uncovered "a gigantic plot to undermine the American Federation of Labor and convert it into a Communist organization for the purpose of overthrowing the United States Government." The raid, as a Department of Labor official wrote in a "strictly confidential" memo to his superiors, was the "culmination of a plan to furnish conservative [AFL] leaders with the 'dope' [on TUEL members]." In the wake of the raid, and with such "dope" in hand, Los Angeles's AFL officials conducted a "general housecleaning" and expulsion of TUEL militants from the city's AFL affiliates (Johanningsmeier 1994, p. 214).

[23] Until Edward P. Johanningsmeier's dissertation (1988) and book (1994), and Foner's works at almost the same time (1991, 1994), "not a single book, dissertation, or article, scholarly or otherwise" had ever been devoted to the TUEL or TUUL or to any of TUUL's constituent unions (Draper 1972, p. 371). Important details had appeared, however, in Cochran 1977; Draper 1957, 1960; Foster 1937; Galenson 1940; Klehr 1984; Starobin 1972.

[24] Foster (1947, pp. 198 ff.); Keeran (1980b, p. 137); Draper (1972, p. 374).

[25] Keeran (1980a, p. 37); Cochran (1977, p. 63).

the most brutal terror was reserved for the Communist unions." With no "revolutionary wave" to ride, "the TUUL had to depend on the straining, sweating, and plodding of its own organizers. They were too few, and they tried to do too much." So the Red unions organized during these strikes typically"went to pieces afterward."[26]

TUUL's Jack Johnstone lamented in early 1930 that "The objective conditions were never better for building militant revolutionary unions, *but objective conditions do not create organizations.*" By 1932, even the few more or less durable Red unions became "for all intents and purposes, moribund." With the upsurge of labor led by the CIO bypassing their own "dual unions," TUUL leaders formally disbanded in mid-1935; and its unions, so it is said, "faded away."[27]

In some struggles (such as Harlan County, Kentucky), Draper suggests, the revolutionary intransigence and plain incompetence of the Communists had been so disastrous for the workers involved that once the Communists were driven out, they could never return; in the end, "for all their fortitude and determination, they had nothing concrete to show for their efforts." But in other struggles in the auto, transport, electrical, lumber, and shipping industries, for instance, Communists and their radical allies apparently succeeded in putting together and holding on, as Irving Howe and Lewis Coser suggest, to "a kind of skeleton apparatus. In this way the Communists were able to begin functioning in the CIO with an embryonic structure of organizers who knew each other from 'the old days' and, though assigned to different industries, could help one another with regard to both party interests and their own status." If nothing else, the TUEL and TUUL experiences served "as a training ground for the Communist unionist in organization techniques and in administering unions." Also, "aside from these organizational advantages," as Glazer emphasizes, "the Communists were in fact founding fathers, with all the moral authority that gives a leader."[28]

On balance, even if nearly all of the Communists' "revolutionary unions" were stillborn and some of the struggles they led were politically disastrous for them, these hard years of Red organizing, we suggest, created in some industries a cadre of experienced Communist organizers and effective,

---

[26] Draper (1972, p. 392); Klehr 22(1984, p. 133). The IFLWU was the only CIO Communist-led union that grew directly out of earlier Red unionism. Ben Gold and other top officers were "avowed" members of the CP who had originally won the New York district leadership in 1925 when they ran on a TUEL slate (Kampelman 1957, pp. 215–16).

[27] Klehr (1984, pp. 41, emphasis added, 47, 133).

[28] Draper (1972, pp. 392, 389); Howe and Coser (1957, p. 373); Taft (1964, p. 16); Glazer (1961, p. 111).

even charismatic, leaders with a legitimate claim to many workers' support. If so, then Communists should also have had a better chance of winning the leadership of CIO unions established in industries where their earlier Red comrades had tried to organize (i.e., before the CIO's founding) than in unions established in industries where no earlier Red organizing had occurred.[29]

Our findings are more or less consistent with this hypothesis. First, 52 percent of the twenty-one CIO international unions in the industries where earlier Red organizers had been active compared with 41 percent of the seventeen in the other industries turned out to be led by Communists. Second, the contrast is sharper when we examine the effect of earlier Red organizing on the subsequent success of the *anti*-Communists: In the industries that Reds had *not* tried to organize in the pre-CIO era, twice as many internationals, proportionately, eventuated in the "anti-Communist camp" as in the industries penetrated by Reds: 35 versus 19 percent.[30]

---

[29] CIO organizing strategy, whether or not it was implemented by Reds, or occurred where earlier Red unionists had been active, also drew on the experiences of earlier Red unionism. Foster's 1935 pamphlet, *Organizing Methods in the Steel Industry,* "became a blueprint for CIO policy" (Cohen 1990, p. 502n39).

[30] As we see below, earlier Red organizing also had significant *in*direct effects in determining whether Communists later won leadership in CIO unions. We can think of no convincing line of argument that the other insurgent political practices which are examined in the following analysis (secession through a workers' insurgency, independent organizing, and amalgamation) themselves somehow "reflected" an industry's specific "structure," "economic conditions," or social characteristics of the workers in it. But in the case of Red unionism, it is plausible that an industry's structure did have a bearing on the very existence of that insurgent organizing practice and on the success or failure of the Communists in penetrating that industry. The Communists were inveterate seekers after the appropriate "objective conditions" in which to carry out their activities. For this reason, the TUEL and its successor TUUL did target certain industries because they considered organizing them critical in the struggle to organize all industrial workers (e.g., core mass production industries such as steel, auto, chemicals). In short, it could be argued that earlier Red union organizing had an impact precisely where the "industry structure" favored it. If so, the apparent direct and indirect effects of earlier Red unionism on the chances of subsequent Communist union leadership could be spurious. Both might reflect, instead, the "objective conditions" of the industries at the time the Red unionists were organizing them.

Yet Communists often tried to organize industries that were neither "strategic" nor characterized by obviously favorable objective conditions for industrial unionism. As Levenstein (1981, p. 71) emphasizes, "Often their egalitarian impulse led [the Communists] to expend inordinate energy on organizing those least powerful and least strategically placed: tragic cases such as the migrant workers, 'losers' such as southern textile workers, the infinitely replaceable Macy's salesclerks, or hospital workers." Howe and Coser, assessing the

Secession from the AFL

In the fall of 1936, the AFL "suspended" ten unions affiliated with the CIO (then still the "Committee for Industrial Organization") on charges of "dual unionism" (the same charge the AFL had used to throw out the adherents of the TUEL eleven years earlier) and of "fomenting insurrection." The ten unions immediately started making their per capita payments to the now-independent CIO. These founding unions of the CIO came into the new industrial union movement as the result of what we term "a revolt from above," and others soon followed the same path.[31] Their top officers broke away from the AFL and joined the CIO with their staff and organizational hierarchy – and much of their union jurisdiction – intact.[32] As a result, they "had a continuity of leadership," as Jack Barbash suggests, "that [was] proof, by and large, against Communist domination."[33] Or as Mills remarks in a related context, their "machines were already built and fenced in" before any organizing campaigns were undertaken.[34]

Red unionists' activities during the revolutionary "Third Period," make the same point. In their view, the Communists bowed to Comintern decisions that ignored the real situation in the United States. "TUUL leaders and members often displayed a heroism and self-sacrifice which no amount of political disagreement should deter anyone from admiring." But time after time, in one industry after another, from coal mining to textiles, they say, the Reds led workers into disastrous strikes and senseless efforts, where the objective conditions were heavily, and obviously, against them (1957, pp. 257, 272).

For these reasons, we doubt that "industry structure" in the extraordinarily diverse industries organized or hazarded by the TUEL and TUUL could account for their enduring impact. Communists went on to win the leadership of unions in a broad range of entirely different industries, and to lose and win in others whose objective conditions appear to have been quite similar (also see Glazer 1961, p. 120). Most important, "objective conditions," as TUUL leader Jack Johnstone said, do not organize workers. The Red unionists' decision to try to organize an industry, for any reason ("strategic," "revolutionary," or "egalitarian impulse"), is itself a political act which has its own independent political consequences, whatever the "objective conditions." Withal, to assess the effects of industry structure on early Red unionism other scholars will have to do primary historical research on the TUEL and TUUL's varying organizing successes and failures and on the nature of the industries in which they occurred.

[31] A couple of examples: The URW's leaders, who came chiefly right out of the company union (Saposs 1959, p. 123), won an AFL charter in 1935. But they bolted to the CIO later that year and went on to lead some of the bitterest recognition strikes of the time in any industry. The International Woodworkers originated as a dissident group among the "unskilled" in the AFL's Brotherhood of Carpenters, where they had no voting rights; they and their leaders seceded and joined the CIO with their own organization intact.

[32] Bernstein (1970, pp. 422–23).   [33] Barbash (1956, p. 342).   [34] Mills (1948, p. 197).

In contrast, most other CIO unions grew out of local and district battles between craft and industrial unionists over the control of its AFL precursor. Such workers' insurgencies split many AFL unions. The workers in these AFL locals and districts then came into the CIO to form the core of new international unions. This happened, for instance, in the AFL's Upholsterers International Union in 1937, where a number of locals defected from the AFL and combined with some other independent craft unions and a few CIO locals to form the CIO's United Furniture Workers. Other struggles "from below" took place in the newly chartered AFL "federal labor unions," that is, the newly organized locals given a temporary AFL charter to "store workers" until they could be "parceled out" to AFL craft affiliates.[34] Some seceded from the AFL to become the nuclei of a new CIO union, rather than be parceled out and subordinated to craft control. Of the eighteen CIO internationals that originated in a workers' insurgency, fourteen took place in various locals and districts of regular AFL affiliates, and four in AFL federal unions.

Many leaders of these local rebellions against the craft leadership were radicals, and some were Communists. Unlike the situation in the former AFL unions that came into the CIO from above, these left leaders had the opportunity to gain secure political bases in the new CIO unions that they built in struggles from below. This was the pattern among longshoremen, for example, with the Australian seaman Harry Bridges. An outstanding leader in the epic 1934 West Coast maritime strike and in the San Francisco general strike, Bridges rose, with Communist support, from ordinary dockworker to president of the San Francisco local and then, in 1936, to president of the entire Pacific Coast district of the International Longshoremen's Association (ILA). The next year, he led 17,000 West Coast dockworkers out of the ILA into the CIO, to form ILWU.[35]

For these reasons, we suggest that far more of the unions that had been born from below, in a workers' insurgency, than from above, in an officers' revolt, turned out to be Communist-led. We find, indeed, that the numbers of Communist-led internationals in these categories differ sharply. Of the eighteen that seceded from the AFL through a workers' insurgency, 72 percent turned out to be Communist-led, but this was so of only 15 percent of the thirteen internationals whose top officers had bolted from the AFL to join the CIO. Now seven other CIO internationals had been independent non-AFL unions before the CIO was established (e.g., the Federation of Architects, Engineers, Chemists and Technicians) or had been organized in an industry

---

[34] Peterson (1944, p. 135); Bernstein (1970, p. 355).   [35] Levinson (1956, pp. 262–63).

that had no prior AFL union (e.g., the Farm Equipment Workers (FE)). FE originated when a number of locals in farm equipment manufacturing broke away from the CIO's Steel Workers Organizing Committee (SWOC) to set themselves up as the core of an independent organizing committee (and, later, an independent union) in that industry.[36] Because they also joined the CIO with their leaderships intact, we added these seven to the thirteen in the "from above" category. Among these twenty internationals, the proportion of Communist-led unions increases to 25 percent. The effect of the type of secession on the chances that *anti*-Communists would win union leadership was especially sharp: 45 percent of these twenty internationals that joined the CIO with their leaderships intact but a mere 5 percent of the eighteen internationals that seceded through a workers' insurgency ended up in the *anti*-Communist camp.

Independent Organizing

Forged in the earlier Red union-organizing drives, thousands of experienced Communist organizers dedicated to industrial unionism formed a ready but recalcitrant and even politically dangerous reservoir of organizers who could be tapped by the CIO's founders. CIO President John L. Lewis and other CIO leaders "had no choice but to accept the support of the Communists," as Saul Alinsky gives Lewis's thinking on the matter. "Even after the debacle of 1933 and 1934, when the American Federation of Labor smashed the spirit of unionism, it was the left-wingers who zealously worked day and night picking up the pieces of that spirit and putting them together." S. Martin Lipset also emphasizes that "John L. Lewis was forced to employ many young Communists as organizers for the C.I.O. when it first started because they were the only people with the necessary skills who were willing to take the risks involved for low pay."[37]

The CIO's founders, notably Lewis, tried both to use Communist organizers to build the new CIO unions and to hobble them so that they could not take power in them. Responding to warnings that hiring Communists meant trouble for the CIO, Lewis asked sardonically, "Who gets the bird, the hunter or the dog?" But just in case the "dog" got other ideas, Lewis and other CIO officials exerted tight control over every "CIO organizing committee" that they put in charge of organizing the unorganized in an industry.[38]

---

[36] Peterson (1944, p. 120).
[37] Alinsky, as quoted in Cochran (1977, p. 97); Lipset (1960, p. 386).
[38] Cochran (1977, p. 97); Taft (1964); Bernstein (1970, p. 616).

What happened in SWOC, for instance, is instructive. SWOC had 200 full-time organizers and another 233 part-time organizers on its payroll, paid out of CIO funds (mainly contributed by the unions of the miners and the clothing workers); 60 of the full-time organizers were Communists (including the head district organizer in Pittsburgh, Bill Gebert, a Polish-born member of the party's national committee).[39] "With Philip Murray [who later replaced Lewis as head of the CIO] and his superbly competent, experienced, and anti-Communist lieutenants in charge of the steel organizing campaign," according to David Saposs, "... when Communists were spotted, or became too dangerous a threat, they were discharged." SWOC organizers were all hired, paid, and fired by the head office. When they organized a local, the SWOC moved them to another area, allowing SWOC officials to take control. Local autonomy was not allowed to emerge: "[D]espite the Communist workers in the steel mills, despite the Communist organizers who worked in the drive, the party gained no important sphere of influence in the union. A skillful anti-Communist administration," Nathan Glazer points out, "keeping close reins on local unions and preventing the development of local autonomy, also prevented the establishment of a Communist base" in SWOC and, as a result, the USWA. "Thus, a Communist who had helped to organize twenty-five SWOC locals lamented," says Levenstein, "that despite a few successes, Communists 'weren't too successful' in wooing the leaders of the locals they helped to organize." Communists played an important role in the four-year battle to organize "Little Steel," the violently antiunion steel companies that held out long after the U.S. Steel Co. capitulated. "But when the struggle was over, they were quietly fired by SWOC head Philip Murray."[40]

In the auto industry, in contrast, a host of contending radical, Communist, socialist, Coughlinite Catholic, and other "outside groups" were involved in the organizing and then in vying for power in the new UAW–CIO. The UAW financed much of its own organizing drives by collecting dues from the workers, so top CIO officials had little direct influence on the conduct of the campaigns against the big auto companies. Even when CIO influence in

---

[39] Foster (1952, p. 349); Walker (1982, pp. 184–85).

[40] Saposs (1959, p. 122); Taft (1964, p. 57); Glazer (1961, p. 113); Levenstein (1981, p. 51). It ought to be noted, though, that the fight in Steel was, according to Levenstein, entirely one-sided, constituting a rather clear illustrative instance of the independent causal relevance of "the political": CP leaders, following the "Popular Front" line, never "challenged the purges or sought to increase Communist power by calling for the democratization of the SWOC," because they feared alienating their liberal allies (1981, p. 51).

the internal affairs of the UAW was at its height, the CIO was unable to impose "outside leadership."[41] Also, the major auto companies bitterly resisted unionization. Both GM and Ford agreed to bargain with the CIO union only after engaging the workers in a tenacious conflict and unleashing company strong-arm men against them. In the GM drive, especially in some of the hard-fought sit-down strikes – including the one in Flint in 1937, "the first great victory" for the UAW "and one of the epic confrontations in American labor history" – and in the over decade-long siege and the final storming of the Ford ramparts at River Rouge in early 1941, Communists gained a reputation as superb organizers and combative and courageous leaders. Consequently, they were able to create strong rank-and-file groups in the auto industry.[42]

So the chances that Communists could build their own base and later win the union's leadership were better, we suggest, when they were involved in independent organizing than when they worked as staff members of a CIO organizing committee. Where they earned moral authority among the workers and had no CIO organizing committee standing in their way, Communists could also "bring in reinforcements on the lower levels who could provide a solid layer of support for its people on top."[43]

In fact, we find that Communists won the leadership of only 17 percent of the twelve international unions that were organized by a CIO committee, but of 61 percent of the twenty-six that had been independently organized. In contrast, anti-Communists took power in 42 percent of the internationals organized under the tutelage of a CIO committee, but in only 19 percent of the independently organized internationals.[44]

---

[41] Galenson (1960, p. 133). The CIO contributed money and organizers to the drive to organize the Ford Rouge megaplant, but longtime local organizers and leaders were crucial in planning and leading it. See Chapter 4.

[42] Zieger (1986, pp. 46–47); Galenson (1960, p. 150); also see Chapter 4.

[43] Howe and Coser (1957, p. 377).

[44] When a CIO organizing committee in an industry was run by men who were not hostile to the Communists or the committee was short-lived (or both), Communists were able to form their own nuclei of support in the new union. The Shoe Workers Organizing Committee, for instance, fits into both categories. Its CIO-appointed head, Powers Hapgood (who had joined the party secretly in 1923 but apparently left sometime later), was willing to work with Communists (Levenstein 1981, p. 108; Johanningsmeier 1994, p. 237). The organizing committee lasted barely a year before it succeeded in establishing the fledgling union, in 1937, and went on to fight, the next year, a "series of heroic strikes in the corrupt and vigilante-ridden New England shoe towns" (Stolberg 1938, p. 230). The United Shoe Workers Union was, consequently, led by Communists and their allies until the great purge a decade later.

Amalgamation

The formation of unions took either a unitary or amalgamated path. A unitary organization (i.e., centralized and typically hierarchical) tends, as it grows, to incorporate new members and units (whether local or national) into its existing structure, "with the new subordinate officials and groups deriving their authority from the summits of the organization." In contrast, an amalgamated organization grows through the merger of a number of existing independent units that retain their own leaders.[45]

In the early days of the CIO, some unions amalgamated because their "jurisdictions," despite what their CIO charters stated, were still mixed and shifting. Sometimes several unions were organizing in different parts of the same industry. Sometimes a single union branched out and organized locals in several closely related industries.[46] How CIO officials responded to these disparate drives, allowing the cross-industry locals (say, in radio, electrical, machinery, and utilities) to merge and remain in the same international or compelling some or all of them to split off into their "authorized" industrial jurisdictions,' was always a political question. For the international unions and

---

[45] Lipset, Trow, and Coleman (1962, p. 442). Only if an international was the result of mergers during the 1930s of two or more independent units do we classify it as formed through "amalgamation." So if an established ex-AFL union merged with one or more other unions, we classify the new CIO international as amalgamated only if the merger resulted in a substantial reorganization of the ex-AFL union's administrative or political structure. Only three unions had any record of mergers after joining the CIO: (1) MM, which added a Die Casting Division in 1942, five years after it bolted the AFL to become a charter member of the CIO; (2) the IFLWU, formed of a merger of the existing unions of furriers and leather workers; and (3) the ACW. Because the MM merger occurred long after its political structure had been established, it does not qualify, in our terms, as an amalgamated union. (Classifying it as amalgamated would strengthen our findings.) As to the ACW, it became a unitary highly centralized union long before 1936, when it absorbed the Journeymen Tailors Union (and its some 6,000 members) and, later on, the CIO Laundry Workers (and its nine locals). No significant reorganization of the ACW's administration occurred after these mergers (Galenson 1960, p. 285; also see Bernstein 1970, pp. 73ff). So, despite its name, it does not qualify as having been formed through amalgamation. In contrast, the merger of the International Fur Workers Union in March 1939 with the National Leather Workers Association resulted in substantial reorganization of both. The new union was constituted of two relatively independent divisions, fur and leather; each elected its own officers and managed its own finances. Their combined executive boards constituted the executive body of the new amalgamated International Fur and Leather Workers Union (Foner 1950, p. 556; Brown 1947, p. 135). So, we classify it as having been formed through amalgamation.

[46] Analysis would show, we suggest, that what came to be considered an "industry" in capital–labor relations was itself at least in part a political artifact of these organizing struggles.

locals involved, it was, of course, also a political question, as well as a matter of organizing strategy.

Long before the CIO's birth – in 1912 under the Syndicalist League and then followed by the TUEL a decade later – as we know, radicals had made the "amalgamation" of existing craft unions into industrial unions their watchword. So CIO officials were wary of any similar strategy of organization, especially when they saw earlier Red unionists among its bearers. They ordered UE, for example, to relinquish the locals the union's organizers had been building among utility workers (albeit with CIO assistance), and established a new jurisdiction, which they allocated to a new Utility Workers International Union, whose "constitution contained one of the most drastic bans against Communists ever adopted by a labor union," Kampelman notes, "specifically excluding Communists and providing for their expulsion from membership." UE leaders probably accepted the CIO order because, although UE was in charge, paid CIO staff had been doing most of the organizing, and some organizers from the Association of Catholic Trade Unionists (ACTU) were also active there. So refusing to let go of the utilities locals would have been both costly and destructive of labor unity. This may also have been a political concession, a gesture of unity by UE Communists with their erstwhile antagonists but now new CIO allies, in tune with the "Popular Front" line of their party. Similar events occurred in the auto and steel industries.[47]

A strategy of amalgamation among independent unions, by bringing their leaders, members, and finances into one organization, strengthened the new, larger union. So, for the same reasons, where radical or Communist-led locals or unions were incorporated into the new union through amalgamation, their leaders also had a chance to compete for its international leadership. A strong local led by Communists could become a "base of operations, its officers assuming a guiding role in relation to other party-led groups in the union."[48]

In the UAW, one of the most influential of the organized factions was led by Communists. They were among the leaders of several important locals, including the huge local at the Ford Rouge megaplant in Dearborn, Michigan. They also had political bonds to powerful non-Communist allies forged during the sit-down strikes. But although they were highly influential, the Communists made no effort to take over the UAW's leadership.[49] Not only the Communists but other factions, including the one led by the Reuther brothers (Walter, Roy, and Victor) and ACTU, were successful in winning local centers of power and using them as bases for further operations, in an

---

[47] Galenson (1960, p. 253); see Keeran (1980a); Levenstein (1981, p. 51); Kampelman (1957, p. 46).

[48] Selznick (1960, p. 213).   [49] Glazer (1961, p. 112); Keeran (1980a).

effort to forge alliances and build their own "political machine" within the union.

In contrast, in the relatively diversified electrical industry, the UE – whose name (United Electrical, Radio and Machine Workers Union) reflects its amalgamated origins – was organized and led mainly by Communists and their allies. Among the latter were many older radical and socialist workers. Reds had organized one of the major unions (the TUUL's Steel and Metal Workers Union), and the TUUL had some members and significant influence among several other independent and local unions (e.g., in GE's Schenectady plant) that amalgamated in 1936 to form the new union. Communists consequently succeeded in winning the new union's international leadership. "Because it was essentially a coalition of independently-organized unions," as Levenstein explains, "the UE had a relatively democratic constitution with many features ensuring local autonomy and decentralization of power." UE districts, which paid the salaries of their own elected officers, were "exceptionally powerful," and much of the support for the Communists rested at local and district levels.[50]

In sum, we suggest that amalgamation increases the chances that the leaders of the merged units, whatever their politics, will retain local political bases within the new union, from which they can try to extend their influence and contend for its leadership; in a unitary organization, in contrast, their chances of survival as leaders, once their union has been incorporated into the new organization, stripped of its autonomy, and subordinated to the existing officialdom, are minimized. So, for the same reasons, we suggest, Communists who won their spurs and gained adherents in the industrial battles that forged a CIO international union had a better chance of becoming leaders in it if it was formed through amalgamation.

And that is what we find: 67 percent of the twelve amalgamated internationals but only 38 percent of the twenty-six unitary internationals turned out to be led by Communists, and the remaining percentage in both of these categories was split evenly between the "shifting" and anti-Communist camps (17 vs. 17 among the amalgamated and 31 vs. 31 among the unitary unions).

What were the relationships among these four constellations of events and political practices? Put differently, what were the relatively independent effects of each insurgent practice, if we take account of, or "remove," the effects of the others? To get at this, we use "logit analysis"; it is a method for regression analysis when the dependent variable is a dichotomy, like "Communist/non-Communist." What is nice about this method of analysis is that it provides a coefficient of the relative effect of each independent variable that can be

[50] Levenstein (1981, p. 62).

46

restated in "everyday language" as the comparative odds of alternative political outcomes.[51]

[51] Swafford (1980, p. 672). A logit analysis estimates the probability of an event; that probability is converted into an odds; and the natural "log of the odds" is taken to get the "logit." The difference between "probability" and "odds," as any gambler knows, is crucial. The odds of an event is defined as the probability that it will occur divided by the probability that it will *not* occur. Take the throw of a die. The probability that it will come up a 1, 2, 3, 4, or 5 rather than a 6 is five sixths, or 0.83. The probability that it will come up a 6 (i.e., that it will not come up 1, 2, 3, 4, or 5) is one sixth, or 0.17. So the odds of a die coming up on one of these five numbers (1, 2, 3, 4, or 5) is 0.83/0.17 or 5 to 1. Now, in our analysis, for example, we found that 72 percent of the CIO's internationals that seceded from the AFL through a workers' insurgency went on to become Communist-led and 28 percent turned out to be led by non-Communists. So the odds of a union that seceded through a workers' insurgency turning out to be Communist-led were 72 to 28, or 2.57 to 1. Similarly, 25 percent of the internationals that seceded through a top officers' revolt went on to become Communist-led and 75 percent turned to be led by non-Communists. So the odds of a union that seceded through an officers' revolt turning out to be Communist-led were 25 to 75 or 0.33 to 1. The "comparative odds" of a union turning out to be Communist-led if it seceded through a workers' insurgency as opposed to a top officers' revolt were 2.57 to 0.33, or 7.79 to 1. As we see below, the comparative odds were reduced somewhat taking into account (or holding constant) the effects of the other insurgent practices.

Using logit analysis may not be fully appropriate here because our data do not meet all of its crucial assumptions. A much larger number of cases than ours may be needed to be sure the approximations are adequate. Our N of 38 (or, in later chapters, usually 36) is far from "asymptotic." But the logit formulation provides a convenient technique for describing relationships among binary (either/or) events, as in our analyses of winning or losing union leadership and, in later chapters, winning prolabor or procapital provisions in collective bargaining agreements. Further, we do not rely on the logit models alone to test our substantive theory, but also carry out contingency analyses; and the results of the logit and contingency analyses are, as they shoul be, consistent with each other.

Although we present tests of "statistical significance" (e.g., the log odds ratio), assessing how unlikely a relationship is to happen just by chance, we question whether it is appropriate to use significance tests in the multivariate analyses in this book as a criterion for accepting or rejecting a given finding. We have allowed ourselves to think seriously about theoretically salient relationships that fall below the conventional acceptable 0.05 confidence level. First, some of these analyses use data on the entire population. Second, the small number of international unions in the population means that even strong relationships could be rejected at the 0.05 confidence level. Third, relationships of determination ("causal relationships") are not uncovered by tests of significance. A large enough sample can yield small effects that are statistically significant but substantively unimportant (Swafford 1980, p. 687). Rather, a process of determination is revealed by demonstrating, in successive approximations to the underlying realities, the existence of a coherent set of theoretically relevant empirical relationships. Fourth, the analyses in this book are, in a sense, exploratory, not confirmatory.

Table 2.1. *Logit estimates of the direct effects of the insurgent political practices in determining the comparative odds that CIO international unions were Communist-led*

Insurgent practice	Logit coefficient	Odds multiplier
Earlier Red organizing	0.19	1.21
Workers' insurgency	1.95*	7.05
Independent organizing	2.14*	8.51
Amalgamation	0.21	1.23
Intercept	−2.77	
Likelihood ratio chi-square (df)	14.67 (4)	
(N)	(38)	

$^*p < 0.05$.

Of the four insurgent practices, only secession via a workers' insurgency and independent organizing each had a substantial direct effect in determining which CIO international unions were led by Communists. Controlling for the effects of the other three practices, the comparative odds of Communists winning the leadership of a union that seceded from the AFL through a workers' insurgency versus one that seceded through a revolt of its top officers were 7.1 to 1, and the comparative odds were 8.5 to 1 that independent organizing versus a CIO organizing committee resulted in Communist leadership. On the other hand, the comparative odds of the Communists' winning the leadership of an international in an industry that had earlier Red organizing versus an industry that had none were only 1.2 to 1, and the comparative odds were also 1.2 to 1 for an amalgamated versus a unitary international (see Table 2.1).

What are the implications of these findings, that neither earlier Red organizing nor amalgamation seems to have increased the odds much in favor of

Indeed, they are "designed to find out what was not even guessed at before" (cf. Lipset et al. 1962, p. 430). So it makes sense to try to think through the implications of all theoretically salient, empirical relationships.

We have not applied a full path-like model because its applicability to our data is especially problematic. To apply structural equations and path analysis to discrete data, we would have to make several untenable assumptions. For instance, the models developed by Winship and Mare (1983) assume a recursive structure, but, again, it is not possible to test this assumption. In addition, in their "Model Four" (i.e., the model for binary variables without an underlying continuum), which is the closest to our own situation, it is assumed that no measurement error exists. But this would be a silly assumption in a sociohistorical analysis, especially one based on secondary sources. Overall, the use of logit modeling to describe independent effects stretches our data but, we think, permissibly so.

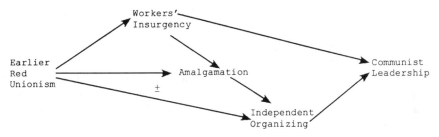

Figure 2.1. Substantive theoretical model of the determination of Communist leadership in CIO international unions by insurgent political practices.

the Communists winning power in an international union? Does this mean that these two insurgent political practices were hardly of importance? In particular, were the long, hard years of earlier Red organizing wasted, scarcely leaving any legacy of industrial unionism, let alone radicalism, among workers for the CIO organizers who followed in their footsteps? In the end, did the Red unionists, as Draper suggests, have almost nothing concrete to show for their efforts? The short answer is a complicated "no."

Our "substantive theoretical model" suggests (see Fig. 2.1) and our findings tend to confirm that these "premature" struggles to build industrial unions had complex and sometimes contradictory indirect political effects in shaping the two decisive political practices – a workers' insurgency and independent organizing – that allowed the Communists to win the leadership of the new CIO unions.

We suggest three closely related hypotheses about the indirect effects of earlier Red organizing.

1. It had contradictory effects on independent organizing. On the one hand, the presence of any number of experienced Red organizers in an industry should have improved the chances that the workers could independently organize a CIO union there. On the other hand, past battles there between Red unionists and the then-AFL officials who later founded the CIO reduced the chances for independent organizing in that industry. (During the Reds' so-called Third Period of "revolutionary upsurge," the TUUL had defined the AFL as "fascist" and denounced even a leader such as Sydney Hillman, head of the militant ACW, as a "fascist gangster leader.")[52] Remembering those battles and knowing whether or not Reds had been active in an industry, top CIO officials such as Lewis, Murray, and Hillman must have tried (as Saposs said they did in SWOC) to put a CIO organizing committee in charge of that industry's

---

[52] Draper (1960, pp. 302–6); TUUL (1930, p. 17); Klehr (1984, pp. 39, 17).

campaign to "spot" Communists and keep them from gaining a hold on power in the new union being built there. If so, this nullified much of the impetus that earlier Red organizing gave to subsequent CIO independent organizing.

Consistent with this reasoning, we find that 38 percent of the twenty-one CIO unions in the industries that witnessed earlier Red organizing, as opposed to 23 percent of the seventeen in the other industries, were built under the aegis of a CIO organizing committee, rather than through independent organizing.[53]

2. Amalgamation occurred more often in industries with a history of earlier Red unionism than others. Some former Red unions or their tight-knit remnants held on, despite repression (e.g., James Matles's Metal Workers International Union (MWIU)), and managed to amalgamate with others like themselves, with AFL federal locals, or with independent unions as a strategy for building new CIO unions. Amalgamation in turn, we suggest, enhanced the capacity of these unions to go it alone (without CIO tutelage) in unionizing their industry. This reasoning is strikingly supported by our findings: Among the twenty-one internationals in industries where earlier Red organizing had occurred, 52 percent were formed through amalgamation. But among the seventeen in the industries untouched by earlier Red unionism, 94 percent were unitary organizations.[54]

3. Perhaps most important, by creating a local sympathetic base in an AFL affiliate, earlier Red organizing paved the way for a later workers' uprising and secession to join the fledgling CIO. In the earlier TUEL phase, Communists had won adherents inside AFL affiliates, and although their main organizing efforts after establishing the TUUL in 1929 had been aimed at building independent "revolutionary unions," many Red unionists had ignored the current party line and continued to work to organize oppositions and win independent followings in the AFL.

In 1934, a year before the dissolution of the TUEL and the party's decision to have it return to the AFL, a confidential CP memorandum reported that Communists were in the leadership of 135 AFL locals with a combined membership of over 50,000 as well as of "several" entire union districts; the memo said they also led organized opposition groups in another 500 locals.[55] In 1935, with the TUUL's formal dissolution, these Communist bases in 635 AFL locals and entire districts were reinforced and new ones were established when Red union remnants rejoined the AFL, as intact units if they could or, otherwise, as individuals.

[53] Log odds ratio (uniform association) = -0.63, $p < 0.20$; standard error = 0.70.
[54] Log odds ratio (uniform association) = 2.49, $p < 0.01$; standard error = 0.95.
[55] Klehr (1984, p. 225).

The evidence is consistent with the hypothesis that they were among the main agitators and organizers involved in "fomenting insurrection," as AFL officials charged, and leading the secessionists into the CIO. In industries that had experienced earlier Red unionism, 62 percent of the internationals were born in a workers' insurgency, whereas in industries with no history of earlier Red organizing, 71 percent were led into the CIO from above by a revolt of their top officers.[56]

Now, as we already know, a workers' insurgency in turn yielded high odds (7 to 1 over an officers' revolt) in favor of Communists' winning power in the new CIO union. So earlier Red unionism had a decisive *indirect* effect – that is, as mediated by a workers' insurgency – in bringing Communists to power in the CIO. What's more, and as our substantive model suggests, far more of the unions that seceded as the result of a workers' insurgency than of those that were led out by their top officers merged with others to form a new, amalgamated international union. An amalgamated union was also more likely than a unitary union to carry out its own strategy of independent organizing in the industry rather than falling under the aegis of a CIO organizing committee; and again, this, in turn, strengthened the odds that the Communists would win union power. Among the twelve unions formed through amalgamation, 83 percent did their own organizing, without the intervention of a CIO organizing committee, as compared with 61 percent of the twenty-six formed as a unitary organization.[57] The eighteen unions that joined the CIO as the result of a workers' uprising split half and half between becoming an amalgamated or unitary CIO international union, but among the twenty that either seceded in an officer's revolt or joined with their leadership intact, 85 percent became unitary CIO internationals.[58] In sum, earlier Red unionism in an industry and the resulting later presence there of veteran Communists and their adherents had contradictory direct effects on independent organizing, but their presence also spurred secession from the AFL through a workers' insurgency and, subsequently, a strategy of amalgamation, both of which in turn increased the chances that Communists would win the leadership of the new CIO internationals.

Conclusion

Our analysis has shown that the organizing strategies and concrete political practices of rival workers' factions and parties during the industrial battles and union drives of the long Red Decade, wittingly or not, determined whether

[56] Log odds ratio (uniform association) = 1.28, $p < 0.05$; standard error = 0.67.
[57] Log odds ratio (uniform association) = 0.98, $p < 0.08$; standard error = 0.81.
[58] Log odds ratio (uniform association) = 1.61, $p < 0.01$; standard error = 0.74.

Communists, "uncertain and shifting" coalitions, or anti-Communists won and held "power and trust" in the new industrial unions for the duration of the CIO era.[59] In particular, the four insurgent practices of earlier Red organizing, secession from the AFL via a workers' insurgency, independent organizing, and amalgamation increased the odds of the Communists' winning the workers' leadership.

None of this, however, implies a "voluntaristic" theory of how history is made. The original *historical opening* for the left among the nation's industrial workers was provided by an extraordinary crisis of American capitalism, the consequent political upheavals at all levels of government – local, state, and federal, legislative, executive, and judicial – and the unprecedented, primarily spontaneous, "labor upsurge" of the 1930s. "Such times," Frances Piven and Richard Cloward put it well, "are rare and certainly not of anyone's deliberate making." And it was in these rare times that "the few Communists who had been working in factories and mines and shops found themselves," as Glazer says, " . . . carried like corks riding a flood to top positions in a host of unions."[60]

---

[59] We have not tried to assess how the "unintended, unanticipated, or unrecognized consequences of purposive social action," in Robert K. Merton's well-known phrase, bear on this substantive analysis. We have avoided this question intentionally, because we cannot address it empirically, while signaling our awareness of it by an occasional parenthetical phrase, for example, "wittingly or not."

[60] Brody (1980, pp. 103, 130–44); Piven and Cloward (1977, p. 173); Glazer (1961, pp. 100–101). Unfortunately missing from our analysis is an attempt to assess the effects on subsequent CIO organizing and the eventual Communist leadership in CIO unions of the activities of the Depression's Communist-led Unemployed Councils (Leab 1967) – which constituted "the largest 'cover' organization of the depression period," according to Harold D. Lasswell and Dorothy Blumenstock. TUUL cadres were heavily involved in organizing and leading the Unemployed Councils. "We, the Unemployed Council and the Trade Union Unity League, we say, let us organize and fight, why should we starve?" asked Nels Kjar, the Communist candidate for mayor of Chicago, in January 1931. "Well, because they have got a lot of watchdogs around the food, so we shall not get this food, but we say this, when a man is hungry, he has a right to eat, regardless of the capitalist law." The Unemployed Councils, with their TUUL cadres in the lead, served, we suggest, as a base or training ground for later CIO organizers in plants located where the councils had been active. In Chicago, the focus of Lasswell and Blumenstock's study, and a city in which TUUL *a*typically had strong ties to the existing AFL leadership, the Unemployed Councils had "at least 80 locals" that were "effectively established." Among the strongest TUUL unions in Chicago were the Packing House Workers Industrial Union, the Needle Trades Workers Industrial Union, and the Fur Workers Industrial Union, which, Lasswell and Blumenstock note, "were industrial unions, and in this sense were forerunners of the CIO type of organization." TUUL cadres were instructed to hold protest rallies both among employed workers outside factories and among the unemployed to try to unify them to demonstrate "side by side" to demand "work

But the Communists and other radicals of the 1930s involved in the leadership and organization of the working class were not mere "corks riding a flood." They were active, self-conscious men and women, and they were not merely "riding" but struggling to give shape to the sudden social eruption in which they were leading participants. This eruption, this insurgent "flood" flowing over the land, did not itself determine what happened, except in the sense that it constituted, as we emphasized at the outset, an immanent realm of possibility, a choice of possible worlds. Which one was suppressed, and which one realized was determined by the struggles of real men and women, acting both individually and collectively. Indeed, this realm of possibility was itself the partial creation, within (unknown) objective limits, of what they and other men and women before them already had done in the real past, as they fought to make their employers recognize their right to self-organization and concede them a modicum of social justice.

or wages" and insurance and relief "under the direct control of the workers themselves" (1939, pp. 73, 157, 75–76, 191–92). Lizabeth Cohen, writing on Chicago labor history, also emphasizes that the Unemployed Councils taught many of the city's "depression victims that being unemployed was not their fault and that they should join together to demand help, a lesson these workers would put to good use when they began to organize their factories several years later. *Many organizers in the CIO would come directly out of the unemployed movement*" (1990, p. 265, emphasis added). We discuss the role of the TUUL and Unemployed Councils in the struggle for interracial unity in Chapter 9.

3

INSURGENCY, RADICALISM, AND DEMOCRACY

Five years into his presidency of the UAW, and four years after he launched his swift political "fumigation" of the UAW's Red "filth," Walter Reuther still found himself encountering too much dissidence. "Everybody has a right to his own opinion . . . ," he pleaded at the UAW's 1951 convention. "You are going to have contests for offices. . . . But let's have democratic contests without factionalism. Let's have democracy but not factionalism."[1]

Real, contingent political struggles like the ones that had elevated Reuther to the UAW's presidency in 1946 and through which his faction had then defeated the "center-left" coalition in 1947 – and which, despite his steel grip on power, he was still being compelled to wage four years later to consolidate his new "one-party political machine" – have no place in the conventional organizational paradigm inspired by Robert Michels.[2] Instead, an "inevitable current," fed by hidden, and undemonstrable, organizational "needs" for stability, security, and continuity, carries labor unions toward their preordained destiny.[3] The "spread of bureaucracy and the decay of democracy in trade unions" is an inherent "tragedy of organization." The "quest for union democracy" is thus "futile." In sum, oligarchy is an "immanent necessity," dictated by an "iron law."[4]

What used to pass as "evidence" for this putative "iron law of oligarchy" was the "fact" that, in mid-twentieth-century America, "most unions" in the United States were ruled by an "entrenched oligarchy" facing no "internal opposition."[5] It was indeed a fact that autocracy reigned in organized

---

[1] As Lichtenstein comments, "This was an absurd distinction, and it soon drove Reuther to the most autocratic measures" (1995, pp. 309–10, 311).

[2] Michels ([1915]1949); Meyer (1992, p. 226); Halpern (1988, p. 230).

[3] Herberg (1943, p. 413); Magrath (1959); Jacobs (1963, p. 151); Selznick (1943, p. 49; 1949, p. 9).

[4] Michels ([1915] 1949, pp. 402, 382); Lipset et al. (1962, p. 12); Magrath (1959).

[5] Galenson and Lipset (1960, p. 203).

labor: A 1950 study of the constitutions of 154 national and international unions (virtually the entire union population) found that two thirds had clauses expressly restricting internal political action, and these clauses covered "a wide range of activity – from slandering union officers to issuing circulars to the members." A 1948 study of 115 unions also found that most were not even "nominally democratic": Three out of four had a constitution that explicitly prohibited "the existence of factions, cliques, or political parties organized to discuss union business outside of official meetings as proof of the establishment of a dual or opposition union which can be penalized by expulsion," and the constitution also endowed the "chief officer" with "extensive and many sided powers," for instance, to sanction strikes, intervene in disputes with the employer, preside at conventions and appoint its committees, control the content of the union's newspaper, and discipline members.[6]

But none of the Michelsian writers on the governance of American unions seems to have noticed another "fact": "Entrenched oligarchy," consecrated by a constitution that restricted political activity and arrogated power to the executive, although typical if not preponderant among AFL and independent unions, was not at all typical among CIO internationals during its heyday. So, when we break down the 115 national and international unions into two groups, 86 AFL and independent unions versus 29 CIO unions, we find that, as of 1948, the chief officer held "considerable power" in 51 percent of the AFL and independent unions but in only 21 percent of the CIO unions, and he held "routine power" in a mere 17 percent of the AFL and independent unions but in 48 percent of the CIO unions.[7]

On our own comprehensive "constitutional democracy scale," described below, about seven out of ten CIO international unions, as of that same year, were democratic: either highly (29 percent) or moderately (40 percent); only three out of ten (31 percent) were ruled by an autocrat or "entrenched oligarchy." If the same analysis, using our scale, could be made of the constitutions of AFL affiliates and independents, we think it would show that they, unlike CIO internationals, were typically or even preponderantly autocracies or oligarchies. Many, if not most, CIO unions were characterized, then, not by "one-party oligarchy" but (to borrow a description of major unions in England) by a

---

[6] Summers (1950, p. 513); Taft (1946, p. 252); Taft's category of "extensive" power includes two subcategories: "considerable," held by the chief officer in 44 percent of the unions, and "moderate," held in 31 percent (1948, p. 460).

[7] Taft (1948, pp. 459–66). We found a similar pattern on reanalyzing Summers's data on eligibility for union membership (1946). Unfortunately, his constitutional data on restriction of political activity were not published in his later report (1950).

"fluid and fragmented 'multi-party' political system," whose government involved "an uneven and uneasy coalition between representatives of different ideological tendencies." The dynamics of such intraunion coalitions was determined by the relative strength of the contending factions. In a word, the government of many if not most CIO international unions was a "polyarchy," in which "multiple minorities" having their own independent political bases competed for power.[8]

Now if our Michelsians had taken serious notice of the fact that concentrated executive power and restrictions on political activity were typical of AFL and independent unions but not of CIO unions, this alone might have made them suspicious of the notion that oligarchy is an immanent necessity of organization. It might also have rendered prima facie suspect a method of analysis whose unstated assumption it is that *reality* mirrors *theory* and that, therefore, it is proper to posit a case as "deviant" from an "iron law" while imagining that all the rest of the cases conform to it.[9]

The "fact" that the likelihood of democracy in America's labor unions was slim should merely have provoked the question, Why was it so, and not otherwise? The search for an answer begins with the recognition that oligarchy in organized labor is no more immanent than democracy. Rather, both are the product of determinate, though contingent, political struggles among rival workers' factions and parties over who shall lead their class and decide how, and through what political forms, its interests are to be articulated and advanced. In particular, as we see below, the opposed political strategies and actual practices involved in the industrial battles to organize the unorganized, determined not only who won "power and trust" in the CIO's international unions, but also how that power was exercised and that trust fulfilled. Democracy in the CIO's international unions, much as democracy in nation-states, was rooted in insurgency and nourished by radicalism.[10]

---

[8] Martin (1971, p. 244); Dahl (1956).   [9] As in Lipset et al. (1962).

[10] See, e.g., Moore (1966); Therborn (1977); Zeitlin (1984); Stephens (1989). We abstract here from differences in the industrial base of the CIO internationals. No union-specific data on industrial organization and labor force composition exist for these years; and the available U.S. Census data (four-digit SIC) are quite incomplete. The jurisdictions of many CIO unions were not confined within a single refined SIC category but criss-crossed several categories. The available SIC data do not allow precise measures of the industrial base of CIO international unions. At best, only learned "guesstimates" of the industrial mix of a union's jurisdiction are possible. Nevertheless, and bearing these strictures in mind, we did construct necessarily crude measures of some features of the union's industrial base that have been mentioned in the literature as possible "factors" affecting the chances for

But these intraworking-class struggles took place within the class struggle. Inherent in the class struggle is an imbalance of class power between capital and labor; and this, in Max Weber's metaphor, is what "loads the historical dice" against the thriving of democracy both in workers' parties and in their unions.

Put plainly, the snuffing out of dissidence and opposition, and thus the tendency toward oligarchy, in organized labor is dictated not by the "needs of organization" but by the real-world wants of union officials, especially those who – succumbing to the pressures applied by employers (and the state) – have become, in Michels's apt phrase, *strangers to their own class*. In general theoretical terms, this can be stated as the proposition that union oligarchy and the hegemony of capital tend to reinforce each other.[11] Indeed, Michels himself argued (although this has been ignored by his American epigones) that the mainspring of "aristocratic tendencies" among labor officials in the United States was "the unrestricted *power of capital*" and the "corruption" that came with it. The "leaders of the American proletariat," Michels wrote in 1910, were "in many cases . . . no more than paid servants of capital." So, given the "evidence," Michels might well have transformed *this* observation into an "iron law": "*Who says 'the unrestricted power of capital,' says 'oligarchy.'*"[12]

---

union democracy. For industrial organization, (1) the size distribution of plants and (2) the level of concentration in the industry. For labor force composition, (3) skill, (4) sex, and (5) "race." Controlling separately for each of these variables did not make any substantive difference in the relationships that are shown here. These tables are available on request.

[11] See Chapter 5, for an analysis of one side of this double-edged process – the effect of union democracy on capital's hegemony at the point of production.

[12] Michels (1915, pp. 310–11; emphasis added). Long before its academic apotheosis, a TUEL handbook on the "misleaders of labor," by William Z. Foster, first told American workers about the lessons contained in Michels's *Political Parties*. Foster listed what Michels said were "the many devices used by Social Democratic bureaucrats [in Germany] to maintain themselves in office" and said: "But American trade union leaders use not only most of the tricks that Michels touches upon but many more of which he never dreamed. To hang on to their jobs they appeal to the gun and the knife, they make open alliances with the employers and the state against the workers, and they ruthlessly suppress democracy in the organizations" (1927, pp. 270, 273–74, 312, 316, 324). Foster was not exaggerating. In the fur trade in New York City, for example, where "the Fur Workers Industrial Union fought the A. F. of L. International Fur Workers to a standstill, 'vicious fights on the picket lines, in the shops and on the streets were a daily occurrence. Few weeks passed by when workers, slashed with the knives of their trade or trampled by the boots of rival unionists, did not fill the emergency wards and night courts'" (Galenson 1940, p. 10, quoting Scheyer

The "Divided Soul"

Analysis of the social origins of democracy or dictatorship necessarily implies a conception of the democratic ideal against which any real system of rule has to be measured. The meaning of democracy is not a mere matter of definition, but involves contentious political questions. We take our lead from critical democratic theory, in which democracy's essence, and constitutive principle, is that the aims, methods, and uses of political power are decided through juridically protected, freely self-determined political activity. Ordinary men and women "take upon themselves collectively" the responsibility for governing; they do not merely show up to vote, as John Stuart Mill sardonically remarked long ago, and commit "a political act, to be done only once in a few years."[13]

So by what standard should a labor union's inner political life be measured? Assuming the aspiration to be democratic, an unavoidable tension still exists between democracy and "the discipline necessary for militant action," including the capacity to resist and punish "acts of treason" (e.g., strike-breaking) in the ranks.[14] So framing a concept of *"union* democracy" and trying to measure it is doubly difficult. For even assuming agreement on the concept of democracy, the question remains whether a labor union "ought to" be democratic, and if so what that means in practice. For the union's sine qua non is that it is supposed to be a fighting organization of workers that is in constant readiness to defy the "sway of property" over their daily working lives.[15] Any union worth its salt is, minimally, a sort of irregular (if unarmed) workers' "army" engaged in "a guerrilla war against the effects of the existing system" and "the encroachments of capital."[16] Certainly, CIO unions had to confront belligerent and often violent employer opposition – including assaults by company goons and spying by company finks – not just during their early organizing battles but throughout much of the CIO era.[17]

1935). Or take the 1936 East Coast maritime strike: AFL thugs "got some money from the shipowners," as Joe Ryan, head of the AFL International Longshoreman's Association (ILA) boasted, "and drove them [the strikers] back with baseball bats where they belonged. Then they called the strike off" (Kempton 1955, p. 95).

[13] Neumann (1957, pp. 186, 189, 173–76); Pateman (1970); Mill (1963, p. 229).

[14] Mills ([1948] 1971, p. 5); Williams (1954, p. 831).   [15] Mills (1948, pp. 4, 8).

[16] Marx ([1865] 1973b, pp. 75–76).

[17] The most infamous postwar episodes of antiunion violence were the attempted assassinations of Walter Reuther and his younger brother Victor. The blast of a 12-gauge shotgun through Walter's kitchen window ripped into his arm and chest on April 20, 1948; thirteen months later, another shotgun blast, from an identical make, caught Victor at home reading the newspaper, hitting him in the face, throat, and right shoulder. Both men survived, but

So asking what determines union democracy implies that a union not only can but also should be both an "army" and a "town meeting": The union's "irregulars," its rank and file, should freely argue the issues, decide on a battle plan, elect their officers, and themselves vote on the "declaration of war" (strike) and on the terms of each truce (contract).[18] This is scarcely a universal view, however. As V. L. Allen argues, "trade union organization is not based on theoretical concepts prior to it, that is, on some concept of democracy, but on the end it serves.... [T]he end of trade union activity is to protect and improve the general living standards of its members and not to provide workers with an exercise in self-government."[19]

Withal, we reject this view, and (for reasons that become clearer in Chapters 4 and 6) apply the same standard to the CIO's international unions that any political system qualifying as a democracy has to be measured by. A democratic union's political system must combine three basic features: a *democratic constitution* (i.e., guarantees of basic civil liberties and political rights), *institutionalized opposition* (i.e., the freedom of members to criticize and debate union officials and to organize, oppose, and replace officials through freely contested elections among contending political associations, such as parties or factions), and an *active membership* (i.e., maximum participation by its members in the actual exercise of power within the union and in making the decisions that affect them). In this chapter, for lack of appropriate data, we attempt to measure only the first two features: a democratic constitution and institutionalized opposition. In the next chapter, however, we also take a close look at how workers lived democracy in "the biggest local union in the world," UAW Ford Local 600.

Walter lost much of the function in his right arm and hand and Victor lost his right eye. Their assailant was paid by Santos Perrone, a gangster and veteran company goon employed in the battles of the 1930s to smash unionization on Detroit's east side and the CIO's efforts in 1941 to organize Ford's car haul business; in 1945 and 1946, Perrone and his minions also brutally beat up six leaders of the UAW's Briggs local. When the FBI, after a notorious delay of two years, got around to interviewing Walter Reuther in 1950 about the assassination attempts, he was not, alas, above speculating that "individuals from the old Addes–Communist alliance must have had a hand" in the attempts. (J. Edgar Hoover refused to have the FBI enter the investigation; when Truman's attorney general Joseph Clark called for the FBI to do so, Hoover responded that he was "not going to send the FBI in every time some nigger woman gets raped.") In 1953, one of Perrone's gunmen, in return for UAW's $5,000 reward, confessed to being the shotgun triggerman, but somehow he managed to slip away from his police guards and disappear. No one was ever convicted of the assassination attempts (Lichtenstein 1995, pp. 271–74).

[18] Muste (1928, p. 187); Mills (1948, p. 4).   [19] Allen (1954, p. 15).

Constitutional Democracy

Equal franchise and equal access to all public offices and equality of treatment without regard to class or calling are the most basic political rights, without which open, freely self-determined political activity, and thus real accountability of political officials, is impossible. In turn, these political rights presuppose civil liberties, both personal and societal, without which equal suffrage is a sham and political representation an illusion. Any abrogation of civil liberties necessarily vitiates political rights, though not vice versa.

By *personal* civil liberties, we mean those liberties pertaining solely to the person, such as security of the person, of his or her home, papers, and effects, the right to a fair trial, and protection from unreasonable searches and seizures. In contrast, *societal* civil liberties pertain to associations and organizations: the freedoms of religion, speech, and assembly. One limitation, however, is inherent in societal liberties. Their exercise must not deprive others of the same rights. Societal liberties presuppose personal liberties: Without security of the person, freedom of association is impossible. If citizens are subject to arbitrary or capricious arrest and punishment, they can neither associate nor assemble freely.[20]

In accordance with this concept of constitutional democracy, we reviewed the 1948 constitution or, if no constitution was published in 1948, the one for the nearest year, of each CIO international union to assess whether or not it guaranteed basic civil liberties and political rights (or their equivalent) to its members.[21] We selected the year 1948 because it was the last year before the CIO launched its all-out attack on its "Communist camp."

In assessing the provisions of the CIO's constitutions, we were also guided by relevant legal scholarship and, in particular, "a bill of rights for union members," couched in terms of the rights of an industrial worker, that the American Civil Liberties Union drafted in 1947.[22]

Our measure of a union's level of constitutional democracy is a "constitutional democracy scale" meant to assess the extent to which an international union's constitution guaranteed basic civil liberties (personal and societal) and political rights ("franchise" and official "accountability"). The scale consists of

---

[20] Neumann (1957, pp. 173–76).

[21] The analysis in Chapter 2 used data on the CIO's original thirty-eight durable international unions. But mergers among four of them had reduced the total to thirty-six by 1948, the year we used to gather the constitutional data, and we could not locate a copy of the constitution of one other union. This reduces the number of internationals in the present analysis to thirty-five.

[22] ACLU (1948).

four separate scales (two sets of liberties and two sets of rights); each scale is constructed to weigh the items included in accord with their relative order of importance as a constitutional guarantee.[23]

Here are a few examples. On the five-point scale of personal liberties, a constitution was awarded the highest score of 5 points if it stipulated that charges against a member had to be signed by the maker of the charges, and 4 points if it stipulated that the trial committee had to be elected (a score of 4 or 5 points is "high"). On societal liberties, the highest score of 3 points was awarded if the constitution had no clause allowing the suspension of a member on charges of "slander" against the union (a score of 3 points is "high"). On the scale of the right of franchise, a constitution merited the highest score of 3 points if the constitution prohibited political discrimination, and 2 points if it did not bar Communists or members or advocates of any other party from union office (a score of 2 or 3 is "high"); on accountability, the highest score of 4 points was awarded if the constitution stipulated that convention committees had to be elected, and 3 points if it required convention committees to be broadly representative (a score of 3 or 4 is "high"). The specific provisions and scoring for each of the four scales and of the entire constitutional democracy scale are given in Table 3.1.

We classified an international union as having a "highly democratic" constitution if it scored "high" on at least three of these scales, "moderately democratic" if it scored high on two scales, and "oligarchic" if it scored high on no more than one scale. The question, of course, is whether any measure of democracy based on constitutional provisions can provide a valid and reliable measure of the immeasurable, that is, of the "real" level of union democracy. As David Dubinsky, then president of the International Ladies Garment Workers Union (ILGWU), exclaimed at the tumultuous founding convention of the UAW, "In my union, we have democracy too – but they know who is boss!"[24]

---

[23] This is usually termed a "Guttman scale," after its creator, Louis Guttman. We simply split the scores received on each of these four separate scales into "high" and "low" and then added the number of "high" scores on these four scales to get the unions' total score on the constitutional democracy scale. We split the scores on each scale so as to gauge the presence or absence of democratic guarantees on that scale, rather than simply using the actual scores, because the values (and the ranges of values) on each of the four scales are not uniform across the scales. (The number of items is not the same on each scale; one scale has five items; one has four; and two have three apiece. The personal liberties scale, for instance, consists of five items, and the scores are dichotomized 4–5 points, "high," and 0–3 points, "low." The scale for the right of the franchise consists of three items, dichotomized 2–3, high, and 0–1, low) (Table 3.1).

[24] Cochran (1977, p. 339).

Table 3.1. *Constitutional democracy scale in CIO international unions, as of 1948*

Scale score		Constitutional provisions
Civil liberties scale		
Personal	5	Constitution stipulates that charges against a union member be signed.
	4	Constitution stipulates that the trial committee be elected.
	3	Constitution establishes time limits on trial duration.
	2	Constitution allows an appeal to the union convention against the trial committee's verdict.
	1	Constitution stipulates that charges against a union member be in writing.
	0	None of the above.
Societal	3	Constitution has no provision for suspension of an individual union member on charges of "slander" of the union.
	2	Constitution has no provision for suspension of a union local for criticism of international officers.
	1	Constitution has no provision for putting a local under administratorship or trusteeship.
	0	None of the above.
Political rights scale		
Franchise	3	Constitution prohibits political discrimination.
	2	Constitution does not prohibit Communists (or affiliates or advocates of any other party, e.g., Fascists) from holding union office.
	1	Constitution does not prohibit Communists (or affiliates or advocates of any other party, e.g., Fascists) from being union members.
	0	None of the above.
Accountability	4	Constitution stipulates that convention committees be elected.
	3	Constitution stipulates that convention committees be broadly representative.

Table 3.1. (*cont.*)

Scale score	Constitutional provisions
2	Constitution has a provision for recall of international officers.
1	Constitution requires audits of expenditures by international officers.
0	None of the above.

[a] Personal: dichotomized, 4–5 high, 0–3 low.
[b] Societal: dichotomized, 3 high, 0–2 low.
[c] Franchise: dichotomized, 2–3 high, 0–1 low.
[d] Accountability: dichotomized, 3–4 high, 0–2 low.
Note: Scale of constitutional democracy: very high = high on four scales; high = high on three scales; medium = high on two scales; low = high on one scale; very low = high on none. Item analysis indicates that each of the four scales has an acceptable scalar pattern, i.e., at or above the acceptable scalar level measured by the coefficients of reproducibility (0.90) and scalability (0.60). Given our conception of democracy as a hierarchy of basic rights and liberties, a measure of constitutional democracy itself constructed as a Guttman scale from the scores on each of the four separate scales for rights and liberties is ideally preferable, but this is not technically permissible, because a Guttman scale cannot accommodate a hierarchy within a hierarchy.

Any realistic analysis has to recognize that discrepancies necessarily existed between the letter of the law and political actualities in America's unions. But it makes no sense to simply assume, as the authors of a path-breaking work on union democracy do, that in "nominally democratic [unions] . . . the *clauses in the constitutions* which set forth the machinery for translating membership interests and sentiments into organizational purpose and action *bear little relationship to the actual political processes.*"[25]

[25] Lipset et al. (1962, pp. 2–3, emphasis added). Their book, *Union Democracy*, "began to take shape" during the late 1940s, at the tail end of the CIO era, and was published in 1956, a year after the CIO's merger with the AFL. Which "clauses" they have in mind here, they do not say; they present no evidence of their own (aside from some anecdotes), and they do not cite the "studies of social scientists" that, they say, "tend to confirm" the "generalization" that clauses in union constitutions "bear little relationship" to what really goes on in union political life. They do, however, provide one salient, and important, example of the discrepancy between formal constitutional provisions and actual practice in a union: Although the International Typographical Union had an institutionalized two-party system, its constitution explicitly

Their comment is about constitutional clauses *protecting* basic rights and liberties; but if such clauses were mere shibboleths, would this not also be true, by the same dismissive reasoning, of clauses that *restrict* rights and liberties? Are we to assume that clauses endowing the executive with extensive power over its members are also "little" related to "the actual political processes" in the union? Take, for instance, the authority given to the president of the CIO's conservative Steel Workers or the radical FE. The USWA president had "the authority to appoint, direct, suspend, or remove, such organizers [and] representatives . . . as he may deem necessary." FE's had "the power to suspend local unions for violation of the laws of the Constitution of the International union, or to suspend the officers or Executive Board members of such local unions."[26]

We do not consider it sensible or prudent to simply assume that such clauses, which concentrate arbitrary power in the hands of top union officials, "bear little relationship to their actual political processes."[27] If antidemocratic clauses

prohibited ITU members from joining a "combination composed wholly or partly" of ITU members "with the intent or purpose to . . . influence or control the legislation of this union." Strangely enough, by the end of the book, they come up with a proposition that undermines their earlier claim that constitutional rights are unimportant: "The greater the protection for the rights of political opposition included in a union's code of law, the greater the chances for democracy" (1962, p. 468). This proposition is indeed the implicit assumption underlying a crucial part of our constitutional democracy scale, and it is consistent with a close reading of the history of the CIO unions, as we discuss below.

[26] USWA (1948, p. 8); FE (1949, p. 27). These examples of restrictive provisions pale compared, for example, with the dictatorial powers with which the constitutions of the AFL International Brotherhood of Electrical Workers (IBEW) or of the Musicians Union endowed their presidents. IBEW's authorized him to remove any officer for "non-performance of duty"; to suspend or expel locals; to "suspend the cards and membership of any member who, in his judgment, is working against the welfare of the I.B.E.W. in the interests of any group or organization detrimental to the I.B.E.W. – or for creating dissension among members or among L.U's [local unions] . . ."; and to decide all "questions of law and organization disputes" (Taft 1948, p. 468). The constitution of the Musicians Union vested its president with the power to "annul and set aside constitution, by-laws, or any portion thereof . . . and substitute therefor other and different provisions of his own making; the power to do so is hereby made absolute in the president. . . . " (Shister 1945, pp. 105, 104).

[27] In fact, despite their blanket denial of the relevance of constitutional clauses, Lipset et al. themselves specifically point to such authoritarian clauses as evidence of "the power of top officials": "Most unions have given their executive boards the right to suspend local officials for violating policies of the central bodies . . . " and thereby increase "their monopolization of internal power." They specifically refer to constitutional provisions that

really matter, then clauses that provide guarantees of democratic freedoms should be taken no less seriously, as meaningful if imperfect measures – and determinants – of the internal political life of America's unions. If the letter of the law and "knowing who is boss" in the CIO's unions must sometimes have differed – or, more prosaically, if constitutional provisions and political actualities were discrepant – the likelihood is that they were systematically related, for three main reasons.

1. The pattern of basic rights and liberties in the constitutions of CIO international unions was distinctively different from, and was incomparably far more democratic than, the pattern in the constitutions of AFL and independent unions.
2. The judiciary, throughout the CIO era, regularly upheld the provisions of union constitutions against legal challenge.[28]
3. Whatever the situation might have been in the AFL and independent unions at the time, the constitutions of CIO internationals typically were living political documents, written and rewritten over the years to embody the conceptions and objectives of the winners in intraunion political struggles.

The constitutions of CIO internationals were originally written, remember, at a moment of escalating capital–labor conflict and workers' self-organization, and in the aftermath of the CIO's split from the AFL. So a union's constitution tended to define its distinctive identity, reflect its organizers' social

---

forbid "slandering union officers," distributing circulars to union members, or forming internal factions, cliques, or parties as restrictions on union democracy (1962, pp. 8, 271–72, 290).

[28] In intraunion disputes concerning members' rights brought before the courts, from the early years of the twentieth century through the CIO era, the source of the court's decision was usually based on the relevant provisions of the union's constitution (Shister 1945, p. 79; Williams 1954, p. 829; Summers 1955, pp. 604–6). The courts often protected union members by demanding literal compliance with the union constitution (Summers 1955, p. 605). In some instances, therefore, the courts even have upheld the right of a union – in order to defend itself against slander and libel and as a means of punishing deliberate violations of union rules – to invoke provisions in its constitution forbidding criticism of its officers, printing and distributing leaflets to union members without the consent of its officers, or forming factions within the union. On the other hand, the courts were prompt to set aside union provisions when they had been used to take revenge against defeated political opponents and suppress criticism (Aaron and Komaroff 1949, p. 657). In sum, the courts tended to ensure that clauses in a union constitution and the union's "real" political procedures were systematically related.

consciousness, and embody their decisions about its aims, structure, and political system.[29]

Typically, as a close reading of the history of CIO international unions suggests, the original drafting of a union's constitution at its founding convention – by not constitutional lawyers but working men and women – involved heated, lengthy, and detailed debates and political infighting among contending factions over each crucial provision; and it was then amended and revised repeatedly in the midst of serious political struggles over the years. So a union's constitution was, we believe, a rough reflection of its real internal political dynamics.

The regular convention of a CIO international union was simultaneously a legislature, a supreme court, and a constitutional assembly. It was at a union's conventions that its major political battles were fought to a formal conclusion, compacts made, officers elected, and, as a result, its constitution often amended or revised.[30] Decisive political shifts, especially in the balance of power among a union's contending factions, were usually sealed at the convention by new constitutional provisions affecting the members' rights and liberties, local autonomy, executive authority, rank-and-file power, and even the union's aims and political philosophy. So if a gap existed between constitutional provisions and inner political realities, the constitution was, nonetheless, an "effective force" – as men and women on opposing sides agreed – in a union's factional struggles.[31] "Correct constitutional laws are vital," William Z. Foster – onetime Wobbly, founder of the Syndicalist League in 1912, leader of the Great Steel Strike of 1919, and then founder of the TUEL in 1922 – said in 1937, "as they place in the hands of the rank and file effective democratic weapons, if they will but use them."[32] In sum, we are convinced (and show below) that the constitutions of CIO international unions "paint...a very vivid picture" of the unions' inner political life and of their "dominant political machine...in action."[33]

Factionalism: The "Decisive Proof of Democracy"

Constitutional rights and liberties are intended, above all, to guarantee the freedom of political activity, especially the freedom to oppose the existing

---

[29] Cf. Neumann (1944, pp. 8–9).
[30] Taft (1962, p. 125); Leiserson (1959, p. 122); Shister (1945, p. 78); Seidman (1953b, p. 227).
[31] Herberg (1943, p. 408).   [32] Foster (1937, p. 258).
[33] Shister (1945, p. 78); Seidman (1953b, p. 227).

regime and to struggle for political power: to form, join, and participate actively in organized political associations (e.g., blocs, caucuses, factions, or parties). The legitimacy of "factionalism" or organized opposition in a union, as in a state, is the "decisive proof of democracy."[34] "Institutionalized opposition" is democracy's "life blood," for it sustains, and in turn is sustained by, the union's democratic constitution.[35]

So, aside from our constitutional democracy scale, we also draw on historical data to estimate the freedom of oppositionists to organize freely in a union and vie for power. Much has been written about the same handful of CIO international unions, however, but little or nothing about most of them, and even the information on the inner political life of some of the major CIO internationals is spotty. So we have a *rough* measure of the existence of factionalism in only twenty-three international unions, each of which we were able to designate as having "organized factions," "sporadic factions," or "no known factions."

In ten internationals, such as the American Newspaper Guild (ANG), the UAW, and UE, the incumbent leadership appears to have regularly faced serious internal opposition. Organized caucuses or blocs (really, parties in all but name) regularly contended for power within these unions, and their governments rested at different times on uneven and uneasy electoral coalitions among the rival factions. Eight internationals, such as the longshoremen and warehousemen (ILWU), the Oil Workers International union (OWIU), and the rubber workers (URW), had sporadic factions: Internal factional struggles appear to have occurred more or less irregularly over the years or were not sustained by lasting opposition organization, or both. Five internationals, such as the International Union of Marine and Shipbuilding Workers (IUMSBW) or USWA, had no factions and no significant, or even sporadic, organized oppositions.[36]

---

[34] Howe and Widick (1949, p. 262); also see McConnell (1958); Lipset et al. (1962, pp. 7–11, 13); Cochran (1977, p. 340).

[35] Lipset et al. (1962, p. 13); Martin (1968, p. 207).

[36] Lipset et al. refer to "the manifest impermanence of factional opposition in American trade unions" and term this "faction" to distinguish it from "party": "In a party system, opposition is organized and challenges the incumbent administration continuously" (1962, p. 277). This conception of "party" – organized, continual, that is, institutionalized, opposition – is equivalent to our conception here of "organized factions," so we could just as correctly have termed them "organized parties." "Sporadic factionalism" is more or less the same as their conception of "faction."

Remarkably, even using these crude data on a truncated universe, with small numbers in the categories compared, reveals a striking association between factionalism and constitutional democracy in the CIO's international unions. Among the ten with organized factions, only one was oligarchic, three were moderately democratic, and six were highly democratic. Among the eight unions with sporadic factionalism, four were oligarchic, one was moderately democratic, and three were highly democratic. In contrast, among the five that had no factions, four were oligarchic, one was moderately democratic, and not one was highly democratic.[37]

Intraclass Struggle

The CIO, as we know, itself emerged originally as an organized, if minuscule, faction within the AFL, and when AFL officials threw the committee's members out, this was merely the formal culmination of a long-raging conflict.[38] The CIO's split with "reactionary AFL leaders" over the issue of "organizing the unorganized" in mass production industries was a momentous but not solitary act.[39] Rather, it was another blow in the battle for industrial unionism being waged since the early 1920s by thousands of workers, both within and outside the AFL.

The CIO was thus born as an amalgam of disparate, often hostile, elements: The organizers of CIO unions were both the new, young, and inexperienced and the battle-hardened survivors. They were ex-AFL officials, "pure and simple" unionists, Catholic activists, liberals, Communists, and radicals of all stripes, and most were involved in some "outside organization" determined to take charge of the new unions.

This intraclass conflict, remember, can be visualized as made up of four different types of polar political practices and internal relationships among rival political tendencies involved in the organizing of the CIO's international unions: whether the industry had a history of earlier Red organizing or not, whether the union seceded from the AFL in a workers' insurgency or a top officers' revolt, whether the union was organized independently or under the tutelage of a CIO organizing committee, and whether the union was formed through amalgamation or as a unitary organization. Now, as we know from Chapter 2, earlier Red organizing, secession via a workers' insurgency, independent organizing, and amalgamation, or what we have called the four "insurgent political practices," tended – directly or indirectly – if they were

---

[37] Not incidentally, this finding of a close association between our constitutional democracy scale and such a decisive expression of inner political life as factionalism also enhances our confidence in the verisimilitude of the scale.

[38] Bernstein (1970, pp. 422–23).   [39] CIO (1949, p. 3).

involved in an international union's organizing, to increase the likelihood that Communists won its leadership.

Perhaps paradoxically, these same insurgent practices, though not in exactly the same way, also tended to increase the likelihood both that an international had opposition factions and that it was democratic. It is to an investigation of this possibility that we now turn.

Earlier Red Organizing

"Industrial unionism" and "revolutionary unionism" had been virtually synonymous for many years before the CIO took up the call, and they were embodied, as we know, in two successive union leagues, TUEL and TUUL, whose affiliated Red unions were met with "the most brutal terror" by employers.[40] Some of the terror came, however, from hostile AFL unionists, who collaborated in trying to break Red-led strikes and destroy the Red unions.[41] Characteristic, for instance, were the clashes between Red unionists and AFL adherents: in the "garment industry wars of the 1920s"; in the anthracite coal fields, where, in Walter Galenson's words, "one of the bloodiest fratricidal wars in the history of trade unionism" was waged during the late 1920s and early 1930s; and among furriers, sailors, longshoremen, and many other rival unionists on the East Coast during the same years.[42]

Some of the ablest and toughest opponents of the Red unionists were themselves other radicals, in particular, elements of the Socialist Party and ex-Reds who had quit or been expelled from the CP after the late 1920s. Some ex-Red unionists even found themselves battling former comrades with whom they had suffered through earlier Red organizing struggles. Among the participants in early 1930s clashes between rival unionists in the auto industry, for example, were members of the "CPUSA–Opposition" (led by Jay Lovestone), who had been expelled from the CP in 1929 and were bitter enemies of the Red unionists (and of such Red "tools" as the Reuther brothers!).[43] Then these anti-Communist radicals were joined, from the late 1930s on, by ACTU's Catholic activists (or "Actists"), who, in these years, still saw it as their double-edged mission both to root out Communist unionists and to participate in working-class struggles for dignity and "economic democracy."[44] The Actists' earliest

---

[40] Draper (1972, p. 392).   [41] Galenson (1940, pp. 40–41).

[42] Levenstein (1981, pp. 107–8); Galenson (1940, pp. 12–13).

[43] Saposs (1959, pp. 136–41, 150); Levenstein (1981, pp. 107–8, 110–20); Seaton (1981, pp. 144, 153–59).

[44] One of the earliest major defeats suffered by Communists in the UAW came at the hands of a "Socialist/ACTU alliance," which drove them out of the leadership of the Michigan CIO's

rank-and-file caucus activity, often in alliance with CIO socialists, was usually targeted against former TUUL organizers and their comrades now in a union's leadership.

So the CIO unions that were established in industries in which earlier Red organizers had been active inherited both the experienced Red nuclei of effective organizers and leaders and many others like them who were in other, rival political camps, ready, willing, and able to engage in battle with each other over the destiny of the union, no matter which of them had won its immediate leadership. In this sort of motley and explosive political mix, factionalism was second nature. So we expect to find that proportionally more of the international unions built in industries targeted by earlier Red unionism than of those in other industries, had organized factions.

For the same reasons and more, earlier Red unionism contributed to the formation of constitutional democracy. If some factions, and the outside organizations involved in them, fought in principle for basic constitutional guarantees, others did so out of self-interest (i.e., because of their own vulnerability to attack) or both. (Actists were not among them; they consistently fought to undermine or abolish such guarantees insofar as they protected "left-wing CIO members.")[45]

Red unionists especially bore the brunt of repression and expulsion during their fight to form "revolutionary oppositions" inside AFL unions or to amalgamate existing AFL trade unions, and to organize the unorganized, into industrial unions. The result was that, as other opposition groups, they developed a hostility to "bureaucratic machines," a commitment to real "trade union democracy," and "an insistence on specific minority rights, as a means of legitimating their own right to exist."[46]

So, did earlier Red unionism in an industry contribute to the levels of factionalism and democracy in CIO unions? Bearing in mind the small numbers in these categories, the answer is mixed: The seventeen internationals in the earlier Red-organized industries were more likely than the six in other industries to have organized factions: 47 percent versus 33 percent; but they were also more likely to have no factions: 23 versus 17 percent.[47] The pattern was similar with constitutional democracy: The twenty unions

---

Industrial Union Council in 1943. This alliance, although tenuous, was critical in Walter Reuther's ascendancy to the UAW presidency (Rosswurm 1992, pp. 119–20, 126–27).

[45] Seaton (1981, p. 192).

[46] Foster ([1936] 1947a, p. 208; 1927, pp. 286, 296–97, 299); Lipset et al. (1962, p. 16).

[47] Log odds ratio (uniform association) = 0.11, not statistically significant; standard error = 0.61.

in the earlier Red-organized industries were far more likely than the fifteen in the other industries to be highly democratic: 40 versus 13 percent, but they were also slightly more likely to be oligarchic: 35 versus 27 percent.[48] One reason for this pattern is explored below, in our analysis of how the contrasting types of organizing practices (in this instance, under an official CIO committee or an independent cadre) were related to earlier Red unionism.

Secession from the AFL

The twenty internationals that enlisted in the CIO's drive for industrial unionism led by their top officers joined with their staff and organizational hierarchy – and much of their union jurisdiction – intact.[49] Given the continuity of their officials and minimal internal dissension, few changes were made in the relatively autocratic constitutions they inherited from the AFL. In contrast, the CIO internationals that were born in a workers' insurgency inside the AFL usually had to write their own, new CIO constitution from scratch.

Plenty of Communists and other radicals were involved the anti-AFL insurgencies, and these also gave rise, we guess, to a "colossal overproduction of organizers" and of experienced and able leaders at all levels of the new unions who threatened "the stability of the ruling group."[50] Rebel beginnings, we suggest, endowed a union with an ample pool of capable activists, with their own personal ambitions and differing political commitments and conceptions of workers' interests. The first political act of unions born in a workers' rebellion was often to tear up their old AFL constitution, which had endowed a handful of top officials with power, and write a new one that broadened representation, strengthened accountability, and provided guarantees against the kinds of organizational abuses suffered by its own organizers as dissidents or radicals in the AFL.

So, we expect to find – and, in fact, do find – that proportionally many more of the dozen unions born in a workers' insurgency than of the eleven led into the CIO by their top officers had organized factions and were highly democratic:

---

[48] Log odds ratio (uniform association) = 0.31, not statistically significant; standard error = 0.45.

[49] Remember, seven independent, non-AFL unions joined the CIO with their organizational hierarchies intact and are also included here with the unions that seceded from the AFL in an officer's revolt.

[50] The words in quotes are Nikolai Bukharin's, from his work, *Historical Materialism*, as cited in Lipset et al. (1962, p. 454). Bukharin, a leading Bolshevik, was defeated by Stalin in an innerparty struggle and executed in 1938.

Among the former, 58 percent, and among the latter, 27 percent had organized factions. The contrast in the absence of factions was even sharper: 8 versus 36 percent, respectively.[51] As to constitutional democracy, 47 percent of the seventeen internationals originating in a workers' insurgency but only 11 percent of the eighteen led into the CIO by their top officers were highly democratic. Similarly, 23 percent of the insurgents but 39 percent of those whose top leaders took their union into the CIO were oligarchic.[52]

Independent Organizing

Most of the CIO international unions were organized from the bottom up by an independent rank-and-file cadre, consisting both of workers who organized clandestinely on the inside and of their comrades on the outside. They devised their own organizing strategy and actual tactics, and decided whether to call strikes, what demands to make, and when and how to make them. Top CIO officials, such as the UMW's John L. Lewis and the ACW's Sidney Hillman, often had no alternative but to leave these independent organizers alone, for without their hard work, courage, commitment, and sacrifice to organize the unorganized, the CIO could well have been stillborn. Among the most effective organizers were radicals of all kinds: from the battle-hardened old hands, "the flotsam and jetsam of years of sinking radical dreams" – ex-Wobblies, homegrown and immigrant class-conscious unionists, and Reds – who had been baptized in earlier organizing battles to the many more young men and women who came of age in the Great Depression and were drawn to the cause of industrial unionism by the mass misery and the open class war then being waged in America.[53]

Although CIO officials had to give some leeway to the radical organizers, who usually took the lead in organizing the new unions, they also did what they could to retain control. So, as we know, they set up organizing committees – in steel, textiles, oil, meatpacking, shoes, and other industries – and put their own men in charge.[54] The organizing committee's staff members who daily went out to organize were not allowed to make policy, call strikes, negotiate contracts, or vote on any issue. CIO officials at the top made these decisions. If any of the committee's members, whatever their political coloration, but especially if they were radicals of any hue, began to gain an independent following among the local workers, or became "too dangerous

---

[51] Log odds ratio (uniform association) = 1.06, $p < 0.05$; standard error = 0.61.
[52] Log odds ratio (uniform association) = 0.91, $p < 0.05$; standard error = 0.48.
[53] Levenstein (1981, p. 63).   [54] Bernstein (1970, p. 616).

a threat, they were discharged."[55] Under the CIO's thumb, such organizers were rarely able to put down roots or nurture an independent opposition that could challenge the anointed leadership and enliven the new unions' political life.

In contrast, the unions that were organized independently by a mix of Reds, radicals, and "pure and simple unionists," competing both to organize the unorganized and to win their trust, provided the conditions in which rival blocs or caucuses could flourish. The self-interest of these rivals, if not principle, committed them to trying to protect dissent and limit executive power.

These contrasting patterns of organizing are exemplified by, on the one hand, the CIO's SWOC, set up in 1937 under Philip Murray, which waited until 1942 to transform itself into a formal union, the USWA (with Murray as its president), and, on the other, the independent organizing in the auto industry by a host of contending political cadres that founded the UAW.[56]

What we find is somewhat mixed: First, organized factions existed in 40 percent of the fifteen independently organized internationals but in half of the eight established under a CIO organizing committee. Second, and crucially, 37 percent of the latter internationals had *no* factions versus 13 percent of the former.[57] The effects of these contrasting organizing practices in determining the level of constitutional democracy were similar: Nearly identical proportions of the twenty-four independently organized and eleven CIO-organized internationals were highly democratic: 29 versus 27 percent. But, as expected, they differed substantially in the proportions having an oligarchic regime: 25 percent of the independently organized internationals versus 45 percent of the CIO-organized.[58]

This disparity in the absence of factions resulted, we suggest, from CIO officials putting their own committees in charge of the organizing precisely in those industries where (as AFL unionists) they had fought the Reds in the past. But in so doing they hobbled not only Communist organizers but other dedicated non-Communist unionists that would have contributed to the sort of political mix that bred factionalism and democracy. Consistent with this reasoning, and as we pointed out in Chapter 2, a higher proportion of the twenty-one internationals in industries where earlier Red organizing had

---

[55] Saposs (1976, p. 122).

[56] Galenson (1960, pp. 133, 150, 171–72); Leiserson (1959, pp. 154–63).

[57] Log odds ratio (uniform association) = 0.23, not statistically significant; standard error = 0.56.

[58] Log odds ratio (uniform association) = 0.38, not statistically significant; standard error = 0.48.

gone on than of the seventeen internationals in industries where it had not were organized under the tutelage of a CIO committee: 38 percent versus 23 percent. This is also, we suggest, why Red unionism had contradictory effects in determining both factionalism and democracy: The self-conscious political strategy of CIO officials aimed at preventing Reds from getting a foothold in these earlier Red-organized industries and also kept out other dedicated but non-Communist unionists who were unduly restive, recalcitrant, or radical; as a result, whether intentionally or not, this policy also undermined the chances of opposition factions taking root and constitutional democracy flourishing.

Amalgamation

CIO unions, remember, were formed as either a unitary or amalgamated organization. To amalgamate or not to amalgamate was always a political question in the organizing strategy of the international unions and locals involved. To allow two or more unions to coalesce or not was also a vital question for the CIO's executive, because they had to be careful not to strengthen the Communist left in this way. This was an issue that also cropped up occasionally throughout the CIO years, when a merger with or absorption of another union might disturb the balance between left and right in an existing international. A fight of this kind took place within the UAW over a proposal in 1947 to bring the Red-led FE's 80,000 members into the UAW, but as a separate, more or less independent, farm equipment division of the UAW. Its entry into UAW in this way, rather than local by local as the CIO officials and UAW president Walter Reuther advocated, would have tipped the political balance against Reuther and his allies. The Reutherites not only successfully defeated the proposal at the 1947 convention, but defeated the center–left coalition majority on the executive board.[59]

Obviously, then, in contrast to the relative internal seamlessness of unitary unions, amalgamation tends to result in a redistribution of power within the new union: Depending on their relative size and resources, amalgamation can reduce some officers of the previously independent unions, at best, to

[59] Levenstein (1981, pp. 202–4). The UAW (and CIO) officialdom reversed itself, of course, once Reuther and his allies had won control of the UAW, and its concerted attack on its "Communist-dominated" affiliates hit full throttle. In May 1949, the CIO ordered FE to merge with the UAW. FE's officers ignored the CIO's order and merged instead with the UE ("Will C.I.O. Split Apart?").

secondary officers of the new, coalesced international, while others emerge as its top officers. But whatever the outcome for individuals, the amalgamation of once independent unions tends to preserve autonomous centers of power in the new union, and thus fosters political competition if not factionalism. In turn, this tends to enhance the chances for union democracy.

Amalgamation does not emerge, however, as the "natural" product of industrial organization or market relations. This is illustrated, for instance, by the contrasting organizational forms taken by the CIO's three largest unions, or the "Big 3." Even though they arose in industries with a similar scale of production and level of concentration, two of them (UAW and UE) came into existence through amalgamation, and one (USWA) did not.

The UAW "was formed out of an amalgamation of a number of existing automobile unions, and a number of its other local units were organized independently of national control. . . . Most of the factional leaders in the UAW were leaders in the early organizational period of the union, and the different factions have largely been coalitions of the groups headed by these different leaders jointly resisting efforts to subordinate them to the national administration."[60] Long before the CIO was even a glint in John L. Lewis's eye, a number of rival unions had been involved for years in trying to organize auto workers, among them the Red-led AWU, a TUUL affiliate. In 1937, the battered remnants of these rivals, revivified by the decade's mass struggles, amalgamated to form the UAW. In turn, they formed the basis for the UAW's major warring factions, each of which had its quota of leaders who had been involved in the earlier lean years of organizing.

UE grew out of the three-fold amalgamation of locals of the TUUL's Steel and Metal Workers Industrial Union with several independent electrical worker locals organized by skilled immigrant English Socialist unionists and the Philadelphia-based Radio and Allied Trade Union Workers (led by young James Carey, an active anti-Communist).[61]

In contrast, the USWA was formed – by hardly more than rebaptizing the tightly ruled SWOC – as a unitary organization, in which "power [was] firmly concentrated at the top. Indeed, despite its enormous growth, . . . the union's top officers [retained] total administrative power . . . [in the] still highly centralized union." The USWA became the very model of a unitary organization, with little if any local or district autonomy, and it also remained bereft of organized internal dissent and real rivalry for its top leadership.[62]

---

[60] Lipset et al. (1962, p. 443n3).   [61] Levenstein (1981, p. 60).

[62] Ibid., p. 51; Lipset et al. (1962, p. 443).

75

Or take the counterexample of textiles. Although the heterogeneous structure of this industry – vast diversity in geography, technology, markets, and labor force – "should" have nourished either several CIO international unions fitting its major niches or a single, highly decentralized, amalgamated union, the strategy used to organize the new TWUA had its own relatively independent effects. In the pre-CIO era, a host of unions had long competed in the tangle of textile industries. "No industry had so much dual unionism": AFL, independent, IWW, and other syndicalist and radical unions had fought each other for years to organize and win the allegiance of textile workers.[63] In fact, the textile industry was "simply not an industry," as Irving Bernstein observes. "It was cotton, woolen and worsted, rayon and other synthetics, silk, hosiery, carpets and rugs, thread and braid, dyeing and finishing. Each of these 'industries' had its own geographic distribution its own markets, its own technology, its own distinctive labor force," and, often, its own union.[64]

But Sidney Hillman and his CIO Textile Workers Organizing Committee (TWOC) prevented any preexisting unions (especially those led by radicals) from having a voice in it. TWOC established industry conferences and joint boards to provide "the internal coordination that was essential in so diversified an industry . . . *without permitting the rise of permanent functional suborganizations which might eventually challenge the authority of the national union.*"[65]

So, contrary to this variegated industry's presumed "objective conditions" or "underlying tendencies," Hillman intentionally forged a union that was centralized and hierarchical – with, of course, his own subalterns in control. They would not be bothered in the future by organized opposition, for TWUA became a lasting oligarchic union whose members surely came to "know who is boss!"

As TWOC illustrates, the shotgun marriage of several unions through enforced amalgamation from above can vitiate amalgamation's inherent democratic potential, by quashing or eliminating the separate, more or less independent organizational bases (or functional suborganizations) which it otherwise tends to reproduce within the new union. Only to the extent, then, that amalgamation occurs on terms of rough parity among the merging unions, and in this way produces alternative centers of power or political bases from which their own leaders can try to extend their influence and counter or

---

[63] Foster (1927, p. 155).

[64] Ibid., p. 155; Galenson (1940, pp. 15–16); Bernstein (1970, p. 616).

[65] Bernstein (1970, p. 616); Galenson (1960, p. 333, emphasis added).

challenge the new union's top leadership, will it enhance the chances for union democracy.

We find that among the dozen amalgamated internationals, half were highly democratic as opposed to 8 percent that had an oligarchic regime; but among the twenty-three unitary unions, only 17 percent were highly democratic, while a 43 percent plurality were oligarchic. Similarly, among the ten amalgamated internationals, 70 percent had organized factions, while 10 percent had none; but among the thirteen unitary unions, only 23 percent had organized factions, while 31 percent had none.[66]

So far we have treated the constellations of political practices and their consequences as if they were isolated from each other. In part this was necessary just to make a sensible exposition of each one and its hypothesized and actual measurable consequences. So breaking them down analytically into these four separate constellations partly distorts or even falsifies reality, because they were closely related or interacted, or both. Take the four insurgent practices. Many of the same organizers (though no one knows the actual number) who had "fomented insurrection" and *secession* from the AFL and went on to become or were simultaneously involved in *independent organizing* of a fledgling CIO union and trying to cement alliances with other organizers and eventual *amalgamation* with other unions were also veterans of *earlier Red organizing*. So the reader should keep this in mind in the following analyses.

We try to assess the relatively independent effects of each insurgent practice in determining constitutional democracy through a "logit analysis."[67] But, unfortunately, we cannot do the same for factionalism, because the number of internationals on which we have relevant data (only twenty-three of the thirty-six) is too small. As to analysis of interaction effects, even the population of thirty-five (remember, constitutional data are missing on one) is too small to allow a statistical analysis. So, though it is only indicative, we use a simple additive "index of insurgent origins" to try to get at the cumulative impact of the four insurgent practices in the making of factionalism and democracy.

The logit analysis reveals that, of the four insurgent practices, only secession from the AFL in a workers' insurgency and, especially, amalgamation had measurable relatively independent direct effects in the making of democracy. The comparative odds of an international union turning out to be highly

---

[66] Log odds ratio (uniform association) $= 1.31, p < 0.05$; standard error $= 0.68$ for factions; Log odds ratio (uniform association) $= 1.28, p < 0.01$; standard error $= 0.56$ for democracy.

[67] For a brief description of logit analysis, see Chapter 2, note 51, on page 47.

Table 3.2. *Logit estimates of the direct effects of the insurgent political practices in determining the comparative odds that CIO international unions, as of 1948, were highly democratic*

Insurgent practice	Logit coefficient	Odds multiplier
Earlier Red organizing	−1.33	0.26
(standard error)	(0.93)	
Workers' insurgency	1.12	3.06
(standard error)	(0.76)	
Independent organizing	−0.29	0.75
(standard error)	(0.78)	
Amalgamation	2.30*	9.97
(standard error)	(1.00)	
Alpha 1[a]	0.56	
(standard error)	(0.73)	
Alpha 2	−1.57*	
(standard error)	(0.79)	
Likelihood ratio chi-square (df)	9.89 (4)*	
(N)	(35)	

$*p < 0.05$.

Note: An alpha coefficient is not substantively interpretable here. It refers to the distribution of the cases in the various categories of the dependent variable (but not to the distance between the categories). The alphas allow us to assess whether using the trichotomy here (i.e., highly democratic, moderately democratic, and oligarchic) is justifiable relative to a simple dichotomy (democratic vs. oligarchic).

democratic, holding constant the effects of the other insurgent practices, were: if it seceded through a workers' insurgency as opposed to a top officers' revolt, 3.1 to 1, and if it grew through amalgamation as opposed to unitary incorporation of other units, 10 to 1 (see Table 3.2).

Now did multiple insurgent origins matter in the making of democracy in a union? To answer this, we constructed an insurgency index, allocating a point to each of the four separate insurgent practices that was involved in organizing an international union. Given the small numbers, we trichotomized as follows: A score of 0 or 1 is "low," of 2, "medium," and of 3 to 4, "high." This index, despite the small numbers at each insurgent level, indicates the cumulative impact of the insurgent practices in determining both factionalism and democracy. Organized factions emerged in only one of the six internationals that had a low level of insurgent origins, but in three of the six with a medium level and in six of the eleven with a high level.[68] The pattern was virtually the same for constitutional democracy: 46 percent of the thirteen internationals with a high insurgency level and 44 percent of the nine with a medium level, but none of the thirteen with a low level turned out to be highly democratic.[69] The pattern appears as especially sharp and clear in the inverse relationship between insurgent origins and the absence of both factionalism and democracy: 50 percent of the internationals with a low level of insurgent origins, but only 17 percent of those with a medium level and 9 percent with a high level, had *no* factions. Similarly, 46 percent of those with a low insurgency level but only 33 percent of those with a medium level and 15 percent of those with a high level were oligarchic.

Weighing the four insurgent practices as if they were separate marbles on a scale obscures the intimate historical connections among them. So, as we know, earlier Red organizing tended to both foster later secessionist insurgencies from the AFL and encourage a strategy of amalgamation among the industry's unions but, at the same time, also tended to have contradictory effects on independent organizing.[70]

In the long hard years before the CIO's birth, the organizers and workers involved in, or at least influenced by, battles for the cause of industrial unionism, especially Reds and other radicals, considered amalgamation a "burning issue." They called, in the words of TUEL's head in 1927, for the "concentration of the forces of organized labor [through] amalgamation of the six score craft unions into a few industrial unions"; amalgamation, they believed, was a "life necessity of trade unionism."[71] So they had both practical and principled reasons to try to amalgamate the new CIO unions they were building and "concentrate their forces" against capital.

AFL leaders vehemently opposed industrial unionism, both in principle and in practice, and had "made so little effort to organize the unorganized" that the major new industrial unions probably were established, with rare exceptions, only where radicals and, particularly, Red unionists had been active in the pre-CIO era.[72] If most of the Red unions had become "moribund" or had "faded away" by the time of the CIO upsurge, some of them or their remnants

---

[68] Log odds ratio (uniform association) = 0.67, $p < 0.05$; standard error = 0.37.

[69] Log odds ratio (uniform association) = 0.73, $p < 0.01$; standard error = 0.31.

[70] See the quantitative measures of their connections in Chapter 2.

[71] Foster (1927, pp. 32, 22).

[72] Draper (1972, p. 374). As of 1937, 103 unions belonged to the AFL, but a dozen at most were organized along industrial (rather than craft) lines, and of the dozen, eight were not founded until the late 1930s (Daugherty 1938, p. 350).

had survived with enough independence and cohesion to be able, once the CIO drive began, to amalgamate with other such remnants, or independent unions. Red unionists also successfully established local oppositions in many AFL affiliates: At least 635 AFL union locals as well as "several" entire districts, remember, had radical or Red nuclei within them at the time of the CIO's launching,[73] and they must have been involved in "fomenting insurrection" against the AFL (as AFL officials charged) and leading their fellow workers into the CIO.

Earlier Red unionism indirectly contributed in these ways to the formation and consolidation of union democracy, but also had contradictory effects on the way the unions were organized. For if earlier Red unionism in an industry "naturally" tended to foster independent organizing, it also made that industry a ready-made target of a CIO organizing committee, tightly controlled by CIO officials who wanted to prevent the establishment of Communist-led unions there. In turn, such top-down organizing under a CIO committee tended, as we have seen, to produce a unitary union and thus to diminish the chances that opposition factions and democracy would emerge within it.

In contrast, independent organizers in an industry were able to establish their own local bases of support, through the struggles they initiated and led, and to build their unions by allying themselves with other organizers, pooling their resources, devising a common strategy, and engaging in more or less unified industrial battles. Such alliances among various unions or locals in turn also tended to eventuate in their actual amalgamation. So independent organizing, by encouraging amalgamation, also indirectly nourished factionalism and democracy.

The time-order between the "variables" of independent organizing and amalgamation was not – like that between earlier Red organizing and subsequent secession in a workers' insurgency or independent organizing – only one-way.[74] In specific cases, either one could have preceded the other. So while 83 percent of the dozen amalgamated unions compared with 61 percent of the twenty-six unitary unions were independently organized, 38 percent of the independently organized internationals compared with 17 percent of the internationals organized by a CIO committee were formed through amalgamation.[75]

---

[73] Klehr (1984, pp. 47, 133, 225).

[74] That the marginals for the two dichotomous variables here are identical and symmetrical ($N = 26$ for independent organizing versus $N = 12$ for CIO Committee, and $N = 12$ for amalgamation versus $N = 26$ for unitary) is one of those mysterious coincidences whose origin it is beyond this chapter's purview to seek.

[75] Log odds ratio (uniform association) = 0.98, $p < 0.08$; standard error = 0.81.

Yet we want to emphasize again that thinking about these insurgent practices as separable "variables" with a fixed time order among them tends to
obscure the fact that in the lives of many individual CIO organizers, as well
as in the process of organizing some international unions, all four insurgent
practices were concretely inseparable, reciprocal, and self-reinforcing experiences. Often the same individual organizers were veteran Red unionists
who were now involved in "fomenting insurrection" and secession from the
AFL, out-organizing other unorganized workers in the industry, sometimes
even while also on the staff of a CIO organizing committee in another industry, and trying to amalgamate their forces with others all at the same
time.

William Senter, a man who, from the time he joined the John Reed
Club in 1934, openly and proudly proclaimed that he was a Communist, is exemplary of this sort of individual. Still in his twenties, he took
the lead in TUUL organizing drives in several different industries in St.
Louis (one of them among the black women workers in the city's nut-
shelling shops). Then, in 1937, while he was on the payroll of SWOC, he
also became the guiding force behind the independent organizing at Emerson Electric. Soon switching to UE, he had a hand in the fifty-three-day-
long sit-down strike there (the second longest in American history), out
of which came the UE local there and the city's UE district 8; he was
elected president of that district later that year (1937) and served until he
resigned in 1948.[76]

The UE itself is exemplary of a process of dialectical self-determination
involving the four insurgent practices. In 1934, William Turnbull, an immigrant British socialist, and Julius Emspak, both employed at the GE plant
in Schenectady, New York, and Albert Coulthard, a skilled tradesman and
veteran unionist employed at the Lynn, Massachusetts, GE plant, all three
of whom from the early 1930s on had been organizing independent electrical appliance unions, got together with other independent organizers inside
the Philco plant in Philadelphia, chief among them James Carey and Harry
Block, and agreed to merge their fledgling unions. But this coalition itself gave
added impetus to continued independent organizing, under their leadership,
while they pushed for, but were refused, an AFL charter as an industrial union.
Two years later, in March 1936, they formally merged to found the independent
United Electrical and Radio Workers.

Then in late 1937, at the union's convention, where its new president
Carey denounced the AFL leaders as "palsied traitors," another crucial phase of

---

[76] Feurer (1992, pp. 96, 100); Filippelli and McColloch (1993, p. 37); "A Yaleman and a
Communist" (p. 213).

amalgamation was consecrated: Earlier in the year, in June, James Matles had led fourteen insurgent International Association of Machinists (IAM) lodges, of which he was then Grand Master, out of the IAM, and they now formally joined UE. Most of the insurgent lodges, which had joined the IAM less than two years earlier, in March 1935, had belonged to Matles's independent Machine Tool and Foundry Workers Union – itself mainly a reincarnation of his MWIU, which had been an affiliate of the TUUL until its dissolution in the spring of 1934.

What had "finished it up" for Matles and his fellow industrial unionists, was a letter dated April 30, 1937, from IAM president Arthur Wharton to IAM officers. Wharton informed them that he had already conferred with several employers and now directed IAM officers to do the same: to ply employers with the "benefits" of recognizing IAM affiliates. Rather than having to deal with the CIO's "gang of sluggers, communists, radicals and soap box artists, professional bums, expelled members of labor unions, outright scabs and the Jewish organizations with their red affiliates," he wrote, they will get an organization that lives up to its agreements and prevents "sitdowns, sporadic disturbances, slowdowns and other communistic CIO tactics of disruption and disorganization."[77]

With Matles now this UE's new director of organization, the newly amalgamated union then continued to organize on its own; soon other insurgent IAM locals and independents elsewhere in the country followed Matles's lead and also joined the UE. As the UE concretely exemplifies, then, the four insurgent practices interacted in producing political variety and organizational diversity in a union, and in this way produced a rich soil in which the fragile flower of democracy could take root and grow.

Communism, Anti-Communism, and Union Democracy

But these same insurgent origins, as we know, also (paradoxically?) increased the likelihood (although not quite in the same way) that the Communists rather than their rivals would win these unions' leadership. Two insurgent practices, remember, especially favored the Communists' winning union leadership: first, if a union had seceded from the AFL in a workers' insurgency, and, second, if a union had been organized independently. But both earlier Red unionism and amalgamation also indirectly favored the Communists.

So, given this, the immediate question is, What was the connection between Communist leadership, factionalism, and democracy? Writing at the

---

[77] Matles and Higgins (1974, pp. 34, 53, 48–49); Filippelli and McColloch (1995, pp. 29–31, 39–41).

Cold War's dawn, when the Communists' defeat and purge from the CIO was imminent, the answer was already close to axiomatic among scholars as well as liberal and socialist anti-Communist activists, that, as Mills wrote in 1948, "Communist rule within the U.S. unions they control is dictatorial"; their unions were, moreover, "the most undemocratic in the labor movement." The Communists, in Philip Selznick's words in 1952, were "especially prone to use patently undemocratic tactics because of their inability to depend on winning victories in a free political arena.... Reliance on membership apathy, arbitrary expulsions, milked treasuries, and centralized control is the hallmark of the communist just as it is of racketeering leadership in trade unions...." All in all, it was "fairly obvious," S. Martin Lipset, Martin Trow, and James Coleman assert, that U.S. "Communist labor leaders" were "totalitarian."[78]

Who can doubt that, despite a "meticulous adherence to the outer forms of democracy," Communist unionists sometimes "manipulated democratic procedures" or perverted them, as the head of the ACLU charged, "to gain control"?[79] Unquestionably, when American Communists were pushing the (latest) party line on an issue, they included in their political arsenal the well-worn weapons of "personal defamation and intrigue" and "campaigns to bury gainsayers under an avalanche of denunciations and slander."[80]

Yet the conduct of liberal and socialist anti-Communists can also be accurately described in similar terms; they too intrigued against and defamed opponents they deemed Communists or their allies, and carried out Red-baiting campaigns.[81] If Communists in a union usually met or caucused "in

---

[78] Lipset et al. (1962, p. 87); Mills ([1948] 1971, pp. 198–99); Pitzele (1947, p. 31); Selznick (1960, p. 214); also see Moore (1945).

[79] Howe and Coser (1957, p. 383); Baldwin (1946, p. 58).

[80] Mills ([1948] 1971, p. 199); Cochran (1977, p. 379).

[81] So, for example, long before CIO president Murray declared open war on the Communists and their allies, he secretly plotted against them with anti-Communist UAW executive board members, and also funneled USWA money to UE's anti-Communist "Members for Democratic Action," although UE was then (according to nearly every serious observer) a highly democratic union (Levenstein 1981, pp. 211, 334). Once the battle was in the open, Murray called Communist unionists "sulking cowards ... [and] apostles of hate," who were forever "lying out of the pits of their dirty bellies" (Zieger 1986, p. 131). UAW president Walter Reuther's *United Auto Worker* labeled Reuther's opposition in early 1949 "a strange compound of Communists, Trotskyists and free booting opportunists with no political ideology and no moral principles." Reuther called at the CIO convention later that year for "fumigating" the CIO of Communist unionists and combating the "filth" printed in their publications; they were not part of the left, he declared: "They are the phoney Left, they are the corrupted Left, and they are the morally degenerated Left" (Lichtenstein 1995, pp. 309–10). Or take UE president James Carey's attack on his fellow UE leaders (showing

advance of rank and file meetings to plan strategy," it was also true that their opponents "long practiced this policy."[82] If the Communists often packed meetings to get their way, so did their opposition.[83] Most important, they, too, contributed to the actual "perversion of democratic procedures," especially when they purged Communists and "fellow travelers" from the leadership of organized labor, and collaborated with the government in denying them basic civil liberties and political rights.

The fight by "anti-Stalinist leftists" against the Communists and their allies in the CIO, as the (anti-Communist) historian Robert Zieger points out, did not consist only of "vigorous, democratic competition on the shop floor and in the union halls"; rather, it was characterized by "sordid episodes of reckless charges, personal violence and intimidation, and collaboration on the part of anti-Communists with some of the most disreputable congressional witch hunters and antilabor publications."[84]

So any effort to carry out a sustained empirical analysis of the role of the Communists in organized labor, and specifically of whether Communist rule of their unions was dictatorial, has to confront abundant "myth, exaggeration, and nonsense." Until our analysis, the mid-1950s lament by the authors of *Union Democracy* was still correct: "No one has attempted either a qualitative or quantitative analysis of the relationship between diffuse political [that is, socialist or

---

a certain flair, at lest, for political satire): "The performance of a trapeze artist in a circus is entertainment, but political acrobats in pink tights posing as labor leaders are a disgrace to the union and an insult to the intelligence of the membership" (Critchlow 1976, p. 232). Similarly, liberal historian Arthur Schlesinger, Jr., describes Communist labor leaders as "dreary fanatics and seedy functionaries, talking to themselves in an unintelligible idiom" (1957, p. 22). CIO officials put eleven unions on trial and expelled them, based on "elaborate, pseudolegal 'cases' against the accused organizations," for which the "evidence" was that their officers "parroted the pro-Soviet line" (Zieger 1986, pp. 131–33). For details on the collusion of liberals in the violation of the civil liberties of accused Communists, see Caute (1979, esp. chs. 18–21).

[82] Ozanne (1954, pp. 103–4).

[83] For instance, Kampelman ([1957] 1971, p. 136), who was then a liberal anti-Communist (and years later was to become a close advisor of President Reagan), refers approvingly to the "hard-headedness" of an ACTU tactical manual's instruction on how to pack a meeting. Had it been a Communist manual, it surely would have been seen as evidence of how party members manipulated democratic procedures to gain control: "Place your people carefully in the meeting hall. Try to have a good-sized bunch down front. . . . Place others on each side and place a nice contingent in the back . . . . It makes it look as if the entire meeting is filled with your people." The 1949 manual, "How to Decontrol Your Union of Communists," was written by ACTU's chaplain in Pittsburgh, Father Charles Owen Rice.

[84] Zieger (1986, pp. 132–33).

Communist] or specific business–union ideologies and the presence or absence of political conflict [and thus of factionalism and democracy] within trade unions."[85]

Two closely related propositions, suggested by Lipset, Trow, and Coleman, guide this part of our analysis. If the political consciousness, or world outlook, of union leaders is "diffuse" rather than narrow, this tends to provoke opposition, and if "political cleavages" within a union are "ideological," or based on opposing types of political consciousness, rather than on instrumental allegiances alone, this tends to sustain democracy. In contrast, "business unionism, as a set of ideas justifying the narrowest definitions of a union's role in society," discourages controversy, "for it implies that union leadership is simply the administration of an organization with . . . undebatable goals: the maximization of the members' income and general welfare," so it also "helps to legitimate one-party oligarchy."[86]

These general ideas certainly seem to apply to the CIO's Communist unionists. They viewed unions as "a weapon for the liberation of the working class."[87] This was a "diffuse" and transcendent conception of the unions' mission that must have provoked controversy. Their politicization of everyday life, their intense commitment to confront a broad range of public issues (from the poll tax and lynching of black Americans to Spanish fascism, "imperialism," and the "defense of Soviet socialism") transcending the matters dealt with in collective bargaining made it likely that conflicts would arise over these issues in the unions they led; this, in turn, encouraged organized opposition to them and, consequently, factionalism and democracy.

Second, unions whose leaders supposedly followed the party line were targeted by anti-Communist activists. So organized opposition in Communist-led unions was often produced not by spontaneous generation from within but by a self-conscious policy of penetration by the Communists' enemies, such as the formidable "Actists."[88] Third, forging industrial unions by merging the existing craft unions in an industry was, as discussed, the Communists' strategy long before the CIO's emergence.[89]

So, for these reasons, it is understandable that the Communist-led unions typically had "opposition factions too strong to be intimidated, too large to

---

[85] Bernstein (1970, p. 783); Lipset et al. (1962, p. 456).

[86] Lipset et al. (1962, pp. 457, 468, 456).

[87] Foster (1927, p. 23); Marx (1973b, pp. 75–76).   [88] Levenstein (1981, pp. 87–90).

[89] In fact, and as a probable result, 44 percent of the Communist-led international unions ($N = 18$) compared with 20 percent of the internationals in each of the non-Communist camps ($N = 10$ in each) were formed through amalgamation. (Log odds ratio (uniform association) $= 0.665$, $p < 0.08$; standard error $= 0.468$.)

be expelled," whereas organized opposition was rare in the anti-Communist unions.[90] In fact, among the twenty-three unions for which we have data on factionalism, all ten of the Communist-led unions had factions: five organized, five sporadic. Among the seven shifting unions, four had organized factions, two sporadic, and one none. But among the six in the anti-Communist camp, which were precisely the ones most dedicated to the narrowest business unionism, only one had organized factions, another had sporadic factions, and four had none.[91]

If the "diffuseness" of Communist "ideology" provoked opposition, the ideology itself was a peculiarly contradictory blend: It was, as it has been well said by Mark Naison, both "the legitimate heir of American radicalism" and "the bastard child of Soviet totalitarianism."[92] Sycophancy toward Stalin's dictatorship, if not apologetics for his regime of terror, coexisted uneasily with an elemental democratic impulse and egalitarian passion. The weight and mix of these elements in this contradictory amalgam – and how deeply held they were as motivating commitments in the political consciousness of Communist workers, union organizers, activists, and officers – is not known. But the classical socialist (and syndicalist) elements in American Communist views, emphasizing the self-reliance of the working class – that "the liberation of the working class," in the words of the old United Front song, "is the job of the workers alone" – probably had a special immediacy and meaning for Communist unionists.

In their conception, "oligarchy" in unions has its roots not in "organization" as such but in "the class collaboration policies" of union officials; by "rigidly suppress[ing] all union democracy, [they] poison the very class soul of the unions."[93] Specific homegrown ideas of rank-and-file power forged in earlier organizing and political struggles also had a direct bearing on the Communists' commitment to union democracy. They and other radicals had long advocated

---

[90] Cochran (1977, p. 380).

[91] Log odds ratio (uniform association) $= 0.908$, $p < 0.02$; standard error $= 0.428$.

[92] Naison (1985, p. 101).

[93] Foster (1927, pp. 94–99). Among the specific measures Foster advocated repeatedly throughout the era of Red unionism and during the first years of the CIO's emergence were the following: "admit Negroes" without discrimination; "reduce officials' exorbitant salaries"; "establish a free press in the unions"; "secure the right of free expression by minorities"; "abolition of the expulsion policy"; "right of all members to run for and hold office"; "right of all members to hold any political belief"; biennial national conventions; "broad rank-and-file delegations"; "strict financial reports"; "all convention committees to be voted on . . . by convention delegates"; "free discussion of all economic and political questions and opinions in the local meetings and official union journals"; and so on (1927, pp. 319, 222–23, 333–34; [1936] 1947a, p. 208; [1937] 1947b, pp. 251, 253, 259, 274).

constitutional reforms aimed at ensuring democracy in the new industrial unions.[94] They especially opposed "very great centralization of authority [because] union suspensions and receiverships . . . [could] also be used to enforce conformity of opinion within a union; and this weapon . . . [was] used mainly against Communists' [views]."[95]

So, we suggest, all of these processes cumulatively converged to enliven factionalism and ensure stable constitutional democracy in Communist-led unions, and our findings are consistent with this hypothesis: 44 percent of the sixteen Communist-led internationals were highly democratic as opposed to 20 percent of the ten in the shifting camp and 11 percent of the nine in the anti-Communist camp. Only 6 percent of the internationals in the Communist camp were oligarchic, compared with 50 and 55 percent, respectively, of those in each of the two non-Communist camps.

These findings, not incidentally, are buttressed by the 1948 study on constitutional power that we cited earlier, which distinguishes "routine," "moderate," and "considerable" power held by the "chief officer." Breaking down the 1948 data by political camp shows that the internationals in the Communist camp had the least autocratic rule by far: 69 percent of the thirteen internationals in the Communist camp but not one of the eleven in the other camps granted the chief officer only "routine" power, and only 8 percent in the Communist camp but 45 percent in the other camps endowed the chief officer with "considerable" power.[96]

---

[94] For specific democratic measures and constitutional guarantees advocated in the pre-CIO years by earlier Red unionists and by Communists once the CIO was born, see Foster (1927, pp. 319, 322–23, 333–34; 1947a, p. 208; 1947b, pp. 251, 253, 259, 274).

[95] Davis (1953, p. 236). *Union Democracy*'s authors assert that it is "fairly obvious" (1962, p. 87) that the reason that Communists "made strenuous efforts to increase interest in the union by establishing various forms of union-controlled leisure-time organizations and making attendance at union meetings compulsory" was not, as it might seem, "to encourage and deepen internal democracy," but rather because they were "totalitarian." But why is this "fairly obvious"? After all, if these authors open their book by quoting (on p. 3) the infamous and pernicious nonsense uttered on the issue by ILWU head Harry Bridges, extolling (in 1947) the virtue for unions of "totalitarian government" (where there are "no political parties. People are elected to govern the country based upon their records"), 146 pages later they observe that: "The east coast [right-wing, AFL longshore] union is one of the worst dictatorships in American unionism, whereas the West Coast union [ILWU], though Communist-controlled on the international level, is very democratic. The San Francisco local [the heartland of Harry Bridges's support] has two permanent political groups, which alternate in power much as do parties in the ITU" (Lipset et al. 1962, p. 149n).

[96] Log odds ratio (uniform association) = 1.32, $p < 0.01$; standard error = 0.53. Taft refers to 29 CIO internationals, but gives the names and classification of only 24. He says that 14 were in

We now must ask whether the apparent causal nexus between Communist leadership and a high level of constitutional democracy is spurious. We know that Communist leadership, factionalism, and constitutional democracy were each also the refracted product of the insurgent practices involved in an international's creation. So the question is, if we take account of, or remove, the effects of the insurgent practices and of organized factions, does the apparent effect of Communist leadership in enhancing the likelihood of democracy tend to disappear?

The problem with trying to answer this question is that the insurgent practices were so integral to the making of the Communist-led internationals and so important in carrying Communists into their leadership that the attempt to disentangle and assess their "independent" effects, alongside the effects of factionalism and Communist leadership, in determining democracy may be misguided. From a historical standpoint, such an attempt may exemplify (to coin a phrase) "the fallacy of misplaced controls": That is, analytically removing the effects of the insurgent practices would tear asunder what history had put together and distort, rather than illuminate, the characteristic uniqueness of the reality of constitutional democracy in the CIO's international unions.

But we are reluctant to let this question hover in the arras unanswered, even though, leaving aside the historical question, missing data and small numbers restrict the quantitative analysis. We assess the relatively independent effect of Communist leadership in determining democracy first, by controlling for the presence of factions (see Table 3.3); second, by controlling separately for each insurgent practice and also for our insurgency index (see Table 3.4); and third, by doing a logit analysis to assess the relatively independent effects of Communist leadership, organized factions, and amalgamation (which, remember, among the four insurgent practices, had by far the biggest effect on the comparative odds of Communist leadership) (see Table 3.5).

Even with very small numbers in the categories compared, the critical relationships are as predicted: Among the internationals with factions, the Communist camp had a much bigger percentage that were highly democratic

---

the "routine" category, but names only 10 (1948, p. 460). He comments with implicit dismay that all but one of the internationals in his category of "routine power" were "recognized as members of the leftist faction, and their policies have been largely determined by well-entrenched communist groups operating within the unions. Does the absence of a strong executive," he asks rhetorically, "make political domination easier, in that it eliminates the possibility of the defection of the chief officer changing the policy of the union?" As an afterthought, he adds that "other reasons" might be that the Communist "chief executives have either lacked the will or the opportunity to appropriate much power." The question, of course, is, what explains such differences in "will" and "opportunity"?

Table 3.3. *Level of constitutional democracy in CIO international unions, by political camp and the presence of factions (in percent)*

	Unions with organized or sporadic factions Constitutional democracy			
Political camp	Highly democratic	Moderately democratic	Oligarchic	(N)
Communist	60	30	10	(10)
Others	37	13	50	(8)
Log odds ratio		$.90^x$		
Standard error		.61		
	Unions with no factions Constitutional democracy			
Political camp	Highly democratic	Moderately democratic	Oligarchic	(N)
Communist	0	0	0	(0)
Others	0	20	80	(5)
Log odds ratio		$-^a$		
Standard error				

$^x p < 0.07$.

^{a} Log odds ratio cannot be computed.

Note: The numbers in parentheses in the (N) column refer to the number of international unions in a given category. The log odds ratio can be interpreted as a way to express magnitude of association and (knowing the log's standard error) to test a relationship's statistical significance. All log odds ratios given in tables assume uniform association (or equal distance between categories).

and a far smaller percentage oligarchic than in the non-Communist camps combined. Every Communist-led international had factions, so none appear in the category of internationals without factions. But it is worth emphasizing that the faction-free non-Communist internationals had by far the highest percentage oligarchic of all internationals (see Table 3.3).

When we hold constant either the specific type of political practice involved in organizing the unions or the overall level of insurgent origins, the Communist-led international unions continue to stand out as highly democratic: Whether or not their industry had earlier Red unionism, whether

Table 3.4. *Constitutional democracy in CIO international unions by type of political practice in union organizing, and CIO political camp (by percent)*

Part 1. Earlier Red organizing

Political camp	Some				None			
	Highly democratic	Moderately democratic	Oligarchic	(N)	Highly democratic	Moderately democratic	Oligarchic	(N)
Communist	54	36	9	(11)	40	60	0	(5)
Others	11	22	67	(9)	10	50	40	(10)
Log odds ratio	1.83**				1.90*			
Standard error	0.78				1.15			

Part 2. Source of secession

Political camp	Workers' rebellion				Top officers' revolt			
	Highly democratic	Moderately democratic	Oligarchic	(N)	Highly democratic	Moderately democratic	Oligarchic	(N)
Communist	50	42	8	(12)	25	75	0	(4)
Others	40	0	60	(5)	7	43	50	(14)
Log odds ratio	0.97^x				1.83*			
Standard error	0.70				1.34			

Part 3. Organizing strategy

Political camp	Independent				CIO committee			
	Highly democratic	Moderately democratic	Oligarchic	(N)	Highly democratic	Moderately democratic	Oligarchic	(N)
Communist	43	50	7	(14)	100	0	0	(2)
Others	10	40	50	(10)	11	33	55	(9)
Log odds ratio	1.72**				—[a]			
Standard error	0.78							

Part 4. Union formation

Political camp	Amalgamation				Unitary			
Communist	50	50	0	(8)	38	50	13	(8)
Others	50	25	25	(4)	7	33	60	(15)
Log odds ratio	0.60+				1.68**			
Standard error	0.24				0.78			

Part 5. Index of insurgent origins

Political camp	High and medium				Low			
Communist	50	43	7	(14)	0	100	0	(2)
Others	37	13	50	(8)	0	45	55	(11)
Log odds ratio	1.18+				0.79*			
Standard error	0.18				0.66			

[a] Log odds ratio cannot be computed for CIO organizing committee.

+ $p < 0.25$.

x $p < 0.10$.

* $p < 0.05$.

** $p < 0.01$.

Table 3.5. *Logit estimates of the direct effects of organized factions, amalgamation, and Communist leadership in determining the comparative odds that CIO international unions, as of 1948, were highly democratic*

	Model 1		Model 2		Model 3	
	Logit coefficient	Odds multiplier	Logit coefficient	Odds multiplier	Logit coefficient	Odds multiplier
Amalgamation	1.30^x	3.67			1.10	3.00
Standard error	(0.76)				(0.99)	
Organized factions			2.18*	8.85	1.73^y	5.64
Standard error			(1.03)		(1.09)	
Communist camp[a]	1.83*	6.23	1.76^y	5.81	1.65^z	5.21
Standard error	(0.90)		(1.14)		(1.17)	
Shifting coalitions	0.32	1.38	−0.51	0.60	−0.33	0.72
Standard error	(0.92)		(1.28)		(1.32)	
Alpha 1	−0.36		−0.91		−1.21	
Standard error	(0.68)		(0.88)		(0.96)	
Alpha 2	−2.63**		−2.29*		−2.65*	
Standard error	(0.85)		(1.00)		(1.11)	
Likelihood ratio chi square (df)	11.85(3)**		11.28(3)**		12.49(4)**	
(N)	(35)		(23)		(23)	

[a] The unions in the Communist camp and the "shifting" camp are separately compared with those in the anti-Communist camp. If this variable is dichotomized so that the unions in the Communist camp are compared with the unions in the other camps combined, then in model 2, $p < 0.05$ for organized factions and for Communist camp; in Model 3, $p < 0.10$ for organized factions and $p < 0.057$ for Communist camp.

$^z p < 0.16$.

$^y p < 0.12$.

$^x p < 0.10$.

$^* p < 0.05$.

$^{**} p < 0.01$.

Note: An alpha coefficient is not substantively interpretable here. It refers to the distribution of the cases in the various categories of the dependent variable (but not to the distance between the categories). The alphas allow us to assess whether using the trichotomy here (i.e., highly democratic, moderately democratic, and oligarchic) is justifiable relative to a simple dichotomy (democratic vs. oligarchic).

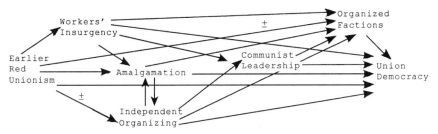

Figure 3.1. Substantive theoretical model of the determination of constitutional democracy in CIO international unions by insurgent political practices, organized factions, and Communist leadership.

they joined the CIO from below or from above, whether they were organized independently or under the aegis of a CIO organizing committee, and whether the level of insurgent origins was "high" or "low," the Communist-led international unions in each of these categories (despite the small numbers in them) had a bigger percentage highly democratic and a far smaller percentage oligarchic than their non-Communist counterparts (except among the amalgamated unions). So, for example, in the industries that had earlier Red unionism, 54 percent of the eleven Communist-led internationals but only 11 percent of the nine others were highly democratic; and 9 percent of those in the Communist camp but 67 percent of the others were oligarchic (see Table 3.4).

The logit analysis also reveals that, controlling for organized factions and amalgamation (which was the insurgent practice whose effect on the comparative odds of the Communists' winning power was biggest), the comparative odds that the internationals in the Communist camp as opposed to those in the anti-Communist camp would be highly democratic are as follows: 6.2 to 1 with only amalgamation controlled (Table 3.5, model 1), 5.8 to 1 with the presence of organized factions controlled (Table 3.5, model 2), and 5.2 to 1 with both amalgamation and organized factions controlled (Table 3.5, model 3). Both amalgamation and organized factions, alongside the Communist camp, also had sizable independent effects in determining the odds that an international was highly democratic: For the amalgamated as opposed to unitary internationals, the comparative odds were 3.0 to 1, and for organized as opposed to no factions, 5.6 to 1.[97]

To sum up these analyses, we present a substantive theoretical model (Fig. 3.1), which graphically represents the hypothesized effects (both direct and indirect) of each of the four insurgent political practices, organized factions,

[97] For a brief description of logit analysis, see Chapter 2, note 51, on page 47.

and Communist leadership in the making of democracy in America's industrial unions.

Conclusion: An "Iron Law of Democracy"?

The findings in this chapter consistently contradict the Michelsian theory that oligarchy is the "outcome of organic necessity ... affect[ing] every organization."[98] Rather, as our findings reveal, oligarchy and democracy are alternative possible paths of union development. Which path a union takes is determined not by any "iron law," but by specific, relatively contingent, political struggles among workers' parties and factions over the aims, methods, and uses of union power, and by both the resultant pattern of the unions' internal political relations and the political consciousness, radical or conservative, of their leadership.[99] Where these struggles are waged through insurgent political practices, resulting in durable internal bases for opposition factions and allowing radicals to put down deep roots and win and hold their leadership, the unions tend, consequently, to be democratic. But where the opposite political constellation prevails, they tend to be oligarchic. If this expresses an underlying "law," it is that democracy in labor unions is the product of both insurgency and radicalism in the working class.

[98] Michels ([1915] 1949, p. 402).
[99] Cf. Gouldner's brilliant critique of the Michelsian theory of bureaucracy (1955).

4

LIVED DEMOCRACY: UAW FORD
LOCAL 600

Sprawled on the banks of the Rouge river in Dearborn, Michigan, "the Rouge,"
as the workers called it, was unique in both size and complexity. UAW Local
600, based at the Rouge, was the world's largest local union; it was also one
of the most militant, radical, and egalitarian unions in America – and one of
the most democratic. The local's "lived democracy" of self-governing workers
incarnated, in its own way, some of the same underlying patterns already
revealed in our analysis of the insurgent origins and radical sustenance of
democracy in the CIO's international unions.

The Rouge was the single largest, fully integrated industrial unit on earth.
It combined and integrated every basic operation involved in the production
of an automobile.[1] Trains hauled raw materials and equipment over the plant's
twenty-four miles of railroad tracks, and ships laden with ore and fuel directly
discharged their cargoes into huge concrete storage bins with a capacity of
two million tons, to be processed and transformed into finished products. Its
foundry and 500,000 h.p. electric powerhouse were the biggest in existence.
The new cars that rolled off the Rouge's massive assembly line were produced
"from the ground up": All of the major phases of the production process
involved in the manufacture of an automobile, from blast furnace to assembly
line, were carried out by workers in some twenty-one different "building units"
and subunits.

Rouge's highly rationalized, integrated system of production under central
management surely seemed to constitute a hostile environment for the flowering of union democracy.[2] The immensity of the Rouge alone appeared to be a

---

[1] No other industrial unit anywhere has employed as many workers: Ford had 87,000 hourly-
rated production workers on its Rouge payrolls in 1941 (Wayne State University Archive,
Leonard to Roosevelt 1941), when Local 600 won its first contract (and far more during
World War II), and, according to the Company, it still had some 70,000 a decade later, after
Ford started to "decentralize" (Allen 1951, p. 8).

[2] Some leading authorities on unions have even argued, in a functionalist vein, that, in contrast
to the decentralized and small scale of craft production (epitomized, e.g., in the printing

formidable obstacle to its flowering. UAW Local 600, "the biggest local union in the world," had more members than most international unions. At its membership high in 1948, only eleven of the CIO's thirty-six internationals were bigger than Local 600, and in 1950 Fortune magazine commented that it "is the single most important slug of Communist strength remaining in the C.I.O."[3]

The production regime at Rouge was designed by Ford to be the epitome of hierarchical administration, technical perfection, and optimum profitability. Yet by design of the workers themselves, it also became the bedrock of their local union's system of constitutional self-government and enduringly contentious, democratic political life.

Local 600's record of vibrant democracy during its heyday compares favorably in every way with the celebrated case of the enduring "two-party system" in the International Typographical Union (ITU).[4] UAW Local 600, a local union, was for much of its history comparable, in both the size of its membership and the complexity of its internal governmental system, to the ITU international union. The ITU grew from 28,000 to 85,000 members between 1900 and 1942, and then rose to 100,000 in the early 1950s.[5] In Local 600, of the 83,500 Rouge workers who voted in the NLRB representation

---

industry at the time), the large-scale, centralized, and rationalized system of mass production requires predictable and, therefore, bureaucratic and centralized union leadership (e.g., Lipset et al. 1962, pp. 166–67).

[3] In 1950, Fortune reported that Local 600 had 63,000 members; "it is larger, in fact, than at least fifteen C.I.O. internationals" ("Anti-Communists in High at Ford," p. 48).

[4] Philip Taft (1944) originally brought scholarly attention to the ITU's unusual durable two-party system among American labor unions; by then, ITU already had a record of nearly half a century of competitive presidential elections. Lipset et al.'s subsequent study of the ITU posited it as a "deviant case" in regard to Michels's "iron law of oligarchy" as if that were really a scientific law (i.e., a general theoretical statement whose diverse empirical implications had been replicated so thoroughly as to attain the status of an accepted, if always tentative, conceptual reconstruction of an objective or immanent pattern of being and becoming). As we showed in the previous chapter, however, Michels's "iron law" is not a law at all – although, shorn of its fatalistic language, it can be a valuable admonition about the forces tending to subvert democracy.

[5] Lipset et al.'s quantitative analysis of the determinants of union democracy in the ITU, however, was based only on the New York local, which contained 10 percent of the total ITU membership, or about 10,000 members in the early 1950s (1962, p. 91). Three of Local 600's political units were about the same size as the ITU's New York local, which was the ITU's biggest local: The production foundry, according to the General Council's allocation of delegates (July 9, 1950), had 9,756 full-time dues-paying members; pressed steel, 10,058; and the motor building, 10,697.

election on May 21, 1941, some 58,000 cast their ballot for "UAW–CIO Local 600." (some 23,000 voted for "UAW–AFL" and fewer than 2,500 voted "no union.") During World War II, the local's membership rose to somewhere around 90,000; after the war, the local's full-time dues-paying membership hovered over 60,000 (63,450 in 1947, 62,000 in 1949). In mid-1950, the local had 60,725 full-time dues-paying members, but by mid-1952, as a direct result of Ford's concerted efforts to "decentralize" Rouge's production and reduce its work force – and to, not incidentally, weaken the local – the number of members fell sharply to 49,302. The full-time dues-paying membership continued to fall as Ford cut down the Rouge work force until, by the end of the decade, in 1960, the figure was down to around 42,000 – where the membership remained, with ups and downs, through 1975.[6]

Of the ITU in the mid-1950s, Lipset, Trow, and Coleman say: "It is the only American trade union in which organized parties regularly oppose each other for election to the chief union posts, and in which a two-party system has been institutionalized."[7] This statement was factually accurate at the time only in the narrowest sense, that the ITU's organized political blocs referred to themselves as "parties." For by that same year, Local 600's political life already had been governed for fifteen years by a de facto "two-party system," consisting of two major rival "caucuses" of left and right: the "Progressive" and the "Right-Wing."[8] Political parties in all but name, they continued – despite

---

[6] Conot (1974, p. 372). These figures on full-time dues-paying members, who were eligible to vote in the local's elections, do not include part-time or laid-off members or members in good standing holding withdrawal cards. These membership counts are based on the General Council's allocation of delegates by unit: 1947: ACTU Box 24, Local 600 – conference 1947; 1949: a progressive caucus election flyer and a Locke flyer on the 1949 strike (WPR 88–16 "factionalism"); 1950: *Ford Facts*, July 9, 1950; 1952: *Ford Facts*, August 9, 1952; 1960–75: Walter Dorosh (the local's president, 1965–75) interview. Irving Howe and B. J. Widick (1949, p. 106) give a membership figure for the late 1940s of around 90,000. They say that in 1948, some 98,989 Rouge workers were eligible to vote in an NLRB election, under the provisions of the Taft–Hartley Act, on the issue of continuing the union shop or ending it; 90,157 workers cast ballots, of whom 88,943 voted to continue the union shop. We suspect that these figures refer to all Ford workers in the Detroit area, and not only to Rouge workers.

[7] Lipset et al. (1962, pp. 1–2).

[8] Indeed, as we pointed out in the previous chapter, throughout the CIO era, ten of the twenty three CIO international unions on which we had appropriate information had rival organized factions or political blocs, ordinarily split between the "left" and "right," that – whatever their political self-identification – were actually durable parties that regularly contended for power and engaged in electoral contention. Lipset et al. (1962, p. 149n6) implicitly recognize this in their comment about the San Francisco longshore (ILWU) local: "The San Francisco local has two permanent political groups, which *alternate in power much as do parties in the ITU*"

the UAW leadership's open assaults on the Progressives and repeated attempts to strip them of office – to fight an unending battle for the trust and loyalty of the Rouge's workers and power in the local for many years to come, at least well into the 1970s.[9] (Alongside the two major caucuses and inhabiting the political terrain somewhere in between them were several small, sporadic caucuses. So, the local's political system might more accurately be termed a "multicaucus system.") The Progressive Caucus, whose core leadership consisted of Communists and their radical allies, held Local 600's elected leadership for most of the CIO era, but the local's elections were always hotly contested and frequently brought defeat and turnover in office for incumbents in both major caucuses. The core of the Right-Wing Caucus was made up of supporters of Walter Reuther; in the late fall 1946, Reuther defeated the "center–left" incumbent, R. J. Thomas, and won the UAW presidency. In the next year's elections, in which Reuther's allies won control of the executive board, even Local 600 "gave a majority to Reuther."[10] But soon the local's so-called right-wingers and left-wingers were uniting in opposition to Reuther's program. From 1950 on, the local was engaged in a sharpening battle to stop Ford's decimation of the Rouge through "decentralization." Yet Reuther negotiated and signed, on September 4, 1950, a five-year contract with the auto maker. "We raised hell with him," said Walter Dorosh, a Communist tool-and-die maker who was on the local's bargaining committee (and later was the local's president). "We said he had no right, without a

---

(1962, p. 149n, emphasis added). As we noted earlier, they also explicitly define "faction" as characterized by "manifest impermanence," as opposed to "party," whose "opposition is organized and challenges the incumbent administration continuously" (1962, p. 277). Certainly this latter conception of "party" – organized, continual opposition – applies precisely to the political system in UAW Local 600. Eight internationals had "sporadic" factional struggles that appear to have occurred irregularly over the years, and which may or may not have been sustained by durable opposition organization – they were, in Lipset, Trow, and Coleman's terms, "manifestly impermanent" (given the available information). Others have found evidence of a similar form of sporadic union democracy; for example, Cornfield (1989) showed that turnover on the Furniture Workers Union general executive board varied by historical period; it was especially high in the union's formative period, low in its period of stability, and then higher again (though not at the level of the formative years) during the era of decline. Similarly, Craig and Gross (1970) found that in the Saskatchewan Wheat Pool recurrent bouts of electoral contention were followed by long periods of uncontested elections. It may well be that the types of unions that, like Local 600, have systems of stable democracy and organized opposition and those that have only sporadic or periodic episodes of such contention are qualitatively different in their internal structures, as well as their "external" circumstances.

[9] Dorosh (1984).   [10] Howe and Widick (1949, p. 169).

convention decision, to sign a five-year contract. . . . 'Who the hell made you God?'"[11]

The local's fight to abrogate the UAW's five-year contract with Ford brought the left and right together;[12] long afterward, despite the Reutherites' relentless drive during the 1950s to expunge the Reds in their midst, the local continued to be a thorn in the side of the UAW's international leadership. At the time of Reuther's accidental death in a plane crash in 1970, Local 600 was still a lonely bastion of rank-and-file activism and socialist consciousness in organized labor.

In this inseparable coupling – of activism and socialism – we find the main clue to Local 600's rich and contentious political life: Its leaders, who were predominantly socialists of one or another hue, were – like their counterparts elsewhere in the United States – "more accessible to the membership, more aggressive in their tactics, more concerned with violations of a union ethic of service to the membership, and [had] greater personal integrity" than run-of-the mill unionists, right-wingers, and, especially, "business unionists."[13]

Insurgent Origins

Indeed, Local 600 had roots planted by earlier Red unionism, as well as by the local's distinctive blend of other insurgent political practices. Long before the CIO's formation, the Red union leagues, TUEL and then its successor TUUL, had been fighting to penetrate the plant and to bring their then-radical vision of industrial unionism to Rouge workers. From the mid-1920s on, the TUUL affiliate, the AWU, targeted the auto industry and, in particular, the Rouge plant, where it published a widely circulated shop paper called *The Ford Worker.* Sold for a penny or given away by Communist leafleters at the plant gates, it provided the only news of Rouge conditions and workers' grievances. In the spring of 1932, the AWU spearheaded the organization of the Ford Hunger March, in alliance with the Detroit Unemployed Councils; the March was joined by some 3,000 to 5,000 marchers demanding jobs for laid-off workers, a slowdown in the Rouge plants, and a halt of foreclosures

---

[11] Stepan-Norris and Zeitlin (1996, p. 22). Ford's five-year contract with UAW was its version of the "Treaty of Detroit" that UAW signed earlier with GM ("The Treaty of Detroit," p. 53).

[12] Especially crucial in unifying the local was the battle against Ford's "decentralization" program, which the local dubbed "Operation Job Runaway" (or "Operation Runaway"). we discuss this in Chapter 5.

[13] Gouldner (1947); Lipset et al. recognize that for socialists and radicals of all kinds, including Communists, union leadership was a "calling," but they consider Communists, virtually by definition, anti-Democratic (1962, pp. 263, 282).

on ex-Ford workers' homes. After an exchange of words and a thrown piece of slag, Ford's "servicemen" opened fire on the marchers and killed four of them. Several days later, tens of thousands of men and women marched in a funeral procession to honor the four fallen workers. If, despite its heroic efforts, the AWU never was able to put together much more than a skeleton organization at the Rouge, these early Red unionists and the many workers they influenced in these earlier struggles at Ford constituted a relatively compact, class-conscious, oppositional cadre committed both to radical social objectives and "rank-and-file democracy."[14]

A peculiar twist on the pattern of revolt from below was also involved in the local's organization. In the summer of 1938, with the infant local already split into warring factions, UAW head Homer Martin entered into secret negotiations with Ford in a gambit intended to consolidate his control. In exchange for Ford's recognition, Martin agreed to drop the NLRB actions that the union had brought against the company and, with Martin as UAW president, to take the local out of the CIO and join the AFL. When word of this got out, the local split asunder, and most members "seceded" from Martin's now UAW–AFL local to stay with the fledgling UAW–CIO. Three years later, in the May 1941 NLRB elections following the great strike, 70 percent of the workers voted to join the "UAW–CIO," 3 percent voted for "no union," and 27 percent voted for the AFL.[15] These rank-and-file AFL supporters also probably formed a minor current of working-class conservatism and a right-wing base within the local.

The UAW itself was independently organized at GM and other auto plants, as we know, but cracking Ford took the combined force of both independent and CIO organizing. In the wake of the defeat of several earlier UAW organizing drives led by "inside organizers," many of them Communists, in cooperation with Walter Reuther's westside Local 174, the UAW made an agreement with the CIO in late 1940 to launch a new Rouge campaign, under the "joint prosecution" of the UAW and the CIO. At the time, some 900 Rouge workers were UAW members; they formed a tightly knit group spread through many of the Rouge's major units and were ready and waiting. They formed the core of active cadres who carried out the directives of the joint organizing committee, headed by CIO appointee Michael Widman. The drive's strategy was devised in a cooperative effort between the UAW, the CIO, and Local 600 veterans. (Outstanding among these veteran organizers, and a leading strategist of the final drive, was "Brother Bill McKie," an open Communist and AWU organizer who had gone to work in the plant as a tinsmith back

[14] Stepan-Norris and Zeitlin (1996b, pp. 9–11).
[15] Galenson (1960, p. 183); Conot (1974, pp. 369–72).

in 1927.)[16] Many of these independent organizers, who won the trust of their fellow workers in the course of this final drive, went on to become elected officers in both the local's general council and the governments of its various building units.

Various "outside groups" and organizations – including nationality clubs, especially those allied under the umbrella of the Red-led International Workers Order (IWO),[17] the National Association for the Advancement of Colored People (NAACP) and its youth branch in Detroit,[18] various black churches, the CP, the Socialist Workers Party (SWP),[19] a women's auxiliary, followers of Father Charles Coughlin (the fascist "Radio priest"), the Knights of Columbus, the ACTU (which, as Seaton says, formed the "Catholic vanguard in the conflict with the radicals"), Masonic lodges, and other fraternal associations, as well as some neighborhood-based groups – had been represented among the Rouge's workers for years and took part, in one way or another, and often in hostile contention, in various assaults on Ford's union-free citadel, in successive, failed organizing drives and the final, victorious campaign.[20]

Out of the separate, cellular amalgamations that occurred among workers belonging to these various outside groups sprang some of Local 600's enduring,

[16] Bonosky (1953, p. 22); Stepan-Norris and Zeitlin (1996b, pp. 70–74).

[17] The IWO, which split off from the Workmen's Circle in 1930, was led by "avowed Communists"; the organization ran a national network of welfare, health, and death-benefit societies for "foreign-born" workers. As of 1945, IWO had a membership of 136,000 and published just short of thirty foreign-language newspapers that closely followed the party line and had a total circulation of 400,000 (Moore 1945, p. 38). In Detroit alone, the IWO had some thirty nationality sections, and perhaps as many as 1,500 Rouge workers were IWO members. IWO lodges also organized cultural events, such as choruses and dance groups, as well as educational forums. Some IWO lodges took part in leafleting during the earliest AWU organizing drives. Saul Wellman, who headed the CP's auto commission in Michigan after the war, called the role of the IWO "the key secret of why the Communists were able to make the contribution that they did in the organization of the mass production industries" (Stepan-Norris and Zeitlin 1996b, pp. 10, 88–89; Stepan-Norris 1988, p. 178).

[18] So, for example, the NAACP's senior leadership and many black clergymen in Detroit vocally opposed the unionization of the Rouge, but its youth branch actively supported it.

[19] A group of Trotskyists belonging to the SWP formed the core of the so-called Independent Caucuses. One of their leaders was Larry Yost, who headed the aircraft unit during the war (the unit was disbanded after the war) and also led the "anti-Stalinist" and anti-Reuther "Rank and File Caucus," founded in 1945; it ran candidates that year in the presidential elections of two of the biggest units, press steel and the production foundry, on a ten-point program that included revoking the wartime "no strike pledge" and organizing an independent labor party (Preis 1972, p. 24; *The Militant*, April 26, 1941, pp. 1, 4; August 19, 1944, p. 2; May 18, 1946, p. 1).

[20] Seaton (1981, p. 24); Stepan-Norris and Zeitlin (1996b, pp. 11–18); Stepan-Norris (1997).

rival political cadres. Over the years of the CIO era, several of these groups – chief among whom were the CP, the Socialist Party, and ACTU – repeatedly brought their own independent resources, objectives, "organs of information and opinion," and dedicated agitators and organizers into the political fray within the local.[21]

In sum, these insurgent practices endowed Local 600 with a lasting, rich, and restive political mix and a "colossal overproduction" of experienced organizers and proliferation of indigenous leaders spanning the political spectrum, which nurtured political contention and a lively democratic life.

E Pluribus Unum

Rouge's workers formed a veritable microcosm of the American working class. They came from all over the country and all over the world, in all sorts of colors, creeds, and religions. Some fifty-three nationalities – Poles, Bulgarians, Italians, Chinese, Syrians, Jews, Greeks, and Maltese – were represented at the Rouge. Unique, too, among manufacturers, the Rouge had a large contingent of black production workers, employed mainly in the production foundry; they constituted around 10 percent of the megaplant's labor force. Ford, alone among the nation's automakers, had gone out of his way to hire black men (and, reluctantly also some black women).[22] Many black workers, who had been working there since the Rouge went into operation in 1920, were loyal to "Mr. Ford" and hostile to the "white-man's trade unions." A large number of recent migrants from the South were also mixed into this workers' brew, bringing with them ingrained white-supremacist and reactionary conceptions

---

[21] As Lipset et al. observe, outside groups can fructify democracy by providing resources that enable the membership to challenge the incumbent leadership: "an opposition party with finances or motivation provided by outside groups and loyalties, such as the ACTU or various radical political parties, could perhaps by itself offer sufficient competition to the administration's control of the organs of information and opinion" (1962, p. 116; also see Craig and Gross 1970). To the left/right division in Local 600 between "outside" Communists at one pole and "outside" ACTU activists at the other was also added a peculiar, ostensibly "religious" cross-cutting division of that era, that between the Masonic Order and ACTU: a "sizable Masonic group" was active around the local, and in the local's "elections, if the [ACTU] were supporting one slate of candidates," Walter Dorosh recalls, "the Masons were supporting the other, automatically" (Stepan-Norris and Zeitlin 1996b, pp. 185, 168, 172).

[22] A year after Pearl Harbor, as of December 23, 1942, the Rouge employed 150 women, compared with the following numbers at other auto plants: none at Chrysler Dodge Main or Chrysler Highland Park; none at GM Cadillac; ten at all Hudson plants; seven at Packard; and two at Briggs-Conners (Foner and Lewis 1983, pp. 357–58).

(reinforced by the notorious anti-Semitic and racist radio agitator of the day, Detroit's Gerald L. K. Smith).

Local 600's workers were employed less in the "automobile industry" than in many highly diverse industries combined and integrated in Rouge's megaplant. Workers in the "steel unit," including the production foundry, jobbing foundry, open hearth furnace, and rolling mill, made the steel that was then stamped into automobile bodies in the press steel unit; in the rubber unit, the workers made the tires; in the plastic unit, the steering wheels; in the glass unit, the windshield and windows; and so on for the other major components that were then fit together to become the latest Ford models. In a sense, then, the "occupation" of the workers at the Rouge was not "auto worker" but blast furnace operator, tinsmith, puddler, carpenter, steel worker, assembly-line worker, tool-and-die maker, machinist, electrician, glassworker, warehouseman, trucker, pattern-maker, or rubber worker – or one of the other "*et ceteras* and so forths who did the work" at the Rouge.[23]

The diverse national origins and ethnic, religious, and racial composition of the Rouge's "native" and "foreign-born" workers, coupled with an unparalleled breadth of occupational differentiation among them within the same immense, integrated industrial complex, provided a double-edged realm of possibility: either as a source of division, setting worker against worker and taking a centralized, bureaucratic union to discipline, coordinate, and unify or as a source of a severalty of constituencies and rival political factions, united in a solidary and democratically self-governed union. Neither of these paths was pregiven or "natural."[24] Rather, these alternative paths confronted Local 600's founders, most of whom were self-conscious radicals, with a stark choice, and they self-consciously chose the path of democracy. They set out to build a union based on rank-and-file participation in making and carrying out the local's policies, whether in daily shop-floor battles or major strikes against the company or in staking out and fighting for their positions on national and international political issues.

[23] A line from Latouche and Robinson (1939).

[24] The TWUA, as we discussed in Chapter 3, is a salient example of how conscious and deliberate political choices at historical junctures can shape (although not always as intended) the form of government. As we know, a host of unions, some led by radicals, had long competed in this extraordinarily variegated congeries of related industries. Rather than choose to establish a system of decentralized government that based itself on, and tapped, the democratic potential inherent in this structural and organizational diversity, the men in charge of the CIO's textile industry organizing committee chose instead to exclude the preexisting unions from the organizing campaign and to create a centralized regime that would not permit "the rise of permanent functional suborganizations which might eventually challenge the authority of the national union" (Galenson 1960, p. 333).

They designed their system of constitutional, representative government to tap the potential that inhered in the workers' highly differentiated occupational and ethnic, religious, and racial identities and to foster multiple, contending sovereignties and thereby ensure the representation of the diverse, specific needs, grievances, and demands of the local's members.

In particular, they based the local's formal system of representative government on the industrial organization of the plant itself. The workers in every building unit elected their own delegates to the "general council." In addition, the local's constitution guaranteed the workers in each unit "a full measure of self-government . . . within the confines of Local 600." In each unit, the workers adopted their own unit bylaws and elected their own officers and delegates to three unit elective bodies: a set of nine regular officers (unpaid except for the chairman, who got the same pay that he, and rarely she, was earning before becoming an officer), an executive board of at least fifteen members, and a council ranging, depending on the size of the unit, anywhere from fifteen to 100 members. Each department and unit also elected its own "committeemen" to represent them on the shop floor.

Workers' Political Consciousness and Union Democracy

Electoral contention was so intense in Local 600 that the only time during the CIO era that a winning candidate for its presidency gained a majority of the votes in every single unit was in the election of 1953, which came right after Reuther reluctantly ended the "administratorship" he had imposed on Local 600 a year earlier so as to root out the local's Communists. This unprecedented vote reflected the members' overwhelming rejection of any further interference in their affairs by Reuther and his international executive board.[25]

In Local 600's twenty-five presidential elections between 1942 and 1984, the winning candidate received an average of 62.3 percent of the vote. The runner-up received an average of 48 votes for every 100 received by the winner. In the twenty-three elections between 1898 and 1942, the ITU's heyday, the winner's average was about the same as that in Local 600, or 64.1 percent. The runner-up in the ITU got an average of 62.5 votes for every 100 received by the winner. ITU elections, however, were strictly two-party battles (with a few exceptions), while Local 600 elections typically meant splitting the total vote among three or more contending candidates (which explains the lower number of votes to the runner-up). The races for next-to-top offices were also as close in Local 600 as they were in the ITU: Winners received an average of 64.4 percent in Local 600 elections compared with a similar 60.5 percent of the vote in the ITU (see Table 4.1).

[25] *Ford Facts* (May 16, 1953, p. 4).

Table 4.1. Closeness of presidential elections in UAW Local 600, 1942–84, and the ITU, 1898–1942

	UAW Local 600							ITU				
Year	No opponent	Number of candidates	Total votes cast	Votes to runner-up/100 winner	percent vote to winner		Year	No opponent	Number of candidates	Total votes cast	Votes to runner-up/100 winner	percent vote to winner
1942		7	45,269	110.0[a]	33.0		1898		4	19,076	59.3	58.6
1944		3	30,000	65.0	50.9		1900		2	23,759	67.9	59.6
1945		3	26,227	87.0	48.7		1902		2	27,765	34.6	74.3
1946		2	25,657	54.5	64.7		1904		2	33,505	66.7	60.0
1947		5	31,578	34.4	66.3		1906	X	1	24,420	0.0	100.0
1948		4	30,125	61.2[b]	44.3		1908		2	34,447	63.4	61.2
1949		5	44,391	62.3	56.8		1910		2	37,833	72.0	58.1
1950		5	37,194	94.9[b]	38.2		1912		2	43,169	79.5	55.6
1951		4	37,871	55.6[b]	48.4		1914	X	1	33,921	0.0	100.0
1952	X	1	22,898	0.0	85.9		1916	X	1	37,127	0.0	100.0
1953		3	35,749	41.7	64.8		1918		2	41,997	56.0	64.0
1955		3	35,375	17.3	79.9		1920		2	55,184	94.9	51.3

Year				
1922	2	52,971	84.2	54.3
1924	2	56,153	91.0	52.3
1926	2	58,552	93.2	51.7
1928	2	58,001	56.5	63.9
1930	3	47,576	39.0	71.9
1932	2	55,030	83.3	54.6
1934	2	47,897	74.3	57.4
1936	2	50,734	72.0	58.1
1938	2	60,563	62.7	61.5
1940	2	59,198	93.2	52.0
1942	2	56,844	93.0	52.8
Mean	2.0	44,162	62.5	64.1
1957	6	32,994	15.8	73.6
1959	3	27,572	56.1	60.8
1961	4	26,399	84.4	51.7
1963	3	25,773	98.4[b]	49.6
1965	2	30,061	86.3	53.7
1967	3	26,331	12.9	84.2
1969	4	25,633	61.0	57.1
1971	2	23,312	20.5	82.9
1973	3	23,617	16.4	76.7
1975	3	20,358	19.4	71.9
1978	X	21,468	0.0	71.5
1981	3	20,694	41.3	58.7
1984	X	15,002	0.0	83.9
Mean	3.3	28,862	47.9	62.3

[a] Candidate with more votes in the primary lost.

[b] Run-off election.

Note: Local 600 data missing for 1943.

Sources: Ford Facts, 1941–84 for UAW; Taft (1944) and Lipset et al. (1962) for ITU.

So the vitality of democracy, and of electoral contention, in Local 600 was comparable if not superior to the acclaimed democracy of the ITU.

In Local 600's democratic political life, "outside political organizations," mainly radical parties, played a crucial role from the start, and it was taken for granted that their UAW members could freely express their views. Back in 1937, in the struggle that led to the split the next year between his "UAW–AFL" and the UAW–CIO, Homer Martin, then head of the fledgling UAW, had inaugurated an attack on an "outside organization trying to seize control of the union," by which he meant the CP, and then fired several organizers, among them Walter Reuther's brothers, Roy and Victor. Such Red-baiting availed Martin nothing at the time; union activists knew that Communists had worked hard and long to build the union, and "even the dissident Marxist groups still considered [Communists] part of the radical community"; so Martin was defeated by a coalition of Communists and socialists (led by the Reuthers). Ten years later, however, Walter Reuther launched his own attacks on "outside groups" and "outside political interference" in the UAW.[26] This time, it worked: He won, and went on to purge Communists and their allies from UAW positions everywhere. But he failed in Local 600; it remained a recalcitrant "Red local," in which "outside organizations" continued to participate in the struggle for power for years afterward. Irving Howe and B. J. Widick go so far as to say that "the Communist Party . . . controlled Local 600."[27] Certainly, throughout the CIO era, Communists and their allies

---

[26] Reuther never did question the outside influence of the ACTU, while no one doubted its connections to the Catholic Church. Even the church's central leadership was interested in the ACTU's progress in the CIO: "In 1947 Pope Pius XII sent a congratulatory message to A.C.T.U.'s tenth anniversary meeting" ("The Labor Priests," p. 152).

Howe and Widick comment that Martin's cries of "outside influence" had "dangerous overtones for the union's political life. All too often talk in unions about 'outside influence' is demagogic; what matters is not whether people are 'outside' or 'inside' but whether they are right or wrong, honest or dishonest, intelligent or stupid. . . . A union has the right to exert union discipline: that is, when a strike is called, it can insist that all its members stop working. But does it have the right to insist on political conformity among its officials and leaders? This is a dangerous notion. The same might be said for the proposal to expel CP members from the CIO. . . . No union member should be expelled, and deprived thereby of his livelihood, unless specific and grave charges such as scabbing can be proved against him." They add that the way to "win union members away from the CP [is] by exposing it politically, in the arena of intellectual debate. . . . This seems both a more democratic and effective means of fighting the Stalinists than the view advocated by Walter Reuther" (1949, pp. 70, 73, 158, 268–69).

[27] Howe and Widick (1949, p. 157; also see p. 169).

were an integral part of the leadership of Local 600's leading Progressive Caucus.[28]

The progressives offered the local's members a compelling program of political activity sustained by a radical social vision: The core of that program dealt, of course, with the Rouge, with the workers' daily lives on the job and basic "bread and butter issues" of wages and working conditions, and often put forward innovative ideas that challenged the collective bargaining and other positions taken by the UAW's Reutherite leadership. The progressives opposed the restricting of workers' influence on job standards, and fought against the reduction of the number of shop stewards and the replacement of them with far fewer "committeemen," who were scarcely able to recognize the hundreds of workers each of them were now compelled to represent. The Progressive Caucus demanded that the international rescind its "company security" agreements, first signed in 1946, which gave Ford the right to discipline or discharge union shop officials who took part in "unauthorized" work stoppages, thus disarming the workers of the most effective weapon the stewards had been able to wield when they were not able to resolve a grievance satisfactorily: the shutting-down of their departments. The progressives took the lead in denouncing the "Treaty of Detroit" and led the charge against Ford's "Operation Runaway."[29] Beyond contract issues, the progressives stood, as their slogans declared, for a "strong democratic union," "open negotiations," "no discrimination," and "independent political action."[30]

They also took stances on a broad agenda of issues in local, state, and national politics, from matters such as taxation and foreign policy to racial segregation in housing. They made special appeals to the large contingent of black workers, and sought to address their distinctive, oppressive burdens and interests. As a result, black workers, even older ones who had been loyal to "Mr. Ford" and antiunion, came to provide the progressives with sustained support and filled important positions in their caucus's leadership.[31] In turn, of course, the

---

[28] Carl Stellato, first elected to UAW Local 600's presidency in 1950, was, reported *Fortune*, "the most determined anti-Communist the local has ever had for president." Since he joined the union at Ford in 1940, he had been "associated with the U.A.W. left-wing caucus and was for a time an assistant to [Percy] Llewellyn; however, he was never a Stalinist" ("Anti-Communists in High at Ford," p. 48). Although he was initially elected with the support of the Reuther leadership, he quickly switched his allegiance to the left wing, and became Reuther's nemesis.

[29] Stepan-Norris and Zeitlin (1996b, pp. 20–25).

[30] "Save Our Union" (n.d. but probably 1946).

[31] Stepan-Norris and Zeitlin (1996b, pp. 5, 130–49); Meier and Rudwick (1979, pp. 106–7); Howe and Widick (1949, p. 227). On the question of interracial solidarity in the CIO's international unions, see Chapters 8 and 9.

progressives' advocacy of black rights also provoked plenty of active opposition
to them among white workers who might otherwise have stayed out of the
political fray.[32] By widening the sphere of the union's role, by trying to educate
and spur the local's members to action on a host of issues transcending their
own immediate interests and circumstances, the Progressive Caucus stimulated
their fuller participation – both for and against them – in its political life.

The Right-Wing Caucus's electoral platforms sometimes looked a lot like
the progressives' platform, but in practice, the right-wingers spent their energy
on Red-baiting. As the ACTU's *Wage Earner* pointed out after one campaign,
in early 1947, "Anti-Communists made much of the Communist issue during
the campaign, but the two most prominent Communists, John Gallo, guide,
and William McKie were winners."[33] Aside from the issue of ridding the local
of Communists, "the right wing generally wanted to just leave things alone,"
as Walter Dorosh puts it, "and things [would] take care of themselves." So,
although the Right-Wing Caucus was a crucial actor in the local's political
system, as a "second party," in opposition to the program of the left, it rarely
put any new proposals in defense of workers' interests on the agenda.[34] As a
result, it was less likely to arouse workers' interest and participation.

Communists pushed the Progressive Caucus to take an expansive conception of the Local's mission and to advocate programs on a broad range of issues
that resonated with the workers. But ACTU's main political objective was to
challenge and eventually throw out the Communists, not to offer a genuine alternative to their program.[35] Actists were conspicuously involved in the right
wing's leadership. On the national scene, ACTU advocated both "social peace
and social justice," which meant "cooperative" labor relations involving the
"reciprocal rights and duties of employers and workers." The ACTU chapter
in Detroit was founded not by priests, as were many other chapters, but by lay

---

[32] In 1943 and 1944, for example, the progressives sought to end Jim Crow practices in
housing in Dearborn, Michigan, where many of the Rouge's workers lived. This became a
divisive issue in the next Local 600 election and, according to Saul Wellman, then head of the
CP's auto commission in Michigan, contributed to the defeat of the progressive president,
W. G. Grant, and other progressive leaders (Stepan-Norris and Zeitlin 1996b, p. 149).

[33] *Wage Earner* (April 4, 1947).

[34] Many of the former Local 600 leaders interviewed made this point, and it is confirmed by a
close reading of the campaign platforms of the opposing caucuses (Wayne State University,
Walter P. Reuther Archives, ACTU Collection, Box 24, and Andrew Ignasiak Collection).

[35] John Cort, one of ACTU's administrators in New York, responded to liberals' warnings that
ACTU was acting dangerously: "When St. Francis kissed the lepers, there were doubtless
many who pointed out that it was a highly dangerous activity. The A.C.T.U. may not have
the reckless courage of St. Francis, but in a smaller way it is risking contamination to bring
Christ into the dirty streets of the industrial world" ("The Labor Priests," p. 152).

workers, who "tended to be more radical" and to oppose "collaboration with companies."[36] If the Actists' presence as a vocal, often effective, opposition itself contributed to democracy in the local, they themselves were not enamored of that democracy, especially its constitutional protections of dissidents and dissenters. As an internal ACTU memo noted with dismay, when Reuther put alleged Communists in the local's leadership on trial, "The [Local] Union's democratic procedures guaranteed under its constitution which give all the breaks to the defendants and put the entire onus on the accusers is a guaranteed bar against railroading anyone out of the Union or out of office. In fact, if these defendants are found guilty they can only be removed from their Union positions and not from their jobs. The Taft–Hartley law protects the commies from loss of their jobs if nothing else does." Other than expunging the "Communist menace" in Local 600, the ACTU clubs at the Rouge, like other ACTU clubs elsewhere, espoused no union program and no long-term union objectives.[37] Once Reuther routed UAW's Communists, ACTU disappeared from the scene.

Electoral Contention

Now, to assess the effects of the programs of the contending caucuses, and thus of the political consciousness they embodied, as well as the role of rival "outside groups" in democratizing the Local's internal political life, we turn to an analysis of electoral contention in the local's twenty-one units. We examine the voting pattern for the offices of president, vice president, recording secretary, financial secretary, sergeant-at-arms, guide, and trustee, in the 1,006 elections held in these twenty-one units yearly between 1948 and 1953 and every two years between 1954 and 1959. (Except for some random missing cases, these 1,006 elections are all of the unit elections held from 1948 through 1959.) Organized left/right factionalism was intense during the era when these elections were held. Nine of the local's units at Rouge were under progressive leadership, five "center" units split the leadership between progressives and right-wingers, and seven units were under right-wing sway.[38] Communist

---

[36] Seaton (1981, p. 29); Goode (1994, p. 127).

[37] Seaton (1981, pp. 95–7, 108–9).

[38] The electoral data come from reports in *Ford Facts*, the local's newspaper, as well as from information in the files of the Wayne State University Archives of Labor and Urban Affairs (WSUA). The progressive units: production foundry, press steel, glass, motor, plastic, tool and die, job foundry, engine, frame, and cold heading. The "center" units: axle, casting, assembly (also called "B" building), miscellaneous, open hearth. The right-wing units: maintenance, rolling mill, transportation, spring and upset, specialty foundry, central parts,

clubs were active, as of 1952, in ten of the local's twenty-one units, according to HUAC. By ACTU's own account, its clubs were active, as of 1944, in six units.[39]

This analysis of electoral contention in the local's self-governing units allows us, so to speak, to hold constant over time the workers' specific "occupational community" (with its particular mix of jobs, skills, and work pace, as well as the size of the workplace) in order to assess the effects on electoral contention both of the political polarities of radicalism versus conservatism represented by the Progressive and Right-wing caucuses, respectively, and of the parallel, closely associated "outside groups": the CP and the ACTU.

Yet it should be borne in mind that midway in this period, the Progressive Caucus was wounded and weakened considerably by the combined assaults of HUAC, the FBI, the Detroit police department's Red Squad, and, above all, the UAW's executive board. HUAC's hearings on "Communist infiltration" of organized labor – which came in the midst of the massive U.S. "police action" against "Communist aggression" in Korea – not only generated a lot of suspicion of progressives but resulted in indictments, as "unfriendly

Lincoln–Mercury parts. We classified the political alignment of the units based on information taken from documents in the WSUA and interviews conducted by Stepan-Norris with seven retired former Local 600 officers.

[39] The Communist Party had formally dissolved its "fractions" (or clubs) in CIO unions at the time of the Popular Front and had reaffirmed this decision during World War II (see page 155 below). But at the Rouge, Communist clubs apparently were again active as of 1952, according to HUAC, which identified the following Rouge units as having Communist clubs: axle, B building (assembly), production foundry, open hearth, motor, plastic, press steel, tool and die, spring and upset, and miscellaneous (United States Congress 1952b, p. 2763). HUAC also said that a Communist club was active in the local's women's auxiliary. ACTU claimed to have active clubs in the following Rouge units as of 1944: axle, press steel, transportation, tool and die, rolling mill, spring and upset, maintenance, new steel foundry, and rubber (only 1941–45) (ACTU n.d. [c. 1944], pp. 5–6). Obviously, information on ACTU clubs as of 1944 and Communist clubs as of 1952 provides a crude measure of the presence of these clubs during the entire period 1948–59, but no other relevant information is available. To fill in some of the missing data on the clubs we made the following adjustments: The jobbing foundry was similar in having mainly black workers and was close by to the production foundry, which had one of the biggest Communist clubs; so we assume that it, too, had a Communist club until the unit was shut down in 1949. The engine plant was opened in 1952, during the height of the period when Communists were under attack, so it is unlikely that they tried to establish a club at that time; with no Communist club there, ACTU had no reason to establish one there. So we classify the engine unit as having neither club. For the same reason, we also classify the following units as having neither club: frame and cold heading (opened in 1950), specialty foundry (opened in 1952), central parts (opened in 1948), and Lincoln–Mercury parts (opened in 1951).

witnesses," of several progressive leaders. At the same time, in 1952, Reuther imposed an administratorship on the local, during which he stripped the "Ford Five" – five alleged Communists – and others in several different units of their elective offices.[40] The political analyst B. J. Widick, once a Reuther fan, now remarked: "It's amazing! Walter Reuther points out a thousand times in a thousand speeches that Stalinism cannot be defeated by force alone – superior ideas and a better program for the workers is the only answer! Yet in the UAW today, the only answer to Stalinism is bureaucratic force!"[41]

In fact, after the six-month administratorship was removed, and the local, as David Saposs notes, "was restored to full self-government, the old officers [excepting the Ford Five, who remained barred from office] were immediately re-elected." In 1959, Saposs was still lamenting that the "Reuther administration still finds itself stymied in its efforts to clean out the Communists completely from the UAW. Its chief difficulty has been the case of Local 600. This Ford local flaunts the International by adopting pro-Communist resolutions and by taking other actions of a similar nature." In 1961, when an open Communist candidate ran for office in the local against a Reutherite incumbent, he lost by only a razor-thin margin. In 1964, faced with the threat of a lawsuit, Reuther finally lifted the ban prohibiting the Ford Five from holding office. Within a few months, all five were promptly reelected to their former offices by overwhelming margins. The next year, Walter Dorosh, a prominent, longtime progressive leader, was elected local president. "At the time they took us out, they couldn't defeat us," Paul Boatin recalled.

> They had been trying to defeat us all the time, with candidates running against us. I know, I don't think, I know, what kept us in office. Despite the pressure, despite the awesome power of the UAW . . . , and despite the FBI, and despite the Red Squad in the city of Detroit, and despite all the federal and local county agents who at that time were just looking for every Red under a bed, we stayed in office. We got elected, . . . based on what . . we have stood for in organizing the UAW in the first place.[42]

---

[40] The five were Paul Boatin, Nelson Davis, John Gallo, Ed Lock, and Dave Moore (Stepan-Norris and Zeitlin 1996b, pp. 18–20; Buffa 1984, p. 147). The same sort of "evidence" and the same sort of "trial" was used against them as the CIO had used in throwing out eleven "Communist-dominated" international unions two years earlier: The five held views close to those appearing over the years in the *Daily Worker*. Boatin actually was reinstated as a full member in 1956, but the other four were not reinstated until 1964 (Stepan-Norris 1988, pp. 249, 220–21).

[41] Widick's article appeared under the nom de guerre Walter Jason, in *Labor Action*, October 16, 1950, as quoted and cited in Lichtenstein (1995, pp. 314, 518n48).

[42] Saposs (1959, p. 202); Stepan-Norris and Zeitlin (1996b, p. 226).

Findings

So, as our discussion of the local's political life suggests, in both the units led by progressives and those in which Communist clubs were active, the elections should have been hardest fought or had the highest average level of electoral contention over time. That is, we expect that the left-wing units typically (1) had more candidates competing for office (if no candidate ran against the incumbent, this indicates that the unit's leadership had no durable opposition) and (2) the winner's margin of victory was narrower (the winner's share of the total vote was lower and the runner-up's share was higher) than in the units led by their rivals on the right and in the units where Actists were active.[43] We also expect to find that in the units that had active ACTU and Communist clubs, which confronted each other directly, the average level of contention was highest, and in the units with no clubs, the lowest.

These measures of electoral contention are meant to reflect the depth of democratic life, on the assumption that when elections are typically hard-fought, democracy is the better for it: The less contentious the political life in the unit – or the higher the winner's typical margin of victory over time, the less the leaders are challenged by an opposition, and thus the more secure they are – the less likely its leaders are to be accountable to the members and effective in representing their interests. Put differently, if union leaders are regularly faced by opponents who can threaten their hold on power and who stand a realistic chance of defeating them in this or the next election, they are more likely to keep in touch with their members and fight to defend and advance their interests.

In fact, during the years 1948–59, the elections in units led by progressives were the closest, with the "center" units in the middle and the right-wing units lowest in the level of electoral contention: (1) the average number of candidates was highest in the progressive units, the "center" units were in the middle, and right-wing units, lowest (2.6 versus 2.3 and 2.0); (2) the winner typically received the smallest share of the total vote in the progressive units (progressives, 55 percent; center, 60 percent; right-wing, 68 percent); and (3) the winner's margin of victory over the first runner-up was narrowest by far in the progressive units (the runner up got an average of 68 votes for every 100 received by the winner in the progressive units versus 62 in the center units and 51 in the right-wing units).

---

[43] On the measurement of electoral contention, see Edelstein and Warner (1976, pp. 66, 95). The actual measures are the number of candidates in the election, percent of the vote to the winner, and the number of votes for the first runner-up for every 100 votes received by the winner. This latter measure captures the extent to which the elections were real contests, in which an opposition candidate was realistically capable of winning office.

Now, when we assess how "outside organizations" affected unit elections, our findings, though a bit mixed, are also substantively clear. Comparing (1) units in which both rival clubs, Communist and ACTU, were active; (2) units that had only a Communist club; (3) units that had only an ACTU club; and (4) units that had neither club, we find the following: The average number of candidates was highest in the units that had an active Communist club (2.6 for the Communist units versus 2.3 for the units with both clubs, 2.1 for the units with only an ACTU club, and 2.2 for those with neither). The winner received the smallest average share of the total vote in the units that had both clubs, but this was nearly identical to the average in the units that had only a Communist club (57 versus 58 percent). In the other units, those with only an ACTU club and those with neither club, the winner received a higher and nearly identical percentage of the vote (64 versus 63 percent). The winner's margin of victory over the first runner-up was by far the narrowest in the units that had both rival clubs (the runner up got an average of 71 votes for every 100 received by the winner), followed by those in which only a Communist club was active (61.5:100), and those which had only an ACTU club (58:100) or neither one (57:100).

That the units with only an ACTU club or neither club had the lowest levels of contention on all three measures (and were nearly identical on two of them) shows that the mere presence of an outside group per se does not contribute to the sustenance of organized opposition or electoral contention. Rather, both the outside group's political character and objectives and the quality of political competition between rival groups had independent effects in deepening democracy in Local 600 (see Appendix Table 4.2).[44]

Conclusion

The authors of *Union Democracy* assert that Communists have a "corrosive effect ... on trade union democracy. ... Communist ideology does not tolerate the existence of an organized opposition, so that any rise to power by Communists also means an attempt to destroy the opposition. These antidemocratic goals seem to pervade any intraunion dispute to which the Communists are a party."[45] Nowhere in *Union Democracy*, however, is there any examination (apart from an occasional anecdote) of the actual inner political life of any Communist-led union. Whatever forms of unfreedom "Communist ideology" was transmogrified into elsewhere, the homegrown American workers' version of "Communist ideology" as it was expressed in practice in Local 600 and in the other unions in America where Communists held power and

[44] See the Appendix to Chapter 4.   [45] Lipset et al. (1962, p. 282).

trust certainly did "tolerate the existence of an organized opposition."[46] Local 600, like every Communist-led international, had organized opposition factions or what amounted to an established "party system" and regular, hard-fought and contentious elections. In Local 600, as in the UAW as a whole, not Reds but the UAW's international leaders, who were adherents of a liberal or social-democratic "ideology," as well as their Actist allies, were the ones whose actual political practices had a "corrosive effect" on union democracy; they were the ones who would not tolerate and sought to destroy organized opposition from the left.

They failed, fortunately, in Local 600. Throughout the CIO era and long afterward, Local 600 remained a democratic political cauldron, in which a campaign of some sort for some office or over some issue, pitting the progressive and right-wing caucuses against each other (assisted by their allies in outside groups), seemed to be going on all the time. These were workers electing not remote "union bosses" or "bureaucrats," but workers. In this alert, active, and solidary workers' political community – in the biggest self-governing local union on earth – militancy, radicalism, and democracy proved to be inseparable.

[46] To impute the causation of Communist dictatorship to "Communist ideology," as do Lipset et al., requires us to ignore the specific historical circumstances and relationships in which the Soviet and Chinese Communist dictatorships arose; it also requires us to ignore the contrasting experiences of the freely elected and reelected constitutional Communist governments of the states of Kerala and Bengal in India and many of the northern cities in Italy over decades as well as the short-lived Socialist–Communist coalition government of Chile (1970–73, whose overthrow and replacement by a military dictatorship was instigated by the U.S. government).

APPENDIX TO CHAPTER 4

We also carried out several "ordinary least squares" (OLS) multiple linear regression analyses to control for three variables often said to be determinants of electoral contention in unions: (1) the importance of the office at stake in the election (the presidency vs. lesser offices); (2) the characteristic skill level of the workers in the unit; and (3) the number of workers in the unit. OLS is a statistical technique for analyzing the relationships among one or more independent variables, such as these three, and a single continuous, quantitative dependent variable (such as electoral contention). The point of using OLS is that it is supposed to allow us to assess whether an independent variable has an independent effect on the dependent variable, taking into account ("holding constant" or "removing") the effects of the other independent variables, and to estimate the size of that effect. The results of these OLS analyses, with slight differences, are substantively equivalent to the results of the cross-tabular (or contingency) analyses. The cross-tabular tables show the results of the empirical analysis in an intuitively understandable form, whether or not the reader is trained in regression diagnostics. See note 21 to Chapter 6 for further discussion of OLS.

We present the results here of our OLS analyses of electoral contention in Local 600's units (see Appendix Table 4.2), prefaced by a concise summary of the reasons (and rare relevant previous findings) that various authors have given for including the four control variables in the regression models.

The presidency of a unit not only brought with it greater authority than other offices, but also modest privileges and perquisites, the most important of which was being released from factory work. Once elected to the unit's presidency, a worker became a full-time union leader, whereas the other elected unit officers remained on the job while attending to their union duties. So we expect that the elections for the presidency of the unit were the most contentious.

It is often assumed that bigness per se tends to increase the social distance between union officers and rank and file workers and enhance the monopoly of

Appendix Table 4.2. *Standardized OLS regression coefficients of Local 600 unit election contention on measures of the political orientation of unit leaders, the number (and type) of clubs, and other control variables*

Independent variables	Model 1 Natural log of the number run	Model 2 Natural log of the number run	Model 3 Percent vote to winner	Model 4 Percent vote to winner	Model 5 Votes to the runner-up	Model 6 Votes to the runner-up
Skill	−0.12***	−0.05	0.07*	−0.00	0.03	0.08
	(−3.48)	(−1.23)	(2.06)	(−0.01)	(0.84)	(1.87)
1951–53	−0.16***	−0.16***	0.18***	0.18***	−0.17***	−0.17***
	(−4.69)	(−4.48)	(5.22)	(5.04)	(−4.95)	(−4.80)
1955–59	−0.07*	−0.06	0.11***	0.11**	−0.14***	−0.14***
	(−1.97)	(−1.73)	(3.25)	(3.03)	(−4.03)	(−3.86)
Medium size	0.12**	0.24***	−0.19***	−0.32***	0.21***	0.31***
	(3.10)	(5.87)	(−5.04)	(−7.81)	(5.47)	(7.51)
Large size	0.22***	0.31***	−0.23***	−0.32***	0.17***	0.24***
	(4.72)	(6.84)	(−4.98)	(−7.10)	(3.69)	(5.27)
Presidential election	0.13***	0.13***	−0.06*	−0.06*	0.03	0.03
	(4.27)	(4.25)	(−2.03)	(−2.02)	(0.94)	(0.95)
Progressive units	0.12***		−0.12***		0.10***	
	(3.51)		(−3.47)		(2.95)	
ACTU club		−0.15***		0.18***		−0.16***
		(−3.78)		(4.45)		(−3.91)
CP club		0.02		−0.01		−0.00
		(0.57)		(−0.27)		(−.08)
ACTU and CP Clubs		−0.06		0.04		0.01
		(−1.50)		(1.06)		(0.28)
Intercept	0.68***	0.67***	64.28***	64.37***	56.15***	56.27***
Adj R²	0.10	0.10	0.10	0.11	0.09	0.10
(N)	(1006)	(1006)	(1006)	(1006)	(1006)	(1006)

* $p < 0.05$.
** $p < 0.01$.
*** $p < 0.001$ (two-tailed).

Note: T-statistics are in parentheses, except in the last line, where the number of elections, 1948–59, analyzed in each model is in parentheses.

political resources in the officers' hands, and thus result in oligarchy (Summers 1984). But as we have seen, Local 600, despite its immensity, was – for the reasons we explored earlier – an extraordinarily democratic union. In fact, the findings of other studies on the effect of size on union democracy have been mixed. We found data on the number of workers employed in the various units for only two years, 1950 and 1952, and we simply trichotomized unit size into small, medium, and large. Although the absolute unit sizes changed during the 1948–59 period, their relative size probably was more or less stable. The variables medium and large are included in the regression model, and small constitutes the comparison category.

It has been suggested that the relative skill of workers affects their degree of participation in union politics and, as a consequence, the union's overall level of democracy. Skilled workers, both because of their mastery of their trade and their having more education than unskilled workers, tend to have less social distance or a smaller status gap between them and their union leaders than do the unskilled; they also tend to form "occupational communities" of their own, based on shared experiences and pride in their specific skills. Therefore, they are supposed to be more likely than the unskilled to have democratic unions (Strauss 1991, pp. 226–29). Now at the Rouge, most skilled workers were spread out all over the plant, rather than being situated in one physical locale, but two units probably consisted mainly of skilled workers: the tool and die unit and the maintenance and construction unit. Except in these two units, the formation of a distinctive occupational community among the skilled seems to have been unlikely. We have simply coded these two units as "skilled" and the rest as "unskilled" (which is at best a crude measure of the differential skill levels of the workers in the various units).

A few authors have argued that as unions "evolve" or "age" and collective bargaining becomes institutionalized, they tend to slough off the "superfluous political ideologies" present at their birth and to don the "mature" integument of "business unionism." The putative result is that union representation tends to become routinized, bureaucratized, and centralized over time, and to result in "machine control" (Lipset 1960, p. 392; Lester 1958, pp. 21–34, 103–4, 120, 42; also see Herberg 1943; Kornhauser et al. 1954, pp. 507–10). So, taking only the intraunion political conflicts into account, we demarcate three periods: 1948–50, when there was little direct threat to the local from the international leadership; 1951–53, when the local was under attack by the international leadership; and 1955–59, when there was a heightened political conformity and significant lessening of the left's influence and, in this specific historical sense, an increase in the international's centralized "machine rule" over the local. (We include the latter two periods as control variables and allow the first period to provide the comparison.)

Overall, including these three variables as controls does not change the findings we already have presented on the effects of caucus leadership: More candidates competed in the elections in the progressive units (Appendix Table 4.2, model 1); the winner got a significantly lower percentage of the votes (Appendix Table 4.2, model 3); and the ratio of the runner-up's votes to the winner's votes was also higher in the progressive units (Appendix Table 4.2, model 5) than in the other units. In other regression models (not shown here, but available upon request), we also take into account the distinction between "center" and right-wing units. These models show that both the progressive and center units were significantly more contentious than the right-wing units, but the progressive and center units' levels of contention barely differed from each other.

As to the effects of the clubs, the findings of the regression analyses are somewhat mixed. In the units that had only an ACTU club, electoral contention was low: Fewer candidates competed in the elections (Appendix Table 4.2, model 2); the winner got a significantly higher percent of the vote (Appendix Table 4.2, model 4); and the ratio of the runner-up's votes to the winner's votes was also lower than in the units that had neither club (the comparison category) (Appendix Table 4.2, model 6). But the units that had a Communist club and the units that had both an ACTU club and a Communist club were not significantly different from those that had neither club on any of these measures of electoral contention. We also ran other models that contrast the units that had only a Communist club and the units that had both clubs with a comparison category of the units that had only an ACTU club or neither club, and these show that the units that had only a Communist club and the units that had both clubs had significantly higher levels of electoral contention. A table showing these models is available upon request.

As to the effects of the control variables themselves: The number of candidates was significantly higher in the presidential elections than in the elections for lesser offices, but the share of votes that went to the winner was lower in the presidential elections (again, this might reflect the fact that the large units had the most candidates competing for the presidency), and in both types of elections, the ratio of the first runner-up's votes to the winner's votes were about the same.

In two models, the units with skilled workers had significantly fewer candidates in the elections (model 1) and the winner got a higher percentage of the vote (model 3) than in the "unskilled" units.

In the large and medium units, significantly more candidates competed than in the small units (the difference was greatest in the large units). This is consistent with John Anderson's (1978) suggestion that the larger the unit, the larger the pool of potential candidates. The victor's percentage of the votes and the ratio of the runner-up's votes to the winner were both significantly higher in both the medium and large units than in the small units. But (like Lipset et al.'s finding in their analysis of elections in the ITU's New York local), we also find a curvilinear relationship here: The ratio of the runner-up's votes to the winner's votes was higher in the medium units than the large units (but, again, this may be a function of the fact that the large units also had more candidates competing).

Consistent with the "union maturity" hypothesis, elections with significantly less contention occurred in the latest period (i.e., when the union was "oldest") than the earliest period (when it was "young"), but, contrary to that hypothesis, no linear decline of contention occurred; rather, on each measure, the middle period, 1951–53 (when it was "middle aged") had the lowest level of electoral contention. This was not the result of a supposedly inexorable process of ideological disenchantment or bureaucratization as the local aged, however; rather, the 1952 election came right after Reuther's executive board ended the almost universally despised administratorship over the local, and Local 600's members used that election to send the international's Reutherite leadership a pretty blunt, nearly unanimous message of solidarity against it for having violated their right to self-government: They overwhelmingly reelected many of the incumbents whom Reuther had tried to get rid of.

5

"RED COMPANY UNIONS"?

When UAW president Walter Reuther signed a five-year contract with Ford on September 4, 1950, over the vehement and united opposition of Local 600's leadership, it was identical in substance to the five-year GM contract he had negotiated and signed in complete secrecy four months earlier, making organized capital's spokesmen both incredulous and ecstatic. *Business Week* extolled the GM settlement as "industrial statesmanship of a very high order," and *Fortune* famously dubbed it "The Treaty of Detroit." Reuther declared that the 1950 settlement represented "the most significant development in labor relations since the mass production industries were organized," although it is questionable whether he really understood or intended what its real historical significance was. For the "Treaty" signaled, and not only for the big automobile corporations and the UAW, "a great political settlement," a class accord ending nearly two decades of workers' insurgency, self-organization, and open class warfare.[1] The accord came in the immediate wake of Reuther's defeat of the UAW's center–left coalition and his ensuing purge of Communists and their allies from positions of responsibility and trust in key UAW locals as well as from the international itself (although he still had and would have, for years to come, the recalcitrant and powerful Red Local 600 to reckon with).

Two years earlier, in the battle over the 1948 contract, General Motors had already launched an offensive – over a union principle as basic as seniority – to halt what a GM executive termed "the tendency of watering down management's responsibility to manage the business."[2] Now, the UAW's 1950 contracts with

---

[1] Lichtenstein (1995, p. 276); Harris (1982, pp. 112–18); Maier (1987); Nissen (1990). Now this was the kind of "collective bargaining" employers could relish, for it called, as labor economist Frederick Harbison put it bluntly, "for internal union discipline rather than grass roots rank and file activity" (cited in Lichtenstein 1995, p. 292).

[2] Lichtenstein (1995, pp. 280, 288–89). The war had barely ended when GM refused, in late 1945, to negotiate certain UAW demands that would, in GM's words, compel it to "relinquish its rights to manage its business." GM referred to its mid-1934 statement of

GM and Ford signaled the triumph of that offensive and sealed the UAW's acceptance, in principle, of the corporations' "right to manage." "GM may have paid a billion for peace," *Fortune* recognized, "but it got a bargain. General Motors has regained control over . . . crucial management functions. . . . "[3]

The companies saw their detente with the UAW as an opportunity to try to reimpose their control over production processes which their managements believed they lost during the years of workers' insurgency and self-organization and then of government wartime labor regulation.[4] Ford, in particular, set out with a vengeance to "decentralize": to downsize and relocate production from the Rouge to new plants elsewhere in the country. But Local 600 was not about to acquiesce and deliver the "lengthy period of stable and peaceful relations" that Reuther had personally assured Ford's managers that they would get if, like GM, they, too, agreed to a five-year contract.[5] The local sought to abrogate and renegotiate the contract, as part of its battle to put a stop to what it derided as Ford's "Operation Runaway." Its leaders predicted that decentralization would result in the disappearance of upward of 19,000 jobs from the Rouge. The local fought one of its initial battles over Ford's farming out of maintenance and construction work. The company was taking a varying number of jobs from the Rouge and giving them to AFL building trades locals. The local's position on decentralization was vindicated, so its leaders thought, when umpire Harry Shulman supported it on a related problem in July 1950.

principles opposing management's delegation of "authority to anyone [such as a union] whose interests may be in conflict with those of the owners of the business" (quoted in Chamberlain 1948, p. 133).

[3] "The Treaty of Detroit" (p. 53). *Fortune* hailed the GM contract, which the Ford contract emulated, as "the biggest labor event of . . . the entire post-World War II period. . . . [The contract] goes further in its affirmation of both the free-enterprise system and of the worker's stake in it than any other major labor contract ever signed in this country [and] . . . unmistakably accepts the existing distribution of income between wages and profits as 'normal,' if not as 'fair.' . . . It is the first major union contract that explicitly accepts objective economic facts − cost of living and productivity − as determining wages, thus throwing overboard all theories . . . of profit as 'surplus value.' Finally, it is one of the very few union contracts that expressly recognize both the importance of the management function and the fact that management operates directly in the interest of labor" ("The U.S. Labor Movement," p. 92). The GM and Ford "treaties" established the precedent of multiyear contracts, annual cost-of-living adjustments, "productivity-factored wage adjustments," and union cooperation to improve "efficiency" and "productivity" (Harris 1982, pp. 150–51).

[4] Lichtenstein (1995, p. 288).

[5] A Ford calculation put the number of production hours lost through strikes and walkouts at the Rouge at more than a hundred times the number lost at GM (Lichtenstein 1995, p. 315).

But "[t] he issue of [decentralization] became so exacerbated," *Fortune* reported a few months later, "that, on three separate occasions, settlements worked out by the local leadership were turned down by the membership."

Over Reuther's opposition and refusal to cooperate, the local then went to court, in an unparalleled suit against the company. On November 11, 1951, the local voted to seek "an injunction against further removal of operations from the Rouge plant and against further farming out." This suit, as the local's president, Carl Stellato, wrote Reuther, had "the unanimous approval of every member of the Local and of the chairmen of all 17 building units. There is no difference of opinion on this issue."[6] Reuther's own UAW general counsel, Harold A. Cranefield, considered the proposed suit "novel in its conception," as he informed Reuther in a confidential memo on November 8: It would be unprecedented, he said, if the UAW proceeded with it. The suit rested on the legal theory that the UAW's contract with Ford "should be construed as carry-ing a commitment by Ford against such practices [i.e., removal of operations and farming out jobs] or that the Court should reform the contract in accor-dance with the actual understanding of the parties though it was not written into the agreement." In Cranefield's view, the theory, "though novel, . . . [was] very carefully thought out"; it was "within the realm of possibility that the court might entertain the complaint." He was "sure the suit would be taken seriously and would attract national attention among labor lawyers on both sides of the table and in the labor press and trade journals." Most important, Cranefield concluded, it was "undeniable" that if the court could be persuaded "to move even an inch in the direction of the theory of this complaint it would be a great gain for labor. It is equally undeniable that such advances are usually generated in the courts in such circumstances as these rather than legislatively."[7]

But Reuther and his executive board not only offered no help against Opera-tion Runaway but, in a speech at the UAW convention later that year, charged

---

[6] "Anti-Communists in High at Ford," p. 50. With Reuther's backing, Stellato had narrowly won election as the right-wing candidate for the local's presidency in May 1950, and had made sure during his campaign and subsequent policy statements to denounce not only Communism but "monopoly capitalism" and "the greed and ignorance of capital" (Stellato press release, July 10, 1950, WSUA: Stellato 1950). But he soon came to have a cooperative working relationship with progressives in the local.

[7] Cranefield (1951) reviewed a draft of the proposed suit (Goodman 1951). Although no author is given, it is known that Ernest Goodman (of the firm of Goodman, Crockett, Eden and Robb), who represented the local before the court, drew up the suit. We have not found any document with Reuther's (or the UAW executive board's) specific reply either to Cranefield or to Local 600.

that the local was "dominated by the Communist Party" and that its program was "Communist-inspired." The local's newspaper, *Ford Facts*, retorted in an editorial, on January 19, 1952, that "Brother Reuther evidently forgot that 30,000 members of Local 600 sent him cards requesting the immediate negotiation of a thirty-hour week with forty hours' pay. In his opinion, he believes that 30,000 of us in Local 600 are members of the CP." On November 14, 1951, Local 600 filed the suit against Ford.[8] It charged that the company had perpetrated a "fraud" upon the union, and asked that the UAW–Ford contract be either reformed to prohibit the decentralization or declared null and void, because the company had falsely assured the union that it had no plans to decentralize.[9] The suit was "perhaps unique in the history of American labor–employer relations." For at "the very heart of this case," as Ernest Goodman, counsel for Local 600, told the court nearly two years later, was the question of ". . . the rights of workers under a contract with an employer extending over a long period of time to have some security in the retention of the work processes on which they are employed for the duration of the contract, and the accumulation of the rights which they can only acquire if the employer continues his operations at that particular place where they are employed."[10]

On June 5, 1953, the U.S. district court ruled against the local; it declared that the local's allegation that Ford committed a fraud upon the union was "render[ed] doubtful" because Reuther and the other UAW officials who signed the contract with the company were not parties to the local's suit "complaining of the alleged fraudulent conduct on the part of the company." The court also ruled that the contract had no implied commitment against decentralization

---

[8] Two months later, Stellato reported to the local's membership: "The Company's attorney argued, time and time again, that since the international union and not the Local was on the contract, the case could not be continued without the International. We pointed out in reply that the Local and its members were the only workers affected. While we believe that we are correct on this argument, the case would be strengthened if the International Union joined in. I again urge the International to come into the case . . . because the issue involved is one which affects every member of the UAW–CIO, as well as every union member in the country" (*Ford Facts,* January 19, 1952, pp. 1–4).

[9] "The assurances were false and the Company's representatives well knew at the time that they were false [and constituted] a fraud upon the [union], in that at no time prior to, or during the negotiations which led up to and culminated in the current agreement, was there any communication or intimation . . . that the defendant was planning, or had planned or intended any substantial transfer or contracting out of the usual and customary production operations, maintenance and construction activities and facilities . . . then being carried on at the Rouge plant . . . but, on the contrary, were denied by the defendant" (*Local Union No. 600 v. Ford Motor Co.* 1953, p. 839).

[10] *Local No. 600 v. Ford Motor Co.* (1953, p. 844).

because it "unequivocally vest[ed] in the company, and only in the company, the right . . . 'to manage its business, including the rights to decide the number and location of plants'. . . . " So, because Reuther's executive board had ceded "the right to manage its business" to the company and refused to join the local's suit, the "realm of possibility" of "a great gain for labor" never had even a fighting chance to become a reality.[11] Instead, with Ford and other corporations retaining the unrestricted "right" to freely dispose of their property (and their workers), Detroit and the downriver communities soon became, as Local 600 leaders had foreseen and tried to prevent, "industrial wastelands."[12]

Ford's "decentralization" had not been a mere technical decision, based on criteria of efficiency or productivity. On the contrary, it was inherently political: It was one tactic in a strategy aimed at once to undermine Local 600 and find a more docile work force and more accommodating local union leadership elsewhere in the country. Ford had ruled out building another plant in Detroit, for fear that the UAW's "position in the Detroit area would be further strengthened."[13] Ford also deliberately avoided relocating to other sites where the company would have to face strong working-class organization as a whole (not only that of auto workers). For Ford's planners, cities with a highly organized working class such as Chicago or Pittsburgh surely would not have been the best location for a new plant.

In the words of a Ford executive memorandum, there was one consideration that deserved special emphasis in relocating production:

> . . . the ominous mixture of the United Mine Workers, the United Steel-workers and the United Electrical Workers in the Pittsburgh area; the combination of the United Steelworkers, the radical Farm Equipment Workers and the United Automobile Workers in the Chicago area; and the entrenched position of the United Autoworkers [*sic*] in the Detroit area, should cause any company considering the establishment of a new plant at these locations to pause. There is no question but that the union

---

[11] As is implied in Local 600's struggle to put a halt to Ford's decentralization – and the judge's explicit ruling – its leadership had long opposed UAW's ceding so-called management prerogatives to Ford. As Paul Boatin, who had been the president of the local's motor unit, told us: "They [the International] consciously recommended to the workers that the Company shall retain the sole right about the location and the kind of things the plants do. . . . [They] allowed a trade-off – 'We'll give you three percent annual wage increases but [we keep] the prerogatives, the rights of management.'. . . This is carried to the ridiculous extreme where even the pension money of the workers is managed by the Company" (Stepan-Norris and Zeitlin 1996b, p. 154n84).

[12] WSUA, Averill (1950, p. 8).   [13] Ford Industrial Archives (1949; also see 1946).

influences in these areas at these locations are much more powerful than in the Buffalo area, where the C.I.O. has not been able to establish a dominating position against the old, traditional A.F. of L. building trades unions and the railroad unions. . . . Introducing aggressive United Auto Workers unionism into a community that is the stronghold of the United Mine Workers and the United Steelworkers, and where the radical United Electrical Workers has one of its strongest units, in the turbulent Westinghouse local, could result in the combination of these explosive forces which over a period of time could well create an atmosphere of tension and strife in which industry could not hope to progress.[14]

"The Class Struggle in Production"

Implicit in this consultant's blunt warning to Ford about the "ominous mixture" of major industrial unions in these cities and the "explosive forces" inherent in an organized working class is the theoretical issue we address empirically in this chapter: In "the class struggle in production [over] the technical and social organization of the labor process," what difference can "aggressive" and "radical" unionism make? Put differently, what limits can unionism impose on the capitalist's power – or on how "the workers are subjected to domination by employers" – and what is the character of those limits?[15]

The class struggle in production in the advanced capitalist countries tends to be explicitly political: The capital/labor relation in the immediate labor process is ruled by a regime based on collective bargaining agreements (as well as other forms of class mediation), reinforced by the coercive power of the state.[16] The question, then, is whether "aggressive" and "radical" union leaders can build their own conceptions of working-class interests into the "political regime of production," through which capital's subordination of labor is defined, regulated, and enforced, and, in so doing, expand labor's "frontier of control."[17]

---

[14] Ford Industrial Archives: Bethlehem Steel Company (1949, pp. 2–3).

[15] Magaline (1975, p. 60); Weber ([1925] 1956, p. 78). "The *will* of the capitalist is certainly to take as much as possible," in Marx's words. "What we have to do is not to talk about his *will*, but to enquire into his *power*, the *limits of that power*, and the *character of those limits*" ([1865] 1973b, p. 33, emphasis in original).

[16] The 1947 Taft–Hartley Act, which amended the 1935 Wagner Labor Relations Act to require a "non-Communist affidavit" of union leaders, also transformed "collective bargaining" agreements into "contracts," specifying "rights" and "obligations" in production, enforceable in the courts.

[17] Goodrich (1920, p. 61). The term "political regime of production" appears in Burawoy (1985, pp. 19, 68); we have given it somewhat different conceptual content (see Brighton 1977, pp. 4, 14, 16), especially below in our delineation of its "contradictory tendencies." For

So the central question addressed in this chapter is, How did the Communist-led internationals differ from the internationals in the rival camps, in sustaining or subverting the immediate subservience of labor to capital?

Within the prevailing functionalist paradigm of "labor relations," the answers to these questions are not in doubt. Both "pluralist" and self-described "Marxist" analysts of labor relations, despite "sharply opposed valuations" of the outcome, argue that the labor union, by routinizing conflict and containing discontent, and thus reducing labor market uncertainty and regulating labor costs, "incorporates" the working class and tends to stabilize the capitalist system. As Hugh Clegg, a leading British pluralist, remarks, "The pluralist can accept every word of . . . the Marxist theory of economism, or incorporation, or institutionalization. . . . The terminology may differ. . . . But translation is easy."[18]

Translation is easy since both sets of analysts, whether phrasing their arguments in the language of social harmony or of radical critique, share the same paradigmatic presupposition, namely, that the systemic needs of "modern industrial society" or of "corporate capitalism" generate the means of their own satisfaction. They assume, in particular, that the "institutionalization of class conflict" necessarily contributes to the maintenance of the capitalist system.[19] Once "industrial unionism establish[es] itself in the corporate sector," as Michael Burawoy says, it is *shaped in accordance with the needs of capital*," and thus tends merely to consolidate "factory regimes which *reproduce the capital–labor relationship more efficiently*." Unions cannot challenge capitalism, Perry Anderson avers, but can merely express it, for they are confined within "insurmountable" limits that are "inherent in the[ir] nature." In sum, as Stanley Aronowitz puts it, "unionism can be [none] other than a force for integrating workers" into the "corporate capitalist system."[20]

This "Marxist" argument and the "pluralist" argument are, except for differences in "terminology," as Clegg says, virtually identical. Collective bargaining is a bulwark of "democratic capitalism," says Frederick Harbison, because it "provides a drainage channel for the specific dissatisfactions and frustrations which workers experience on the job." Similarly, Daniel Bell tells us that "in the

---

kindred formulations in different theoretical terms, cf. Dahrendorf (1959, pp. 64–67); Dubin (1958, p. 153); Flanders (1968, p. 8); Marshall (1965); Selznick (1969, p. 154); Slichter (1941, p. 1).

[18] Jonathan Zeitlin (1985, p. 6); Clegg (1979, p. 455).

[19] Cf. Aronowitz (1973, p. 218).

[20] Burawoy (1981, p. 104; 1983, p. 587n, emphasis added); Anderson (1967, p. 264, emphasis in original); Aronowitz (1973, pp. 256, 217); cf. Losche (1975).

evolution of the labor contract, the union becomes part of the 'control system of management'" and performs "a vital function" as "a buffer between management and rank-and-file resentments."[21]

Collective bargaining, it is assumed, must result in merely marginal changes in the employment relation, because in principle both union and employer must concede a legitimate sphere of interests to the other side. Demands that threaten either side's basic interests are thus unavoidably excluded. Further, this form of "mutual dependency" of union and employer produces a "common interest in the survival of the whole of which they are a part."[22] As unions "evolve" or "age," says S. Martin Lipset, they slough off "superfluous political ideologies" and don the "mature" integument of "business unionism."[23]

"The *contractual logic itself*," historian David Brody argues, makes it " . . . into a pervasive method of containing shop-floor activism." By displacing "class struggle" from the shop floor and reconstituting it in "a framework of negotiation," in Burawoy's formulation, collective bargaining results in *"an institutionalized creation of a common interest* between the representatives of capital and labor." It is "a form of class struggle [that] revolves around marginal changes which have no effect on the essential nature of the capital–labor relationship."[24] In sum, "the modern labor agreement is the principal instrument of class collaboration between the trade unions and corporations," and must, therefore, normally serve "to strengthen, rather than weaken, capitalist relations of production."[25]

Anything that retrospectively appears compatible with the development of capitalism is thus explained as a fulfillment of its reproductive needs. This sort of explanation compels even its radical or Marxian adherents to ignore the effects of the actual class struggle within production, for these effects are pregiven and thus already known. Unions, asserts Anderson, are a mere "passive reflection" of the organization of production, necessarily taking on "the *natural* hue of the closed, capital-dominated environment of the factory itself. . . . No matter whether the trade union movement in question adopts a 'revolutionary' or 'reformist' stance, it tends to encounter the same *structural limits* to its action."[26] Radical unionists, as Aronowitz says, cannot "transcend the

---

[21] Harbison (1954, p. 274); Bell (1961, pp. 214–15); cf. Drucker (1950, pp. 134–35); Dubin (1954a, b).

[22] Fox (1966, p. 4).

[23] Lipset (1960, p. 392); see also Kornhauser et al. (1954, pp. 507–10); Lester (1958, esp. pp. 21–34, 120, 142).

[24] Brody (1980, p. 201, emphasis added); Burawoy (1979, pp. 114–15, emphasis in original).

[25] Aronowitz (1973, p. 218); Clarke (1978, p. 18).

[26] Anderson (1967, pp. 264–65, emphasis in original).

institutional constraints of trade unionism itself." Rather, as Michael Mann puts it, for the "union militant and official . . . there is lack of fit between his ideology and his action": Because "the framework of a capitalist market is implicitly accepted by the very activity of compromise economic bargaining . . . the practical relations with management entered into by Communist unions may be indistinguishable from those of reformist unions."[27]

Given the premise of predetermined structural "limits" and institutional "constraints" necessarily corresponding to the system's imperatives, it follows that no matter whether organized labor makes any self-conscious efforts to probe or test them, the result, a null effect, is also preordained. In this sort of theory, the possibility is excluded that unions, given the political commitment, might be able to "bend" or "stretch," if not break through, the "limits" or "constraints" it posits. The theory must deny that the union's political objectives, strategy, and actual practices really matter in *shaping* the plant's "capital-dominated environment."

But these, of course, are precisely the critical substantive issues. For even if we concede that unions can "never become fully anti-capitalist organizations," as Richard Hyman argues, the possibility remains that under the appropriate political leadership – especially one committed to "socialist objectives" – they can inscribe "anti-capitalist" tendencies into the political regime of production in their domain.[28] How far such encroachments on capital can go, "beyond which the mechanisms of private capital accumulation are threatened, and disinvestment occurs, unleashing another kind of class struggle, of an extra-production character," can be discovered only in practice, by probing and testing the "theoretical" limits.[29]

Our premise here, in Antonio Gramsci's words, is that "a trade union is not a predetermined phenomenon. It becomes a determinate institution, i.e., it takes on a definite historical form, to the extent that the strength and will of the workers who are its members impress a policy and propose an aim that define it."[30] So, rather than being the protean expression of systemic functions, the political regime of production is an artifact – within specific circumstances and (unknown) objective limits – of both class *and* intraclass struggles. Its contours are determined in part by the distinctive political strategies and actual practices of union leaders, concretely expressing their "reformist" or "revolutionary" (or even "conservative") political consciousness.

---

[27] Aronowitz (1973, pp. 21, 219); Mann (1973, pp. 37, 22).

[28] Hyman (1985, p. 123). Referring to legislation on "workers control" under advanced capitalism, Stephens and Stephens (1982) argue, in terms similar to our own argument, that the "ideology and action of working-class leaders" affects both its enactment and implementation.

[29] Anderson (1990).   [30] Quoted in Hyman (1985, p. 118).

Historiography

Before turning to our empirical analysis of whether the CIO's unions could and did, "impress a policy" on collective bargaining, it is germane to review what the writings by historians, other specialists, and journalists on U.S. labor have to say. For although the theoretical and historical questions are inseparable, the writings addressing them often exist on different planes of discourse, passing unaware like ships in the night.[31] Until recently studies of the actual achievements of Communist-led CIO unions have been rare, and few have dealt in any detail with their collective bargaining gains.[32]

The prevailing historical claim, in labor economist Jack Barbash's words, is that "where the Communists are able to control a going union there is no evidence of any relationship between collective bargaining and revolutionary ideology. The contracts negotiated by an established, Communist-dominated union are indistinguishable from any other contract negotiated by any other union."[33] Here are representative statements by distinguished historians: "It is remarkable," says David Brody, "how little difference [radicals] made on the direction of the . . . unions they controlled." "All indications," Harvey Levenstein suggests, "point to the fact that the politics of neither group [Communists and anti-Communists] played any major role at the bargaining table." "In their pursuit of union recognition, higher wages, and better working conditions," says George Lipsitz, ". . . Communists in the CIO functioned as enthusiastic, but largely conventional, trade unionists."[34]

Some authorities, however, implicitly or explicitly reject the idea that the politics of union leaders are irrelevant to their union's achievements. On one

---

[31] The work of historian James Prickett on the CIO is a rare exception. He specifically rejects the "contention that the institutional demands of the trade union make the politics of its leadership irrelevant" (1975, p. 443).

[32] The handful that have dealt with collective bargaining consists of: Filippelli and McColloch (1995); Gilpin (1988); Jensen (1954); Keeran (1980a); McColloch (1988); and Ozanne (1954, 1967). Other studies of specific unions include Dix (1967); Filippelli (1970); Huntley (1977); Kimeldorf (1988); Prickett (1975); and Schatz (1977, 1983).

[33] Barbash (1956, p. 350). Barbash was then the Research and Education Director for the AFL–CIO.

[34] Brody (1980, p. 132); Levenstein (1981, p. 334); Lipsitz (1994, p. 194). Similar explicit or implicit claims that the politics of union leaders did not affect their union contracts, or that the Communist-led unions did not differ from other CIO unions in their "actual trade union practice," appear in Aronowitz (1973, pp. 25, 342, 350); Bernstein (1971, p. 782); Caute (1979, p. 353); Cochran (1977, pp. 355, 379); Draper (1985c, p. 45); Kampelman (1957, p. 254); Karsh and Garman (1961, p. 113); Lichtenstein (1980, p. 128); Oshinsky (1974, p. 125); Ozanne (1954, p. 215); Saposs (1959, pp. 184–85).

side, this is stressed by those who charge that the Communist-led unions were subservient to an "alien power," and thus pursued policies that, as CIO officials charged, were "subversive of sound trade union objectives." So, for instance, Walt Disney testified before HUAC in October 1947 that the Screen Cartoonists Guild was "Communist-dominated and had tried to take over his studio with a view to having Mickey Mouse follow the Party line."[35]

The Communists' union policies, says C. Wright Mills, were determined not "by their judgment of the changing needs of the working people, or by pressures from these people, but by the changing needs of the ruling group in Russia." "Communists in the labor movement," Walter Galenson asserts, "were committing a fraud. . . . The evidence [historians] have already gathered is overwhelming. . . . There is simply no doubt that in general the unions that remained in the CIO were far more responsive to the views of their members than the expelled [Communist-dominated] unions, and never sacrificed their economic interests at the behest of an alien power."[36]

On the other side are barely a handful of historians who assert that the Communist-led unions were, in the words of Richard Boyer and Herbert M. Morais, "the pace-setters for the whole trade union movement by reason of wage scales and conditions won . . . and sound trade union practices. . . . [They] insisted on membership control in drawing up contracts, in declaring contracts, or in settling them."[37]

A similar assessment, though with a sharply opposed valuation, was made in 1946 in a "special report" on how to "deal with . . . Communist-controlled unions." The report by the RIA warned that "[b]argaining with a CP union is a more tight-fisted affair than with any other union." It advised employers "dealing with a Communist-controlled union, or with a union in which Communists may win control, [to] give particular attention to clauses" dealing with the "management prerogative," "no-strike commitments," and the "grievance procedure." The RIA report advised management to "insist on no-strike clauses," "keep committeemen to a minimum," and "limit [the] working time stewards may spend on grievances."

---

[35] Caute (1979, p. 493).

[36] Mills (1948, p. 199); Galenson (1974, pp. 236, 242). Similar claims that Communist-dominated unions made a habit of betraying their members appear in Boulding (1953, p. 103); Gates (1944); Goldberg (1964, p. 7); Lens (1949, pp. 228, 244–45); and Stolberg (1939, p. 5). Barbash, in some confusion, wants it both ways, that Communist "ideology" did not matter in collective bargaining, but that, anyway, "Communist penetration of unions . . . along with racketeering [is] a form of union pathology" (1956, pp. 350, 324).

[37] Boyer and Morais (1955, p. 361); also see Emspak (1972, pp. 366–67); Prickett (1975, p. 419).

It was "especially important (though more difficult) to strengthen the management prerogative clauses," the report said. Similarly, Lee Hill (secretary of Rustless Iron and Steel Corp.) and Charles Hook (vice-president of Allis-Chalmers Manufacturing Company) also warned: "Left-wing militant unions consider management rights as obstacles to be overcome in order that the unions may have more freedom of action. . . ."[38]

The Hegemony of Capital

Inherent in the political regime of production are a set of inseparable contradictory tendencies, which are codified in labor–management agreements, specifying each party's rights and obligations within the workplace. The balance of these contradictory tendencies represents the relative hegemony of capital or of labor's "consent to exploitation."[39] (This balance is also partly determined, of course, by other labor legislation and statist, or corporatist, forms of mediation that coexist with collective bargaining, e.g., codetermination in Germany.)

On the one side, the production regime defines, regulates, and enforces the domination of workers by employers: It aims to ensure the formal rationality of production – to ensure that the workers carry out the tasks allotted to them in the division of labor – and thus to provide the optimum profitability of the so-called effort/reward bargain.[40] On the other, the production regime

---

[38] RIA (1946, pp. 14, 16). Hill and Hook (1945, pp. 58–59, 60). Writing in the *Harvard Business Review*, Benjamin M. Selekman also warned that "the communist and left-wing unions of today" were committed to "the most undeviating and ineradicable conflict pattern in present-day industrial relations. . . . [O]nly by ousting party-line leaders from positions of union leadership, whether by legislation or by employer resistance or by intra-union action, may this source of conflict be minimized" (1949, pp. 179–80).

[39] Gramsci ([1929–35] 1971, pp. 18, 133, 182); Przeworski (1980, p. 24).

[40] Weber ([1925] 1956, p. 78; 1946, p. 261). Put in Weber's terms, the production regime embodies an inherent opposition between the "formal rationality" of capital and the "substantive rationality" of labor. In his words: "That the maximum of *formal* rationality in capital accounting is possible only if the workers are subjected to domination by employers, is another specific instance of the *substantive* [*materiale*] irrationality of the modern [capitalist] economic system" (Weber 1968, p. 138, emphasis in original, translation slightly reworded). Or, put in Marx's terms, ([1844] n.d.; [1867] 1906) these contradictory tendencies also bear on the objective relationship of alienation (*Entausserung*) within the immediate production process. Weber's "formal rationality" is what Marx might have termed "alienated production rationality." Alienation inheres in the immediate production process to the extent that control and organization of the process (not only what is produced but how it is produced) are the prerogative not of labor but of capital. Capital thereby usurps the collective rationality – the "knowledge, judgment, and will" – of the producers themselves. This "separation of the

embodies the effects of the workers' resistance to their employer's domination and of their struggles to enhance their own "negative freedom" and thus minimize the exploitation inherent in the effort/reward bargain.[41]

Consequently, the hegemony of capital, as it is embodied in the political regime of production, is relational, practical, and dynamic. Any real production regime is continually being constructed and reconstructed in and through concrete struggles between workers and employers. Under advanced capitalism, the collective bargaining agreement codifying the resultant balance of procapital versus prolabor tendencies, is the form taken by the so-called employment contract.

The Employment Contract

"Organizational discipline," as enshrined in the employment contract, is indispensable for guaranteeing the effort of free workers. In the "capitalist enterprise, . . . [or] large firm run with free wage labor, [the specific historical] form of valorization of capital [is] the exploitation of other people's labor on a contractual basis." On this contractual basis, the employer acquires the legal "right," having bought the workers' capacity to produce, to decide not only what they produce but how they produce it: "[T]he optimum profitability of the individual worker is calculated," in Max Weber's words, "like that of any other material means of production."[42] Free wage labor's subordination, then, is the essence of the employment contract, and it clothes with the color of law, as Anthony Giddens puts it, the "exploitative class relation [that is] part of the very mechanism of the [capitalist] productive process itself."[43]

Three types of provisions in union–management agreements codify the actual form taken by this exploitative class relation in a given political regime of production. First, the so-called *prerogatives of management*.[44] Does the agreement restrict or protect management prerogatives, by guaranteeing specific

intellectual powers of labour" from the producers converts "these powers into the might of capital over labour"; thus "all means for the development of production transform themselves into means of domination over, and exploitation of, the producers" (Marx [1867] 1906, pp. 396–97, 462, 708–9; [1844] n.d., 71–73, 78–80).

[41] Hyman (1974, p. 245).   [42] Weber (1961, p. 209; 1988, p. 50; 1946, p. 261).

[43] Giddens (1982, p. 169); also see Weber (1968, p. 213); Halaby (1986, p. 635); Klare (1977/78, p. 297). So long as the employment contract consisted of an individual and so-called voluntary agreement between employer and worker, that is, until workers were able to organize and win some collective demands, the balance of class power embodied in the employment contract was so heavily weighted in capital's favor that it was all but bereft of contradictory tendencies.

[44] Chamberlain (1948, p. 144); Dubin (1958, p. 151).

functions exclusively to management? Second, *the union's freedom of action*. Does the agreement protect or restrict the workers' rights to resist and their ability to impose sanctions on the employer's use of their labor and, specifically, their right to strike?[45] Third, the *methods for handling disputes* under the contract.[46] Does the grievance procedure protect or restrict the employer's right to discipline the workers and the workers' rights (individually and collectively) to oppose such discipline – even to impose contrary practices, which in effect become unwritten supplements to the contract?

The rights to strike, to resist employer discipline, and to get fair treatment through established grievance procedures are hard-won workers' rights. How fully the terms of the collective bargaining agreement as the workers understand them are applied daily on the factory floor is partly determined not only by the workers' militancy and leadership, but also by the features of the grievance procedure itself. Fulfillment of the contract's terms will vary with the extent to which the grievance procedure enables workers to have their individual gripes or common troubles taken up by the shop steward, "committeeman," or other union representative and addressed directly by the immediate supervisor on the job.[47]

Management Prerogatives

The issues workers can raise and the demands considered legitimate in collective bargaining depend on how the issue of management prerogatives (the so-called right to manage) has been resolved. What these prerogatives are has long been "at the storm center [of battles over] ... the frontier of control."[48] For how they get defined in the agreement touches all of its other provisions bearing on capital's immediate power over production. This is stressed by managerial spokesmen and radical critics alike.[49] Mann suggests that "[t]he employer will yield on economic bargaining more readily than he will on the sacred 'managerial prerogative.' ... "[50] Similarly, an American Management Association publication declares that "the *struggle for power* must automatically be *focused* [on] the *management rights* clause" because it is essential, as

---

[45] Giddens (1982, p. 170); Dubin (1958, p. 151).

[46] Dubin (1958, p. 151); Lens (1947, p. 716).

[47] For instance, the grievance procedure determines whether individual workers get the specific wage rate they are entitled to under the contract, get first refusal for a job opening to which their job seniority gives them claim, are not laid off out of turn, or can call their foreman to account for discriminatory treatment or unwarranted discipline (Chamberlain 1958, p. 631).

[48] Goodrich (1920, p. 61).   [49] Harris (1982).   [50] Mann (1973, p. 21).

corporation executives Hill and Hook argue, for "protecting [management's] freedom and authority."[51]

So, in this analysis we *assume* common employer hostility to union encroachments on management prerogatives, and thus abstract from any actual internal variation in employer resistance against such encroachments during these years.[52] This is not merely a heuristic assumption, however, but is buttressed by the available evidence on the stance of American management throughout the CIO era. There was "no question . . . [what] the prevalent management position, as presented by company spokesmen" was, or what a majority of the ranks of management believed, in the struggle over managerial authority during these years. The widely held moral convictions of managers in large corporations, expressed both privately and publicly, as Neil Chamberlain remarks in his now classic study of the union challenge to management control, were that they had to resist the encroachment by labor on managerial prerogatives. They were convinced that such

---

[51] McMahon (1969, pp. 266–67, emphasis added); Hill and Hook (1945, pp. 58–59). The theory behind management prerogatives was stated bluntly by Ben Moreel, then chairman of the board and president of Jones and Laughlin Steel: "Under our system of free enterprise . . . we obtain a division of labor by a process of natural selection. Each person gravitates to the place where his talents are best employed. . . . This process of natural selection has given us the best industrial management and the highest standard of living the world has ever seen. We believe, therefore, that *management* should continue to *manage* – because it can do the job better than anyone else" (quoted from a radio address, January 11, 1952, in Chamberlain 1958, p. 598, emphasis in original).

[52] Employers in some types of industrial work, it has been suggested, may have an interest in ceding managerial control to unions, as they ostensibly do in some types of craft work. But this supposition is not supported by any evidence in the historical works we have read or in our own independent research on relations between the companies and the unions during the CIO era. In contrast to craft unions, as Chamberlain (1948) observes, industrial unions have "immense significance [for potential] encroachments on managerial prerogatives. . . . [W]here organization proceeds on a craft basis, with a number of unions bargaining only for their memberships, it is impossible for such individuated unions to establish terms applicable to all the employees of that company. They are concerned only with terms for the craft. . . . [O]n matters affecting the operation of the company as a whole no one union has any more standing than the others. . . . This limitation does not apply in the case of a company-wide union, or council of unions, however. Representing all the production employees, it may speak authoritatively in the interests of all. . . . It is not surprising, then, that *the question of union participation has arisen most importantly where unions may speak on behalf of all the employees in the company or industry. . . . It has been with the entry of the CIO, with its predominantly industrial structure, into the mass production industries that the question of managerial authority has become such a pressing one*" (1948: 163–64, emphasis added).

encroachment held "grave dangers for our social economy, and that it . . . [had to] be halted."[53]

The "inherent rights of management," in the prevailing managerial view as stated and endorsed by Wayne L. Morse in 1941, were not "negotiable or arbitrable."[54] Defending these inherent rights against an invasion by unions had aroused *employer solidarity*, a leading management official declared in 1945, "in never giving in on anything which *jeopardizes the institution* of their company and of management."[55] The struggle over the frontier of control in American industry, Chamberlain observes, "*date[d] back for many, many years.* . . . [But it] was particularly acute in the period following World War II, when unions – which had been restrained by the War Labor Board for four years – displayed their newly acquired strength in a number of demands which led a suspicious management to question whether it would all end in 'socialism.'"[56]

For working-class radicals or socialists, "management rights" are neither "inherent" nor legitimate; on the contrary, such alleged rights constitute, in their view, a quasilegal form of illegitimate class power. As an officer of the Communist-led FE bluntly told an interviewer, "The philosophy of our union was that management had no right to exist. Therefore our policy was to offer no quarter. . . . "[57] "Offering no quarter" to management and ceding it no "prerogatives" extends the principle of self-government to the "economy" and challenges, in Giddens's words, "the broader 'political' subordination of the working class within the economic order."[58] The warning by GM head Charles E. Wilson right after World War II carried the same message, but with a rather different valuation: Labor's "attempt to press the boundary farther and farther into the area of managerial functions," Wilson declared, threatened the "American system" with a social revolution "imported from east of the Rhine."[59]

In the CIO's heyday, according to Chamberlain, a management expert who interviewed "union activists" of all stripes, they made "little distinction between the *political philosophy* underlying the *state* and *industry*. In both spheres they see the necessity of controlling authority in the interests of those who take the orders . . . [in the] firm conviction that *those in control must themselves be controlled.*"[60] We turn now to see how and to what extent this political philosophy was actualized in the employment contracts won by the unions under the leadership of the CIO's rival factions and parties – and inscribed as a result in the political regimes of production in which they were involved.

---

[53] Chamberlain (1948, pp. 3, 129, 166, 8).
[54] Quoted in Chamberlain (1948, p. 4n6).   [55] Bakke (1946, p. 40, emphasis added).
[56] Chamberlain (1958, p. 593, emphasis added).   [57] Ozanne (1967, p. 214).
[58] Giddens (1973, p. 206).   [59] Quoted in Brody (1980, p. 181).
[60] Chamberlain (1948, pp. 166–67, emphasis added).

The Sample of Contracts

Our analysis is based on a sample of 236 contracts negotiated by the locals of CIO international unions in California from 1937 to 1955. This California sample is a subsample of a refined national sample of 431 taken from an original batch of 596 CIO local contracts provided by the Industrial Relations Center (IRC) at the California Institute of Technology. Basing this analysis on only the California sample holds constant some of the so-called objective conditions outside the workplaces in which these agreements were negotiated.[61]

---

[61] Our sample is drawn from a batch of nearly 2,000 collective bargaining agreements collected for a survey by the California Institute of Technology's IRC. The survey began soon after the Wagner Act was upheld in 1937 and continued until the mid-1970s, with the aim of providing employers with systematic information on the types of provisions being included in collective bargaining agreements. The IRC sent requests for their contracts to unions (AFL, CIO, and others) and companies throughout the United States. The clauses of each agreement were coded on McBee Keysort cards. We located three persons who had been involved in the contract survey: Victor V. Veysey, director emeritus of Cal Tech's IRC; Joseph W. Lewis, research assistant on the survey; and Verna P. Steinmetz, secretary and coder, but none could provide a copy of the mailing list or further details about the method of collection.

We constructed our sample from this original batch as follows. First, we separated out the batch of 596 CIO agreements. Second, we excluded thirty-two agreements that had been negotiated between a major employer and an "international" union. Third, from this collection of local agreements, we also excluded all but one (which was randomly selected) of any set of successive agreements between the same parties. We did this because of the likelihood that such agreements had the same or similar provisions, and so possibly biased the sample. These steps resulted in a refined national sample of 431 local contracts. This national sample is a fund of primary historical data, whether or not it might be representative of the contract universe.

Finally, we surmise that the prestige of Cal Tech in California most likely gave the institute access to some California companies and unions and increased the likelihood that these union locals would send copies of the requested collective bargaining agreements to the IRC. Because of the probable higher response rate in California, and to hold some objective conditions constant, we extracted the 236 California agreements. To assess the representativeness of this sample, we compared its division into political camps as of 1946–47 with that of a known population, namely, the member unions of California's CIO locals in the 1940s that belonged to California's Industrial Union Council. Here is the distribution by camp of locals, delegates, and votes versus sample locals: Communist, 54, 59, 48 versus 59; "shifting," 21, 15, 23 versus 19; anti-Communist, 25, 26, 30 versus 22 (CIO 1945). As can be seen, the sample's distribution of CIO local unions by political camp is virtually identical to the actual distribution of locals and delegates by political camp. So this sample is, we are confident, roughly representative of California's population of CIO contracts (although, in fact, a sample need not be representative to serve as a basis for an analysis exploring

The question, of course, is whether *local* contracts constitute a valid measure of the *international* union's achievements in collective bargaining. Obviously, as UAW Local 600's continual clashes with Reuther illustrate clearly, the politics of the international union and its locals did not always coincide. Yet the locals of CIO international unions generally had to negotiate within guidelines set by international officers, or the international's constitution specifically required locals to receive approval of their agreements from the international's executive board, national office, or president.

In thirty-one of the CIO's thirty-six durable international unions, our survey reveals, the union constitution specifically provided for the international's guidance or supervision in local bargaining or actually required its approval of local agreements. For example, a provision in the 1947 UAW constitution states: "After the Local Union has approved a contract at a meeting called especially for such purpose, it shall be referred to the Regional Director for his recommendation to the International Executive Board for its approval or rejection."[62] In other international unions, the authorization for the international's involvement in local negotiations (as can be seen from their proceedings) was provided by delegates at its annual convention. So, for example, although UE's constitution had no specific provision concerning the international's involvement in local negotiations, the union's conventions regularly dealt with the issue of local bargaining.[63] Despite differences between the tenor of the inner political life of some locals and their international as a whole, it seems safe to assume that the internationals' leaders were always involved, either directly or indirectly, in their locals' part of the collective bargaining process.

Measuring the Contradictory Tendencies

The procapital versus prolabor tendencies of a specific political regime of production, as they are formally codified in the relevant provisions of a union's agreements, are measured as follows.

theoretically relevant relationships, so long, of course, as the scope of the sample is appropriate and the relationships tested are not introduced into the data by selective sampling).

We have deposited the complete Cal Tech batch in the University Research Library, Department of Special Collections, at UCLA.

[62] UAW (1947, Article 19, p. 50).

[63] For instance, a resolution at the UE's 1946 convention specified what types of provisions locals should try to include and avoid in their contracts (UE 1946).

Management Prerogatives

A clause (or clauses) in which a union cedes the right to manage ordinarily stipulates that "management has the right to hire, the right to discharge for just cause, the right to discipline, the right to plan production, the right to change the process of production, etc."[64] A union's acceptance of management prerogatives is indicated by a clause in the contract explicitly ceding them. Absence of such a clause leaves labor free to challenge and encroach upon them. Our measure, then, is a dichotomy: whether or not a local union explicitly cedes management prerogatives.

The Right to Strike

A no-strike provision prohibits strikes entirely or it specifies the limited conditions under which strikes are permissible during the term of the contract. Such a provision might prohibit strikes when the disputes involved are subject to settlement by the grievance machinery or arbitration or when they are "unauthorized" by the international. So, we measure restriction of the right to strike as a trichotomy: no prohibition, a conditional prohibition, or a complete prohibition of strikes.

Contract Term

The practical impact of a no-strike clause in restricting workers' abilities to resist their employers or prevent workers from enforcing their understanding of the contract depends to some extent on its duration (or term) and on the provisions of the grievance procedure. The longer the contract's term, other things being equal, the longer the workers are prohibited from using the strike, either conditionally or totally, as a weapon of struggle; and so, the longer the term, the more disabling is a strike prohibition, even a conditional one, of workers' power in the immediate production process. If long-term agreements serve as "a management tool to stabilize production and labor costs," Aronowitz suggests, "militant unionism has always fought for one-year contracts based on its view of contracts as per se a limitation on workers' power to deal effectively with problems on the job."[65] So we measure the length of the contract as a dichotomy: short-term (one-year) versus long-term (18 months or more) (no contracts in the sample were for a term between one year and 18 months).

[64] California Institute of Technology (n.d., p. 21).
[65] Aronowitz (1973, p. 252); also see Mills (1948, p. 255).

Trade-off Provision

A union might be willing to accept a conditional or even total strike prohibition as a trade-off for a short-term contract; so we also include a trade-off variable. The trade-off is prolabor if the contract has no prohibition or a conditional prohibition against strikes during the term of the contract or is short-term (one year); if it has a total strike prohibition and is long-term (18 months or more), the contract has no trade-off.

Grievance Procedure

A complex and lengthy grievance procedure also reduces the pressure on an employer to try to resolve contract disputes and grievances quickly.[66] An employer's ability to discipline workers is enhanced, in Aronowitz's words, by "a bureaucratic and hierarchical grievance procedure consisting of many steps during which the control over the grievance is systematically removed from the [hands of the workers on the] shop floor." Conversely, from the workers' standpoint, a preferred grievance procedure would involve the union, through a steward or committeeman, from the first step, and would resolve the grievance speedily and "at the lowest levels," that is, within the workplace unit itself.[67] This sort of grievance procedure makes it easier for workers to enforce the terms of the collective agreement and redress what they see as inequities and abuses.[68]

A provision that a union rep must be present at the first step of a grievance procedure immediately transforms it from an individual complaint into a collective demand backed by the union. This not only increases the chances of settling it favorably, but also protects workers from retaliation by management. Settling a grievance with the least delay is facilitated by allowing only a minimum number of steps in the process and by imposing a time limit on each step and on the entire procedure. In contrast, a procedure involving many steps delays settling a grievance and also cedes its settlement to higher levels in management and the union (whether the latter are local or international officers).

[66] Mills and Wellman (1987, p. 194).

[67] Aronowitz (1973, p. 217). A grievance could be settled in a series of "steps," from the lowest to the highest levels of union representatives and company management: at the first step, in the workplace, by negotiations between the union "rep" (shop steward or committeeman) and the foreman or another immediate supervisor, or further up the hierarchy to involve top union officials or their representatives of either the local or international union, and the company's labor relations officials or other representatives of top management (or, if provided for in the contract, by an arbitrator) (Chamberlain 1948, p. 85).

[68] Lens (1947, pp. 716–17).

So, to measure the prolabor versus procapital tendencies embodied in a contract's grievance procedure, we dichotomize each of three variables: whether or not a shop steward or other union rep must be present at the first step; the number of steps in the grievance procedure (one to three versus four or more), and whether or not each step has a time limit.

Prolabor Index

We also constructed a simple index counting how many of the six contract provisions in a contract were prolabor: the possible "score" ranges from a low of zero to a high of six. (The trade-off measure, which is not per se a provision but a combination of the provisions on the right to strike and the term of the contract, as explained earlier, is not included in this index.)

The relationships to be shown here using these measures, we want to emphasize, are of both theoretical and historical relevance, for they constitute "simple historical facts" about our recent past that bear on our understanding of the present. What our analysis shows about the prevailing theory of labor unions and reveals about the "realm of possibility," and what it discloses about the era of the CIO, are conceptually separable issues. But they are inseparable historically.

The Effects of Political Leadership

What, then, are the effects of a union's political leadership on the production regime? How different were the provisions codifying the political terms of the immediate capital/labor relation (i.e., management prerogatives, the right to strike, the grievance procedure, and contract duration) in the contracts won by the locals of the international unions in the CIO's rival camps? Was the pattern of contractual provisions in these camps roughly the same? If the functionalist consensus, whether in its "pluralist" or "Marxist" variant, as well as the prevalent views of historians, labor economists, and other specialists, were correct, then the answer to the last question (our null hypothesis) would be a definite "yes." But the answer is, to the contrary, a definite "no." For the contracts won by the unions in the CIO's rival camps differed sharply.

The local contracts of Communist-led international unions were consistently more likely to be prolabor on the entire set of provisions codifying the crucial political terms of the immediate capital/labor relation than those won by locals affiliated with internationals in the shifting and anti-Communist camps. The contracts in the shifting camp also were more likely to be prolabor than those in the anti-Communist camp, though not consistently. But the vast majority of the contracts of the Communist-led unions were prolabor on each of these provisions. Of the Communist, shifting, and anti-Communist contracts, respectively, the percentages of those that did not cede management prerogatives were 59, 41, and 22; of those that had a total no-strike provision, 35, 65, and 70 percent; of those that were short-term, 84, 74, and 54 percent; of those that specified a shop steward had to be present at the grievance's first step, 79, 32, and 34 percent; of those that allowed no more than three steps in the grievance procedure, 84, 64, and 67 percent; and of those that put a time limit on each step, 65, 43, and 46 percent (see Table 5.1, part 1).

If, for the moment, we disregard what each provision specifies, and just count how many of them were prolabor, the results are dramatic. Some 20 percent of the Communist unions' local contracts were prolabor on all six provisions: They were a virtual actualization of the "ideal type" of the "counterhegemonic" production regime, but none of the contracts of the unions in the other camps were prolabor on all six provisions. Another 29 percent of the contracts in the Communist camp, but only 3 and 2 percent, respectively, of those in the shifting and anti-Communist camps had five prolabor provisions. All in all, then, half the Communist camp's contracts but less than 3 percent of the contracts in the rival camps had at least five prolabor provisions. At the low end, none of the contracts in the Communist camp but 11 and 21 percent, respectively, of the contracts in the shifting and anti-Communist camps had no more than one prolabor provision (see Table 5.1, part 2).

The local contracts in our sample are not evenly distributed among the various international unions, so to check the possibility that one or another international was overrepresented among the local contracts and distorting the real political pattern, we sorted and examined the local contracts by international. For every international having at least five local contracts in the sample, we calculated the percentage of these contracts that were prolabor on the set of crucial provisions. Although this gave us only a handful of unions in each political camp to compare on each provision, the relationships are sharp, clear, and in the same direction as the relationships already shown. On all of the provisions, the average percentages of prolabor local contracts were much higher for the Communist-led internationals than for those in the other political camps (combined). So, for example, on the management prerogative, the mean percentage of the contracts that were prolabor was 72 percent for the six Communist-led unions and 44 percent for their six non-Communist counterparts; and on the strike prohibition, the prolabor mean percentages were, respectively, 52 versus 24.

Table 5.1. *Prolabor provisions in CIO local union contracts in California, 1938–55, by CIO political camp (in percent)*

Part 1. Specific prolabor provisions

Political camp	Management prerogative	(N)	Strike prohibition[a] None	Cond'l.	Total	(N)	Short-term contract[b]	(N)	Trade-off[c]	(N)	Grievance procedure Steward	(N)	Steps	(N)	Time limits	(N)
Communist	59	(91)	25	40	35	(91)	84	(81)	91	(91)	79	(70)	84	(91)	65	(69)
Shifting Coalitions	41	(78)	10	24	65	(78)	74	(65)	80	(78)	32	(62)	64	(78)	43	(54)
Anti-Communist	22	(67)	13	16	70	(67)	54	(50)	57	(67)	34	(59)	67	(67)	46	(54)
Log odds ratio	0.80**		0.77**				0.75**		1.04**		0.99**		0.44**		0.40**	
Standard error	0.18		0.17				0.21		0.22		0.20		0.18		0.18	

Part 2. Number of prolabor provisions

Political camp	0	1	2	3	4	5	6	(N)
Communist	0	0	10	20	22	29	20	(51)
Shifting Coalitions	0	11	27	30	30	3	0	(37)
Anti-Communist	4	17	33	17	26	2	0	(46)

[a] Dichotomized for log odds ratio; no and conditional prohibition vs. total prohibition.

[b] Data are missing on the term of the contract of the prewar contracts. To retain them in the sample, and not lose the data on their other provisions, we coded all prewar contracts as short-term. It is a safe assumption, we think, that they were really short-term.

[c] The trade-off is prolabor if the contract has no prohibition or a conditional prohibition against strikes during the term of the contract or is short-term (one-year); if it has a total strike prohibition and is long-term (18 months or more), the contract has no trade-off (and is procapital). This trade-off measure is *separate* from the six contract provisions included in the prolabor index.

**$p < 0.01$.

Note: The numbers in parentheses in the (N) column refer to the number of contracts in a given category.

From "Red Unionism" to "Red Company Unionism"?

So far, we have seen that throughout the CIO era, taken as a whole, the contracts won by locals of the Communist-led internationals were far more likely than those won by their rivals to be prolabor or to counter capital's hegemony in the sphere of production. This was an era, however, of abrupt transitions and profound changes, which carved out four distinctive periods within it. The critical events of these periods deeply affected the immediate political agenda, and thus the strategy, tactics, and actual practices of the rival factions and parties vying for leadership within the organized working class. In particular, the "line" of the Communists went through acute turns ("zig zags") and sudden reversals ("flip flops") during these years, as their party sought to cope with sharp changes in the current situation both at home and abroad, while also not straying "too far for too long" from "the 'general line' . . . set in Moscow."[69]

The question, then, is whether the contractual pattern in any of these four periods differed substantially from the others and from the general pattern for the entire CIO era. These periods were (1) the immediate pre–World War II years of the Great Depression, working-class insurgency, the rapid growth of industrial unions, and the New Deal; (2) World War II, the "anti-fascist alliance," and state regulation of capital/labor relations; (3) the immediate postwar offensive of organized labor coupled with the right-wing resurgence in Congress and passage of the Taft–Hartley Act in 1947; and (4) the advent of the Cold War, the establishment of the "national security state," and the heightened attacks on the Communist-led unions, culminating in 1950, as the "police action" in Korea was under way, in their purge or expulsion from the CIO.

In the pre–World War II years, as most serious observers agree, "Communist trade union leaders long [had been] among the most militant in the country"; "they worked hard to build unions," in Mills's words, "to fight in the class struggle against the bourgeoisie and its government."[70] But once Nazi

---

[69] Draper (1985a, p. 37).

[70] Seidman (1953a, p. 80); Mills (1948, p. 23). Recurrent in the writings on the immediate prewar period is the issue of the alleged "political strikes" provoked by Communist unionists during the twenty-two months of the party's "the Yanks are not coming" peace campaign, from the signing of the Stalin–Hitler Nonaggression Pact on August 23, 1939, until the German invasion of the Soviet Union on June 22, 1941. Sidney Hook, for one, wrote in "Heresy, Yes; Conspiracy, No," in the *New York Times Magazine* (July 9, 1950) that "in labor organizations, the existence of Communist leaders is extremely dangerous because of their unfailing use of the strike as a political instrument at the behest of the Kremlin" (reprinted in 1953, p. 33). The most notorious purported Communist-led political strike was the one by the UAW local at North American Aviation in Los Angeles in June 1941. President

Germany attacked the Soviet Union, and for the war's duration, the CP officially subordinated the "class struggle" to "national unity" in the war effort.

Roosevelt dispatched the army to break the strike because of its purported interference with "defense mobilization"; the army suspended the local's officers; and the UAW executive board, pushed by the Reuther faction, which made the most of the smashed "wildcat strike" to go on the offensive against the UAW's Communists, never reinstated the suspended leaders and also fired the local's organizers. In one stroke, this put an end to Communist influence there. It also led, at the UAW's convention later that year, to the overwhelming adoption of an amendment to the UAW constitution brought by the Reuther faction to bar Communists from union office. Whatever the truth of the charge that this strike or others under Communist leadership during those twenty-two months were political strikes – a careful, detailed examination of which by Bert Cochran shows to be of little or no substance – it is notable that John L. Lewis denounced the dispatch of troops, and the highly regarded magazine *Labor*, published by the conservative railroad brotherhoods, asserted that "in the space of a few hours, labor was deprived of rights which had been won in more than a half century of struggle" (Cochran 1977, pp. 156–95, 183). Of crucial if not decisive evidential relevance, the record of UE, the biggest Communist-led international, lends no credence to the charge that Communist unionists were provoking political strikes at the time. In 1952, at the height of the Korean War, in hearings before a Senate subcommittee, chaired by Hubert Humphrey, on anti-Communist labor legislation proposed by GE and Westinghouse, this charge was revisited and made against UE by John Small, chairman of the government's Munitions Board (and former president of Emerson Radio): "There is not the least bit of doubt that if the policy of the Soviet Union called for strikes in various industries in the United States, then the leadership [of UE] would subjugate the membership to a strike." In reply, UE's James J. Matles told Humphrey, in testimony before his subcommittee, that Small was a "damnable liar." He showed Humphrey "a clipping from *The New York Times*, dated June 12, 1941, which reported that of all strikes in industries holding military contracts from January to June 1941 – before the Soviet Union was attacked by Hitler – not one strike had involved the UE; and that of more than 2 million man-hours lost in labor disputes in war industry, the UE was responsible for none." This left Humphrey, a reporter wrote later, "remarkably speechless" (Matles and Higgins 1974, p. 207). Four years earlier, Matles had already confronted and documented the falsity of the same charge in his testimony before a subcommittee of the Education and Labor Committee chaired by Congressman Fred Hartley (of Taft and Hartley) investigating "Communist infiltration" of the UE: "It may be of interest to you, sir, on the question of [Communists' alleged infiltration] of the union," Matles said, "that in 1939 and in 1940 and in 1941, the outstanding record of peaceful relationship between any union – any industry or major union in a mass production industry – prevailed in this industry in this union, sir.... [I]n 1941, from January 1 until June 11, 1941, the War Department issued a release of strikes affecting defense industries in America, and this union did not have a single strike during that period, sir. I don't mean to say by that that people were not entitled to strike, ... but I do mean to say by that, in accordance with some of the insinuations made here by the chairman at the very beginning of this hearing, we

Committed to production "without interruption," party officials vehemently supported organized labor's "no-strike pledge." The party's chairman, Earl Browder, even proclaimed himself proud to be a strikebreaker: It would be "the greatest honor," he declared in the midst of a coal miners' strike in April 1943, "to be a breaker of this [strike] movement"; and he denounced UMW head and CIO founder John L. Lewis as "playing the so-called 'labor part' of the long planned effort of his America First associates to shift the fire away from Hitler." The irrepressible Browder, as late as January 7, 1945, was still denouncing "advocates of strike threats or strike actions in America [as] ... scabs in the war against Hitlerism, ... scabs against our armed forces, ... scabs against the labor movement."[71]

were supposed to have strikes and violence and revolutions and bomb throwing, in 1939 and 1940 and the beginning of '41 – where we made radar, and we made defense material and equipment, we were supposed to have chaos. But we didn't, under the present leadership, and under the present constitution of the union, sir. . . . Those are facts, sir. Those are not stories." The "infiltration" that concerned Matles, he added, was "employers' infiltration into our union – that is the only thing we are concerned about. . . . Employers infiltrating our unions and converting them into company unions. That is right, sir; that is the greatest danger that we are confronted with, and the Taft–Hartley law permits that" (U.S. Congress 1948, pp. 129–30). Matles could have reminded his interrogators also that "while the leadership of the union was supposedly following the Communist line, James Matles urged 475 workers in a Brooklyn torpedo plant to delay a strike because of the importance of the plant to the defense effort. He asked that the United States Conciliation Service be given an opportunity to try to effect a settlement" (Filippelli 1970, p. 91).

[71] Isserman (1982, p. 169); Prickett (1975, p. 274). In January 1942, at the beginning of the war, the party's chairman, William Z. Foster, who had led the Great Steel Strike of 1919 and founded and led the TUEL and TUUL, had carefully hedged his support of the no-strike pledge. "In this war emergency," said Foster, "labor should contemplate using the strike only when the basic economic needs of the workers are involved or the very life of trade unionism is threatened" (1942, pp. 60, 64, 65). Browder's conception of "national unity" shifted ever rightward during the war. Following the 1943 Three-Power Tehran Conference's pledge to continue Anglo–American–Soviet unity into the postwar era, he declared in the party's theoretical organ that "class divisions have no significance now except as they reflect on one side or the other of this issue"; consistent with this logic, he presided a few months later, in May 1944, over the official dissolution of the CP and its reconstitution as the "Communist Political Association" (Levenstein 1981, pp. 163, 164). The famous critique by French Communist leader Jacques Duclos, condemning Browder and the party for "revisionism" and abandoning the class struggle, which precipitated Browder's fall from grace and expulsion from the party, was not published until April 1945 in *Cahiers du Communisme* (and included quotations from Foster's letter). Duclos's letter was published in English translation by the *Daily Worker* on May 24, 1945, two days *after* it had already appeared in the New York *World-Telegram and Sun* (Starobin 1975, p. 66; Levenstein 1981, p. 187). Yet Foster, who

So, according to the prevailing interpretation, the Communist-led unions, in adhering to this party line, abandoned "a militant defense of labor's interests" for the duration of World War II.[72] Typical is the claim that the Communist-led unions "moved so far to the right . . . in support of the war effort that the traditional left–right spectrum no longer accurately measured the real differences between factions of the CIO." "[I]n every union," as columnists Joseph and Stuart Alsop summed it up, "the communists became the great reactionaries."[73]

In the postwar years, after an immediate moment of militant unity among its rival camps, the CIO began to split apart, over issues of both domestic and foreign politics. The Communist-led left and their liberal opponents in the CIO differed over how to fight against resurgent reaction and new antilabor legislation, chiefly the Taft–Hartley Act.[74] They also disagreed, far more sharply, over whether to form a labor-backed third party and to oppose the Truman Administration's emerging Cold War policy of Soviet "containment." CIO executive board members wavered for some time over whether to endorse Truman's presidential candidacy or launch a third party. Meanwhile, the CP was instrumental in forming the new Progressive Party, and running the presidential campaign of its candidate, Henry Wallace. But in January 1948, the CIO's board lopsidedly voted to endorse Truman, and it enforced adherence to this policy throughout the organization and purged anyone from positions in CIO Industrial Councils and other CIO agencies who opposed it.

After Truman's surprise election victory, and Wallace's poor showing, CIO liberals launched an effective assault on the Communists' power. In late 1949, the CIO's executive board, now entirely shorn of Communists and their allies, voted to expel unions found to "consistently follow the Communist line." By late 1950, eleven "miscreant unions . . . had been drummed out of the CIO."[75]

---

was soon enough to replace Browder and don the mantle of revolutionary inflexibility, had himself joined Browder and other party officials in proudly denouncing "strike incitements" during the war.

[72] Lichtenstein (1974, xvi; but cf. 1982, p. 144). Germany's invasion of the USSR on June 22, 1941, abruptly ended the twenty-two-month surreal interlude, begun with the Hitler–Stalin nonaggression pact of August 23 1939, during which the U.S. Communists – with the slogan, "The Yanks are not coming!" – opposed U.S. entrance into the "imperialist war."

[73] Davis (1980, p. 66); Alsops (1947b, p. 118; see also 1947a); Mills (1948, p. 23); Lens (1949, p. 345).

[74] The Taft–Hartley Act, remember, required union officers to sign a "non-Communist affidavit" and allowed the employer to call for a bargaining election to try to "decertify" the union (i.e., deprive it of NLRB representation) if its officers refused to sign such an affidavit. If an officer openly resigned from the party but did not renounce Communism, and then signed a non-Communist affidavit, as some officers did, he was promptly put on trial for perjury.

[75] Levenstein (1981, p. 306).

The CIO executive board was forced to resort to the trials and expulsions, as David Oshinsky observes, "because the anti-Communist factions within the various left-wing affiliates were unable to dislodge the Communists from power. In only three . . . of the pro-Communist unions were the right-wingers successful in gaining control – an indication, perhaps, that despite their pro-Soviet, anti-Truman position, the Communists were still respected for their ability to run effective trade unions. . . ."[76]

After their expulsion from the CIO, the Communist-led unions were continually subject to raids by other CIO unions and attacks by an array of government agencies and congressional committees. The latter held hearings on "Communist infiltration" throughout the country between 1950 and 1952, subpoenaing and interrogating "unfriendly" witnesses active in locals of the expelled unions. The coup de grace came in 1954 in the form of the Communist Control Act, which authorized the Subversive Activities Control Board to define a union as "Communist-infiltrated" and deprive it of the protection of the Wagner Act and representation before the NLRB.[77]

What, then, were the effects of the events of these periods – immediate prewar, World War II, immediate postwar (through 1947), and later postwar years (1948–55) – on the comparative odds that unions in the rival camps would

---

[76] Oshinsky (1974, p. 125). If by "right wingers" Oshinsky means the anti-Communist victors, then, in point of fact, this was true of four of the sixteen Communist-led international unions: maritime (NMU), transport (TWU), Furniture Workers, and Shoe Workers, but in each of these it was mainly because men in the CP (such as TWU's Mike Quill) or close to it (such as NMU's Joe Curran) now broke with it, and kept their hold on union power. As Saposs observes: "Where such an outstanding leader as Curran or Quill undertook to rally the anti-Communist forces and wage battle with the Communists, the outcome was bound to be favorable. . . . On the other hand, in contrast to the NMU and the Transport Workers where the outstanding leader staunchly adhered to his Communist affiliation, as [Harry] Bridges did, the opposition remained weak and control was retained by the Communist" (1959, pp. 198–99). We have not found evidence to support C. Wright Mills's widely repeated claim that the struggle against the Communists, in the unions they led, was "in most cases . . . not merely a struggle of cliques [but] . . . was also a rank-and-file uprising." Even after the expulsion of eleven "Communist-dominated" unions from the CIO, none faced a serious internal "uprising," and UE; mine, mill, and smelter workers (MM); and longshoremen and warehousemen (ILWU) proved to be extraordinarily resilient in the face of combined CIO, government, and corporation assaults. When UE was really beset by a so-called uprising, "the sting came from within." For it was led by *Communists* in its New York–New Jersey district who, in 1955, followed the party leadership's order to desert the UE and "return to the mainstream" (Aronowitz 1973, pp. 348–49). See the detailed discussion of the CP's instigation of this secession, in Chapter 11.

[77] See Caute (1979, chs. 18–21).

win prolabor provisions in their contracts? Did World War II transform the "Red" unions, as has been charged, into "Red company unions"?[78] How effective were the Communist-led unions in the immediate postwar period, after the CP renounced "revisionism" and "class collaboration," and then during the later postwar years, when they were under relentless siege?

We find that in all four periods on almost every provision examined, the local contracts won by Communist-led unions were far more likely to be prolabor than those won by the unions in the "shifting" and anti-Communist camps. In fact, most of the contracts won by locals of Communist-led internationals were prolabor on almost every provision in every period. This was so even during World War II, when the CP advocated "class collaboration," and even in the late postwar period, when the Communist-led unions were besieged by enemies on all sides.

The Antifascist War and Class Struggle

But these findings on World War II, which are contrary to the nearly monolithic consensus among writers spanning the political spectrum, must surely leave many readers incredulous. The simple historical fact revealed here is that – whatever the demands of the antifascist war effort and the rhetorical extremes of CP officials – the wartime contracts won by the Communist-led unions were far less likely than those of their rivals on the right to cede "management prerogatives," to sign away the "right" to strike, or to have cumbersome grievance procedures: 65 percent of the wartime agreements won by locals of the Communist-led unions did not cede management prerogatives, and only 27 percent entirely prohibited strikes for the duration of the contract. But, in contrast, 55 percent of the wartime contracts negotiated by locals of the shifting camp and 67 percent in anti-Communist camp *did cede* management prerogatives, and 54 and 73 percent, respectively, banned strikes entirely for the contract's term.

The pattern among the locals in the rival camps is also more or less the same for each of the three components of the grievance procedure. And the same is true of the prolabor index: 53 percent of the wartime contracts won by the Communist camp's locals had at least five of the six prolabor provisions, as opposed to 10 percent of those won by locals in the shifting camp and to none of those in the anti-Communist camp (see Table 5.2).[79]

---

[78] Aronowitz (1973, p. 350).

[79] According to Frank Emspak, "even during the Second World War, none of the left-wing [international] unions signed company security clauses like GM clauses [or]...a clause which gave the company the right to fire a shop steward if he interfered with production as the Ford contract did" (1972, pp. 366–67).

Table 5.2. *Prolabor provisions in CIO local union contracts in California, 1938–55, by historical period and CIO political camp (in percent)*

| | Management | | Strike prohibition[a] | | | | Short-term | | | | Grievance procedure | | | | | | 5–6 Prolabor | |
	prerogative	(N)	None	Cond'l	Total	(N)	contract	(N)	Trade-off	(N)	Steward	(N)	Steps	(N)	Time limits	(N)	provisions	(N)
Political camp																			
Prewar																			
Communist	100	(8)	25	37	37	(8)	—[b]		—[b]		100	(4)	100	(8)	0	(8)	50	(4)
Shifting coalitions	56	(9)	11	56	33	(9)	—		—		17	(6)	100	(9)	0	(8)	0	(6)
Anti-Communist	20	(15)	0	33	67	(15)	—		—		31	(13)	60	(15)	40	(15)	8	(13)
Log odds ratio	2.21**		0.72*								1.16*		—[c]		—[c]		1.46*	
Standard error	0.72		0.38								0.63						0.74	
World War II																			
Communist	65	(40)	25	47	27	(40)	92	(38)	95	(40)	67	(33)	82	(40)	71	(38)	53	(32)
Shifting coalitions	45	(11)	36	9	54	(11)	64	(11)	73	(11)	20	(10)	64	(11)	54	(11)	10	(10)
Anti-Communist	33	(15)	20	7	73	(15)	40	(15)	53	(15)	29	(14)	47	(15)	27	(15)	0	(14)
Log odds ratio	0.67*		0.41*				1.42**		1.36**		0.93**		0.85**		0.93**		2.56**	
Standard error	0.31		0.20				0.39		0.42		0.36		0.33		0.33		0.99	

Postwar (1)

Communist	42	(24)	17	42	(24)	79	(24)	92	(24)	87	(15)	87	(24)	75	(20)	33	(12)
Shifting coalitions	32	(28)	7	21	(28)	83	(24)	93	(28)	35	(20)	57	(28)	50	(28)	0	(16)
Anti-Communist	20	(20)	25	10	(20)	63	(19)	70	(20)	35	(17)	65	(20)	55	(20)	0	(16)
Log odds ratio	0.51^{x}			0.16		0.41		0.93^{*}		1.10^{**}		0.57^{*}		0.42^{+}		$-^{c}$	
Standard error	0.34			0.21		0.36		0.49		0.41		0.34		0.33			

Postwar (2)

Communist	53	(19)	37	21	(19)	74	(19)	93	(19)	89	(18)	74	(19)	100	(3)	67	(3)
Shifting coalitions	43	(30)	3	23	(30)	70	(30)	73	(30)	38	(26)	60	(30)	43	(7)	0	(5)
Anti-Communist	18	(17)	6	18	(17)	56	(16)	65	(17)	40	(15)	94	(17)	100	(4)	0	(3)
Log odds ratio	0.76^{*}			0.73^{**}		0.39		0.92^{**}		1.13^{**}		-0.50		-0.20			
Standard error	0.37			0.28		0.37		0.44		0.41		0.39		0.84			

[a] Dichotomized for log odds ratio: no and conditional prohibition vs. total prohibition.
[b] Missing data.
[c] Log odds ratio cannot be computed.
$+$ $p < 0.10$.
x $p < 0.07$.
$*$ $p < 0.05$
$**$ $p < 0.01$.

What explains this persistence of a distinctive blend of prolabor provisions in the contracts won by Communist-led unions, even at a time when the party was officially committed to "class collaboration" and "relentless production" in the antifascist war effort? First, and most important, although the Communist unionists surely sought to avoid strikes and promote national unity in the war effort, they were scarcely alone in organized labor. Rather, this was also the policy of both the AFL and the CIO. All of the CIO unions were officially committed to "sacrifice" to win the war; they all officially tried to settle their disputes and grievances against management without interrupting production or hurting productivity; they all (except John L. Lewis' UMW, which seceded from the CIO in 1942) officially adhered to the "no-strike pledge" throughout the war; and they all (again except for the UMW) officially moderated their demands for the duration of the war. In short, in this sense, all of the CIO unions shifted "to the right" during World War II.

So the actual practice of the Communist-led unions, in comparison to their rivals, could still have distinctively expressed their radical anticapitalist world view; and the relative place of the political camps with respect to each other, on the spectrum of prolabor contractual provisions won by their unions, should not have changed much from the prewar period, or in comparison with the postwar years – unless, of course, the Communist-led unions went so much further in sacrificing their members' interests and granting concessions to management during World War II that they passed even the right-wing unions on the right to become, as is often charged, "Red company unions." But our analysis of these unions' wartime local agreements, as well as of the UE/GE national agreements in the next chapter, reveals no such drastic shift in practice – to the contrary, not only were the wartime local contracts of the Communist-led internationals to the left of the other camps', but the majority of them were prolabor on each of the six provisions. Even during the war, Communist unionists buttressed and reinforced prolabor production regimes in the industries within their domain.

The "antifascist war" and defense of Soviet "socialism" presented Communist unionists with an odious political dilemma, namely, how to promote "national unity" to push war production while also protecting and advancing their union members' immediate interests. Despite the declarations of CP officials, we suggest, the CIO's Communists and their radical allies at every level, rather than abandoning their union principles, sought in practice to maintain "national unity" without yielding any hard-won union gains.

Not the party line, but the elemental democratic impulse and egalitarian passion (if not socialist vision) of Communist unionists guided them in their permanent struggle against the companies. "We conducted business as usual in the unions," Dorothy Healey, a leading California Communist and union activist at that time, told us. "We never stopped fighting on the shop floor, whatever the national leadership under Browder was saying. I was in the Mine, Mill local at Boniface Aluminum in those days [during the war] – and we never gave anything away. It was the tasks imposed by the day-to-day defense of workers that mattered. We never stopped to ask if what we did violated the no-strike pledge or Browder's incentive plans."

Healey's memory and our findings are consistent with the serious case studies (by writers whose political views differ markedly) that have tried to get at the record of the activities of specific Communist-led unions and of Communist workers in these and other unions. They are consistent also with the report of an FBI informant highly placed in the party (apparently Louis Budenz, former *Daily Worker* editor, 1940–45). Many Communist unionists complained to the party's National Committee during the war, according to the May 16, 1944, FBI report, that the party was "'folding up,' abandoning its role as the vanguard of the working class, allying with the reactionary wing of the labor movement, cooperating with capitalism, and abandoning class struggle."[80] Joseph Starobin, a former leading Communist, reports the same, and stresses that there were many instances of open conflict between party officials and party members in the leadership of CIO unions.[81]

In liberal anti-Communist Robert Ozanne's study of the big UAW Local No. 248 at the Allis–Chalmers plant in Wisconsin, he found that under its "Communist leadership," workers' "grievances were not soft-pedaled [during World War II]. On the contrary, they were magnified . . . in *a bold offensive to enlarge the area of union control.*" Engaged in "a bitter struggle with Allis–Chalmers management," Ozanne remarks, the union's Communist leadership "was *unwilling to be sidetracked* merely to comply with Communist [party wartime] policies."[82]

In 1944, in their zeal for increased war production, the CP's leaders were supporting a bill for compulsory labor service, to "transfer workers from non-essential to essential [defense] plants regardless of seniority, or whether they were unionized. Essentially it amounted to a labor draft." But a January 1945 conference of eight Communist-led internationals, organized by UE, came out against the bill. "The Communists [the Party's leaders], as part of their

---

[80] Levenstein (1981, p. 183).   [81] Starobin (1975, p. 258).

[82] Ozanne (1954, p. 316, emphasis added). Stephen Meyer also observes that during the war, under the leadership of Harold Christoffel and Robert Buse, "UAW Local 248 followed a strategy of relentlessly pursuing shop floor grievances to alleviate management abuses of authority and to expand the boundaries of worker rights. Through the war, the UAW local sought a new variety of union control of the shop floor" (1992, p. 131). Also see Harris (1982, pp. 67–70).

1944 line, were supporting such projects," Joseph Starobin notes. "The unions closest to them were not."[83]

Several other such case studies reveal, as CIO historian Robert Zieger sums up their findings, that Communist unionists were intent on putting "workers' interests ahead of Party shifts, *even during World War II.*" At the minimum, in Bert Cochran's earlier summary interpretation of some of these same studies, "Communist labor officials, enmeshed in the politics and alliances attendant on their wartime position, [nonetheless] . . . conducted themselves like the next set of CIO officials in contract negotiations."[84]

This conclusion will surprise only those who caricature Communist unionists and simplify the relationship that existed between them and the CP itself.[85] No doubt, as Theodore Draper observes, CP officials spent most of their energies bearing down on its members at all levels "to carry out whatever policies or campaigns happened to be uppermost at the moment," especially during World War II.[86] But they were not always successful in getting their way, least of all with their comrades who held positions of power and trust, and had their own political base in major industrial unions. Thus, as Daniel Bell remarks, "tensions between the communist leaders of several unions and the party" were chronic.[87]

"Evidence that the party could not control the Left union leaders as it wanted to," David A. Shannon writes, "is seen in the frequent complaints of John Williamson, who became the party's labor secretary in mid-1946. Although Williamson tried to direct his forces at national CIO conventions from caucuses in his hotel room, he was unable to get all the Left leaders consistently to toe the mark. In his reports, he complained bitterly about the Left leaders' behavior, attributing it to 'Browder revisionism [which] left deep imprints in the thinking and practices of our trade union cadres.' . . . Since the [CIO's] Communists were a minority, they had to accomplish their ends through co-operation with, or at least with the tolerance of, the non-Communists. They had to build and maintain what they so fondly called the 'Left-Center coalition.'"

---

[83] Frank Emspak says UE's Communist unionists "simply refused to accept" the party's advocacy of the labor draft, "citing their responsibilities to their union and its membership" (1984, p. 111). Starobin (1975, p. 259n50) cites a January 29, 1945, letter from Clifford McAvoy, UE's Washington representative, to Louis Budenz, then editor of the *Daily Worker*, expressing "some astonishment" at the paper's support of the labor draft, which the left-union conference opposed.

[84] Zieger (1980, p. 133, emphasis added); Cochran (1977, p. 255).

[85] Starobin (1975, p. 269n).   [86] Draper (1985c, p. 46).   [87] Bell (1952, p. 201).

"[T]rade union Communists," as David Brody observes, "had not normally submitted themselves to regular party discipline."[88] Neither, of course, had their radical allies done so. An aversion to bowing to any party's "line" or submitting to any party's "discipline" was, in reality, often precisely why many of the most important, enduring allies of the Communists, at all levels of union leadership – including prominent left-wing labor leaders such as the ILWU's Bridges, UE's Clifford McAvoy, and UAW Local 600's Shelton Tappes – never joined the party itself or, as often happened, left as quickly as they joined, but continued, more or less, to align themselves with it in practice.[89]

Communist Party officials were also hampered in imposing a line on Communist unionists because, years before the outbreak of World War II, the party had dissolved its "fractions" (or clubs) in the CIO unions. This had been a Popular Front gesture meant to show that the party was not interfering, as its journal *The Communist* stated in July 1943, "with the normal functioning of the trade unions, including those with Left and progressive forces in the leadership."[90] Before the clubs were abolished, all the Communists in a local or in "any given group or in any campaign would map out strategy and tactics together, and a common discipline would be binding on everyone no matter what their echelon or particular task." But dissolution of the party's clubs inside the unions had the paradoxical effect of making the party's officials themselves dependent on the Communist union leaders and their allies; for party officials could no longer exert enough pressure or undercut, let alone "control," them by appealing to rank-and-file Communists in their unions, who were now without an organization of their own.[91]

So, as Nathan Glazer points out, "[d]uring the war Communist union leaders were treated with kid gloves by the party. . . . [E]stablished in the semipermanent tenure of trade-union leadership, they could draw on an independent base of power" and "run their own show."[92] They ran "their own show," our evidence reveals, even when faced with the exigencies of the "antifascist war" and the defense of the Soviet Union, in a way that (however imperfectly) remained consistent with their radical, anticapitalist sensibilities – and, as a result, they won contracts that were typically far more prolabor than those won by their political rivals.

---

[88] Brody (1980, p. 227); Shannon (1959, pp. 105–6).
[89] Starobin (1975, pp. 12, 258n); Tappes (1983).   [90] Glazer (1961, p. 126).
[91] Starobin (1975, p. 39).   [92] Glazer (1961, p. 125).

The Comparative Odds of Prolabor Contracts

Now we estimate the independent effects of the CIO's political camps, controlling for historical period, "aging" of the union-management relation, and the "Big 3" (i.e., removing the effects of the three largest internationals: UE, UAW, and USWA – on which, see the next chapter) in determining the comparative odds that the provisions of CIO local union contracts, 1938–55, were prolabor. The logit models separately compare each of the crucial provisions of the contracts won by locals of the Communist-led unions and by the shifting camp's unions with those won by locals of the anti-Communist camp's unions (see Table 5.3).[93]

The crucial finding is that the comparative odds of the Communist camp's local contracts being prolabor, as opposed to those in the anti-Communist camp, were consistently much higher on each provision, as follows: The comparative odds that the contracts did not cede management prerogatives were 4 to 1 in favor of the Communist camp; that they did not have a total strike prohibition, 7 to 1; that they were short-term, 4.6 to 1; that they had a trade-off, 11 to 1; that a steward had to be present at a grievance's first step, 11 to 1; that the grievance procedure had no more than three steps, 3 to 1; and that each step had a time limit, 2 to 1.

The comparative odds of the shifting camp's contracts being prolabor on each of these provisions and on the trade-off, as opposed to the anti-Communist camp's, were, respectively, 2.4 to 1, 1.8 to 1, 2.5 to 1, 2.8 to 1, 0.9 to 1, 0.9 to 1, and 0.6 to 1, in favor of the shifting camp.[94]

Conclusion

What inherently vitiates both the "pluralist" and "Marxist" variants of the functionalist theory of organized labor is that they are, of course, *a*historical. They either ignore history or, worse, simply postulate an unreal one – from which real men and women, possessing consciousness and the capacity to act, and to make and remake history, though not just as they please, disappear or are

---

[93] Likewise, they compare the contracts of Big 3 locals with those of other locals; they compare, separately, the local contracts negotiated during the prewar period, immediate postwar period (no. 1), and late postwar period (no. 2) with those negotiated during World War II. For a brief description of logit analysis, see Chapter 2, note 51, on page 47.

[94] The estimate of the effect of the "aging" of union–management relations in the logit models shows no "hardening of the arteries" or "sloughing off"; rather, the effect of "aging" on each of the provisions was almost precisely nil. To assess whether the variable, "historical period" was somehow "soaking up" and obscuring the real effect of "aging," we also ran a logit model excluding it, and found that the estimated effect of "aging" was still nil.

Table 5.3. Logit estimates of the independent effects of the CIO's political camps, controlling for historical period, "aging," and "Big 3" in determining the comparative odds that specified provisions of the CIO local union contracts in California, 1938–55, were prolabor

| | Management prerogative | | Strike prohibition | | Contract term | | Trade-off | | Grievance procedure | | | | | | |
| | | | | | | | | | Steward | | Steps | | Time limits | |
	Logit coeff.	Odds mult.	Logit coeff.	Odds mult.	Logit coeff.	Odds mult.	Logit coeff.	Odds mult.	Logit coeff.	Odds mult.	Logit coeff.	Odds multi.	Logit coeff.	Odds multi.
Communist Camp	1.43**	4.18	1.96**	7.10	1.52**	4.57	2.41**	11.13	2.43**	11.36	1.11**	3.03	0.71^x	2.03
Shifting coalitions	0.88*	2.41	0.60	1.82	0.91*	2.48	1.02*	2.77	-0.10	0.90	-0.08	0.92	-0.44	0.64
"Big 3"	-1.46**	0.23	1.25**	3.49	0.47	1.60	0.57	1.77	0.65^x	1.91	0.14	1.15	0.14	1.15
Prewar	0.55	1.73	0.21	1.23	–	–	0.57	1.77	0.53	1.70	0.89	2.43	-1.25^x	0.29
Postwar (1)	-1.06**	0.35	-0.47	0.62	0.69	1.99	-0.11	0.90	0.87^x	2.39	0.26	1.30	0.19	1.21
Postwar (2)	-0.78	0.46	-0.70	0.50	0.98	2.66	0.03	1.03	1.11*	3.03	0.51	1.66	0.63	1.88
Aging	0.02	1.02	0.03	1.03	-0.20	0.82			0.00	1.00	-0.01	0.99	0.07	1.07
Intercept	-1.23		-2.71		8.80		-1.58		-1.80		0.72		-3.21	
Likelihood ratio chi-square (df)	54.11(7)**		45.66(7)**		19.05(6)**		25.47(6)**		47.84(7)**		13.56(7)^x		27.08(7)**	
(N)	(236)		(236)		(196)		(204)		(191)		(236)		(177)	

^{x} p < 0.10.
* p < 0.05.
** p < 0.01.

made into mere bearers of systemic imperatives. So, as penetrating as are some of the specific observations and ideas of individual authors in these schools, their analyses unavoidably beg the decisive question: How was the prevailing capital/labor relation and the production regime regulating and enforcing it actually *constructed*?

For instance, Richard Lester, author of a theory of "union maturity" (or of the "shedding of youthful characteristics in the process of settling down or 'maturing'") that he uses to explain the taming of militant CIO unionism, mentions obliquely that the "Communist-dominated unions have dwindled or disintegrated," but ignores this in his theory of the "underlying forces and impersonal compulsions" which "submerged ideology" and eliminated unions that "stressed hostility toward the . . . capitalistic system."[95] Similarly, Burawoy writes: "After World War II there was much uncertainty as to what would be negotiable in a collective contract, but this *uncertainty* has since been *resolved* in ways that establish management's prerogative to direct the labor process. *Whatever the reasons for this outcome*, the consequences are relatively clear . . .[namely,] an expanding arena of consent . . . through the constitution and presentation of the interests of the corporation as the interests of all."[96]

So, in this sort of grand theoretical design, the men who expelled, raided, and eventually destroyed most of the CIO's Communist-led unions and, in the process, snuffed out much of the "institutionalized opposition" in the CIO rump, aided and abetted by government agencies, as well as major corporations, were merely the bearers of "underlying forces and impersonal compulsions" needed to "resolve uncertainty" and induce "union maturity."

But to ignore "the reasons for this outcome," as functionalists must, is, again, to fail to come to grips with the real issue of sociohistorical causality: What made the "characteristic uniqueness" of the political regime of production "historically *so*," to borrow Max Weber's words "and not *otherwise?*"[97] Put in general theoretical terms, the question is, What are the relatively independent effects of the "class struggle in production" in determining whether the immediate labor process in a given time and place embodies the workers' "consent" to capital's dominion? The answer, as our own analysis and findings imply, can be found only through a substantive analysis of the origins, course, and consequences of capital/labor conflict. But how *this* momentous conflict is fought, and with what consequences, is at least partly contingent upon intraclass conflict: upon who wins power in organized labor, how they hold on to it, and what they do with it.

---

[95] Lester (1958, pp. 21, 22, 32, 104, 120).   [96] Burawoy (1979, p. 120, emphasis added).
[97] Weber (1949, p. 72, emphasis in original).

6

RANK-AND-FILE DEMOCRACY
AND THE "CLASS STRUGGLE
IN PRODUCTION"

For radicals of all hues in American labor, "rank-and-file democracy" and effectiveness in the class struggle have always been inseparable. Certainly, this was a recurrent theme in the political rhetoric of the Red union leagues: "The fight for industrial unionism goes hand-in-hand," as the TUEL's founder declared, "... with the need for genuine trade union democracy." Or, as the 1927 TUEL handbook on the "misleaders of labor" said: Reactionary leaders erect "powerful bureaucratic machines ... to prevent the left wing from mobilizing the discontented rank and file against it ... and to force the workers back under [their] arbitrary direction ... which means under the control of the employers."[1] But the militant autocrat and peculiar Republican who spawned the CIO was not so sure that union democracy was such a good idea. "It is a question of whether you desire your organization to be the most effective instrumentality ...," as John L. Lewis unabashedly put it at a UMW convention in 1936, "or whether you prefer to sacrifice the efficiency of your organization in some respects for a little more academic freedom."

Dave Beck, president of the Teamsters, had a word or two to say on the issue also: "Unions," he said, "are big business. Why should truck drivers and bottle washers be allowed to make big decisions affecting union policy? Would any corporation allow it?"

Walter Reuther's view was more subtle: Bargaining with the most powerful corporations, he explained to dissidents at the 1949 UAW convention, "requires central direction in terms of timing and strategy and tactics, and if we dilute this central direction ... you dissipate the power of the union at the bargaining table." But James Matles, UE's director of organization, to the contrary, equated "the ideology of rank-and-file unionism" with "the ideology of democracy":

> Militant rank-and-file industrial unionism ... is the ideology of members running their own union, of members themselves, through union

[1] Foster (1927, pp. 286, 296–97, 299).

159

organization, learning to handle "local economic issues" that affect their lives as workers. . . . The UE constitution [provides that] all negotiating committees are elected – and negotiations themselves are conducted with the participation of rank-and-file elected representatives of the members; proposed contracts are voted up by the workers they cover; strikes are called and concluded only by membership vote.[2]

Implicit in the contrasting views of these preeminent labor leaders is the critical question, What difference does rank-and-file democracy – "members running their own union" – make? How, in our terms, did democracy and factionalism in the CIO's internationals matter in winning prolabor local contracts?

On the Effects of Union Democracy

In the writings on American labor, there is no consensus as to whether or how democracy or autocracy makes unions more effective in promoting their members' interests. With rare exceptions, too, the relevant theoretical claims are unelaborated; they appear as stray assertions or as implicit ideas embedded in interpretations of the collective bargaining successes or failures of specific unions. So, for instance, Paul Jacobs says, "[W]ith practically no democracy of the ITU type, the Teamsters Union has brought about great improvements in working conditions and wages for its members. As an economic instrument, it has probably been more efficient than the ITU."[3] Or an impressionistic claim takes the form of a kindred theoretical agnosticism. As Walter Galenson and S. M. Lipset assert, for instance, "[t]he leadership of a union may be 'responsive' even in the absence of institutionalized rights for the individual, or of political factions in the union. On the other hand, the presence of opposing factions does not guarantee this kind of representation of the members' interests, although, as in the case of the ITU, where factional interests are stabilized into a two-party system, it may be *said* to do so."[4]

---

[2] Lewis, quoted in Cochran (1977, p. 339). Reuther, quoted in Lichtenstein (1995, pp. 293, 311); Matles and Higgins (1974, p. 10).

[3] Jacobs (1963, p. 146).

[4] Galenson and Lipset 1960 (p. 204; emphasis added). The phrase "may be *said* to do so" is characteristic of the writings on union democracy. For all its concern with union democracy, the study by Lipset, Trow, and Coleman (1962) provides no empirical analysis of how the two-party system in the ITU affected the union's activities in the workplace or its achievements in collective bargaining.

What follows, then, are composites of the two main opposing theoretical claims about how union democracy or oligarchy affects collective bargaining. The underlying premise of the theory that monolithic, bureaucratic unions are superior in winning material benefits for their members is that rationality and efficiency are enhanced by bureaucracy. Or, as Peter Magrath says bluntly, echoing the comment above by Reuther, "Successful union activity vis-a-vis modern industry demands businesslike, i.e., nondemocratic organization. . . . [D]emocracy is as inappropriate within the international headquarters of the UAW as it is in the front office of General Motors."[5] Nondemocratic or oligarchic rule is required for the effective defense of union members' interests, because to cope with "bargaining pugilism" the union needs a centralized apparatus that parallels the structure of modern industry and enables it to countervail the concentration of corporate power. "In the event of strikes, the union has to confront a centrally directed and bureaucratically coordinated national mechanism with its own symmetrical counter force; in negotiations, the union has to control its own camp so that locals do not undercut each other's positions; in contract-keeping, the union has to be in a position to vouch, in return for security grants, that it can and will discipline its ranks to guarantee uninterrupted production."[6]

From the standpoint of critical democratic theory, however, "businesslike" conduct by union officials, (i.e., unaccountable and unrepresentative conduct) results less in the officials' rational and efficient approach to pursuing the interests of union members than in estranging them from members' daily lives and insulating them from members' demands. Simultaneously, businesslike conduct also leads union officials to establish closer and closer relationships with employers. As a result, they are less likely to push for contracts that improve working conditions and, specifically, enhance workers' power in the workplace.[7]

Only where workers are protected by a democratic union constitution and, in practice, can also freely criticize union officials and organize their own political associations, or "factions," to contend for power (caucuses, blocs, etc.), can they "discover for themselves what is possible" in collective bargaining.[8] Institutionalized opposition in turn makes the leadership alert, accountable, and representative and leads to a "vital union program" and the "active guardianship of membership interests."[9]

---

[5] Magrath (1959, p. 525).   [6] Cochran (1977, pp. 336–37).

[7] Leaders of recent dissident movements in some major unions (e.g., the Teamsters and the UAW) make essentially this same argument.

[8] Lipset et al. (1962, p. 461).

[9] McConnell (1958, p. 639); also see Nyden (1985); Howe and Widick (1949, pp. 259–66).

In its radical and critical (or "participatory") variant, democratic theory further holds that union policies are more likely to be in accord with the wants and demands of workers concerning their everyday working lives if not only the leaders of the union but also its rank and file are involved actively in the initiation, formulation, and implementation of policy.[10] By participating in making decisions in common about matters they know intimately and which, once decided, directly affect their daily lives on the job, and by electing their own leaders and knowing that they, too, stand a chance of being elected, workers gain political experience, skills, and political efficacy; simultaneously they gain substantive knowledge and political rationality. "For the union to become an instrument of social transformation . . . ," in C. Wright Mills's words, "[its members] "must think of it as their creature; they must want to know all about it and want to run it in as much detail as possible."[11]

The union, as a result, becomes the members' own immediate political community within which they and their leaders forge and retain closer social ties and identify with each other.[12] This community sustains and enhances the leaders' understanding of and empathy for the workers' everyday travail. Consequently, the chances increase that incumbent officers who lose an election will return to work in the plant and continue to be activists, but likely as part of the rank-and-file opposition.[13] Above all, through their participation in the political life of the union and in debating and deciding the union's objectives, strategy, and tactics, workers develop a common political consciousness as *workers*, as well as the capacity for self-reliant common action.

As David Wellman found in his study of ILWU's San Francisco longshore local:

> The experience of community teaches [longshoremen] . . . to be moral, not just economic, actors . . . [and] their ethical code applies to all workers, not just brothers on the docks. The 'us' that this community practices, . . . is reinforced by the daily fights with employers. . . . The process of defensible disobedience teaches longshoremen how to argue with their

---

[10] Pace Schumpeter's view (1942, 283); and see Pateman (1970); Mills ([1948] 1971, pp. 250–59).

[11] Mills ([1948] 1971, p. 268).

[12] Or the "vertical social distance" or "status gap" separating them is reduced. See Mannheim (1956a, pp. 180–81, 208, 210, 218); Lipset et al. (1962, pp. 240, 460); Nyden (1985, p. 1183).

[13] Lipset et al. (1962, p. 64) point out that in the ITU, because the "income gap" between the wages of rank-and-file printers and the salaries of their union's officers was small, this reduced the "strain" on the officers of returning to the printshop if they failed to win reelection.

employers, how to act when they think they are right and have been wronged . . . [and] not to accept an order simply because it is issued by powerful people. They learn to ask the powerful, by what right is an order issued?

This sense of community is a unifying class capacity that is a far more effective counterforce in any struggle against an employer than are businesslike conduct and bureaucratically imposed directives and discipline. So, for example, in the rank-and-file democracy of San Francisco's longshoremen, says Wellman, the question is regularly posed, in daily practice, in even apparently minor disputes over how to do a job, *"Which class will rule the waterfront?"*[14] So the contracts won by such solidary democratic unions, we suggest, tend to reflect the workers' wants and demands, and subvert, rather than sustain, the immediate sway of capital in production.

In Detroit, a retired auto worker named Dave Moore told us, in his words, the essentials of this same theory. Arriving in Detroit from the Blackbelt South during the Great Depression, Moore went to work at Ford's River Rouge plant in Dearborn, Michigan, got involved early on in trying to organize the union there, and went on to serve as a Progressive officer representing the gear and axle unit in UAW Ford Local 600. "The representatives out at Local 600 were basically honest with their constituents," he said, "because they had to be. . . . "

A person had to be a good representative. Now, some guys got elected, and they weren't; and they didn't last but one term, and they were gone and forgotten. . . . For a worker to see you smiling, as a representative, and a foreman got his arms around you, that was the kiss of death. You couldn't, when you confronted a foreman, you couldn't show any smile on your face. The best thing you could do, if he started to explain to you or something like that, you could just stand there and look at him, and say, "Well, look I want this did, understand, Fred? . . . Now, if I have to come back in this department, God damn it, your production stops." That would happen. The whole department would stop. . . . On the shop floor, around the machines, during the lunch-hour breaks, guys used to come down [and talk] . . . about the rights of workers, and what you had to do, and those things, about solidarity, sticking together, what your rights are. (These are the things we got agreement on. Don't you let nobody take them away from you. . . .)[15]

[14] Wellman (1995, p. 308, emphasis added).
[15] Stepan-Norris and Zeitlin (1996b, pp. 176, 177, 183).

In sum, where workers retain "the power of democratic initiation" in their unions, as Mills puts it, the chances increase that they will try to impose limits wherever they can on "management's power over the social organization of work."[16]

Constitutional Democracy, Factionalism, and Counterhegemony

Our constitutional democracy scale, remember, is a measure of the level of constitutional democracy at the height of the CIO era, in 1948. But shifts in power in various internationals and, consequently, significant constitutional changes sometimes occurred over the era. So, for example, at the Oil Workers' 1940 convention, an insurgent "workers' control" group, which had been active since the union's founding four years earlier, won the union's leadership, and then carried its program into effect by passing a complex of constitutional amendments that aimed to limit the executive power of the union's top officers. These amendments provided that all members, rather than convention delegates alone, could vote on the election of officers and the executive council, and they excluded full-time officers from the executive council. A year later, at the UAW's convention, the delegates passed an amendment to the constitution by a vote of nearly 2 to 1 barring Communists from holding any union office. At the NMU's 1947 convention, the constitution was amended to concentrate more power in the presidency and so in the hands of Joe Curran, at the expense of positions held by Communists.[17]

We were not, unfortunately, able to obtain copies of more than a few international constitutions from the early 1940s, so to provide a rough gauge of the stability of an international's constitutional order, we used published constitutional data from the early to mid-1940s on eligibility for union membership to construct an index of "equality of the franchise." We combined this index with the constitutional democracy scale;[18] and this yielded four categories of

[16] Mills ([1948] 1971, p. 256). Obviously, it is not possible to test this theory adequately here. To do so would require detailed data on each of the aspects of the political process (i.e., data not only on basic constitutional rights and liberties and institutionalized opposition within the union, but also on political participation, political efficacy, political rationality, political consciousness, the sense of identification and the vertical social distance or status gap between the leaders and the led, political community, and class solidarity). Only with such data would it be possible to assess the independent effects of the various mechanisms in determining a union's shop-floor activity and collective bargaining strategy.

[17] Galenson (1960, pp. 417, 423); Cochran (1977, p. 194); Levenstein (1981, p. 257).

[18] (Summers 1946, table b, pp. 92–107). Summers does not give the dates of the constitutions he examined; they were in all likelihood from the early to mid-1940s, as his article was

CIO internationals: *stable highly democratic* (a score of "high" on both the scale and the index), *stable moderately democratic* (a score of "moderate" on both), *stable oligarchic* (a score of "low" on both), and *unstable* (a score that shifted up or down).[19]

Now we find that, in fact, not only were the contracts won by locals of the stable highly democratic international unions consistently the most likely to be prolabor, as compared with their moderately democratic and oligarchic counterparts, but also the preponderant majority of them were prolabor on each of the six provisions.[20] The local contracts of the moderately democratic internationals were, in most instances, also more likely than those of the oligarchic internationals to be prolabor. Of the highly democratic, moderately democratic, and oligarchic internationals' local contracts, respectively, the percentages of those that did not cede management prerogatives were 59, 35, and 46; of those that had a total no-strike provision, 16, 58, and 74 percent; of those that were short-term, 83, 78, and 67 percent; of those that specified a shop steward had to be present at the grievance's first step, 79, 55, and 23 percent; of those that allowed no more than three steps in the grievance procedure, 84, 69, and 65 percent; and of those that put a time limit on each step, 65, 45, and 49 percent. For the trade-off, the respective percentages were 98, 83, and 72.

On the prolabor index, the same pattern is even more indelibly etched. All in all, 48 percent of the local contracts won by the stable highly democratic internationals, but only 4 percent of those won by the moderately democratic and 2 percent of the oligarchic, were prolabor on at least five of the six provisions

published in 1946. "Equality of the Franchise" refers to the constitution's express prohibition of discrimination against potential union members on the grounds of race, creed, citizenship, sex, or political affiliation (or belief). Each explicit provision in the constitution stating that "anyone is eligible" for union membership "regardless of" or "irrespective of" each of these five grounds is scored one point. The level of equality is defined as "high" if a union had a total score of five points, "moderate" if its score was three to four points, and "low" if its score was zero to two points.

[19] We excluded the unstable internationals, that is, the ones that shifted from low on the franchise to moderate or high on constitutional democracy, from moderate on franchise to low or high on democracy, or from high on franchise to moderate or low on democracy.

[20] The findings are statistically significant for five of the six provisions codifying the political terms of the immediate capital/labor relation – management prerogatives, the right to strike, the contract term, and all three aspects of the grievance procedure – as well as for the trade-off. Although the result for contract term is in the predicted direction, it is not statistically significant at the $p < 0.05$ level. We have allowed ourselves, however, to think seriously about this and other theoretically salient relationships even if they do not reach the conventional $p < 0.05$ significance level.

(see Table 6.1). (To ease the exposition, we call a contract with at least five of the six prolabor provisions a "prolabor contract.")

The contractual pattern is similar in relation to intraunion factionalism. The local contracts of the internationals with organized factions were far more likely to be prolabor on four of the provisions and on the trade-off measure than were the contracts negotiated by unions with sporadic or no factions. The local contracts of the internationals with sporadic factions were also typically, though not on every provision, somewhat more likely to be prolabor than those with no factions. Only the pattern on the cession of management prerogatives is an exception, and a startling one, because not the locals with organized factions but those with sporadic factions were the least likely by far to cede management prerogatives.

Of the local contracts of the internationals with organized factions, sporadic factions, and none, respectively, the percentages of those that did not cede management prerogatives were 44, 61, and 19; of those that had a total no-strike provision, 31, 76, and 71 percent; of those that were short-term, 80, 72, and 57 percent; of those that specified a shop steward had to be present at the grievance's first step, 71, 36, and 28 percent; of those that allowed no more than three steps in the grievance procedure, 78, 65, and 66 percent; and of those that put a time limit on each step, 59, 52, and 45 percent. On the prolabor index, the pattern was again sharp and clear: The percentages of prolabor contracts in the internationals with organized, sporadic, and no factions were 29, 8, and 2 (see Table 6.2).

So, as these findings confirm, not monolithic and businesslike but stable highly democratic industrial unions, whose leaders regularly faced lively organized opposition, were the most effective in defying the sway of capital in the sphere of production.

The question now arises as to how much these differences reflected not only the internationals' levels of democracy and factionalism but, crucially, their political camp or their leaders' political consciousness. What, in short, were the relatively independent effects of these three aspects of an international's political life in reconstructing the political regime of production?

Yet this may not be the correct question. For it is possible that, rather than having independent effects, these variables interacted; that is, the hypothesis is that constitutional democracy itself was enough to ensure prolabor contracts, so we would expect little difference between the local contracts of the democratic international unions in the rival camps. In the oligarchic internationals, however, whose officials were insulated from rank-and-file pressures, their own political consciousness would tend to be the main, if not the sole, determinant of the contract provisions they were willing to negotiate. We would

Table 6.1. *Prolabor provisions in CIO local union contracts in California, 1938–55, by the level of stable constitutional democracy in the international union (in percent)*

Level of stable constitutional democracy	Management prerogative	(N)	Strike prohibition[a] None	Cond'l	Total	(N)	Short-term contract	(N)	Trade-off	(N)	Grievance procedure Steward	(N)	Steps	(N)	Time limits	(N)	Prolabor index 5–6	4	2–3	0–1	(N)
Stable highly democratic	59	(56)	39	45	16	(56)	83	(52)	98	(54)	79	(70)	84	(91)	65	(69)	48	28	20	4	(54)
Stable moderately democratic	35	(55)	13	29	58	(55)	78	(45)	83	(46)	55	(47)	69	(55)	45	(40)	4	33	57	6	(54)
Stable oligarchic	46	(46)	6	20	74	(46)	67	(39)	72	(43)	23	(35)	65	(46)	49	(35)	2	17	71	9	(42)
Log odds ratio	0.29[x]			1.35**			0.44*		1.17**		1.37**		0.55**		0.47**		–				
Standard error	0.20			0.24			0.25		0.35		0.29		0.23		0.23		–				

[a] Dichotomized for log odds ratio: no and conditional prohibition versus total prohibition.

[x] $p < 0.07$.

* $p < 0.05$.

** $p < 0.01$.

Table 6.2. *Prolabor provisions in CIO local union contracts in California, 1938–55, by the presence of factions in the international union*

Presence of internal factions	Management prerogatives	(N)	Prolabor provisions																		
			Strike prohibition[a]				Short-term contract	(N)	Trade-off	(N)	Grievance procedure						Prolabor index				
			None	Cond'l.	Total	(N)					Steward	(N)	Steps	(N)	Time limits	(N)	5–6	4	2–3	0–1	(N)
Organized	44	(102)	27	41	31	(102)	80	(91)	92	(93)	71	(82)	78	(102)	59	(75)	29	30	36	5	(100)
Sporadic	61	(66)	5	20	76	(66)	72	(57)	75	(57)	36	(50)	65	(66)	52	(52)	8	23	62	8	(66)
None	19	(59)	14	15	71	(59)	57	(40)	67	(46)	28	(54)	66	(59)	45	(49)	2	19	57	23	(53)
Log odds ratio	0.43**			0.97**			0.54**		0.86**		0.96**		0.33*		0.28		–				
Standard error	0.17			0.19			0.21		0.23		0.20		0.18		0.18		–				

[a] Dichotomized for log odds ratio: no and conditional prohibition versus total prohibition.

* $p < 0.05$.

** $p < 0.01$.

therefore expect a big difference between the local contracts of the oligarchic internationals in the rival camps. Unfortunately, we cannot test this hypothesis because not one of the Communist-led international unions had a stable oligarchic regime.

We assessed the independent effects of an international's political camp, level of stable constitutional democracy, and factionalism by constructing three multiple regression models.[21] For brevity's sake and to lessen the tedium, we use only the prolabor index to uncover the independent effects of radicalism, democracy, and factionalism. Model 1 shows that both a stable high level of democracy and Communist leadership of an international union independently increased the chances that a local won prolabor contracts. Model 2 shows the same for organized factions and Communist leadership. The "complete" model 3 includes Communist leadership and both a high level of stable constitutional democracy and organized factions, and reveals that each of these political variables independently increased the chances that a local won prolabor contracts (see Table 6.3).

"Objective Conditions"

Not all of the CIO international unions were involved in "mass production industries" nor, of course, were these industries even alike in organization, scale of production, or relative economic centrality. The labor process, including the pace, rhythm, and autonomy of work and other "objective conditions" varied considerably – from seamen running ocean-going vessels to teams of hard-rock miners deep in the bowels of the earth to craftsmen making furs or shoes to steel workers tending an open-hearth furnace to workers laying on the parts on an endless automobile assembly line. Such variations in an industry's preexisting structure could have left their own peculiar stamp

---

[21] The point of multiple regression (OLS), as we pointed out in the Appendix to Chapter 4, is that it is supposed to allow us to see whether an independent variable has an independent effect on a dependent variable, taking into account ("holding constant" or "removing") the effects of other independent variables, and to estimate the size of that effect. But in OLS analysis, the relationships are assumed to be additive, whereas, as our substantive theory and specification of mechanisms ought to have made clear, we certainly do not think that the effects of these variables (political camp, the level of constitutional democracy, or factionalism) in determining prolabor contracts are additive. Further, too often in OLS analyses, significance tests per se are misinterpreted to reveal causal relationships and p values become the theoretical arbiter (see Meehl 1978; Freedman 1991, 1999; Sorensen 1998). We much prefer, therefore, to present the results of our quantitative analyses in the form of intuitively understandable contingency tables. Nonetheless, as a courtesy to OLS proponents, we also present the results of three OLS models below.

Table 6.3. *OLS estimates of the independent effects of stable constitutional democracy, the presence of factions, and the CIO's political camps in determining the likelihood that local union contracts in California, 1938–55, were prolabor*[a]

	Model 1		Model 2		Model 3	
	b	Beta	b	Beta	b	Beta
Stable highly democratic	0.75	0.28** (2.7)	–	–	0.83	0.31** (3.02)
Stable oligarchic	−0.16	−0.06 (−0.7)	–	–	0.46	0.16 (1.19)
Communist camp	0.81	0.31* (2.2)	1.08	0.39** (3.0)	0.60	0.23ˣ (1.57)
Shifting coalitions	0.06	0.02 (0.2)	−0.13	−0.05 (−0.4)	−0.11	−0.04 (−0.36)
Organized factions	–	–	0.48	0.18** (2.5)	0.71	0.26* (2.05)
No factions	–	–	−0.20	−0.06 (−0.5)	–	–
Intercept	2.76**		2.63**		2.27**	
Adjusted R²	0.30		0.29		0.31	
(N)	(150)		(219)		(150)	

[a] Prolabor index (0–6): The number of prolabor provisions in the agreement.
ˣ $p < 0.12$ (two-tailed tests).
* $p < 0.05$.
** $p < 0.01$.
Note: Omitted categories are "stable moderately democratic" in models 1 and 3, "anti-communist camp" in all models, "sporadic factions" in model 2, and "sporadic or no factions" in model 3. Numbers in parentheses are t-statistics, except in the bottom row, where (N) refers to the number of contracts analyzed in a model.

on the unions and influenced not only who won the leadership but also the demands their members would make and their chances of winning them.

It is certainly possible that the varying industrial situations actually encountered by the unions might have influenced what types of provisions these unions and their locals tried to win as well as what types they could win. The reality was, however, that the political camps were quite diverse in their internal industrial composition. They do not appear to have been essentially dissimilar in the relative heterogeneity of their productive organization, scale, technology, concentration, sensitivity to economic fluctuations, and so on. None of the three camps appears to be in any way distinctive in these terms. The same applies to the internationals in the democratic and oligarchic columns. So we doubt that these sorts of "objective conditions" can account for the pattern of deep differences our analysis has revealed in the winning of prolabor provisions by democratic and oligarchic internationals in the rival political camps.

Unfortunately, the U.S. census data for this period (1930–50) on the structure and demographic composition of the relevant industries are incomplete. But even if these industry-level data were complete, we would be skeptical of the validity of measures of union attributes based on them. This is why our quantitative analysis has abstracted from such objective conditions or assumed them to be constant. Withal, despite our skepticism of such measures, we did make an effort to assess the political relevance of "industrial structure." We found that the political variables retained their independent effects when the various interindustry differences were controlled.[22]

The "Big 3"

The CIO's international unions varied considerably in the size of their membership, the number of workers their contracts covered, and competition from other unions in the same industry. These aspects of their organization and competitive situation also might somehow have entered into what an international union's leaders thought was possible or "realistic," and might have affected what demands they chose to make and the likelihood of winning them in collective bargaining.

So, as a rough means of "holding constant" such differences, we also analyzed both the local and national agreements won by the CIO's "Big 3": the UE, UAW, and USWA. In 1948, at the height of the CIO era, their full-time dues-paying members numbered as follows: UE, 499,800; UAW, 893,400; and USWA, 880,600. Together, at that time, they comprised 53 percent of the total of 4.3 million full-time dues-paying members belonging to the CIO's thirty-six international unions.[23] In the characteristic features of their internal political life, each of them, especially Reuther's UAW, simultaneously represented and formed the core of the CIO's rival camps and, in their own way, exemplified and incarnated the contrast between oligarchy and democracy.

---

[22] These tables are available upon request.

[23] Calculated from Troy's figures (1965, table A2). Until 1942, when John L. Lewis took the UMW out of the CIO to protest its "subservience" to President Franklin Delano Roosevelt, UMW ranked third in the CIO. (In 1948, UMW had 572,000 full-time dues-paying members.)

UE: The "Red Fortress"

The Communists and radicals in UE's international leadership were supported by a broad base of Communists and their allies spread among its highly independent locals and powerful districts, although several major locals, especially in the Philadelphia district, were led by anti-Communists. The Red-led UE "prided itself on being a rank-and-file union (only 5 percent of its convention delegates were full-time officials) which represented all shades of opinion."[24] The collective bargaining strategy and specific demands "came up from the locals through the various industry conference boards, not down from the top."[25] The UE's negotiating committees were elected, and all agreements were ratified by referendum, as were both the calling and ending of strikes.[26] Throughout its years in the CIO, various factions were active within the UE, and the union's international leadership was regularly challenged by organized opposition. By 1948, with the heightening of Cold War tensions and the widening political split in the CIO between left and right, the UE was already being beset by escalating raiding of its membership by other CIO internationals and by the repressive assaults of government agencies and congressional investigating committees on its leadership. It was, on our measures, a Red-led "stable highly democratic international union" with organized factions.

UAW

In the UAW, the core of the so-called shifting camp, the Communists and their allies formed a "center–left" coalition, which was one of the most important factions that vied for and actually held the union's leadership over most of the CIO era. They also led some important locals (most notably, Local 600). Their immanent defeat came with Walter Reuther's election as UAW president in late 1946. The next year – in a battle that exemplified and incarnated "a democracy that was legendary throughout the labor movement"[27] – Reuther's faction won a majority of the executive board at the UAW's November convention. Reuther then authorized political surgery, as he declared, to "cut out the [Communist] cancer."

Until then, contending "caucuses" in the UAW had held regular meetings, had been represented by their own recognized delegates at the conventions, and had run their own slates of candidates for the UAW's's top offices. But with

[24] Caute (1979, p. 376).   [25] Filippelli (1984, pp. 240–41).
[26] Matles and Higgins (1974, pp. 10–11).
[27] Cochran (1977, p. 259); also see Howe and Widick (1949, pp. 117, 129, 262).

Reuther's ascendancy, he and his cohorts quickly began to suppress the UAW's pluralism by a series of new and tough constitutional rules that were passed under his aegis – rules that enhanced executive power and narrowed members' basic rights and liberties. Already, at the 1949 convention, Reuther moved, and the delegates approved, a constitutional amendment giving the executive board the authority to prefer charges against members "in case of extreme emergency"; and therewith two veteran UAW leaders, neither of whom was a Communist, were expelled on charges of "treason" for publishing a report on alleged racketeering in the union. "Factional debate within the UAW was now virtually illegitimate."[28] The UAW was, on our measures, "a stable moderately democratic union" with organized factions.

USWA

The CIO's SWOC, which organized the USWA, did not disband and officially establish the international itself until 1942. Once a local was organized, SWOC officials, headed by John L. Lewis and Philip Murray, sent its hired organizers elsewhere; so, although Communists led some of the union's toughest organizing battles, they were not able to gain and hold local leadership,[29] and the USWA remained an enduring and powerful bastion of anti-Communism within the CIO. It was run throughout its history by staunchly conservative, devoutly Catholic men, much influenced by Catholic labor doctrines emphasizing social harmony and the achievement of "Christian justice" through class collaboration.[30]

Serious factional disputes rarely if ever occurred within USWA, which was unitary and highly centralized. Throughout the USWA–CIO's existence, "the union's top officers [held] total administrative power" and eliminated "any local center of disturbance" arising in the union.[31] On our measure of stable democracy, the USWA was unstable. It was moderate on equality of the franchise, but low on constitutional democracy. It had no factions.

The Contractual Pattern

Now, we find that the pattern in the local contracts of the Big 3 paralleled both the pattern of the political camp to which each belonged and their relative degree of factionalism and democracy.

---

[28] Cochran (1977, pp. 324–27); Lichtenstein (1995, pp. 310–11).
[29] Taft (1964, p. 57); Saposs (1959, p. 122).   [30] Levenstein (1981, pp. 111–13).
[31] Levenstein (1981, p. 51); Lipset et al. (1962, p. 443).

UE's local contracts were by far most consistently prolabor on the set of crucial provisions; it was followed by the UAW, and then by the USWA, a distant third. Of the UE, UAW, and USWA's local contracts, respectively, the percentages of those that did not cede management prerogatives were 44, 29, and 7; of those that had a total no-strike provision, 6, 53, and 68 percent; of those that were short-term, 93, 78, and 55 percent; of those that specified a shop steward had to be present at the grievance's first step, 93, 48, and 25 percent; of those that allowed no more than three steps in the grievance procedure, 87, 68, and 66 percent; and of those that put a time limit on each step, 65, 43, and 46 percent (see Table 6.4).

What about the Big 3's national contracts, that is, the contracts that were negotiated by the international union's own executive board? Did they exhibit the same pattern as among the local contracts? To answer this question we examined all of the national agreements made (from the earliest in 1937 or 1938 through 1950) between each Big 3 international and the major employer in its industry: that is, between UE and General Electric (GE), between UAW and GM, and between USWA (i.e., SWOC and later USWA) and Carnegie-Illinois (which became U.S. Steel (USS) in late 1950).[32]

Not one of the UE/GE national contracts before, during, or after World War II ceded so-called management prerogatives. But the UAW/GM and USWA/USS national contracts all did. That UE refused to cede management prerogatives in the postwar years is especially significant, for from late 1945 on higher corporate executives and organized big business were demanding that "unions . . . recognize, and not encroach upon, the functions and responsibilities of management." Management resolutely resisted any form of "joint [union–management] control of matters beyond wages and working conditions," as Sanford Jacoby emphasizes, and after the war, "the unions accepted the terms set by management."[33] The most dramatic expression of the corporations' reassertion of the "right to manage" once World War II ended came in the UAW–GM 113-day strike, begun on November 21, 1945, and involving some 300,000 workers nationwide. GM won the strike, after absolutely

---

[32] For each international union and company, by year, our analysis covers the following national agreements. UE/GE: 1938 (actually in force until 1941), 1941–47, 1948 (in force until 1950), and 1950. UAW/GM: 1937, 1938 (in force until 1940), 1940, 1941, 1942 (in force until 1945), 1945, 1946 (in force until 1948), 1948 (in force until 1950), and 1950. SWOC/Carnegie–Illinois (or USS): 1937 ("amended" in 1938, it remained in force until 1941), 1941, 1942 (in force until 1945), 1945 (in force until 1947), and 1947 ("amended" in 1948, 1949, and 1950).

[33] U.S. Department of Labor 1946, pp. 56–57); Jacoby (1981, p. 26); also see Brody (1980, p. 185).

Table 6.4. *Prolabor provisions in "Big 3" local union contracts in California, 1938–55 (in percent)*

"Big 3" union	Management prerogative	(N)	Strike prohibition[a]				Short-term contract	(N)	Trade-off	(N)	Grievance procedure					
			None	Cond'l.	Total	(N)					Steward	(N)	Steps	(N)	Time limits	(N)
UE	44	(32)	25	69	6	(32)	93	(31)	100	(32)	93	(27)	87	(32)	79	(28)
UAW	29	(34)	15	32	53	(34)	78	(27)	85	(34)	48	(31)	68	(34)	32	(25)
USWA	7	(44)	16	16	68	(44)	55	(31)	54	(44)	25	(40)	66	(44)	44	(36)
Log odds ratio	1.08**			0.67*			1.19**		2.25**		1.61**		0.55*		0.67**	
Standard error	0.31			0.18			0.36		0.43		0.33		0.28		0.27	

[a] Dichotomized for log odds ratio: no and conditional prohibition vs. total prohibition.

* $p < .05$.

** $p < .01$.

refusing to bargain over issues (e.g., pricing) that it saw as encroachments on the "sovereign power of corporate management."[34]

Exemplary of the enduring refusal by UE's local and international leadership to cede management prerogatives is its St. Louis district 8. The district was organized and led from the start and almost uninterruptedly by men who proudly avowed their membership in the CP, including its head for most of its years, William Sentner. At its height, UE was the biggest CIO affiliate in the state of Missouri. In 1937, under Sentner's leadership, the UE local at Emerson electric used an arbitration clause in that year's contract to refuse to accept a reduction of wage and piecework rates when a downturn came the next year. UE rejected the company's assertion that matters such as setting wage rates and the "book of rules" were "the sole function of management to decide." When the UE local appealed to the NLRB, the board ruled in September 1938 that the company had the sole prerogative of setting wage rates but not the prerogative to decide alone the "book of rules." At the district's convention later that year, Sentner declared: "This is the first decision of the Labor Board against the management clause." Again, during the war, he saw the NWLB as a potential weapon against managerial power, and self-consciously argued that the NWLB's rulings on setting wage rates "has shattered the so-called management prerogative and has done a service to this country and has extended the democratic rights that labor was given under the Labor Act." And in the postwar years, district 8 continued its explicit challenge to management prerogatives. It is "an error," Sentner said in September 1948, "to maintain that a union is nothing but a pure and simple economic organization." Rather, district 8's leading idea was "that production," as Rosemary Feurer describes it, "should be geared to community labor needs rather than for profits . . . [and] labor unions should be at the center of social change in the community."[35]

When it came to management "rights," UE's international leadership, like Sentner in St. Louis, never "accepted the terms set by management." No postwar UE agreement with GE ceded management prerogatives – not even in 1950, a year after UE's "expulsion" from the CIO and while it was under relentless siege by the government and raiding by other unions.[36] The 1950 UE/GE

---

[34] Harris (1982, pp. 139–43); Cochran (1977, pp. 251–52).

[35] Feurer (1992, pp. 106, 113, 116).

[36] In fact, UE was "expelled" at the CIO's 1949 convention only after UE already had ceased paying its CIO per capita dues, sent no delegates to the convention, and severed its CIO connections. UE withdrew after CIO head Murray and the executive board ignored UE's repeated requests to stop the raiding of UE by other CIO unions (Matles and Higgins 1974, pp. 188, 198, 249).

contract was signed in September 1950. From April to June 1950, while winning forty of ninety NLRB elections at GE, Westinghouse, and other corporations dominant in the electrical industry, UE had lost as many as half its pre-November 1949 members, most of them to International Union of Electrical, Radio and Machine Workers (IUE) and some to UAW and other raiders such as the AFL's IAM and IBEW. A month before the UE/GE 1950 agreement, five of UE's top officers had refused to cooperate with HUAC on the grounds of the Fifth and First Amendments and were cited for contempt of Congress. Yet that UE contract did not cede management prerogatives. (Nor did any afterward.) No wonder, then, that even a labor historian as fiercely anti-Communist as David Saposs exclaimed that the UE was "superlatively combative."[37]

UE/GE national agreements had only a minor condition on the right to strike; before striking, a local was to try to resolve the dispute or grievance through the established grievance procedure.[38] They were all short-term (one-year) agreements, except 1948's (which was for two years). In the grievance procedure, workers, stewards, and the local union retained initiative, and it involved the fewest and least cumbersome steps and the shortest time limits of the Big 3 contracts.

The 1950 UE/GE contract actually strengthened the grievance procedure by providing that the steward had to be involved throughout three designated phases of "step one." UE's stewards were elected by the workers in the shop or small department and, unlike the "committeemen" of the UAW and USWA, were not paid by the company (until 1950, when part of their time was company-paid). The ratio of shop stewards to workers in the UE, which always stressed that "rank-and-file workers" should decide for themselves how to handle grievances, was also higher by far than the ratio of committeemen to workers in UAW and USWA. UE tried to ensure that every shop would have one steward to every company foreman — whatever the size of the shop — and to solve the grievance in open discussion on the shop floor where the problem arose.[39]

---

[37] Levenstein (1981, pp. 310–11); Saposs (1959, p. 251).

[38] Derber (1945, p. 753) mistakenly reports that the 1938 UE/GE contract forbade "sit downs, stoppages and lockouts . . . during the life of the agreement." In fact, it had only the same conditional prohibition that later contracts had, namely, if a dispute could not be solved between the local and its particular plant management, it had the option, before exercising its right to strike, of taking it to higher levels of the union if it wished: "[S]uch cases *may* be referred to the National Officers of the Union and an Executive Officer of the Company who shall arrange a conference (if necessary) with representatives of the Local union" (e.g., 1941, p. 10; 1948, p. 41, emphasis added). This was also true of the wartime UE/GE national contracts (e.g., 1942, p. 11; 1944, p. 25). We examine "period effects" below.

[39] Matles and Higgins (1974, p. 12).

This "made a big difference" in the lives of workers, as a local UE officer explained:

> If a foreman started riding a member, why, all a member had to do [was] to tell the steward and the steward would get after the foreman. It made a lot of difference. Where before [you had a union], why you could stand there and hear a foreman bawl a guy out for something that didn't amount to anything. Make him look like a damn fool. And you couldn't do nothing about it, see? That's before unionism was in the shop.[40]

UAW/GM agreements ceded management prerogatives, stipulating that the corporation had the "sole and exclusive responsibility" to decide what and how to produce. They restricted the right to strike by requiring that no strike be called before a lengthy and complex grievance procedure was exhausted (this included recourse to an impartial umpire whose decisions were final); all stoppages, slowdowns, or strikes also had to be authorized by the international. Until 1946, UAW/GM contracts were for a one-year term or stayed in force indefinitely until revoked, on sixty-day written notice, by either the union or the company. The 1946 and 1948 contracts were for two years and also contained the sixty-day notice provisions. In 1950, UAW signed the famous five-year "treaty" with GM that many thought "signaled the end of an era in industrial unionism."[41] The UAW/GM grievance procedure typically had four complex steps, with specific time limits. At the worker's request, the "committeeman" handled the first step of the grievance.[42]

SWOC/USS and USWA/USS national agreements all ceded management prerogatives, stipulating that the company had the "exclusive rights to manage

---

[40] Lipsitz (1994, p. 254).

[41] Aronowitz (1973, p. 247). The five-year UAW/GM contract, followed quickly by the five-year UAW/Ford contract, had major "pattern-setting" implications, because of the economic centrality of automobile production and the singularity of UAW's strength. But Harry Bridges's ILWU signed a *seven*-year contract with West Coast employers two years earlier, in 1948; in part, ILWU's rationale was that it would protect the longshoremen's jobs against impending mechanization (Levenstein 1981, p. 334).

[42] Aronowitz reports that "the rank-and-file steward was replaced by the [company-paid] 'committeeman' in the United Auto Workers agreement with the 'Big Three' manufacturers of the industry in *1946*" (1973, p. 254, emphasis added). This date, 1946, for the introduction of the paid committeeman, is incorrect. Already in the 1938 UAW/GM contract, it was specified that committeemen would be paid their regular wages by the company (for up to two hours daily) while they handled grievances (1938, p. 3). The 1946 contract increased the number of paid hours permissible, averaged over the week, to five daily (1946, p. 14), and this was the standard in subsequent contracts through 1950 (e.g., 1950, p. 18).

the business and plants and to direct the working forces." They all had definite no-strike clauses, which prohibited strikes and stoppages during the life of the contract. Disputes were to be settled though "earnest efforts" by both the union and the company through the grievance procedure, which ended in compulsory arbitration unless both parties agreed to forfeit it. The earliest national agreement in 1937 left aggrieved workers on their own to settle the grievance with the foreman, but subsequent agreements specified that the steward (or "assistant committeeman") could be present at the first step of the grievance procedure at the worker's request. The grievance procedure had three steps in the 1943 agreement, but later had four or five complex steps, with specified time limits.

So, in sum, our clause-by-clause examination of the local and national contracts won by the three biggest international unions reveals that they exemplified and incarnated the same pattern already found in our quantitative analysis of the effects of political camp, constitutional democracy, and factionalism: The UE/GE agreements were definitely prolabor; UAW/GM agreements were much less so; and USWA/USS were least, by far.

Delivering the Goods

The question remains: Would an analysis focusing on other contract issues and provisions – for instance, on the differences in the actual "wages and benefits" won – disclose a similar pattern of variations among the unions in the rival political camps? Some "pluralists" and left critics of Communist unionists say or imply, for instance, that their unions won inroads on control issues or management rights only at the cost of their ability to "deliver the goods," and, all in all, they served their members less well than conventional unions.[43]

Yet David Saposs, who fully endorsed "the horrendous task of cleansing the CIO of Communist dominated unions," denies that they were inferior in delivering the goods:

> The evidence and arguments of the CIO that the Communist-dominated unions failed fully to pursue pure trade-union procedures are rather tenuous. . . . The ILWU, Fur, and UE had leadership as competent as the most successful unions . . . and their record in securing wages and better working conditions for their members through collective bargaining is at least as favorable as that of any of the outstanding unions. Undoubtedly, their achievements in the trade-union field enabled them to

[43] See Epstein and Goldfinger (1950, p. 42); Yousler (1956, p. 266).

hold the loyalty of their members, the great majority of whom were not Communists.

Even his evaluation of Communist-led unions that he considered "ineffective," such as, for instance, Food, Tobacco, Agricultural and Allied Workers (FTA) or Office and Professional Workers, was hedged: "No other union efforts, however, were more successful in the fields covered by these jurisdictions."[44]

The impact of unions on wages and benefits – a much-debated issue – is beyond the purview of this analysis. But we want at least to look at how the Big 3 fared vis-à-vis each other, as a way of assessing the charge that the left-led unions "traded off" workers' control for wages and benefits. In "economic gains," as a Trotskyist critic of UE's "Stalinist" leadership writes," . . . the UE trailed behind the steel, auto and other major CIO unions. It was generally the last of the CIO 'Big Three' to make settlements and then on the basis of gains made by the others. . . . Plants under UE contract were plagued with piecework systems that led to wages and working conditions inferior to the far-from-ideal standards in auto and steel."[45]

The evidence, however, does not support this charge. In UE's postwar wage negotiations, it generally kept pace with settlements gained in the steel and auto industries. In 1946, the overall wage raises won by each of the Big 3 from the major employers were identical: UE/GE, UAW/GM, and USWA/USS amounted to 18.5 cents an hour.[46] In 1947, UE negotiated agreements with both GE and Westinghouse that amounted to 11.5 cents in wage increases and another 3.5 cents in fringe benefits. The wage settlement in steel was 12.5 cents, and in auto, 11.5 cents, with comparable fringe benefits. Even in 1948, when UE was already being subjected to constant raiding by other unions and to harassment by congressional committees and federal agencies, UE won agreements that compared favorably with those in auto and steel. At GE, UE won an 8 percent increase in total earnings, with a minimum 9 cents an hour raise. (At RCA, UE also won a three-year vacation period after ten years of employment, which was "a first for any major company in the United States.") UAW got 6 cents added to base rates and 8 cents in a cost-of-living float, which could go up or down. USWA won a package that gave steel workers 9.5 cents an hour in general wage increases.[47]

In addition, it should be emphasized that UE's wage and benefits packages were won for workers, about 40 percent of whom were women.[48] UE's leaders

---

[44] Saposs (1959, pp. 189, 184–85).   [45] Preis (1972, p. 398).   [46] Soffer (1959, p. 59).
[47] Filippelli and McColloch (1995, pp. 128–29).
[48] Women constituted 39 percent of all electrical workers in 1946, 38 percent in 1950, and 36 percent in 1958 (Milkman 1987, p. 13). Since some of these women were employed in

were engaged in a relentless struggle with electrical employers to win pay equity and job protection for women, and they led the way in fighting for integration of women into the industry on equal terms with men.[49] So we suggest that an analysis that held the gender gap constant while comparing wages and benefits in the auto, steel, and electrical industries would show that UE's delivery of the goods compared even more favorably with UAW's and USWA's.

Data for the postwar period 1946–57 show that USWA won the highest absolute average increase of $1.33 an hour for their members employed by U.S. Steel; UAW won an average increase of $1.19 per hour for GM workers and, in "pattern bargaining," for Ford and Chrysler workers; and UE cum IUE won an average increase of $1.16 an hour for Westinghouse workers.[50] The 1950–57 figures, however, cover years when UE was being subjected to a raid-and-destroy campaign by the International Union of Electrical, Radio, and Machine Workers (IUE), the newly chartered CIO international, which became for much of this period the major union at GE and Westinghouse. UE was also being raided by the Teamsters, the International Brotherhood of Electrical Workers (IBEW), and IAM, while fending off, often in court, HUAC, Senate committees led by Hubert H. Humphrey and Joseph McCarthy, and other federal government assaults, including, from 1954 on, efforts by Attorney General Herbert Brownell and the Securities Activities Control Board to decertify the union as "Communist-dominated." Despite this, according to a detailed historical analysis, UE proved over the years to be more combative than its anti-Communist rival IUE on all issues.[51]

An analysis of "the effect of rival unionism on wages" in the electrical industry concludes also that there was "a relative decline in electrical manufacturing industry wages in relation to wages in the durable goods industries since 1949. . . . Prior to 1950 [when IUE was chartered] electrical industry wages were increasing more rapidly than those in the durable goods industries; since the advent of rival unionism the increase has been less. . . . The very effectiveness of [GE's 'take-it-or-leave it'] . . . bargaining policy may depend upon the existence of numerous unions [over a 100, according to GE itself] in the GE chain, some of which are intent upon destroying one another."[52]

IUE, it should also be emphasized, was able to start representing electrical workers only because, under Taft–Hartley Act provisions, the companies

small nonunion plants or plants whose workers were represented by the AFL's IBEW, the percentage of UE's members who were women was probably even higher than these figures.
[49] Zieger (1995, p. 256); also see the discussion in Chapter 7.   [50] Maher (1961).
[51] Filippelli and McColloch (1995, pp. 141–66).
[52] Peevey (1961, pp. 57, 53); also see Backman (1962, pp. 250ff.).

themselves could petition for a National Labor Relations Board (NLRB) union recognition election. Not even one of UE's "right wing" locals initiated an NLRB election to choose between the UE and IUE. As *Business Week* reported in early January 1950: "The Company [GE] has petitioned for an NLRB election in all plants to settle rival claims," and GM, following GE's lead, also petitioned for an NLRB election among the company's 27,000 workers who were then represented by UE.[53] And aside from "rival unionism" weakening both UE and IUE, the latter's leadership was divided, and many of its locals considered IUE head James B. Carey (and CIO Secretary-Treasurer) incompetent. At bargaining time over the years, some large IUE locals even refused to heed his call for a strike. In the 1955 contract negotiations, for instance, the *New York Times* reported: "The plain fact is that many observers – labor leaders and management alike – feel that IUE did not win the plan because it did not have the will or the power to strike for it. The same observers feel that the IUE bargaining team was 'outslicked' and outmaneuvered by the GE negotiators. . . . "[54]

The Shop Floor

The contract is "the document that most shapes the daily life of the . . . worker."[55] Yet the contract language may well provide at best "a very limited window into the actual role of unions [in] . . . class struggle."[56] So how closely the contract reflects the situation on the shop floor is a crucial question. What, put theoretically, is the relationship between the juridical and the practical reconstruction of the immediate capital/labor relation?

How the contract shapes the workers' daily life depends on what the union makes of it in practice – whether acting "as night watchman over the collective agreement," as Michael Burawoy says, to "circumscribe the terrain of struggle" or engaging in constant "extra-contractual shop floor activity" and wielding

---

[53] *Business Week*, January 7, 1950, p. 65, cited in Peevey (1961, p. 29).

[54] *New York Times*, August 16, 1955, p. 18, as cited in ibid., p. 41. Jerry Lembcke presents the findings of a comparative analysis of wage increases among eleven unions during the period 1945–48 in British Columbia, a major district of the International Woodworkers of America (IWA), when its leadership was still Communist. The analysis by the Trade Union Research Bureau in Vancouver shows, according to Lembcke, that "the IWA ranked third of the eleven unions compared. The [anti-Communist] White Bloc came to power in 1948 in the B.C. District and the same eleven-union study for the period 1948–51 showed the IWA having fallen to eighth and for the 1951–57 period, the tenth place out of the eleven unions" (1984, p. 188).

[55] Gilpin (1988, p. 2).   [56] Brecher (1990).

the contract, as Toni Gilpin says, "in the workers' defense, employing it when it [is] useful, abandoning it when [it] is not."[57] What we know about the realm of union activity on the job, based on three ethnographic studies as well as two recent comparative historical works, is consistent with the contractual pattern our analysis disclosed in the previous chapter.

Comparing the Big 3's national and local agreements, the USWA's were by far, as we now know, the most procapital. Yet it was on the basis of Burawoy's work as a machine operator in a piece-work machine shop in a USWA local that he elaborated his variant of the theory of labor unionism's irremediably procapitalist role as "night watchman."[58] He also drew extensively on Donald Roy's reports on shop-floor relations in that "very factory" thirty years earlier. Although separated by so many years, Burawoy found that Roy's observations and his own coincided on the role of the union in the shop and on the workers' attitudes toward it. For instance, he quotes Roy's report that "[t]he union was rarely a topic of . . . conversation [in the shop], and when it was mentioned, remarks indicated that it was not an organization high in worker esteem. Characteristic of machine operator attitudes toward the union was the scornful comment: 'All the union is good for is to get that $1.00 a month out of you.'" Roy said that he had little contact with the shop steward. "In his eleven months at Geer," Burawoy reports, "Roy interacted with [the steward] only twice. [First, when] the steward wanted him to sign the checkoff form" and, second, when Roy complained to him about his piece-work payment rate. "The steward showed interest but did nothing." These "attitudes among rank and file," Burawoy says, "remain much as they were in 1945. There is a pervasive cynicism as to the willingness and ability of union officials to protect the interests of the membership. . . . "[59]

Given the close fit between Burawoy's and Roy's observations on the union's role and the men's views about it, it is crucial that the observations by another member of Roy's own three-man research team working elsewhere at about the same time were quite different from Roy's. While Roy was working in his shop, Orvis Collins was also working as a milling machine operator in another factory, in a shop employing 90 to 110 machine operators. (Roy's shop employed only some 50 men.) Collins worked in his shop for about six months and he also spent many months afterward interviewing the men he had worked with there.[60]

But the union steward in Collins's shop – unlike the nearly invisible steward Roy observed in his shop – was highly visible, active, and respected. He

---

[57] Burawoy (1983, pp. 594–95); Gilpin (1988, pp. 14, 25).   [58] Burawoy (1979).

[59] Roy (1952, p. 434); Burawoy (1979, pp. 111–12).

[60] Collins, Dalton, and Roy (1945). This ethnography is not cited by Burawoy.

was the leader of a lunch group of about forty workers who "were CIO." Another lunch group consisted of about fifteen to twenty "AFL men," dominated by several who wanted the AFL to replace the CIO in the plant.[61] Rather than finding depoliticization and "pervasive cynicism" about the union's defense of their interests, Collins found that "union sentiment was strong" in his shop. He also found (unlike Roy's observation that the union, let alone "politics," was rarely a topic of conversation) that the workers often had "heated arguments" about political issues, with the lines drawn between the prounion majority and a few antiunion workers. "These arguments," Collins reports, "were usually political in nature, and on such subjects as whether Russia had any part in winning the war, whether Roosevelt had planned to become a dictator, or whether the workmen had 'the right' to strike."

Collins refers to a typical discussion in which one worker, called "Swede," defends the union against the charge by another worker, called "John," that the union is "all right if you like racketeers." To which Swede responded: "Without a union the boss tells you where you're going to work and if you don't like it you don't open your mouth." Significantly, Swede had begun the discussion "feeling John out by saying that he hoped [Henry] Wallace would become Secretary of Commerce."

John: I suppose from that you like Wallace.
Swede: He and Roosevelt have both done a lot of good for the working
         man.
John: What do you mean he's done a lot of good for the working man?
         Killing pigs and closing banks.[62]

These ethnographic studies of two different machine shops studied at the same time in the same way by two members of the same research team convey sharply opposed images of shop-floor relations and workers' consciousness. They suggest that the shop-floor relations in Burawoy's (and Roy's) shop were not the expression of unionism's inherently integrative and depoliticizing function, as he assumes, but rather the product of the specific political practices of the shop's bureaucratic and accommodationist union, the USWA.

What's more, Collins's observations on the local union's role in shop-floor relations are consistent with our own findings that the political consciousness of union leaders makes a significant difference in what they fight for and win

[61] Collins et al. (1945, p. 8).
[62] Ibid., p. 10. On the 1948 Wallace presidential campaign, the Communists, and the CIO, see Chapter 10.

for their members. For the union in Collins's shop of active, politically alert, and committed union men, as the reader must already have guessed, was a local of the Communist-led UE.

Two historical monographs that compare Communist-led and rival anti-Communist locals in the same industry and the same plant during the same period also found the same sort of sharp contrasts.[63] One study compared the Communist-led FE local and the UAW local, which "went at each other" during the late 1940s and early 1950s at International Harvester in Louisville, Kentucky. The other study compared UE and the IUE – which the CIO's executive board chartered in 1949 to raid, destroy, and replace UE – while they confronted each other at Westinghouse throughout the 1950s.

The International Harvester plant opened in 1946 with FE as the representative of all production and maintenance workers. Three years later, the company began production in a new foundry at the same plant, and it became a separate bargaining unit, represented by the UAW. According to Gilpin, FE consistently fought "speed up" and similar methods of "lowering costs" and raising "productivity." FE officers warned its members, as they did in 1955, already five years after being expelled from the CIO, that such means of raising productivity actually increased the workers' "exploitation" by "widening the spread between what a worker gets paid for his labor and the profit that the company makes on his labor."[64]

The shop-floor practices of the FE and UAW locals sharply differed. The UAW local emphasized "stability in labor relations," while the FE local actively engaged in "the politics of class conflict." Summing up their contrasting relationships with the company, a Harvester official said in 1952 that "[c]ompared with our relationship with FE–UE, our dealings with the UAW could only be called harmonious." In fact, of twenty-two different unions the company dealt with at the time, it put FE in a "separate category." The company accused FE stewards of roaming the plant not to deal with actual grievances, but, in one official's words, "to promote unrest, stir up ill will, harass the company, and convince as many members as it can that labor relations with Harvester is and must be class warfare." Or, as another company official put it, FE's officers were "irresponsible radicals" who were "more interested in disruption than in labor–management peace."[65]

---

[63] Gilpin (1988, 1993); McColloch (1988); also see Filippelli and McColloch (1995).

[64] From an FE pamphlet, 1955, quoted in Gilpin (1988, p. 19). Congress's Joint Labor–Management Relations Committee also "tended to agree," she observes (1988, p. 47n), "at least in 1948, that the FE established the standards for contracts in the agricultural implements industry."

[65] Gilpin (1988, pp. 1, 17, 28, 42).

In Mark McColloch's analysis of UE's and IUE's records on "incentive pay" and "seniority provisions and practices" at Westinghouse in the 1950s, at a time when the isolated UE had shrunk to a fraction of its CIO strength and was under accelerating and constant attack by congressional investigating committees and government agencies, he found a "clear difference" both in how these unions approached these questions and in the working conditions that resulted. "On both incentive and seniority the UE ... consistently resisted take-aways and usually succeeded. ... Measured day work and camera time studies were just two of the Westinghouse-sought innovations which the UE was able to block, while they were being imposed on thousands of IUE members. ... [UE] firmly and consistently resisted ... any watering down of the applicability of seniority" and also fought, in particular, for equal seniority rights for women.[66]

What accounts for the "clear difference in the practice of the two unions" and UE's superior defense of its members, despite its shrinkage and weakened state, compared with IUE during the 1950s? After all, few if any of UE's leaders still had close ties to the CP by 1951.[67] Yet most were radicals who had joined UE during the mass workers' struggles of the 1930s and early 1940s, and "their political personalities," as McColloch puts it, "had been shaped by these struggles." IUE's leaders in contrast, were generally younger and "less influenced by the 'movement' atmosphere of the 1930s and 1940s." UE and IUE leaders had opposed conceptions of the capital/labor relationship, and of the role of their union vis-à-vis the workers and the corporations, and this "did make a difference on the shop floor. ... [I]deology and worldview – and the personalities and actions that they helped produce – counted for much."

Last, but not least, IUE's officers and staffers were "substantially higher paid than those of the UE, often a factor," as McColloch wryly notes, "in easing one's adjustment to the existing order."[68] "Yes, some people think we're just a bunch of nuts": So said James Matles in a talk with rank-and-file delegates at a UE convention about the leadership's egalitarianism and its effects on their adjustment to the existing order. "Why," Matles asked, "do we have an international union where our officers are living the same lives as the rank-and-file?"

> If you want ... to maintain democracy in our organization, if you want officers and representatives to whom no shop grievance is too small to

---

[66] McColloch (1988, pp. 28–29). The contrast between the aims and achievements of UE and IUE on women's rights during the 1950s is discussed below, in Chapter 7.

[67] McColloch (1992, p. 184). On CP strategy concerning the expulsions of "Communist-dominated" unions from the CIO, see Chapter 11.

[68] McColloch (1992, pp. 199, 185).

handle, . . . you must have an organization where your officers and your organizers feel *like* the members and not feel *for* the members. There is a big difference.[69]

In fact, as has been shown elsewhere, the average salary of the highest-paid officer and the income differential between that salary and the average wage in the industry was by far the lowest in the CIO's Communist-led internationals. The same pattern also characterized the democratic internationals and those with factions as contrasted with their opposite numbers. What's more, it was among the biggest internationals, which had more resources to enhance the material rewards of office, that all three of these political contrasts in leaders' egalitarianism – between the Communist-led unions and their rivals, the democratic as opposed to the oligarchic, and those with and without factions – were especially sharp.[70]

Conclusion

The analysis in this chapter has been guided by the theory that union democracy makes a real difference in the daily lives of workers: A union with a democratic constitution, organized opposition, and an active membership tends to constitute the workers' immediate political community, sustaining both a sense of identification between them and their leaders and class solidarity; as a result, the union also tends to defy the hegemony of capital in the sphere of production. Consistent with this theory, we found that the contracts won by the locals of stable highly democratic international unions were systematically more likely to be prolabor on a set of critical provisions (management prerogatives, the right to strike, and the grievance procedure) than those won by locals of stable moderately democratic and stable oligarchical internationals. The contracts won by locals of internationals with organized factions also were far more likely to be prolabor than those won by unions with sporadic or no factions. This pattern also held within the CIO's political camps – left, right, and center. What's more, stable constitutional democracy, organized factions, and Communist leadership each had an independent effect in limiting capital's power in the immediate production process.[71]

Of course, neither democracy nor oligarchy ever comes into the world full blown. Rather, they are alternative possible paths of union development.

---

[69] Matles and Higgins (1974, pp. 12, 11).   [70] Stepan-Norris (1998).

[71] It should be remembered, however, that although the measured effect of radical leadership in the "complete" model is also in the predicted direction, it is not statistically significant at the conventional level (p < 0.12, two-tailed test).

The path a union takes, as we saw in Chapter 3, is determined by relatively contingent struggles among workers' parties having opposed conceptions of working-class interests and differing strategies and actual practices to protect and advance them.

So the results of this analysis, like those in previous chapters, are also consistent with the theory that political relations within classes (given "objective limits and possibilities") are relatively autonomous determinants of the relations between classes.[72]

In industries where employers were confronted by stable highly democratic unions having a vital inner political life, especially those led by radicals, the political regimes of production constructed there tended neither to subordinate the immediate interests of labor to capital nor to embody labor's "consent to exploitation." Rather, by denying management the "right" to exercise unilateral authority over production and by holding employers maximally accountable to the workers under their dominion, these political regimes of production embodied an altered balance of class power in the workers' favor. In a word, these were "counterhegemonic" production regimes, for they tended to subvert rather than sustain the immediate sway of capital over production.

---

[72] As we have emphasized, however, this analysis has abstracted from any actual variations in employers' resistance or accommodation to unionism in general and to specific provisions in the employment contract in particular. The question remains, then, whether differences in the political consciousness, strategy, and practices of employers, in their struggles with workers, affected the workers' own consciousness, strategy, and practices. How in turn did this affect both whether their unions would become democratic or authoritarian and, as a consequence, what the balance of class power would be in the sphere of production? Providing a systematic empirical answer to these questions would require research in primary materials aimed at characterizing both the original stance toward unionization taken by the major employers in each industry (that is, how and to what extent they resisted or accommodated workers' self-organization) and then, once the union was established in the industry, their continuing stance in collective bargaining, during the CIO era, with respect to each of the major contractual provisions. See Stevens (1994) for a preliminary analysis of how the strategy and tactics of employers in four industries confronted by union organizing drives in the 1930s affected the chances that Communists would win the new union's leadership.

7

"PIN MONEY" AND "PINK SLIPS"

Women's employment "outside the home" during the CIO era was always precarious, buffeted constantly by the cold winds of "traditional family values." Women were expected to be submissive mothers and daughters, and men, the breadwinners. Not only employers but also many if not most union leaders, as well as rank-and-file unionists, also held these values dear – agreeing that a woman's place was in the home, not in the nation's offices, factories, mines, and mills.

And anyway, if she had a paying job, it was only to earn "pin money." Once at work, she was carefully taught by "labor relations" counselors, in the words of the title of a syndicated newspaper series in early 1951, "How to Get Along with Men." Sure, a "girl" got paid less than her fellow male employees and was passed over in promotions. But, advised the series' author, Beatrice Vincent, she should just swallow that "bitter pill"; after all, "you can't do a blessed thing about . . . the firmly established order," so why go banging your "attractively coiffured head . . . against stone walls"? Just do your job, treat your boss right, and he'll take care of you, Miss Vincent recommended, like a valued, especially "delicate piece of human machinery."

The wisdom of Miss Vincent's advice provoked a response from Helen Kingery, another woman with a rather different slant on the matter, who was an activist and staff member of the expelled Communist-led United Office and Professional Workers (UOPW). She wrote:

> You can see, sisters – and brothers too – all those struggles waged over the years for the right of women to work at decent hours, and under decent conditions, were completely unnecessary. We can stop worrying and fighting together with our union brothers – because thousands of women still do the same work as men for less pay, because thousands of working mothers have no proper way to care for their children, because hundreds of firms discriminate against married women . . . all this is

radical stuff and all that is necessary is to remind the boss what delicate pieces of machinery we are.[1]

Women's Work

On the eve of World War II, the long-held consensus of so-called efficiency experts and their employers was that "women could excel at jobs requiring a high degree of dexterity, manipulative skill, and speed; those involving patience, attention to detail, and ability to perform well at repetitive tasks; and those that required working to close tolerances."[2] So only these sorts of lower-paying jobs were deemed appropriate for women.

The loss of millions of male industrial workers to military service in the defense buildup and especially during the war compelled employers to tap "the second sex" as a labor pool. Initially, women were mainly hired into unskilled and semiskilled jobs, but as jobs requiring a higher level of skill became vacant, employers began training them for, at least, some skilled jobs, which they were deemed capable of performing. Still, in most plants, de facto gender segregation and lower wages for women were the rule.

At peak war production in 1944, women comprised 33 percent of all manufacturing workers. But even though they had proven their mettle, when the war ended and servicemen came back looking for work, women were given "pink slips" and sent home, and postwar women's employment was vastly reduced: "[W]omen were thrown out of work at a rate nearly double that for men in the manufacturing sector as a whole," even though, as a 1944 survey had revealed, "85 percent of the women war workers who answered the survey wanted to remain in the labor force after the war, and almost all of them preferred to continue doing factory work."[3] By May of 1947, the percentage of all production workers who were women had fallen to 25 percent.[4]

The CIO and Women's Equality

The fledgling CIO did not put women's concerns high on its organizing agenda. But their cooperation and participation was needed in organizing, and women played an important role in many of the CIO's early strikes, especially during the wave of "sit-downs." Although the CIO proclaimed that it aimed to

---

[1] Kingery (1951, p. 24, ellipsis in original; the quotes from Vincent's series are Kingery's).
[2] Quoted in Campbell (1984, p. 115).   [3] Milkman (1991, pp. 489–90).
[4] U.S. Department of Labor, Bureau of Labor Statistics, 1947, Handbook of Labor Statistics, BLS Bulletin 916, p. 17.

organize "working men and women," only four of the delegates at its founding convention were women; that convention did not pass a single resolution specifically addressing the interests of working women, although it did pass one favoring "women's auxiliaries." A major vehicle for involving women in organizing and in support of strikes and other union activities, women's auxiliaries brought the wives, sisters, mothers, and daughters of union men together to educate them on the union cause.[5] They retained their importance even as women themselves became an increasing proportion of union members. An auxiliary was affiliated with a particular union, and served its membership's needs. But since the auxiliary was expected to address women's concerns, this too often gave a union license to ignore them.

The CIO as an organization did little to attend to the specific needs of women in the labor force and largely ignored them in postwar organizing. Few women were employed on the CIO's staff or as organizers. Typically, not more than 5 percent of the delegates at CIO conventions in the late 1940s and early 1950s were women. In the lengthy annual "state of the CIO" addresses delivered at CIO conventions by Philip Murray and Walter Reuther, who (after Murray's death) succeeded him as CIO president, "discussions of special problems or opportunities involving women workers played no role."[6] Still, CIO conventions repeatedly called for "women to have positions of responsibility and leadership in unions." They also "advocat[ed] state equal pay legislation."[7] In 1944, when – pulled by wartime needs for "manpower" – women's employment outside the home had reached a historic peak, the CIO adopted a program to advance women's equality, calling for (1) extending equal pay for equal work to all CIO contracts; (2) enacting state laws prohibiting wage discrimination on the basis of sex; (3) protecting women's employment through special seniority provisions in collective bargaining agreements, and ensuring adequate rest periods; (4) maternity leave without seniority loss, and inclusion of maternity coverage among health benefits; (5) establishing child-care centers, housing, and recreational facilities; and (6) establishing educational programs to bring women into union leadership.[8]

But to the fulfillment of this program, and other ways of advancing women's equality, CIO unions were not equally committed. Some devoted enormous energy to women's issues, but all too many apparently were satisfied with token gestures. The disparity was evident even in the constitutions of the CIO's internationals; in the late 1940s, only fifteen of thirty-five constitutions, or 43 percent, had an explicit provision guaranteeing membership to all eligible workers "regardless of sex" or had preambles welcoming all

---

[5] Foner (1980, pp. 326–27).   [6] Zieger (1995, pp. 349–50).
[7] Foner (1980, p. 374).   [8] Ibid., p. 174.

"working men and women" in the industry.[9] Notably, whether the women's share of union membership was "high" (40 percent or above) or "low" (below 40 percent) apparently did not affect the chances that an international's constitution guaranteed women equal access to membership: Of the thirteen internationals for which we have women's membership figures, the constitutions of three of the seven with a high women's membership as opposed to three of the six with a low women's membership had such a nondiscrimination clause.[10]

The CIO stood in principle for "equal pay for equal work." But women's wages were typically lower than men's, even for the same or similar work, throughout the CIO era. The skills they were thought to possess "naturally" (manual dexterity and attention to detail) were devalued by employers. The battle for gender equality at work – to abolish sexual discrimination in job classifications and wage scales, and to address women's distinctive needs – was fought unevenly by the CIO's international unions; and there was a great disparity among them in winning collective bargaining agreements that guaranteed equal pay for equal work. In our sample of local contracts dating from 1937 through 1955, only 21 percent had such a provision.[11]

Communists and Women's Equality

Socialists everywhere, since the days of Marx and Engels, were advocates of women's social equality. In America, the Industrial Workers of the World (IWW), the TUEL, and its successor the TUUL had emblazoned "the woman question" and the struggle for women's equality on their organizing banners. The Red union leagues had many women leaders and devoted special efforts to organizing women workers and fighting for their interests. In the first big strike initiated and led by the TUEL among wool and silk workers in and around Passaic, New Jersey, in 1926, women made up half of the workers; and in some

---

[9] We examined the constitutions of all of the CIO's durable internationals in 1948, or the nearest year. In the AFL, only 11.5 percent of all affiliates' constitutions had an explicit provision that all eligible workers could join, "regardless of sex" (according to information in Summers 1946, pp. 92–107).

[10] Log odds ratio (uniform association) = 0.17, not significant; standard error = 0.42. This calculation is, unfortunately, based on the membership figures we were able to find for only thirteen internationals, in 1944 – but at least this was a year when women's employment was at an all-time high. The highly incomplete membership data precludes controlling for the size of women's membership in the following analyses.

[11] The total number of local contracts in our sample, remember, is 236; but only 214 had relevant information on the equal pay for equal work provision.

of the other most heroic TUEL-led organizing drives and strikes in the mid- and late 1920s – for example, the strikes of the textile workers in Gastonia, North Carolina; the cotton workers in New Bedford, Massachusetts; and the millinery workers in Chicago and New York – a majority of the striking workers, and their TUEL leaders, were women. Communist Elizabeth Gurley Flynn, who had herself become famous in IWW strikes in Passaic and Paterson back in 1913, was an advisor to and champion of the 1926 strikers.[12] What TUEL organizer Ann Crayton told the militants leading the strikers in New Bedford in May 1928 is exemplary of the TUEL's militant sexual egalitarianism:

> Women are . . . more courageous than men. They will do more and suffer more. . . . [I]n the Passaic strike . . . women with baby carriages [were] leading the picket lines. Organize the women along with the men. Teach them to organize the picket lines . . . and let them learn to speak.[13]

At the TUUL's founding convention in 1929, a special Women's Conference was held in connection with it, out of which came a TUUL Women's Department. Of the 690 TUUL delegates, seventy-two were women, or about 10 percent; and two women were elected to TUUL's national committee. The delegates condemned the AFL's officialdom for neglecting women's needs and interests:

> The trade union leaders have altogether failed to defend the interests of the women workers, barring them from the unions and discriminating against them in industry, as they have done against the youth, the Negroes, and the foreign-born.[14]

The TUUL women's program called for equal pay for equal work; a minimum wage for women workers in agriculture and domestic service; a seven-hour day and five-day week; paid holidays; prohibition of hazardous work;

[12] Foner (1994, pp. 143–50). Flynn was to become a top Communist Party leader; and she was on the party's national board during Foster's disastrous chairmanship (which is discussed in Chapters 10 and 11).

[13] Foner (1994, pp. 115–16, 142–43, 164–72, 168; 1991, pp. 56–62).

[14] Quoted in Foner (1980, pp. 263–64). In the 1920s, over 3 million women worked at trades which came under the jurisdiction of AFL affiliates, but no more than 200,000 were members. The AFL's officials, presented with these figures by women unionists who urged a targeted organizing drive of women, responded that "a separate and distinctive movement confined to organizing women wage-earners . . . would be impracticable" (Foner 1991, p. 62).

paid maternity leave and provisions for nursing mothers; worker-run and employer-funded child-care; women's dressing and wash rooms; and the extension of all forms of social insurance to all women working for wages.[15] This 1929 program was so ahead of its time that it continues to be advanced even today, over seventy years later.

So at the core of earlier Red unionism's vital legacy to the CIO was the struggle for women's equality. This heritage was imparted, directly or indirectly, to over half of the CIO's internationals, but it was honored above all by the Communists and their allies.[16]

Even during World War II, despite the Communist Party's strident calls for "uninterrupted production" and class collaboration in the antifascist war, "the Communists . . . fought to open up employment opportunities for women, to win them equal pay on the job and equal citizenship within the labor movement." Women Communists often sharply criticized the "male chauvinism" of union leaders, including some close to the party, and castigated them for their laxity in bringing women into union leadership. "It is high time that outstanding male leaders, those of the left especially, take a stand on these issues," wrote Elizabeth Gurley Flynn in the *Daily Worker* in the fall of 1942, "and begin to practice what we all preach."[17]

Some, certainly, were already practicing what they preached. The United Federal Workers (which in 1946 merged with the Architects and Engineers to become the United Public Workers (UPW)) was the first national labor union to be headed by a woman, Eleanor Nelson; and when she was elected to the CIO's executive board, Nelson also became the first woman to join the top leadership of any American labor federation. When Marie Richardson Harris was elected as a Federal Workers national representative in 1941, she became "one of the first Black women to work at the national level in a labor union."[18]

And in the Communist-led Food, Tobacco, Agricultural and Allied Workers (FTA), "as in no other CIO union," leadership by women emerged at both the national and the local level.[19] In 1944, when Robbie Mae Riddick was elected as FTA international vice-president, this made her the first black woman to serve on the international executive board (IEB) of any CIO international.

[15] Foner (1980, p. 264).

[16] All nine of the internationals in the study whose findings we report in this chapter (Wilson 1993) were born in industries in which earlier Red unionists had been active or, as in ACW's case, had TUEL activists deeply involved in its inner struggles.

[17] Isserman (1982, pp. 140–41, citing the *Daily Worker*, August 21, 1942, p. 7). The Communist Party itself, as Isserman also notes, was one of the few organizations in the country at the time in which women considered it their right to challenge men's accepted prerogatives.

[18] Richardson (1987, p. 176); Ginger and Christiano (1987, p. 391).

[19] Rosswurm (1992, pp. 4–5).

She joined another female vice-president and three alternate vice-presidents who were already on the board.[20] The FTA also incorporated Mexican women into its local leadership positions to "an extraordinary extent" in Texas and California.[21]

Whatever the flaws Comrade Flynn saw in the "outstanding male leaders of the left," the Federal Workers and FTA, as we see below, were exemplary – to the extent that a modest comparison of nine internationals in three different camps can reveal – of the Communist camp's higher level of integration of women into union leadership. Indeed, all in all, as Robert Zieger puts it, the Communist-led internationals did "the best job among CIO affiliates in accommodating the special bargaining concerns of women workers and developing female leadership."[22] This generalization is buttressed and reinforced by the results of the analyses presented in this chapter.

Measuring the Struggle for Gender Equality

Despite the burgeoning scholarly attention to women and unionism, there is still little detailed information available on the situation of women in the CIO's internationals or their industrial fields. Most historians of the CIO era seem to implicitly assume that only men were industrial workers. As a result of this "myopic focus," as Steve Rosswurm calls it, scant information is available about the extent of women's representation and participation in the leadership of CIO internationals or the overall principled and practical commitment of these internationals to the struggle for women's rights.[23] Few published works even raise these questions and fewer still present hard data addressing them; they often convey the salient information, however valuable, in the form of impressionistic brush strokes, for example, that a given international had "incipient feminism within its ranks" and women were "important in its secondary leadership." We know of only one full-length study of CIO unionism and "gender at work."[24]

Now for two critical issues, (1) women's representation and participation in international union leadership and (2) the commitment to protecting and advancing women's rights and gender equality, we draw on a comparative analysis of nine internationals, three in each political camp, as of 1944 (or thereabouts), when women's employment in manufacturing reached a CIO-era peak. On two other critical issues, we have systematic data covering all of the durable CIO internationals: (3) equality of access to union membership, as provided by the international's constitution and, most important, (4) winning

---

[20] *Labor Fact Book* 7 (1945, p. 74); Wilson (1993, p. 60).   [21] Ruiz (1998, pp. 78–82).
[22] Zieger (1995, p. 349).   [23] Rosswurm (1992, p. xv).   [24] Milkman (1987).

provisions for "equal pay for equal work" in local union contracts, and in the national contracts of the "Big 3."

For issues 1 and 2, two desiderata guided the selection of the set of three internationals in each political camp: that the three had the highest and, if possible, comparable women's membership in that camp; and that they were formed during roughly the same years. The first desideratum was easier to suggest than to find in reality. The internationals were not distributed across the camps with similar percentages of woman members. The mean percentages of woman members for the three internationals selected in each camp were nearly the same in both the Communist and shifting camps – 42 versus 45 percent, respectively – but in the anti-Communist camp, the mean was only 20 percent.[25]

Surely, women's political participation and leadership – as partners in power – is both a vital aspect of women's equality and crucial in the struggle to ensure that the distinctive needs and interests of women workers are addressed. The levels of women's participation and leadership in the nine internationals were assessed by the prevalence of:

1. Women convention delegates, measured by the ratio of the percentage of delegates who were women to the percentage of all members who were women.
2. Women's representation on convention committees, measured by the ratio of the percentage of committee members who were women to the percentage of all members who were women (of course, in both of these preceding measures, a ratio of 1:1 indicates full equality).
3. Women's participation in convention debate, measured by the mean number of women delegates who spoke at the convention.
4. Women's international leadership, measured by the mean number of women who were international officers or on the IEB.

Whatever the levels of women's participation and leadership in an international union, a crucial question, of course, is how committed it is, in principle

[25] The nine internationals and the percentage of women members, as reported in their 1944 convention proceedings, unless otherwise noted, were Food, Tobacco, and Allied Workers (FTA, 50%); UE (40%); United Office and Professional Workers (UOPWA, 35%); Amalgamated Clothing Workers (ACW, 66%);** Retail, Wholesale, and Department Store Union (RWDSU, 40%);* UAW (28%); Textile Workers Union (TWUA, 40%);** USWA (11%); International Union of Marine and Shipbuilding Workers (IUMSBW, 10%).*1942; **1946. Except for the ACW, which was long an independent union before the CIO was founded, these internationals were organized around the same time, in the early drives of the CIO. Valerie Wilson (1993) carried out this study under the direction of Maurice Zeitlin, in partial fulfillment of the requirements for the M.A. in sociology, UCLA.

and practice, to the struggle for women's equality. This commitment in the nine internationals was assessed by the prevalence of convention resolutions supporting any or all of the following contractual provisions to ensure the equal treatment of men and women workers:

> 1. "equal pay for equal work"; 2. "comparable worth" (though that term had not yet entered the discourse, the issue was addressed by some unions), that is, support for making job classifications based only on skill or experience and opposition to job classifications based on sex; 3. women's seniority rights, that is, opposition to separate men's and women's seniority lists; 4. maternity benefits in medical insurance; and 5. making organizing women workers a priority, by targeting workplaces in which many of the workers were women.

Last, but not least, there is the question of support for economic reforms and, specifically, the enactment of legislation to enhance women's rights, employment equality, and overall equality in the nation's economic life. This commitment was assessed by the prevalence of convention resolutions endorsing legislation to ensure any or all of the following points:

> 1. equal pay for equal work; 2. extension of social security coverage to employment in domestic service and agricultural work, in which women predominated; 3. national medical insurance with maternity coverage; 4. increasing the minimum wage, which was to the benefit of women workers who were heavily concentrated in low-wage jobs; 5. government child care programs; and 6. *opposition* to the passage of an Equal Rights Amendment, which many left-wing unionists, men and women alike, saw during these years as a threat to hard-won legislation protecting women in the workplace.[26]

How, then, did the political consciousness of the leadership and the form of government, democratic or authoritarian, enter into determining a union's commitment to women's rights and the struggle for women's equality? Or,

---

[26] The issue divided feminists in the labor movement from their middle-class and professional counterparts from the first day the National Woman's Party called for an Equal Rights Amendment in 1921. The laborites feared that its passage would wipe out the protective legislation for women workers won at great cost over the years; most women were not in unions, and so had no protection at work, in great part as a result of the AFL's neglect; and most AFL affiliates disdained organizing women (and some straightforwardly excluded them from membership) because, after all, their job was "motherhood and family," not competing for work with men (Sealander 1982; Foner 1991, pp. 65–71; Kessler-Harris 1975).

in other words, how did the gender policies and practices of the Red-led and democratic internationals differ from their opposite numbers? We also ask how, and how much, the women's policies and practices of the "Big 3" differed. Given the limitations of our data, these are, alas, questions that we cannot answer adequately. But until other research makes possible more refined and systematic answers, the following rough ones will have to serve.

Women's Political Participation and Leadership

Analysis of the levels of women's participation and leadership in the political life of the nine internationals shows a consistent pattern, sharply differentiating the rival political camps: 1. *Women's delegates:* The ratios in the rival camps were: in the Communist camp, 0.58:1; in the shifting camp, 0.31:1; and in the anti-Communist camp, 0.28:1. 2. Women's representation on convention committees: The ratios in the rival camps were: in the Communist camp, 0.59:1; in the shifting camp, 0.25:1; and in the anti-Communist camp, 0.23:1. 3. *Women's participation in convention debate:* The mean numbers of women delegates who spoke at an international's convention in the rival camps were: in the Communist camp, 16; in the shifting camp, six; and in the anti-Communist camp, three. 4. *Women's representation:* The mean number of women who were international officers or board members in the rival camps were: in the Communist camp, 1.7; in the shifting camp, 0.7; and in the anti-Communist camp, 0.7.[27]

Equality of Treatment

Here, too, the pattern is sharp and clear. Resolutions at the conventions that endorsed one or more of the five proposed contract provisions were passed as follows: In the Communist camp, resolutions endorsed a mean of 3.0 provisions; in the shifting camp, 2.3; and in the anti-Communist camp, 0.33.[28]

---

[27] FTA: In 1944, two women were vice-presidents, and three were alternative vice-presidents (we do not include alternates in our counts). UE: In 1944, one women served on its IEB, and one of them as an alternative trustee. UOPWA: In 1944, two women served on its IEB. ACW: In 1946, one woman was a vice-president. RWDSU: In 1944, one woman served on the IEB. UAW: In 1944, no woman on the IEB (not until May 1966 was a woman elected to the UAW's IEB, as a member at large (Gabin 1990, p. 210)). TWUA: In 1944, two women served as international officers. USWA: In 1944, no woman was on the IEB. IUMSW: In 1944, no woman was on the IEB (Wilson 1993, pp. 59–60).

[28] The distribution of resolutions in support of these points was: FTA, 3; UE, 4; UOPWA, 2; ACW, 2; UAW, 4; RWDSU, 1; TWUA, 0; USWA, 1; IUMSBW, 0.

Economic Reforms

With respect to the call for legislative enactment of economic reforms to benefit women, there was no difference in the relative support of the internationals in the Communist and shifting camps: In both camps, resolutions endorsed a mean of 3.3 of the six proposed reforms, but the mean in the anti-Communist camp was only 1.3.

Constitutional Membership Equality

In guaranteeing membership to all eligible workers, "regardless of sex," surprisingly, the political camps did not line up quite as expected. At 50 percent, the sixteen Communist-led internationals had the highest percentage with a guarantee, but the ten in the shifting camp had the lowest percentage, not the nine in the anti-Communist camp: 30 percent of the former versus 44 percent of the latter.[29] A few years earlier, circa 1945, the pattern was similar, but the Communist-led internationals stood out even more in guaranteeing women's membership equality: 61 percent of the eighteen in the Communist camp, 30 percent of the ten in the shifting camp, and 40 percent of the ten in the anti-Communist camp had a guarantee of women's rights.[30]

Local Contracts

The last but surely most decisive evidence of the difference in the actual achievements of the CIO's rival political camps in winning women's employment equality is the pattern revealed in the local contracts won over the entire CIO era: 34 percent of the eighty-four local contracts of Communist-led international unions had an "equal pay for equal work" clause in them, as opposed to 10 percent of the sixty-seven in the shifting camp and 16 percent of the sixty-three in the anti-Communist camp.[31]

Union Democracy and Women's Equality

What difference did democracy and the presence of factions make? Did rank-and-file democracy – "members running their own union," as James J. Matles put it – and the give and take and open debate that this involves tend to create common understandings and sustain a sense of mutuality and common identity

[29] Log odds ratio (uniform association) = 0.17, not statistically significant; standard error = 0.42.
[30] Calculated from information in Summers (1946).
[31] Log odds ratio (uniform association) = 0.64, $p < 0.01$; standard error = 0.22.

among union men and women? Were women and men who were committed to protecting and advancing women's interests more successful in doing so where all workers' rights and liberties were constitutionally protected and organized factions contended for leadership? The answer is (with one exception) a decided yes.

Women's Rights

Among the set of nine internationals representative of the three political camps, the democratic ones were consistently more likely to encourage women's representation at their conventions and to support equality of treatment and call for economic reforms favoring women. The presence of factions, in contrast, did not have as consistent effects: The internationals with factions were less likely to include women in conventions but more likely to support equality of treatment and economic reforms.

Constitutional Membership Equality

The ten highly democratic internationals stood out: 60 percent of them guaranteed membership to all eligible workers, "regardless of sex," as compared with 43 percent of the fourteen moderately democratic and 27 percent of the eleven oligarchic internationals.[32] But as to factionalism and women's membership equality, the consistency of the pattern suddenly disappears: The eight internationals with sporadic factions were most likely and the ten with organized factions least likely to have a constitutional guarantee of membership equality: 62 percent of the former, as opposed to only 30 percent of the latter, and 40 percent of the five internationals without factions had such a guarantee.[33]

Local Contracts

Here, as expected, the stable democratic internationals and those with organized factions stood out in ensuring women's equal pay for equal work: 38 percent of the fifty local contracts of the stable highly democratic internationals and 30 percent of the fifty-four local contracts of stable moderately democratic internationals but only 13 percent of the thirty-seven local contracts of the stable oligarchies included an equal-pay clause.[34] As to

---

[32] Log odds ratio (uniform association) = 0.69, $p < 0.06$; standard error = 0.47.
[33] Log odds ratio (uniform association) = 0.34, not significant; standard error = 0.54.
[34] Log odds ratio (uniform association) = 0.62, $p < 0.01$; standard error = 0.26.

factionalism, 33 percent of the ninety-one local contracts of internationals with organized factions as compared with 10 percent of the fifty-nine contracts of the internationals with sporadic factions and 13 percent of the fifty-two contracts signed by those with no factions had such a clause.[35]

Now, did both radicalism and democracy have independent effects in determining an international union's commitment to women's equality? When we control for each of them in determining the chances that the constitution guaranteed membership to all eligible workers, "regardless of sex," we find that democracy did have an independent effect but that political camp, to the extent an appropriate comparison is possible, did not. In the non-Communist camps combined, 30 percent of the ten stable oligarchic internationals as opposed to 50 percent of the eight democratic internationals (high and moderate combined) had a constitutional guarantee of equality. The Communist camp had only one oligarchic international, ILWU, and it had no guarantee. So this does not allow a reliable contrast to the democratic Communist internationals. But we can compare the democratic internationals in the Communist and non-Communist camps; and their percentages barely differ: 53 percent of the fifteen stable democratic Communist-led internationals versus 50 percent of the eight stable democratic non-Communist internationals had a constitutional guarantee of membership equality.

On the crucial issue, however, of winning a provision ensuring "equal pay for equal work" in an international's local contracts, both radicalism and democracy mattered. In the non-Communist camp, 21 percent of the forty-two local contracts of the stable democratic internationals but only 13 percent of the thirty-seven local contracts of the stable oligarchic internationals had such a provision. Among the stable democratic internationals, the contrast between the political camps is sharp: 42 percent of the sixty-two local contracts of the Communist-led internationals, as opposed to 21 percent, or half that many, of the forty-two local contracts in the non-Communist camps had an "equal pay for equal work" provision.[36] As to factionalism and radicalism, and to the extent that an appropriate comparison is possible, we find that only radicalism mattered: Among the unions with factions, an equal-pay clause was included in 35 percent of the seventy-eighth local contracts of the Communist-led unions but only 13 percent of the seventy-five contracts of the non-Communist unions. Of those without factions, 13 percent of the

---

[35] Log odds ratio (uniform association) = 0.73, $p < 0.01$; standard error = 0.24.

[36] Because our one Communist-led union that we classified as oligarchic (ILWU) is classified as moderately democratic using Summers data, we could not place it in a "stable" category, and, hence, it drops out of the analysis. So, since the stable oligarchic category has no Communist-led union, we cannot make the appropriate comparison here.

fifty-two non-Communist union contracts included such a clause. None of the Communist-led internationals lacked factions, remember, so no comparison here is possible.

The "Big 3"

The "objective conditions" facing women and the unions in the electrical, auto, and steel industries differed greatly. On the eve of World War II, in October 1940, there were substantial differences in these industries' levels of women's employment. The percentage of all production workers in the manufacturing of electrical machinery was 32.2; in automobiles, 5.7; and in iron and steel, 6.7. The only jobs held by women within the steel mills before the war were in sorting and inspecting tin plate.[37]

Electrical

In the electrical industry, from the early years of the twentieth century on, employers considered women workers appropriate for "light labor, in which either boys or girls or men or women can be employed," and they hired many women, at much lower wages than men, especially in labor-intensive production work.[38] Auto employers, in contrast, resisted hiring women. Henry Ford famously disapproved of women working "outside the home" altogether and declared that women who did hold jobs "did so in order to buy fancy clothes." Yet when women did get jobs in that industry, as Ruth Milkman points out, the jobs they did in "a particular plant came to be viewed as requiring a feminine touch, even though elsewhere the identical operation might be seen as intrinsically suited to men." In the steel industry, despite employers' prewar reluctance to hire women, by 1943, in the middle of the war, women were employed in most divisions.[39]

At peak war production, in 1944, half of all workers in the electrical industry, a quarter in auto, and something over a quarter in steel were women.[40] But in the immediate postwar years, women were thrown out of their jobs in auto and steel to make way for returning servicemen; and along with this came a return to prewar conceptions about the woman's place. So, for example, in February 1946, an auto industry representative said that "reconversion meant that the

---

[37] As early as 1910, over a third of the "operatives and laborers" in the electrical industry were women. That year, women in this category constituted less than 3 percent of all auto workers. Milkman (1987, pp. 50, 12); Foner (1980, p. 342).   [38] Foner (1980, p. 342).

[39] Milkman (1987, p. 19); Foner (1980, p. 342).

[40] Milkman (1987, p. 13); Bureau of Labor Statistics (1947, pp. 17–18).

wartime light assembly work involved in airplanes gave way to the heavy, tiring assembly work of cars. . . . Women can't handle such tough work."[41] In the steel industry, too, the jobs that women did throughout the war suddenly became "unsuitable" for a woman.[42]

The electrical industry had more continuity in women's employment in the postwar period than did auto or steel. At the end of 1945, some 40 percent of the UE's members were women, 28 percent of UAW's, and 11 percent of USWA's.[43] In 1946, women made up just under 40 percent of the work force in the electrical industry, but women's share of the work force in the auto industry had fallen to 9 percent and, in steel, to 10 percent.[44]

So how did the "Big 3" differ in their programs and policies on women?

UE's constitution called for the unification of "all workers in our industry on an industrial basis . . . regardless of sex," and it was a virtual clarion call for the union: UE was in continual conflict with Westinghouse and GE over women's employment equality. As the number of women in the industry swelled, UE fought to prevent the companies from substituting women for men as a way of cutting wages. "Both Westinghouse and GE went to great lengths to do so," according to Milkman, "shifting jobs from one plant to another and changing men's jobs into women's jobs – at substantially reduced pay."

UE's leadership recognized the arbitrariness of the boundaries between so-called men's and women's jobs in electrical manufacturing and challenged the entire basis of wage discrimination by sex. UE's 1945 National War Labor Board (NWLB) case against Westinghouse and GE, for instance, "was the most comprehensive challenge on the issue," says Milkman. "It made the demand feminists [today] . . . call 'equal pay for comparable worth.'" The issue, as the War Labor Board's decision pointed out, was "that the jobs customarily performed by women are paid less, on a comparable job content basis, than the jobs customarily performed by men" and that "this relative underpayment constitutes a sex discrimination."[45]

Women's rights were regularly a focus of UE's conventions, official publications, and contract demands. UE "actively pressed demands for women's job training centers, equal pay for equal work, no sex differentials, and free child care centers." When World War II began, the national staff had only two women; a few years later, thirty-six staff members were women, or one

[41] Gabin (1990, p. 114).   [42] Foner (1980, p. 541).   [43] Hutchins (1952, pp. 65–66).
[44] Milkman (1987, p. 13); Bureau of Labor Statistics (1947, pp. 17–18).
[45] Milkman (1987, pp. 78–80). In 1944, the War Labor Board had already taken an important step in this direction, when it ruled that "a study of job content and job evaluation should afford the basis for setting 'proportionate rates for proportionate work'" (War Labor Board 1944).

fourth of the total.[46] One woman served on the international executive board beginning in 1944, and by 1946, one woman was on the IEB and one was an international representative. In 1952, two women served on the IEB.[47] During this period, women were also prominent in secondary leadership roles. At the 1944 convention, 13 percent of the delegates were women (at a time when women constituted 40 percent of UE's members, or a ratio of 0.32:1).[48]

All women workers represented by UE benefited from the union's struggle for women's rights, but black women apparently were its special beneficiaries. As a whole, in all industries, "the male labor force proved to be more racially flexible than the female labor force"; in part, this resulted from the even more intense white prejudice against black women than against black men.[49] Any CIO union's ability to fight employment discrimination against black women was consequently more limited than it was for black men. In the electrical industry, black women were "the least favored group of workers." In the immediate postwar years, the overall proportion of women production workers employed in electrical manufacturing dropped by over a fifth (from a high of 49 percent of total employment in 1944 to 39 percent in 1950). Yet despite this sharp decline in women's electrical employment, "by 1950, *black* representation among *women* electrical workers was slightly *greater* than among men."[50]

UE, in Milkman's words, had a "radical vision of a transformation in gender relations in industry," and this "vision must have been nurtured by Communist influence in the union." She argues, however, that "*the critical factor* leading to the union's sophisticated approach to the equal pay issue was the structure of the electrical industry itself and its prewar sexual division of labor."[51] But "industry structure" does not produce a "radical vision," let alone a "sophisticated" strategy in accord with that vision. Real, and fallible, men and women do.

---

[46] Critchlow (1976, p. 233).

[47] Labor Fact Book 7 (1945, p. 74); Labor Fact Book 8 (1947, p. 127); Labor Fact Book 11 (1953, p. 89).

[48] Zieger (1995, p. 256); Wilson (1993, p. 59).

[49] The rate of increase of black male employment in all manufacturing from 1940 on was some three times the black female rate. Black workers made their biggest wartime gains in industries that predominantly employed men. But even in traditional female clerical and sales jobs, the gains of black women were negligible. Domestic service, though it declined markedly from the prewar years, remained their primary occupation: In 1944, 45 percent of the black women in the labor force were domestic workers; in 1950, the figure was still 40 percent (Anderson 1982, pp. 82–85; Boris 1998).

[50] Milkman (1987, pp. 55–56, emphasis added).

[51] Ibid., pp. 77, 152, 82, emphasis added.

If "structure" had been the "critical factor," we would expect to find, for instance, that the International Brotherhood of Electrical Workers (IBEW) – UE's counterpart in the AFL – was also as "sophisticated," foresighted, and effective as UE in protecting and advancing women's rights in its own shops. Yet neither the influx of women members into IBEW, who made up somewhere over a third of IBEW's industrial union membership at the time, nor its having to compete with UE – which in head-on organizing battles repeatedly made an issue of IBEW's treatment of women as second class, or "B," members – stimulated a noticeable IBEW commitment, let alone a "sophisticated approach," to the cause of women's rights.[52] Only in 1946 did IBEW drop the word "male" from its constitution and formally grant women full-fledged union membership and the right to hold elective office.[53] Even so, a decade later women at some IBEW plants continued to have seniority lines separate from men or, worse, were still fired when they got married. The UE allowed no such practices in its plants. Not until the 1960s, especially after the passage of the 1964 Civil Rights Act, did women in the IBEW begin "to demand equal rights within the organization, and ... [try] to persuade recalcitrant locals to amend some longstanding discriminatory practices."[54]

Even more instructive is a comparison between the approaches to women's rights by the UE and IUE, the CIO's rival anti-Communist union set up in UE's jurisdiction. One of the major changes UE had won at Westinghouse in thirteen years of struggle, 1936–49, was the solidification of the seniority system; it achieved this both by codifying existing shop-floor practices and strengthening the rules governing layoffs and rehirings as well as upgrading and promotions. It also won broad seniority units, usually departmental, if the unit had over 1,000 workers; but it also often won plantwide seniority in smaller plants; and the seniority units usually were determined not by the national contract but by what the workers on the shop floor extracted through local supplements. UE's international leadership consistently supported these local struggles to win "broad seniority units," as Mark McColloch points out, "because they were equitable and would generate the greatest internal solidarity."

---

[52] By the 1960s, one third of all IBEW members were women (Palladino 1991, p. 248), but because virtually all of them were employed in electrical manufacturing, they probably constituted a far higher percentage of the membership of the Brotherhood's industrial locals in the 1940s. Few women were employed as electricians in the construction trades well into the 1980s.

[53] UE's 1938 founding constitution pledged to "unite all workers in our industry ... regardless of craft, age, sex, nationality, race, creed, or political beliefs" (Palladino 1991, p. 159).

[54] McColloch (1992, p. 198); Palladino (1991, pp. 248, 250).

UE was a pathbreaker in winning unified seniority lists, undivided by race, ethnicity, or – crucially – sex, despite Westinghouse's prewar practice of maintaining separate seniority lists for men and women, a practice relaxed during the war and which the company tried, unsuccessfully, to reimpose in the immediate postwar period. Most UE locals resisted the company's attempt, with strong support by the international leadership. "By 1949, most locals had unified seniority lists. When right-wing local leaders attempted to resurrect or defend the discrimination against married women, the UE opposed them, usually successfully."[55]

After the anti-Communist IUE and Westinghouse signed their first full contract in the fall of 1950, the company tried to take advantage of the union split to narrow and limit the UE's hard-won seniority provisions, especially those protecting women. Women's equality then eroded quickly at IUE locations. In fact, at over a dozen locals, supplements to the national IUE contract specified that "married women will not be considered for employment if their husbands are able to work." If women employees married, they became the first to go in case of a layoff. After decisive IUE local retreats, even where contractual discrimination against married women did not exist, "there were separate seniority lists for men and women at almost every major IUE location in the late 1950s." In sharp contrast, at the same time that UE's top leaders James Matles and Julius Emspak and others in its district and lower echelon leadership still were being harassed by the federal government and fighting off raids by IAM and IBEW, UE continued to press its districts and locals, according to McColloch, to try to win (or retain) a contractual provision prohibiting sexual discrimination. Most important, according to McColloch, there was "no example, in this period, of the UE narrowing seniority units or establishing separate seniority units for women."[56]

The strategy of UE's leadership, as Milkman puts it, anticipated "by several decades the struggles being waged today for 'equal pay for comparable worth.'" But devising and implementing an effective strategy, especially one so far advanced for its time, requires a "radical vision"; and it also takes intelligence, analysis, conviction, discussion among comrades, debate with and, if necessary, organizing and defeating intraunion opposition, as well as an exhausting expenditure of time and energy, working long and hard days.

Auto

Women were relatively new to the automobile industry, and not only the auto companies but UAW leaders initially resisted employing women on "men's

[55] McColloch (1992, p. 194).   [56] Ibid., pp. 194, 196, 198.

jobs." But once the war-induced labor shortage compelled employers to hire women, the leadership put its weight behind the "equal pay for equal work" policy as a strategy for maintaining wage standards.[57] Initially, the UAW argued that jobs performed by men were "male" jobs and that women who performed them should receive the higher male rate.[58] In 1942, though, the UAW, jointly with UE, brought a case against GM to the NWLB, and the board decided in favor of the equal pay for equal work principle.[59] This constituted a landmark decision despite the War Labor Board's weak enforcement and failure to apply it to all industries. Eventually, the UAW made the case for higher wages for women auto workers by acknowledging that the distinction between men's and women's work was arbitrary and irrelevant. But UAW leaders continued to speak (in reaction to NWLB arbitration, for example) of "men's jobs" and "women's jobs," which frustrated its later efforts to challenge occupational segregation by sex.[60] UAW never confronted the overall structure of job segregation and the undervaluing of women's work.[61] So, in the end, although the gender gap in wages narrowed in the auto industry during the war, the UAW "fell short of delivering on the promise of the equal pay principle" with regard to pay equity and wider access to jobs.[62]

Separate seniority lists for men and women were commonly used in the prewar auto industry to limit women's access to jobs. The War Labor Board ruled on several cases brought before it that separate seniority lists were no longer permissible. In the aftermath of this decision, the UAW's IEB adopted a resolution in February 1944 opposing the establishment of separate seniority lists in plants where single lists were already in effect, but it failed to mention – much less oppose – the "more blatantly discriminatory practice of providing only temporary seniority for women employed in "men's jobs" for the duration of the war.[63] This policy deprived women of reemployment rights in the auto industry after the war.

In the prewar period, employers in the auto industry had preferred to hire single women, though they often also hired married women, who were the first to be laid off when production slackened. Employers also routinely discharged women when they became pregnant. UAW's international leadership took no stance on the issue of married women's employment or of job loss as a result of pregnancy; they dodged these issues by leaving them to "local autonomy" to decide on. Late in the war, in February 1944, UAW's international executive board finally "adopted a formal policy defending the rights of pregnant workers and issued a model maternity clause for inclusion in contracts."[64]

---

[57] Milkman (1987, pp. 67, 76)   [58] Gabin (1990, p. 62).   [59] Ibid., p. 63.
[60] Ibid., pp. 67–69.   [61] Milkman (1987, p. 77).   [62] Gabin (1990, p. 69).
[63] Ibid., p. 70.   [64] Ibid., p. 80.

UAW also made a serious effort to integrate women into the life of the union during the war. According to a survey by the UAW's Education Department in August 1944, in 73 percent of the locals surveyed, women were active as shop stewards; in 60 percent, women served as members of the local's executive board; and in 37 percent, women served on the plant bargaining committee and other negotiating committees.[65] In 1944, UAW had no woman international officer (and the international board was to remain an all-male preserve until the 1960s).[66] Slightly over 5 percent of the delegates at the UAW convention were women (at a time when 28 percent of UAW's members were women, or a ratio of 0.19:1); and seven women delegates spoke at the convention. The convention passed resolutions supporting four of the provisions on equal treatment of men and women workers, and five of the six proposed economic reforms favoring women's interests.[67] And that same year, UAW established a Women's Bureau, charged with developing and recommending policies and programs affecting women members.[68]

Still, when the war ended, women were not able to resist being laid off. The employers wanted to bring the men back in, and often, when women were called back to work from layoffs, they used strategies such as placing them on jobs that were physically too demanding for them in order to have reason to discharge them.[69] Although UAW's top leadership and the Women's Bureau were supportive, most local union leaders did not give the women "full support."[70]

Yet women's advances in the auto industry were not insubstantial. The UAW had begun to make a serious "critique of the sexual division of labor" during World War II. The union codified antidiscrimination policies; women unionists consolidated their own network; and the Women's Bureau became an institutionalized, independent advocate of women's rights.[71]

Women auto unionists sought to eliminate barriers to equality in employment through not only collective bargaining but legislation and government action, with the support of UAW's top leadership. But not until 1948 did UAW's women succeed in having the international constitution annotated to say that "[i]n all places in the Constitution in which reference is made to the masculine it should be deemed to include the feminine." In 1951, UAW's women pressed, but failed, to get "sex" included in the federal contract compliance code's existing requirement that government contractors not discriminate

---

[65] Ibid., p. 86.

[66] By the end of the war, though, the UAW claimed to have some 300 local women officers (ibid., p. 93).

[67] Wilson (1993, p. 59).   [68] Milkman (1987, p. 92).

[69] Gabin (1990, pp. 117–18); Milkman (1987, pp. 113–14).

[70] Gabin (1990, p. 119); Milkman (1987, pp. 137–38).   [71] Gabin (1990, p. 142).

against job applicants or employees on the basis of race, creed, color, or national origin. But they could not overcome employer opposition and Labor Department indifference.[72]

Ultimately, as Nancy Gabin observes, "UAW leaders may have committed themselves verbally to extirpating the source of women's separate and unequal status in the auto industry, but in practice they confirmed the codification of that status in contracts."[73]

Steel

Unfortunately, as Mary Margaret Fonow observes, "there is very little documentation about gender and the steelworkers in just about any time period you name."[74] This is so because the advancement of women's interests in the industry, and women's participation and representation in USWA's inner political life, were not prominent on the USWA agenda. In 1944, USWA had no woman international officer; women comprised 3 percent of the USWA delegates at its convention (at a time when women made up 11 percent of the union's membership, or a ratio of 0.29:1); only one woman was represented on a convention committee; and no women spoke. No convention resolutions were even broached in favor of fighting for contract provisions to promote equal treatment of women workers (e.g., equal pay, comparable worth, maternity insurance, or equal seniority protection), although the convention did declare its support to try to organize women salaried employees. Resolutions were passed also in support of government child care programs, extending social security to domestic service and agricultural employment, and raising the federal minimum wage.[75] USWA men remained leery of women workers, and the leadership was especially uneasy about having women in the mills, even though USWA's 1948 constitution stated plainly that the union aimed to serve both "workmen and working women eligible for membership." Fonow's search through the USWA archives turned up little: some information on women's auxiliaries, some complaints from women that the union was not supportive enough, and some remarks from a subdistrict director who thought "girlies" belonged in the kitchen.[76] (As late as the 1970s, USWA's leaders still did not think women's rights were "really worth fighting for," as a woman steel worker reported, because there were "so few of us and our votes don't count so much."[77])

---

[72] Ibid., p. 157.   [73] Ibid., p. 173.

[74] Fonow to Stepan-Norris, August 2000, personal correspondence.

[75] Wilson (1993, p. 61).   [76] Fonow (forthcoming).

[77] Foner (1980, p. 541). Not until 1974 did significant numbers of women begin to enter the steel mills and become members of the USWA. And even then, it was not due to the

"Big 3" Contracts

The overall pattern of differences in the defense and advance of women's interests by the "Big 3" is seen clearly in the sample of local contracts over the entire CIO era, 1937–50: 48 percent of UE's thirty-one, 19 percent of UAW's thirty-one, and only 2 percent of USWA's forty-one included a provision of "equal pay for equal work." But the pattern differentiating the Big 3 is somewhat less sharp in the contracts that the international union's own executive board negotiated over the CIO years with the industry's major employer, that is, between UE and GE, UAW and GM, and USWA and USS: All 10 of the UE/GE national contracts, 1938–50, had an "equal pay for equal work" provision. All four of the UAW/GM national contracts, 1942–48, contained such a provision, as did three of the five USWA/USS national contracts 1937–47.[78]

Conclusion

In sum, the Communist-led internationals stood out, by all measures, in the struggle for women's rights, and in bringing women themselves into the leadership of that struggle. Democracy, too, made a big difference: The highly democratic internationals were far more likely than the oligarchic ones to guarantee women equality of membership and to win local contracts that ensured "equal pay for equal work."

A comparison of the records of the UE, UAW, and USWA – the "Big 3" – with each other also shows that UE had a superior record of fighting for and winning women's employment equality. The electrical industry, in contrast to auto and steel, long had employed and continued throughout the CIO era and immediate postwar decade to employ many women. In this "objective situation," in marked contrast to IUE and the IBEW, UE's radical leadership was ready, willing, and able to fight for and to win major concessions from the companies and make big strides toward women's employment equality in the industry. UAW's leaders, with far fewer women employed in the auto industry, did not expend themselves steadily, as did UE's leadership, to defend and advance women's rights, and won much less. USWA's leadership seemed

---

actions of the unions or the industry management, but a result of "the 1974 'consent decree' instituting quotas, which resulted from a combination of mass pressure and legal action by black workers and women." And these gains have not held steadily in the aftermath (Foner 1980, p. 541; Deaux and Ullman 1983, pp. 82–83).

[78] The contracts were negotiated by SWOC, and then USWA, with Carnegie-Illinois and then U.S. Steel.

almost as resistant as the employers were to hiring women, especially in the steel mills, and the union made little effort to advance women's rights, either during the war or afterward.

The pattern of principled and practical commitments to women's equality revealed here, as we see in the next two chapters, is replicated as well in our analysis of radicalism, democracy, and racial egalitarianism.

8

THE "BIG 3" AND INTERRACIAL
SOLIDARITY

Blacks don't have the "speed and rhythm" for factory work, declared the head of the Michigan Manufacturers' Association on the eve of World War II, and he assured government investigators that "most Michigan employers have the same belief." This was certainly the belief and the practice among auto employers (with the eccentric exception of Henry Ford). They simply refused to hire blacks, except, occasionally, as janitors. Two years into the war, with black employment increasing in many automotive plants – as a combined result of the "labor shortage" and the UAW's push, in cooperation with the FEPC, to open jobs for blacks – auto employers were still complaining that blacks "leave the job easily and are absent a lot." In "automobile equipment," black employment was 3.6 percent in 1940 (overwhelmingly at Ford) and rose to a high of 15 percent in 1945.

"Employers in electrical manufacturing," as Ruth Milkman points out, "were even more hesitant to hire blacks" than in the auto industry. In 1940, 0.5 percent of the workers in "electrical machinery" were black; a year after Pearl Harbor, the figure was only 1.3 percent; and at the wartime employment peak, it was only 2.9 percent.[1]

Black employment was so low in electrical manufacturing because employers relied on reserves of white women workers to meet their requirements. Robert C. Weaver, head of the Negro Employment Office of the War Production Board, observed in 1946 that "those industries which delayed longest the employment of Negroes . . . were usually light and clean manufacturing. They were the industries in which [white] women . . . were used in the largest proportions."[2] Even during wartime, electrical manufacturers "introduced blacks only in localities where they had no alternative."[3]

---

[1] Milkman (1987, pp. 54–55); Weaver (1946, pp. 15–80).
[2] Milkman (1987, p. 55).
[3] Weaver (1946, p. 81).

The steel industry was already hiring more black workers than the auto and electrical industries in the prewar years, especially for otherwise shunned labor in the foundries and furnaces. In "iron and steel," black employment was 5.5 percent in 1940, but by mid-1942 it leaped to 18 percent, and then rose by the end of 1943 to 25 percent, where it stayed through the end of the war.[4]

After three years of war, in December 1944, UE had some 40,000 black members out of a total membership of half a million, or 8 percent of the total. In absolute numbers, though not relatively, both of the other two "Big 3" unions had over twice as many black members. USWA had 95,000, or nearly 16 percent of its total membership of 600,000. UAW had 90,000, or 9 percent of its total membership of 1 million.[5]

In the next chapter, we assess the effects of rank-and-file democracy and radicalism in determining interracial solidarity in terms of three practical expressions of it, namely: (1) equality of access to membership, (2) black representation in the highest councils, and (3) establishment, during the war, of special "equalitarian racial machinery" to combat racism, such as a fair employment committee or committee to abolish discrimination.[6] The question for this chapter is, How did the "Big 3" unions compare on these aspects of solidarity?

Each had a constitutional guarantee against racial discrimination. Yet, according to Sumner Rosen, "segregated locals existed at one time or another" in both the UAW and USWA.[7] Indeed, the UAW's Walter Reuther refused to move resolutely to integrate the Dallas, Memphis, and Atlanta locals because this would have lost him right-wing votes and tipped the balance of strength in the international to the so-called left–center bloc.[8] Neither UE nor USWA established a committee to abolish discrimination during the war, whereas UAW did; but, as in other internationals in the shifting camp, UAW established its "interracial committee" under pressure from black unionists and the strong "Communist left" faction, which was "the most militant on racial issues" in the UAW and was "the main force behind the union's program for combating discrimination."[9] Alone among the Big 3, the UE had an elected black officer, although, according to Donald Critchlow, "it was not until 1945

---

[4] Milkman (1987, pp. 54–55); Weaver (1946, pp. 15–80).
[5] Black membership: Labor Research Association (1945, p. 73); total membership: Huberman (1946, pp. 166–80).
[6] Marshall (1964, pp. 249, 187n40). We discuss each of these as measures of interracial solidarity in the next chapter.
[7] Rosen does not say how many segregated locals each had or when or for how long these locals existed (1968, p. 204).
[8] Rosen (1968, p. 204). [9] Stevenson (1993, p. 50); Record (1951, p. 306).

that the first Black was elected to a national office. . . . " The CP's labor secretary even publicly upbraided UE as late as mid-1949 for being, in his view, laggard in fostering black representation. Most "Left-led" internationals had blacks active in their national leadership, he said, but UE, "despite certain very good [civil rights] activities . . . , has not yet faced up to the task of promoting and integrating Negro members into all levels of leadership."[10]

UE

UE's leaders, according to Sumner Rosen, had "a commitment to racial equality" and a record, according to Harvey Levenstein, of "combating discrimination in both shop and union affairs [that] was generally exemplary."[11] This is disputed by Critchlow, however, who argues that UE's record on "the black question" was not outstanding: "[T]he UE on the national level," he says, "virtually ignored the 'Negro problem' in internal union affairs and in the electrical industry. . . . [T]he national leadership generally ignored the integration of Blacks into the union."[12]

The figures on UE's black membership, however, do not lend support to Critchlow's claim. According to his own figures, black employment in the electrical manufacturing industry fell between 1940 and January 1945 from 5 percent to 2.7 percent.[13] But in December 1944, as we noted above, the black share of UE's total membership stood at 8 percent. In other words, blacks were "overrepresented" in UE by over three times their share of employment in the industry itself.

In contrast, the other major union representing workers in that industry, the AFL's IBEW, excluded blacks. During the war, IBEW became a virtual industrial union in electrical manufacturing and more than sextupled the number of its members, to some 350,000, most of whom joined its industrial locals.[14] IBEW rarely challenged UE in the bigger manufacturing plants, but it organized smaller manufacturing concerns throughout the country, where it engaged UE in a continual running battle.[15] Even during World War II, IBEW

---

[10] Critchlow (1976, p. 236); Williamson (1949a, p. 32). We focus on Critchlow's critique because it is a more or less systematic attempt by a historian to compare the racial policies and practices of two Communist-led international unions, and the one on which many writers rely for their characterization of UE's.

[11] Rosen (1968, p. 205); Levenstein (1981, p. 332).   [12] Critchlow (1976, pp. 231–32).

[13] Ibid., p. 235.

[14] By 1954, 75 percent of IBEW membership would belong to its industrial locals (Palladino 1991, pp. 181, 217).

[15] Ibid., pp. 162–66, 171–73.

continued its prewar "traditional racial policy" toward blacks and excluded them from its new industrial local unions, just as it excluded them from its construction locals. As the president of an IBEW local in Cincinnati explained: "We don't want the Negroes to stick their foot in the door. We don't want them for competitors in the postwar period." Another representative of the same local said: "We represent the voice of the people. The voice of the people is that they will not work with niggers."[16]

In vying with the IBEW to represent manufacturing workers, UE organizers made sure to let them know about IBEW's racism. For instance, a *UE Organizer's Bulletin*, "Some Facts on the International Brotherhood of Electrical Workers" (March 31, 1950), published excerpts from an Urban League report that criticized the IBEW for maneuvering "either to exclude Negro workers or limit the number employed." Indeed, as IBEW's authorized historian herself observes, "it took the rise of a national civil rights movement – and the threat of federal legislation – to persuade the international to act on their [black workers'] behalf."[17]

Critchlow says that the UE international "did not initiate any FEPC actions [during the war] against electrical companies that practiced discrimination." No policy to upgrade blacks or place them in jobs from which they were excluded was ever articulated, he says, in any UE "Officer's Report to a [wartime convention], in any pamphlet, or in any *UE News* editorial."[18] He argues that "the most important factor in determining" the UE international leadership's reticence on issues of racial discrimination was the small percentage of blacks in the electrical industry and, consequently, the small black membership in UE. But, as our quantitative analysis in the next chapter shows, Communist-led internationals that had a small black membership scored much higher in interracial solidarity than those with a large black membership; they also scored far higher than their counterparts in the non-Communist camps. So the small size of UE's black membership per se does not qualify as "the most important factor" determining the apparent reticence of UE's international officials to make the fight for equality of black workers a national priority.

UE's representatives see their own record much differently than Critchlow's characterization. For instance, Russ Nixon, UE's Washington, D.C., representative, wrote to NAACP Chairman Roy Wilkins, in a letter dated January 17, 1950: "As I am sure you know, *throughout its existence the UE has been in the forefront of the fight against discrimination, for fair employment practices and for civil rights legislation.* Since you are well-acquainted with the long history of

---

[16] Hill (1985, pp. 242–43).   [17] Palladino (1991, pp. 252–53).
[18] Critchlow (1976, pp. 232, 234). We have not, alas, been able to study FEPC or UE files to examine this record independently.

these issues, you will know that this is true as far as the UE is concerned on a shop level, in the community, in the states, and here in the Capital."[19]

Critchlow acknowledges that the UE international cooperated closely in "community work with liberal reform organizations, such as the Committee to Abolish the Poll Tax, the NAACP, and the Committee for a Permanent FEPC," and also acted as a potent pressure group in Washington, D.C., in support of the FEPC. But he denies that the international made black employment rights a priority.[20]

In contrast to the situation in the UAW, as we see below, the issues of black representation in the leadership or of active support for civil rights do not seem to have played a role in the intraunion factional conflicts between the "left" and "right" in UE over the years. Because UE was a large, decentralized international union, as we know, whose locals and powerful districts enjoyed considerable autonomy, a systematic comparison of the racial policies and practices of left-led and right-led locals and districts would be especially revealing. Unfortunately, the data are not available to allow a systematic internal comparative analysis. Yet we were able to cull some suggestive information from published accounts and public documents on several locals in UE's New York–New Jersey, Philadelphia, Milwaukee, and St. Louis districts. How representative these are of the general pattern of race relations in UE locals, we do not know.

New York–New Jersey Locals

UE locals in the New York–New Jersey metropolitan area were conspicuous in their commitment to racial justice. Locals in New York city waged a concerted antidiscrimination campaign during World War II. A report by black New Dealer Robert C. Weaver, chief of the War Production Board's Division on Negro Employment, singled them out for praise. UE Local 1225 established a fair employment practice committee of its own to fight discrimination. It investigated "the status of minority group employment . . . [in] all [UE] shops; the local referred Negroes, Jews, and persons of foreign extraction to all shops": If these persons were refused employment, the local took the issue to management; if management continued to discriminate, the workers in the shop met to pass a resolution against discrimination, and then again "sent a qualified worker of the race, color, or creed discriminated against to the plant . . . [and] if this worker was [also] refused employment, the case was sent to the President's [FEPC]."

Other UE locals in district 4 followed this lead. They organized a campaign to raise the black share of employment among the city's electrical workers to

[19] NAACP (1988, Reel 6: 0182, emphasis added).   [20] Critchlow (1976, p. 234).

20 percent. Although that goal was not reached, the campaign succeeded in less than a year (between May 1942 and January 1943) in raising the number of blacks in the electrical machinery plants in the city from 172, or barely 1 percent of the total, to over a thousand, or 3.7 percent of the total. For the electrical industry as a whole, the increase during this same period was "from 1 to only 1.5 percent."[21]

In July 1944, UE's New York–New Jersey district 4 signed a "mutual assistance pact" with the FEPC "to speed up the handling of cases of discrimination in UE shops or those under organization by it." In the immediate postwar years, UE Local 450 (Nassau County and Brooklyn) adopted "a special provision on layoffs for Negroes" and won a contract requiring the company to retain the wartime ratio of black to white workers.[22]

Philadelphia

At the Philco plant in Philadelphia, an enduring pattern of racial segregation and discrimination existed for many years. In 1952, Herbert Hill, then the NAACP's Labor Secretary, sought to meet with the president of Philco Local 101 about this. The president refused and, in a telephone conversation with Hill, "made it clear he would not discuss this matter with any representative of the NAACP." At Hill's request, Harry Block, head of IUE district 1, then met with Hill and the president and other officers of Locals 101 and 102. "A rather lengthy and at times heated discussion ensued," according to a June 4, 1952, memorandum by Hill, "in which I was informed that in the past white women had stated that they would rather quit than 'work with niggers.'" Wielding the threat of a lawsuit against the Philco Corporation and the IUE under provisions of the federal government's Contract Compliance Division and FEPC statutes in Philadelphia's municipal code, Hill was able to arrange an agreement with the Philco management and the locals' officers, through which "for the first time in the history of the Philco plant," as Hill wrote in 1952, "Negroes were promoted to production and assembly jobs."

> This development represents a complete departure from the pattern of Negro employment which had existed in the Philco plant for many years. . . . Negroes [had been relegated] to two segregated departments, salvage (scrap) and shipping. . . . The contract at the Philco plant is held by Locals 101 and 102 of IUE–CIO, District 1. The union contract provides for promotion via plant-wide seniority, however, the

---

[21] Weaver (1946, pp. 220–21); also Critchlow (1976, p. 237).
[22] Critchlow (1976, p. 234); Glazer (1961, p. 237n); Winston (1946, p. 354).

upgrading provisions of the contract were suspended [regarding] . . . the Negro workers[,] and by tacit agreement between the local union officials and management the Negro workers were segregated into [the salvage and shipping departments] . . . and promoted only within these departments.[23]

IUE Locals 101 and 102 and the entire district 1 of which they were part had been among the first to secede from the UE in 1950 to join the IUE. In fact, UE Local 101 had been the home local of the now IUE president and once UE president, CIO secretary James Carey; Block had been Carey's successor as head of UE Local 101 and served also as UE district 1 president. From at least the 1942 convention on, all throughout the bitter battle between the "left" and "right" within UE over the next eight years, district 1, headed by Block, a principled anti-Communist Socialist, "had remained the stronghold of the right-wing forces."[24]

Milwaukee

The "racist practices of UE Local 1111 at the Allen–Bradley Co. in Milwaukee," according to Hill, " . . . began soon after UE got its first contract at the plant in 1937 and continued through all the many years the local [was] . . . under direct

---

[23] Hill (1952, pp. 1–2, 4).

[24] Herbert Hill brought the Philco case (and the Allen–Bradley case to be discussed next) to our attention as what he considered to be a glaring instance of "racist practices" by certain UE locals. He mistakenly assumed, however, that the two IUE locals at the Philco plant in Philadelphia had been "Communist-controlled" during their years in the UE, rather than having been, in reality (and as was pointed out to him by Zeitlin in a subsequent telephone conversation) solid "right-wing" locals (1999a, b; 2000). Block was called in 1946 and 1947 to testify before HUAC on Communist infiltration of the UE but refused, saying that "he and his associates" considered their fight with the Communist-led left none of HUAC's business; it was, he said, an intraunion matter. Carey, however, did testify before HUAC at a later date, and, in 1948, at length before the House Education and Labor Subcommittee investigating "Communist infiltration" of UE, at which time he assured the committee "that the employers find it easy to get along with the Communists because the Communists cannot be aggressive in adjustment of a grievance." Why? Well, Carey explained, "that fellow is awfully easy [for the employer] to get along with, because he has to make compromises to protect his position to serve what I consider another interest" (U.S. Congress 1948, pp. 13, 11). In fact, Carey and other right-wingers had been cooperating with the FBI for years, beginning as early as July 1943, when Carey asked J. Edgar Hoover "to do background checks on certain left wingers. . . . By 1946 Carey [was seeing] . . . Hoover regularly to discuss Communists in the CIO" (Filippelli and McColloch 1995, pp. 141, 71, 126, 130, 104, 123).

CP control."[25] Employment grew at the plant from 792 workers in 1940 to 1,300 in 1945, about a third of whom were women, at its wartime peak, and to 2,959 in 1950. It was not until 1952, apparently, that Allen–Bradley "hired its first Negro employee," even though the company, said the Department of Labor, had not overtly discriminated "against any individual applicant for employment or any individual employee because of race or color."[26]

Rather, UE Local 1111 had wrested an agreement from Allen–Bradley early on and retained it throughout the years, which provided "for promotions and transfers on the basis of seniority when skill and ability are substantially equal and when promotions and transfers on that basis are practical." What's more, that agreement also required the company "to advise the union whenever it fills a job by hiring a new employee rather than by complying with a request for [promotion or] transfer by an existing employee." So "without any overt discrimination against any person who applied for a job," said a Department of Labor report, a system relying on dissemination of information about job openings by the existing "white workers among their friends and relatives, who [were also] . . . typically white . . . [established] a network of communication from which Negroes [were] . . . generally excluded."[27] Organized in a plant that employed not one black worker, in a city with a minuscule black population,[28] Local 1188's encroachment on "the management's exclusive right to hire whomever it pleased" thus had the unintended consequence of perpetuating a virtually all-white work force at the plant.[29]

Now, although Hill claims that Local 1111 at Allen–Bradley was "Communist-controlled," the documentary evidence we have been able to

---

[25] Hill (1999b, p. 1; also 1999a, p. 2).

[26] Allen–Bradley (1965, p. 45); U.S. Department of Labor (1968, p. E-1). A decade later, in 1962, the number of black employees among the company's total of 6,383 employees was still precisely one (Hill 1968b, p. 18).

[27] U.S. Department of Labor (1968, p. E-4).

[28] On the growth of Milwaukee's black population, see note 58 of this chapter.

[29] Robert W. Ozanne points out that, "as industrial unions won union shops in the 1930's and 1940's[,] it was *always* on condition that the union would not interfere with *the management's exclusive right to hire whomever it pleased. The Taft–Hartley Act's (1947) prohibition of the closed shop reinforced *management's exclusive control over hiring*" (1984, p. 163, emphasis added). Although Ozanne says *"always* on condition," this is, as we now know, not correct, for, as we saw in Chapter 5, some 44 percent of UE's local contracts refused to cede so-called management prerogatives, among which is exclusive control over hiring, and *not one* of the UE/GE *national* contracts – before, during, or after World War II – ceded management prerogatives. Local 1111 was thus no exception *among UE locals* when it too refused to cede the "exclusive right" to management "to hire whomever it pleased."

find does not support this political characterization. Both in 1938 and 1939, Local 1111's president Fred Wolter "spoke out clearly against 'the Communist element' in the leadership of Milwaukee's CIO" and was involved in an effort to oust them from leadership of the Wisconsin CIO. Allen–Bradley's own corporate history mentions Wolter's stance, but makes no other mention of the political coloring of Local 1111 during the CIO era.[30] Both of the city's newspapers, the *Milwaukee Sentinel* and the *Milwaukee Journal*, wrote a series of "exposes" of Communism in the CIO during the 1946 internecine "left–right battle," as the *Sentinel* called it, for control of the state and county CIO councils, but neither named Local 1111 as Communist-dominated. In fact, the reporter who wrote the *Sentinel*'s series and actually participated in "secret caucuses with the purpose of ousting the alleged left wingers from power," reported that the electrical worker local was among "the militant locals" in the Milwaukee County CIO that were "sympathetic" to "eliminating Communists from the ranks of CIO circles."[31] Finally, Frank Emspak avers that Local 1111 "never was left-led" but, on the contrary, definitely "was politically conservative then [in the forties]."[32]

---

[30] Ozanne has a detailed discussion of the defeat and "purge" of the left wing in the Wisconsin CIO in 1946, but the only mention he makes of Local 1111 is to note also, as does Allen–Bradley's historian, John Gurda, that from the CIO's beginnings in Wisconsin, Local 1111's president, Fred Wolter, was an anti-Communist activist. Wolter was an avowed participant in the "struggle to retire Communists from active leadership in the CIO," as he wrote in a July 24, 1938, letter to the editor of the *Milwaukee Sentinel,* and to oust them from "control of the State and County CIO" (Ozanne 1984, p. 86). Harvey Bradley, president, and Fred Loock, his general manager, the authorized company history notes, had long "gravitated to the far reaches of the right wing" and were "active supporters" of the John Birch Society and the Christian Anti-Communist Crusade – and friends of Crusade head Frederick Schwarz, a regular visitor who usually left "with a check." That despite the far-right political activism of Allen–Bradley's owner and manager, two different company histories (one published by the company itself and the other by the Bradley Foundation) never suggest or even imply that Local 1111 was "Communist-controlled" *at any time* certainly lends no credence to Hill's unsupported assertion that it was (Gurda 1992, pp. 89, 92, 114, 116, 117; Allen–Bradley 1965, pp. 25, 49).

[31] The *Sentinel*'s reporter, Hugh Swafford, reported that a "twin offensive" among ten USWA and eleven UAW locals aimed to unseat the left leadership of the Milwaukee County CIO Council, and that "electrical worker, hosiery-worker, and brewery worker [newly members of the CIO] locals were 'sympathetic' to the possible CIO purge" (Meyer 1992, p. 166). He did not specially name Local 1111 as the "sympathetic" electrical worker local.

[32] Emspak (2000a).

St. Louis

In St. Louis, one of "the most segregated cities in the nation," even the federal government's Employment Service had two offices, one for "white" and one for "colored" workers, and their staffs had no qualms about sending black applicants to segregated work places and contributed in this way to reinforcing the area's segregated employment pattern. The few blacks who applied at the "colored" office were referred to low-skilled jobs, but only if they passed a series of examinations, including a test for venereal disease.

The new all-black St. Louis unit of the March on Washington Movement (MOWM), founded in May 1942, was one of the most active, and radical, MOWM units. Several hundred black workers were laid off that same month by U.S. Cartridge, the city's major defense contractor, in response to mounting hostility from white workers. MOWM took "to the streets" and led the fight to reinstate them. MOWM "found a valuable ally," as Andrew Kersten observes, "in William Sentner, the Communist leader of the UE at U.S. Cartridge," and head of UE's district 8.[33]

District 8, as Rosemary Feurer puts it, made both "racial and sexual equality a high priority during the war." The district called vigorously for the employment of black and women workers as a solution to the wartime labor shortage and to ensure a "just economy in the postwar period. . . . Sentner was instrumental in getting the mayor to establish a Race Relations commission that dealt with employment as well as segregation issues in St. Louis." District 8 leaders launched a campaign calling for full and equal utilization of black and women workers and helped to open new job opportunities for black workers.[34]

This campaign was part of UE's successful drive to organize U.S. Cartridge. One of the campaign's prime demands was "immediate employment of Negro women in production." The company conceded, and management agreed to rehire 300 black male workers and also "pledged to hire seventy-five 'Negro women matrons . . . to clean the lavatories of the white women production workers.'" In fact, the company hired only twenty "Negro matrons," and it never employed a single black woman among its 23,500 production workers.[35] The next year, with the encouragement of MOWM, 3,600 black workers segregated in building 103 at U.S. Cartridge struck to protest against the company's failure to hire and train more blacks in skilled positions. The walkout was supported by the UE, despite its adherence to the wartime no-strike pledge, and the strike ended when the strikers won a

---

[33] Kersten (1999d, pp. 149, 156; 2000, pp. 261, 262, 265).
[34] Feurer (1992, p. 115); Kersten (1999d, p. 153n8).   [35] Kersten (1999d, pp. 152–53).

"significant concession" from the company to train a few black foremen in building 103. "Up to that point, all supervisors had been white."[36]

MOWM repeatedly challenged the citywide unfair employment practices in defense industries. By early 1943, blacks employed in St. Louis's war industries numbered 18,000, a 225 percent increase over 1942. These gains, according to Kersten, were the result of both a general but momentary labor shortage and the activities of the St. Louis MOWM and its allies, especially Sentner's UE, "which organized black workers and fought to gain more jobs for them."[37]

The city's black newspaper, *St. Louis American* (April 2, 1943), commended UE's leaders for being in "the forefront of racial issues."[38] They consistently supported the demand of St. Louis's black community that FEPC hold hearings there on discriminatory labor practices. When a hearing was actually held, on August 2, 1944, Sentner testified to the fact that from March of 1942 on, UE had been demanding that the labor utilization division of the War Production Board take effective steps to eliminate unfair employment practices in the city's plants. Most important, the UE district insisted, according to Sentner, that all collective bargaining agreements to which UE locals were a party contain a clause stating: "No employee or person seeking employment or job advancement shall be discriminated against because of race, color, creed, or sex."[39]

District 8's leaders appointed a black staff member "to demonstrate the district organization's hostility to any form of prejudice." They were also active in civil rights activities in the community.[40] Yet, according to Kersten, "the UE's leadership [in St. Louis] was unable to sway its rank and file to support fair employment." UE's leaders' efforts to bring in black workers were met by protests and wildcat strikes by their locals' white members. Apparently, white women workers were prominent among the instigators and initiators of the wildcats. For instance, in late 1944, when black core handlers were placed in the McQuay–Norris plant, fifty white female UE members walked out, despite the opposition of the local's leaders, and they stayed out until management removed the black workers. The two top officers in the UE's St. Louis Local 825 at McQuay–Norris urged a resolution to "reaffirm our beliefs in the policies of the union, the CIO and the nation to prevent and eliminate discrimination in employment because of race, creed, or color" and to authorize the local's executive board to "effectuate the policies set forth in this resolution." The

---

[36] Ibid., pp. 156–57.   [37] Kersten (1999d, p. 156).

[38] Filippelli and McColloch (1995, pp. 81, 221n102).

[39] At a speech to the Community Relations Institute of St. Louis, 1946 (cited by Kersten 1999c).

[40] Critchlow (1976, pp. 234–35).

resolution passed initially, but was then overturned "after strong protest from white workers." Dejected by this defeat, the two officers resigned their posts.[41]

Again, the contrast with IBEW enlightens. In January 1945, when the management at St. Louis's General Cable Co. decided to train several black women for production jobs, over 1,000 "white women workers, who were [IBEW] members . . . staged a wildcat strike." They returned to work only when the company agreed not "to train or employ black women or promote black men." Unlike UE's local and district leaders in St. Louis, however, IBEW's counterparts did not oppose the women's wildcat and did not endorse the principle of fair employment, and they "never went to bat" for the black workers.[42]

The contrast of UE with the role of UAW in GM's extensive manufacturing facilities in St. Louis is also instructive. GM there engaged in "systematic discriminatory practices," which were embodied in UAW contracts, including a separate seniority line of progression for black and white workers at its Chevy plant. Under UAW, black workers in St. Louis's GM plants were employed for many years "exclusively in menial jobs, such as porter, sweeper, and material handler."[43]

Explaining Racial Egalitarianism in UE Districts 4 and 8

Critchlow argues that UE's New York and St. Louis districts gave "special consideration" to blacks only because both had a "great number" of them. He estimates that some 25 percent of UE's members in the St. Louis district were black. Yet in the New York–New Jersey district, according to his own estimate, less than 10 percent of the membership was black.[44] Having offered the varying size of the black membership in the international and in these two districts as his explanation of their differing racial policies, Critchlow then mentions, in a footnote, that "Communists were leaders in these districts and being politically conscious of social issues, pressed the black question."

---

[41] Kersten (1999d, pp. 161, 163).

[42] Ibid., p. 163; 1999c. In 1950, when IUE, the CIO's newly chartered right-wing dual union, escalated its raiding of UE members in St. Louis electrical plants and at International Harvester, "the UE retained considerable loyalty among blacks by effectively contrasting its record on race with that of other CIO unions" (Filippelli and McColloch 1995, p. 150).

[43] Hill notes also that more or less the same "racial employment pattern at Ford plants organized by the UAW" in Chicago, Kansas City, Long Beach, California, Atlanta, Dallas, and Memphis characterized the GM plant in St. Louis (1998, pp. 97, 106n73).

[44] Critchlow estimates district 4's black membership based on black employment in the electrical industry in various cities in the district, which ranged, he reports, between 4.6 percent and 8.8 percent (1976, p. 236).

Recall that Sentner, St. Louis district head, was – since his first days as a labor organizer – an open Communist; so, too, was James McLeish, head of UE's New York–New Jersey district 4.[45] Critchlow asserts, unconvincingly, that having politically conscious Communist leadership in both of these UE districts "does not serve as sufficient explanation" for these districts' racial egalitarianism. First, he says, other Communist-led locals (unnamed) were not as active on the black question; second, neither district was *"totally* controlled by Communists."[46]

UE, Race, and Gender at Work

The critical question, of course, is why UE's international leaders apparently did not make the fight for black rights a national priority. Marshall Stevenson's answer is direct and derisive: He asserts that because UE had few black members, its "[white] communists were not willing to risk their position and status . . . by overemphasizing issues that appealed to a small minority of workers."[47] This charge (whatever its applicability to Communists and those close to them in the leadership of other unions) surely does not apply to UE's Julius Emspak, secretary-treasurer, and James Matles, its head of organization, for whom the equality of black and white workers was a lifelong cardinal principle. They were men of unquestionable radical commitment, egalitarian temperament, and well-tested mettle in workers' struggles. If in truth the UE international failed to be a pacesetter in the struggle for black equality, this certainly was not because these men and women were "not willing to risk their position and status."

We suggest an alternative explanation, but one for which there is substantial circumstantial evidence, as presented in Chapter 7: UE's top leaders

---

[45] In 1945, Sentner had openly opposed the CP's decision to abandon the Popular Front, had condemned the party's "lack of confidence in working people," and had called for the replacement of its officials by "workers actively associated with . . . [mainstream] American labor . . . capable of understanding and solving realistically the complex problems" confronting workers. But, despite such grave misgivings, Sentner did not officially resign from the party until early 1957, according to the FBI. In September 1952, Sentner was indicted under the Smith Act; he was tried and convicted in 1954. On December 10, 1958, while still in the midst of legal appeals of his conviction, he died of heart failure (Feurer 1992, pp. 116–17; Filippelli and McColloch 1995, p. 157).

[46] Critchlow (1976, p. 236n18, emphasis added).

[47] Stevenson (1993, p. 50). Like Hill, Stevenson also asserts that such Communist reluctance to push black rights in the North differed from the racial egalitarianism won in the South by "communist-influenced affiliates" whose memberships were heavily, if not mainly, black, such as FTA and MM.

were already embroiled in a sharp struggle against electrical employers for pay equity and job protection for women. They led the way in fighting for integration of women into the industry on equal terms with men.[48] Involved in the unrelenting conflict on this front, they were not able, rather than "not willing," to engage in a conflict on a second front, that is, fighting against employers who, as we noted earlier, were even more resistant to hiring blacks than employers in other mass-production industries.

The strategy of UE's leadership on the gender issue, as Milkman says, anticipated "by several decades the struggles being waged today for 'equal pay for comparable worth.'" But no effective strategy, especially one so far advanced for its time, springs full-blown. Rather it takes an exhausting expenditure of time and energy to devise and implement a strategy that will bring employers into battle in a way that the union can win. Under these circumstances, the fact that UE's international leadership apparently could not muster the will to launch a second front against employers over the issue of black equality – an issue which, as radicals, they surely saw as a moral imperative – becomes understandable (though no less lamentable).[49]

UAW

Beginning as early as the UAW's 1939 convention and recurrently at subsequent conventions through the early 1950s, black activists, consistently supported by Communists and their allies, fought (and were defeated) time and again (most notably at the 1943 and 1946 conventions) to pass a constitutional

---

[48] Zieger (1995, p. 256).

[49] In late 1955, in the midst of defending their union against fierce raids by rival CIO unions and from heavy attacks against its officers by various congressional committees, and despite previous NAACP rebuffs of UE's calls for unity in the civil rights struggle, UE again called on the NAACP to join it in fighting discrimination. The Washington, D.C., representative of UE's Fair Practice Committee, for instance, urged NAACP president Roy Wilkins to support a government "crack down" on companies that were in violation of President Dwight D. Eisenhower's executive order banning discrimination by government defense contractors. "Numerous big corporations like General Electric, Westinghouse, General Motors, Ford and others," Ernest Thompson wrote Wilkins on September 29, 1955, "are practicing widespread discrimination against Negro workers in the South, particularly Negro women, who are totally excluded from production jobs with these companies.... they are in serious violation of the spirit, if not the letter of the Executive Order. In my opinion, the policy of the ... [President's Committee on Government Contract Compliance] and the President ought to be to crack down on all contractors [that discriminate] regardless of whether a particular plant has a defense contract or not, since the corporation does have a [defense] contract" (NAACP 1988, Reel 9: 0175).

amendment reserving a seat on the executive board or a vice presidency for a black representative. August Meier and Elliott Rudwick place the blame for these defeats on the racism of auto workers: "[T]he elevation of a black to the International Executive Board," they say, "[was not] possible so long as *the rank-and-file majority* remained overwhelmingly racist." But they provide no evidence in support of either claim, that is, that the "majority" of UAW members were "racist" and (assuming this was so) that this was the main obstacle to black representation on the board.

On the contrary, as Meier and Rudwick themselves document, Walter Reuther and other top anti-Communist leaders of the UAW vehemently opposed the proposal for a black seat on the board, as they said, on principle and – perhaps even more so – for pragmatic political reasons. Spokesmen of the "Reuther faction" denounced "the special seat as a 'hypocritical' demand for racism in reverse." To this charge, a black delegate replied: "We are getting desperate for real representation on that board and if we have to take it 'Jim Crow,' we'll take it." Or, as Meier and Rudwick observe: "One of the fears of the Reuther faction, in fact, had been that, if [the] proposal passed, the black elected to the Board would be a member of the Addes group [the center–left coalition]; and [Addes's] thirty votes would be enough to place [him] . . . in a dominant position on the closely divided Executive Board."[50] They note also: "Even after Reuther had consolidated his control and attained the presidency, [the issue of black representation] . . . remained intertwined with the union's factionalism and typically was championed by Communists and the union's left wing."[51] Throughout the CIO era, the overwhelming majority of the UAW's black unionists supported the center–left coalition.[52]

Local 600

The most conspicuous and powerful base of the left opposition to Reuther's policies, as we know, was rooted in Local 600, whose officers consistently supported the proposal for a black seat on UAW's executive board. In general, Local 600's commitment to interracial solidarity contrasted sharply with the

[50] In the board's system of voting, members cast multiple and highly varied numbers of votes, ranging from 10 to 82, depending on the size of the constituencies they represented.

[51] Meier and Rudwick (1979, pp. 208, 211, 211n, 220, emphasis added). As early as 1943, Reuther had gall enough to tell Hodges Mason, one of the UAW's most effective early organizers and a prominent black leader, that the UAW had no black "qualified" to be a member of the executive board (Mason interview with Herbert Hill, Detroit 1968, cited in Lichtenstein 1995, p. 490n55).

[52] Lichtenstein (1995, p. 208).

Reuther executive board's. So, for instance, in 1949, a year after Reuther's anti-Communist slate had won control of the IEB, Irving Howe and B. J. Widick singled out the leaders of Local 600 (and of Briggs Local 212) as having "consistently fought for the rights of their Negro members. . . ."

> In other locals, the story is rather unpleasant: leaders who go through the motion of supporting the union policy but do not really exert themselves to defend Negro members. . . . Certainly, the experience of Ford Local 600 stands out as an example of what can be done to establish a sense of fraternity and harmony between white and colored workers. While no one in the local could seriously argue that discrimination has been completely abolished, it is clear to all Detroit observers that it has a qualitatively superior record on race relations. Since its formation, Negroes have actively participated in the local's affairs, holding major positions and exerting powerful influence in its politics. There is no visible discrimination at social affairs or any other social function.

Howe and Widick suggest two sources of Local 600's exceptional record of "racial tolerance": one, that black workers were "so large a part of it that any official who ventured to make overt Jim Crow remarks would be committing suicide," and, two, that "the local's leaderships – of whatever faction – have worked toward that end [interracial fraternity and harmony]." Although Howe and Widick here decide to allocate credit to "leaderships . . . of whatever faction" for this achievement, earlier in their book, they characterize Local 600 (as did Reuther) as being "long under Stalinist leadership" and "controlled" by "the Communist Party."[53]

The unified stance taken by Local 600's rank-and-file unionists on the touchy issue of segregation in public accommodations illustrates how appropriate actions by union leaders can result in what W. E. B. Dubois called "an astonishing spread of interracial tolerance and understanding" among workers.[54]

Dave Moore, vice president of the axle building at the Rouge plant, remembers:

> There were some hotels where black delegates to a UAW convention couldn't get in there. . . . If a black guy was being refused admittance to a hotel or motel . . . that hotel was almost torn apart and would have been torn apart if they didn't give them a room. White guys was doing it for us. And we even had run ins with other locals in the UAW. The white

[53] Howe and Widick (1949, pp. 227–28, 169, 157).   [54] Dubois (1948, p. 236).

guys did, from Local 600, defending black guys. Some of the white guys from other locals around the country [would say], "Just what in the hell are you doing, he's a Negro, he . . . can't eat in this room with the rest of us." . . . [But] these [Local 600] white guys, "God damn it, if he don't eat in here, nobody is going to eat. . . ." And we would put up a picket line, sometimes we did. The white guys themselves would organize.

Even more sensitive and fraught with tension was the issue of "race mixing," as it used to be termed, especially between the opposite sexes. But, as Moore tells it, Local 600's leaders confronted the issue head on, with salutary results.

The local was giving dances, blacks and whites dancing together. They would give picnics, the kids were there playing together, they would . . . have choral ensembles, all of them singing in the choir together, they had bands, they played together, in the Labor Day marches all of them competed for prizes, and this kind of thing. *Even though they weren't living in the same neighborhood together, they would visit each other, and these are the kind of social activities, I think, that went on and helped elevate the brotherhood and togetherness more openly.* . . . We had black beauty queens. . . . Nowhere in the country would you find an organization [that] predominantly whites were sponsoring, that would select a black woman for a beauty queen. . . . It was unheard of. But we had it here.[55]

In the middle of World War II, the head of the local's huge recreational program sought (according to FBI reports from 1943 and 1944) to use that program to "break down the walls between the workers of various national groups and races," and he conducted a campaign to break down "racial barriers" in Detroit-area bowling alleys. The program's head was John Gallo, whom ACTU called one of the local's "most prominent Communists."[56]

---

[55] Stepan-Norris and Zeitlin (1996b, pp. 135–36, 138).

[56] *Wage Earner* (April 4, 1947); U.S. Department of Justice (n.d.), Federal Bureau of Investigation, John Gallo FBI File 100-138889 (quoting the *Daily Worker*, November 18 and 19, 1943; and quoting the *Pittsburgh Courier*, Detroit edition, September 30, 1944). Despite the local leaders' efforts, however, production in the Rouge plant still retained much of the characteristic preunion era's racial division of labor, in which blacks held the worst jobs. In the 1960s, most black workers at the Rouge were still employed in the dangerous and dirty production foundry. In 1965, the local's newly elected president, Walter Dorosh, a veteran activist in the UAW's left faction, set out to break this pattern. He and other top local leaders agreed to raise the issue with Ford of the skewed distribution of black employment toward the most menial jobs, and strike the plant if they had to. They proposed that as new jobs in the plant elsewhere than in the production foundry opened up, they be filled by black workers

Local 248

If Local 600 was the most formidable Red-led local in the UAW, Local 248 at the Allis–Chalmers agricultural equipment plant in West Allis, Wisconsin, the biggest private employer in that state, was also an important base of the UAW's governing center–left coalition until 1947, and the local's president Harold Christoffel and its other "Red-lining" officers consistently supported the call for black representation on the UAW's executive board. In 1937, the local "spearheaded the formation of the Milwaukee Scottsboro Defense Committee," which consisted of a cross-section of black and white civic, labor, and religious leaders; this cemented a tight bond between the local and the city's blacks. As early as October 1940, Local 248 filed a grievance against the company's discriminatory layoff policies. And the Wisconsin *CIO News*, under the aegis of Local 248, attacked racial discrimination by the railway brotherhoods and various AFL locals. This, says Joe Trotter, was "particularly gratifying to black workers."[57] Yet blacks never constituted more than a tiny share of Allis–Chalmers workers and of the local's membership, in a city and county with a minuscule black population.[58] Of 11,250 Allis–Chalmers workers in December 1941, only 110, or barely 1 percent, were black, and by the end of the war, in 1945, the number had increased to only 693 of over 16,500 total workers, or 4.2 percent, employed in the main plant and two others opened during wartime.

with high seniority in the foundry, who would then retain their total seniority in the new job. The foundry committeemen agreed, and the foundry workers, "Oh, they applauded," Dorosh said, "they were happy." Management resisted the idea but finally agreed to implement it. But once workers started taking new jobs outside the foundry, "within two or three days," according to Dorosh, "they wanted to go back." Soon a committee of foundrymen asked to have the plan scrapped. The workers, they said, were used to the work in the foundry, and, besides, that was where "they know everybody, it's just like a community." So although this pioneering agreement with Ford to erode the racial division of labor in the Rouge plant remained in force, according to Dorosh, few black foundry workers took advantage of it (Dorosh interview, 1984).

[57] Trotter (1985, p. 163).

[58] "The wartime black migration to Milwaukee came in a rivulet rather than a flood." In 1940, black Milwaukeeans numbered 8,821, or 1.5 percent of the total city's population. In 1945, the figure increased slightly to 10,200, or 1.6 percent (Meyer 1992, p. 124; Trotter 1985, p. 149). By 1950, the total black population doubled to some 21,750, or about 2 percent or so of the total population of the Milwaukee metropolitan area (Department of Labor 1968, p. E-1). The old and established, small black community in Milwaukee was not "militant" on civil rights, let alone on the issue of racial employment equality, according to Hill (2000). Not until 1968 were there public demonstrations at Allen–Bradley calling for minority hiring, and these were led by the NAACP's Father James Groppi, a white Catholic priest.

Until the war, Allis–Chalmers refused to hire blacks except as "porters, janitors and common laborers," and even when faced with a war labor shortage, the additional blacks the company hired to labor in the foundries, to replace workers serving in the armed forces, were imported contract workers from Jamaica (of the plant's 693 black workers, 387 were Jamaican). Allis–Chalmers housed the Jamaicans in segregated army barracks at the Milwaukee airport. "In contrast to such segregation," as Stephen Meyer observes, "the UAW [Local 248] welcomed the black Jamaicans to union social and cultural activities . . . [and] praised them as models for American workers." Even though most of the company's workers were of German, Polish, and other Slavic origins, who "were known to be openly hostile to blacks," Local 248 leaders conducted a militant struggle to achieve racial equality. In 1941, this Red-led local's membership endorsed a resolution to support the proposed "March on Washington" for equal employment of blacks in defense production. Local 248 established its own Fair Employment Practice Committee (FEPC) with a black foundry worker as chair and, as Trotter says, "vigorously worked for the employment and upgrading of black workers" during the war, against a management that otherwise firmly refused to upgrade them into more skilled and better-paid jobs. Local 248 leaders promoted the hiring of black men and women; when the company refused to hire a black woman they sent to apply for work, they filed an FEPC case and pushed for her employment. Within a month the company hired her and five other black women. The local continued throughout the war to call for black women's equal employment.[59]

USWA

The USWA experienced no such internal factional struggles or open differences in racial policies and practices among its major locals. Basically, the stance of the USWA's international leadership toward black representation was akin to Reuther's. For instance, Philip Murray, president both of the CIO and USWA, told the major black daily, the *Pittsburgh Courier* (August 16, 1947): "We have substantial representation among the Negro elements. . . . You've got to give these guys equality of treatment, you don't pick a man for the job because he's a Negro. That provides a bar to good feeling among various elements within the organization." USWA secretary-treasurer David McDonald added: "He also should be respected for his ability, and not his color."[60]

[59] Trotter (1985, p. 174).   [60] Cited in Williamson (1947, p. 1013).

Conclusion

So, in sum, each of the Big 3 had a constitutional guarantee of membership equality, yet even so both UAW and USWA tolerated the existence of segregated locals at one time or another. Only the UAW established a committee to abolish discrimination during World War II, but this was largely the result of pressure by black unionists and the strong Communist faction. UE, alone in the Big 3, had an elected black international officer. USWA's civil rights record, despite a large black membership, was anything but stellar; its leadership, unlike the UAW's, faced no organized left opposition insistently demanding measures to increase black employment equality. In the UAW, Communists and their allies in the center–left coalition fought for black representation on the IEB – and proposed a special provision to assure this – but the Reuther caucus derided and opposed this as "reverse discrimination." UAW's huge "Stalinist-controlled" Local 600, of all locals, had the most exemplary record of interracial solidarity. Similarly, in UE, the international leadership of which did not make black employment equality a paramount issue – for they had enough on their hands fighting for and winning women's rights against re-calcitrant employers – the strongest Communist-led districts, for example, in St. Louis and the New York–New Jersey area, were the most staunch racial egalitarians, whereas locals singled out by the NAACP for their troubling discriminatory practices, for instance, the Philco local in Philadelphia, were led by UE's most prominent right-wingers.

9

THE RED AND THE BLACK

As racial, religious, and ethnic cleavages faded among the mass of industrial workers in the midst of the naked class war of the 1930s, the overt bigotry and narrow exclusionism that disfigured the AFL isolated it from the newly burgeoning workers' movement of "self-organization."[1] The insurgency inside the AFL's Machinists union (IAM) was exemplary of the enveloping schism within the AFL, in which the issue of interracial unity repeatedly came to the fore. Despite the IAM leaders' announcement in March 1936 that they would extend their union's jurisdiction to include metal and transport workers, skilled and unskilled alike, they refused to abandon their long-standing admissions policy of "whites only."

Later that year, at the IAM's November convention, young "Jimmy" Matles called for the abolition of the IAM's secret initiation ritual restricting membership to "Caucasians." Shutting blacks out, recalled Matles, "was something the industrial unionists didn't intend to live with." When he and his fellow delegates rose to speak for their motion, "the convention became bedlam [and] . . . chairs started to fly. The young delegates could hardly be heard amidst

[1] The AFL's leadership and its affiliates long had been deeply implicated in making "color a caste," or in reenforcing an established "color-caste system" in which black workers, if they were hired at all, were "the last hired, and the first fired," and were relegated, compared with white workers, to the more dangerous, dirty, and menial jobs; on the rare occasions when blacks held the same jobs as whites, they were paid less, based on discriminatory wage scales, and they were excluded (or expelled) from skilled jobs (Stevenson 1993, p. 45; Ross 1967, pp. 3–13; Cochran 1977, p. 222n; Spero and Harris 1931; Noland and Bakke 1949; Hill 1968a, esp. pp. 367–88; 1985, pp. 6–21; Marshall 1967a, pp. 17–23; Myrdal 1944, p. 475). A study of the constitutions of 100 AFL affiliates and independent unions found that, in the early to mid-1940s, 17 still had a clause expressly limiting membership to "whites" or "Caucasians," and 35 excluded noncitizens or admitted only, as the Boilermakers' constitution specified, a "citizen of some civilized country." Other unions had tacit understandings or used Jim Crow initiation rituals to exclude blacks, Indians, and Mexicans (Summers 1946; Peterson 1944, p. 51).

the hooting and hollering [by the old guard]. At the height of the uproar, [IAM President Arthur] Wharton banged his gavel, declared the ritual inviolate and adjourned the session. . . . " The suppression of their call for equal membership rights for black workers aroused Matles and the lodges under his leadership to secede and join UE and the CIO.

The Red-led Transport Workers Union (TWU) was also in the IAM briefly and its leaders, Mike Quill and John Santo, like Matles, "had agreed to affiliate with the IAM only after receiving assurances that its white and black members would be treated equally, in spite of the IAM's normal whites-only policy." At the one-and-only IAM convention in which TWU was represented, Quill and Santo joined Matles and left-wing delegates from other new IAM affiliates in the unsuccessful fight to eliminate the IAM's Jim Crow ritual. The TWU then also bolted and joined the fledgling CIO.[2]

"Like a Bad Dream Gone"

From the moment of the CIO's conception as a rebellious "committee for industrial organization" inside the AFL, its organizers appealed to workers on their own ethnic or racial ground as a way, paradoxically, not of separating them but of "articulating worker unity."[3] Under the old radical banner of "black and white, unite and fight," the CIO would embrace the aspirations of black workers and fight for black–white equality, in the words of Robert Zieger, "as had no previous sustained American labor organization."[4]

At the start of the CIO drive at Inland Steel in 1935, for example, a white steel worker exclaimed to his fellows that he now realized that "you must forget that the man working beside you is a 'Nigger,' Jew or 'Pollock.' . . . [He] is a working man like yourself and being exploited by the 'boss' in the name of racial and religious prejudice. You work together – [So]

---

[2] Matles and Higgins (1974, pp. 46–47); Filippelli and McColloch (1995, p. 40); Freeman (1989, p. 151). Even during World War II, IAM, like other AFL unions that began belatedly to organize along industrial lines, excluded (or even expelled) already employed blacks from both skilled jobs and employment in the mass production industries, by using closed shop contracts, e.g., at Boeing Aircraft in Seattle, or by cooperating with employers who already excluded blacks, e.g., at Vultee Aircraft and North American Aviation in Los Angeles (Foner 1974, p. 235; Northrup 1943, pp. 218–19, 220n58; Hill 1985, pp. 174, 178). Also see note 10 of this chapter.

[3] Cohen (1990, p. 339).

[4] Zieger (1995, pp. 153, 372); Goldfield (1993; 1995). Depending, of course, on the meaning of "sustained" in Zieger's statement; for the TUEL and its successor TUUL, from 1922 through 1935 on the very eve of the CIO's formation, certainly had embraced the aspirations of black workers and the struggle for interracial equality. (See below.)

Fight Together!!!" The CIO's interracial organizing had "done the greatest thing in the world gettin' everybody who works in the yards together," said a black packinghouse worker in 1939, "and breakin' up the hate and bad feelings that used to be held against the Negro." Or as another black worker described the change wrought by the CIO at Armour's slaughterhouse: "The white butchers hated the Negroes because they figured they would scab on them when trouble came and then get good-paying, skilled jobs besides, ... with the CIO in, all that's like a bad dream gone. Oh, we still have a hard row, but this time the white men are with us and we're with them."[5]

For most of the CIO's two decades of independent existence – as both union federation and radical political organization – it was to be a major racially egalitarian force in American life. No less an observer than W. E. B. Dubois – then the nation's preeminent black leader – affirmed in 1948 that the CIO probably had brought about

> ... the greatest and most effective effort toward interracial understanding among the working masses .... [N]umbers of men like those in the steel and automotive industries have been thrown together, black and white, as fellow workers striving for the same objects. There has been on this account an astonishing spread of interracial tolerance and understanding. Probably no movement in the last 30 years has been so successful in softening race prejudice among the masses.[6]

Yet, on this cardinal issue, as on most others, the CIO was anything but a single, seamless piece. In general, CIO international unions carried out "determined and far-reaching efforts to combat racism."[7] The efforts of some, however, were not as determined and far-reaching as others'; they ran the gamut from militant confrontation with entrenched forms of racial inequality to cautious gradualism, if not actual accommodation. The question here is how the political consciousness of the leadership and the form of government,

---

[5] Cohen (1990, pp. 333–34, 337). Black workers in the South, of course, had an even harder row to hoe. Southern CIO leaders, even in heavy industrial centers, were often fearful of taking on specifically "Negro issues." At the first CIO convention in Birmingham, Alabama, for instance, the executive board of the CIO's Industrial Union Council summarily rejected resolutions "endorsing federal anti-lynching legislation and urging the state of Alabama to drop the case against the Scottsboro defendants" (nine young black men falsely accused of raping two white women in Alabama, in 1931) (Kelley 1990, p. 147; also Kelley 1996, p. 110).

[6] Dubois (1948, p. 236).   [7] Rosen (1968, p. 204).

democratic or authoritarian, mattered in determining the racial policies and practices of the CIO's international unions.

Unfortunately, despite the recent efflorescence of excellent historical scholarship on race and labor, this is a question to which a conclusive answer is not yet possible; as historian Judith Stein remarks: "Studies of CIO egalitarianism require more basic research. . . . Existing research is too meager for a synthetic study . . . based simply on the secondary literature." Indeed, the lament made twenty years ago by August Meier and Elliot Rudwick still holds:

> . . . no definitive statement on the practices of CIO unions regarding blacks and racial discrimination can be made at this time. We know of no detailed, scholarly investigations of the dynamics of race relations within the CIO. Even the standard works on the subject of blacks and organized labor speak in general terms about the CIO and a few individual unions, but none of these books makes *a systematic analysis* in any depth.[8]

Withal, although the meagerness of the historical record precludes our making an "in depth" systematic analysis, we were able to find systematic data on three practical manifestations of interracial solidarity in an international union: (1) equality of access to membership, in terms of both constitutional equality and the actual existence "at one time or another" of segregated locals; (2) representation in the highest leadership councils; and (3) establishment of "special equalitarian racial machinery" to combat racism, such as a fair employment committee or committee to abolish discrimination.[9]

Our underlying assumption, of course, is that these manifestations of interracial solidarity did, in fact, make a significant difference in reducing black/white inequality. If the appropriate data were available to address this question, a systematic empirical analysis would show, we suggest, that the greater the interracial solidarity in CIO unions, the more equal the employment experiences and earnings of the black and white workers whom they represented.[10]

---

[8] Stein (1993, p. 62); Meier and Rudwick (1979, p. 27n, emphasis added). An "in-depth" systematic analysis of racial egalitarianism in the CIO's internationals would require data on at least six aspects of equality: (1) access to union membership; (2) pay, job placement, upgrading, and promotion; (3) hiring and layoffs; (4) representation in local and international union office; (5) union social activities; (6) civil rights (cf. Goldfield 1993, p. 6).

[9] Marshall (1964, pp. 249, 187n40).

[10] John Brueggemann and Terry Boswell (1998) argue that CIO internationals generally fostered interracial solidarity among industrial workers; a strategy of racial inclusion (appointing black organizers and encouraging the election of black officers) was crucial in realizing black/white intraclass solidarity. Two especially relevant studies, the first by economist Orley

Constitutional Equality

For black workers, who were long accustomed to being excluded entirely from AFL affiliates or relegated to "auxiliary," segregated units, it was a momentous and salutary event when the CIO and its constituent international unions called on them to join as equal members. By the late 1940s, according to our survey, twenty-nine of the CIO's thirty-six internationals, or 81 percent, had a provision guaranteeing membership to all eligible workers regardless of race or color. In contrast, this was true of only thirteen of the eighty-nine major AFL affiliates surveyed, or 14.6 percent, in the mid-1940s.[11]

Segregated Locals

All told, according to information provided by Ray Marshall and Sumner Rosen, nine internationals – including a small number that had a constitutional guarantee of membership equality – are said to have had one or more segregated locals "at one time or another," mainly in the South – although neither reports how many segregated locals each international had or when or for how long

---

Ashenfelter, the latest by Maurice Zeitlin and L. Frank Weyher, have found that CIO unions overall, that is, without making any internal political distinctions among them, did, in fact, reduce black/white earnings and employment inequality. Ashenfelter's analysis, using relative "occupational position" as a proxy for earnings, found that AFL unions *increased* black/white earnings inequality and CIO unions *reduced* it in the forty-eight contiguous states, in 1940 and 1950. He attributes this to the difference between "craft" and "industrial" unions, the latter supposedly being inherently "less discriminatory (more egalitarian)" than the former, rather than to the AFL's pattern of racial exclusionism as opposed to the CIO's interracial organization. Yet he himself notes that although "the CIO affiliates were all industrial unions and all of the craft . . . unions were AFL affiliates, *a large fraction of the AFL affiliates were industrial unions*" (1972, p. 461, emphasis added; also see Ashenfelter 1973). As we point out below, and contrary to Ashenfelter's argument, AFL industrial unions were not "less discriminatory," even in the midst of World War II, than their fellow AFL craft unions. Analyses of data on the thirty-seven nonsouthern states by Zeitlin and Weyher show that (with labor demand held constant), the bigger the CIO was vis-à-vis the AFL – especially in the subset of fifteen highly unionized states – the closer to equality were the reductions of the unemployment rates of black and white workers during the decade of the 1940s (1997, 1998, 2001).

[11] We examined the 1948 constitution of each international or, if it was missing, the constitution for the nearest year available. For the provisions of AFL constitutions and CIO constitutions as of the mid-1940s, see Summers (1946, pp. 192–207).

these locals existed.[12] That the constitutional guarantee was "real" and not merely formal is indicated by the fact that "only" 21 percent of those with a

---

[12] Marshall names three CIO internationals that "have or *have had* segregated locals": the oil workers (OWIU), textile workers (TWUA), and men's clothing workers (ACW), but notes that his "list is not complete" (1965b, p. 107, emphasis added). In fact, he does not name two others he mentioned a year earlier, as examples of what he calls "radically-led unions" that had segregated locals (1964, p. 185): the Butte, Montana, mine, mill, and smelter local (MM), and the Portland, Oregon, longshore local (ILWU), both of which inherited these locals from their past AFL affiliation. Rosen also cites the OWIU, TWUA, and ACW, and adds the following four in which, he says, "segregated locals existed at one time or another": the UAW; United Paper Workers; rubber workers (URW); and USWA (1968, p. 204). That two "radically-led unions" such as ILWU and MM had segregated locals is anomalous but illustrative of the contradictory cohabitation of "intransigent racism" with "class rebelliousness" among white workers (Montgomery 1989, p. 131). The ILWU was born in a workers' insurgency led by Harry Bridges inside the International Longshore Association (ILA) during the epochal 1934 general strike in San Francisco, and one of the left leadership's central demands, which the local won in the course of the strike, and which was later institutionalized throughout its jurisdiction by the new ILWU headed by Bridges, was for a union hiring hall and an end to racial discrimination, to replace the notoriously corrupt "shape up" system (Solomon 1998, p. 253; Kimeldorf 1988). Yet in December 1943, when the Portland local refused membership to a black worker, the only thing done by the ILWU's international leaders (perhaps because it was wartime) was that Bridges wrote a letter to the local's membership condemning the exclusion of a "man solely because he was a Negro" and urging them to "eliminate any form of racial discrimination from your ranks"; "outside of [this] letter," according to Nancy Quam-Wickham, "the International took no action." ILWU's leaders were not prepared to take concerted action against the local to abolish discrimination, as she points out, because this would have required that they make "a drastic modification of the hiring hall system" (1992, p. 64). In the years after ILWU's expulsion from the CIO, with the union now on its own and under attack, the international leadership feared, as its regional director said in 1952, that if they "kicked the Portland local out of the International because they discriminated," this would drive its members into the ILA and weaken the ILWU, and would "hurt the Negro longshoremen . . . as well as the whites. So we decided to live with it" (Nelson 1998, p. 162). "In time, the ideological commitment to racial equality among left-wing ILWUers prevailed, but only after many highly contested and costly battles in the postwar period . . . " (Quam-Wickham 1992, p. 67).

ILWU's longshore Local 13 in San Pedro, near Los Angeles, did not exclude blacks, but neither did it welcome them: A contingent of Mexican Americans but no blacks were employed on the San Pedro waterfront before the war. When some 500 blacks, or 10 percent of the longshoreman, got jobs there during the war, this sudden influx of "colored guys" affected "the sense of camaraderie" of the "34 men" and the "mutual respect undergirding their working relationships." "Over time, the interaction among black, white, and Mexican American workers bred friendship and respect, as well as tension," but, again, with the

guarantee, but 43 percent, or over twice as many, of those without one had segregated locals "at one time or another."[13]

Black Representation

Genuine interracial unionism means "above all," as former NAACP Labor Secretary Herbert Hill observes, "... sharing power." Union leaders must be willing, as he says, "to accept blacks as equal partners in the leadership of unions ... and to permit them to share in the power that is derived from such institutional authority." Many union activists believed that black representation in a union's highest councils was necessary to ensure that the "most vital needs" of black workers were met, and black unionists saw it as being "at the heart" of racial egalitarianism.[14] We found one survey of black representation, but it covered only twenty-three "well-known C.I.O. internationals," and twelve of them had a black "international officer or member of the executive board" as of 1947.[15]

postwar's layoffs, led to black "exclusion." The layoffs fell mainly on the black workers because of their lower seniority; Bridges and the International leadership refused to assist the aggrieved "Unemployed 500" on the grounds that the local had adhered strictly to its rules of seniority. In 1947, frustrated in their attempts to get Bridges to help resolve their grievances against the local, nearly 100 of the laid-off blacks sought restitution through the NLRB and the courts (Nelson 1998, pp. 163–73).

That MM's Red leaders allowed segregation in its legendary Butte local, atop the country's biggest copper mountain, is also remarkable, for at the same time, in the Birmingham area, in marked contrast to USWA, they "insisted on full equality in Red Mountain, Alabama, locals, in defiance of local custom and the preferences of many white members" (Zieger 1995, p. 255). "More blacks were elected to leadership positions within Mine, Mill," according to Robin D. G. Kelley (1990, p. 145), "than any other CIO union, and its policy of racial egalitarianism remained unmatched" (also see Huntley 1977, 1990).

[13] On the constitutions as effective embodiments of the real inner political life of the unions, see the discussion in Chapter 3.

[14] Hill (1996, p. 199); Stevenson (1993, p. 46).

[15] John Williamson, author of the report on the survey, refers to "23 well-known internationals" (1947, p. 1012). But he lists only twenty-two and mistakenly omits the packing house workers (UPWA) from his list and also misclassifies the UE. We have put UPWA back on the list and corrected the misclassification of UE (see Critchlow 1976, p. 236). Williamson does not say how many black officials an international had nor how long they served. We found no systematic data on black representation at lower union levels, as stewards or committeemen, or members of negotiating teams, grievance committees, and other union bodies. It seems likely, however, that such data would reveal a pattern similar to the one at the international

Committee to Abolish Discrimination

In 1942, in response to criticisms by the NAACP and Urban League and pressure from black unionists, the CIO's leadership created the Committee to Abolish Racial Discrimination (CARD), to do more to promote racial equality in employment.[16] CARD was reincarnated as the Civil Rights Committee (CRC) after the war. Ten internationals also established their own committees to abolish discrimination, and cooperated closely with CARD/CRC and its state and local committees around the country. During the war, they formed alliances with the FEPC and its regional offices, and, we assume, they continued to function, as did the CRC, into the immediate postwar years.[17] In contrast, Marshall observes, "many international unions . . . gave it [CARD/CRC] only token support or ignored it entirely." Indeed, with the dawn of the Cold War, some international leaders even condemned CRC as "Communist-inspired," even though, as Marshall points out, it "actually functioned in part as an organization to fight Communists . . . in the Negro community."[18]

---

level. So, for example, the ILWU had a top black international officer, but, as early as 1940, its main Local 10, in the San Francisco Bay Area, also had three top black officers who served on its executive committee and board of trustees, as well as a dispatcher in its hiring hall (Foner 1976, pp. 231–32).

[16] Stevenson (1993, p. 48).

[17] See Foner (1976, p. 257fn). It was in the face of the all-black MOWM led by Sleeping Car Porters' head A. Philip Randolph that President Roosevelt issued his first executive order establishing the Fair Employment Practice Committee (FEPC) in June 1941, declaring that it was the "duty" of employers and labor unions in "defense industries" not to discriminate. Over 100,000 black workers had been expected to come to the capital, in Randolph's words, to demand, as "loyal Negro-American citizens . . . the right to work and fight for our country" (quoted in Foner 1976, p. 240). When Roosevelt issued his order, Randolph called off the march. Roosevelt issued a second order in May 1943 expanding the FEPC's jurisdiction to all industries affecting the national interest (Hill 1985, p. 179). The FEPC had no direct enforcement power, but its well-publicized investigations, in alliance with the CIO, served to expose racial injustice and spur black activism and often succeeded in pressuring employers to end discriminatory practices (Korstad and Lichtenstein 1988, p. 787; Rosen 1968, p. 189; Reid 1991, pp. 10, 85, 353; Zieger 1995, pp. 157–58). Harry Truman ended FEPC in 1946. In 1944 and again in 1945, in hearings on proposed bills to establish the statutory basis for a permanent FEPC and for a fair employment practice law, the AFL opposed them and actively contributed to their defeat. In contrast, the CIO's leadership and CARD actively supported the proposed legislation (Hill 1985, pp. 374–77).

[18] Marshall (1964, p. 185).

Index of Interracial Solidarity

We also use a simple measure of an international's overall commitment to interracial solidarity. We assigned a "point" for each of the following aspects of solidarity possessed by an international: a guarantee of membership equality, a black officer or executive board member, and a committee to abolish discrimination. The index does not include having segregated locals, because, as we pointed out earlier, the information on this aspect of solidarity was not the product of a systematic review of all CIO internationals.[19]

Black Membership

We found only one published systematic survey of the black membership of the CIO's internationals. The Labor Research Association provides estimates of the number of black members for twenty-two of the CIO's internationals, as of December 1944, and we found an estimate for a twenty-third international elsewhere. We calculated the percentage of blacks per international by dividing the estimated number of its black members by its estimated total 1944 membership.[20]

A "Culture of Solidarity"

Union leaders who embraced black aspirations often found themselves not only fighting against employers and their entrenched discriminatory practices, but also, in Dwight McDonald's phrase, against workers' "grass roots prejudices."[21] Take NMU, for instance. It was a militantly egalitarian seamen's union, whose Communist leaders worked far harder than most others in the CIO to advance black employment equality. But they "often found," according to August Meier and Elliott Rudwick, "the prejudices of both white employers and many white workers serious enough to inhibit [the union's] efforts at promoting

---

[19] We also ran the tables using the index modified to include the absence of segregated locals, and every relationship shown here was strengthened.

[20] Labor Research Association (1945, p. 73). Rosswurm (1992, p. 4) gives black membership estimates for three CIO internationals, but only one was not already on the Labor Research list. The total membership of CIO internationals is given in Huberman (1946, pp. 166–80). The membership of the UPW is the sum of the 1944 memberships of the Federal Workers and of the SCM; they merged with each other shortly afterward to form the UPW.

[21] McDonald (1944, p. 294) was commenting on one of the many "hate" strikes during the war by white workers to protest the employment or upgrading of black workers.

fully egalitarian practices in the industry."[22] In TWU, also, the "Communist-dominated . . . leadership, regardless of its ideals, was dependent on a white membership characterized by pervasive prejudices."[23]

Even the Rouge plant suffered antiblack wildcats during the war, although black workers exerted considerable influence in its politics and blacks held major leadership positions, including recording secretary, in Rouge's UAW Local 600. Archie Acciacca, a left-wing officer in the lily-white pressed steel unit, found himself caught in the middle of a wildcat when he tried to transfer two "high seniority" black workers into his unit: "I gave them a slip to go down there; and they replaced the youngest ones. Holy Toledo, . . . two blacks coming down there, there wasn't a black person in there. . . . All hell broke loose and they had a wildcat over it. Man, I told them, 'No way,' then I stood my guns all the more. I told them, 'Those people are going to go in there.'" Local 600's Ken Roche, a left-wing committeeman, recalls that the "maintenance unit was what you call a real, racist unit": "Rednecks from the South was in the leadership. . . . You would never find any blacks in the maintenance unit." In 1944, as then Michigan Communist leader Saul Wellman recalls, despite Local 600's "progressivism, . . . the left progressive leadership was defeated . . . because the left and Communists in 1943 and '44 had been trying to deal with the problem of Jim Crow in Dearborn."[24]

---

[22] Meier and Rudwick (1982, p. 166).

[23] Ibid., p. 195; cf. Lichtenstein 1997. During World War II, union leaders often found themselves having to oppose and discipline many of their own members who went out on wildcat "hate strikes." For instance, when Packard workers walked off the job in early June 1943 to protest upgrading of black workers, UAW president R. J. Thomas gave them an ultimatum that they had to go back to work or, as he said in a speech to UAW delegates, "if it means that large numbers of white workers are going to get fired, then that is exactly what's going to happen" (Winn 1943, p. 342; also see Keeran 1980, p. 232). Illustrative of the opposite way in which AFL leaders in the same city responded at the time to the struggle to break the color barriers in employment was the then head of a major trucking local. "No nigger," Jimmy Hoffa boasted to the FEPC, "will drive a truck in Detroit" (quoted in Kersten 1999b, p. 98). When violent black–white clashes broke out in the streets of Detroit during the week of June 20, 1943, in which thirty-four persons died and over a thousand were wounded, "no disorder [occurred] within [Detroit] plants, where colored and white men [in CIO industrial unions] worked side by side," as U.S. Attorney General Francis Biddle wrote to FDR, "*on account of efficient {CIO} union discipline*" (quoted in Lee and Humphrey 1943, p. 17, emphasis added). The head of the FEPC's Detroit office observed further that "this behavior in the plants may well be credited to the fact . . . that *these workers know each other better, have mutual interests and recognize their interdependence*" (quoted in Kersten 1999b, p. 93, emphasis added).

[24] Local 600 quotes are from Stepan-Norris and Zeitlin (1996b, pp. 141–42, 134, 148–49). On the left's fight for racial justice in Michigan, see Pintzuk (1997).

Thus, even in unions where the CIO's "culture of solidarity" was at its most vital, there were plenty of white workers who formed a potential or actual opposition to racial egalitarianism.[25] Yet even if and to the extent that such "grass-roots prejudices" set limits on the egalitarian actions of union leaders and activists, how they responded to these limits was not pregiven, nor were the limits somehow fixed in cement. Leaders and activists acted on their own racial prejudices and, more deeply, on their own innermost conceptions and convictions. In turn, we suggest, how they translated these conceptions and convictions into practice, how they dealt with the various issues of racial equality, in the union's own political life and its battles with employers, also shaped the workers' prejudices.

Rank-and-File Democracy and Interracial Solidarity

Remarkably, we have found no previous work that offers an explicit theory of the relationship between a union's internal political life and its substantive racial policies and practices. From what we have said in preceding chapters, our own theory must already be evident. In a nutshell, the more vibrant a union's political life, the more committed its members will be to interracial solidarity. If union leaders and activists are willing, whether as an expression of democratic ideals or egalitarian principles, or both, to challenge and engage the union's members fully and freely in a real give-and-take about the issue of bigotry or brotherhood and try to bring them together, in practice, around common grievances, in common struggles, irrespective of "race or color," then they are bound to develop mutual regard and respect or, in Dubois's words, "interracial tolerance and understanding." In short, as we argued in Chapter 6, rank-and-file democracy – "members running their own union," as Matles puts it – tends to create and sustain a sense of common identity among the union's members, and to transform it into a solidary workers' political community that transcends any racial, ethnic, or religious differences among them.

Constitutional Democracy and Factionalism

What, then, do we find? On every measure except black representation (perhaps because the numbers with the relevant data are even smaller in these categories), the highly democratic internationals were far more likely than the oligarchic to evidence interracial solidarity. The pattern is even sharper for factionalism:

[25] Fantasia (1988); also see Lizabeth Cohen (1990, pp. 333ff), who refers, in a parallel phrase, to "the CIO's culture of unity"; Killian (1952); Sugrue (1996).

On every measure, the level of black/white solidarity was far higher among the internationals with organized factions than among those with none. The deep gap between the internationals in these polar categories is indicated by their average scores on the solidarity index: 1.9 for the highly democratic versus 0.9 for the oligarchic internationals, or a "solidarity ratio" of over 2 to 1 in favor of the highly democratic, and a score of 1.9 for those with organized factions versus 0.75 for those with none, or a solidarity ratio of 2.5 to 1 in favor of organized factions (see Table 9.1).

Size of the Black Membership

It might be argued that to the extent that democracy allows a racial minority to organize and express its demands openly and, especially, to exert pressure through the exercise of its "bargaining power" in the struggle among rival factions for union leadership, our findings are really a mere reflection of the relative size of the black membership. Thus, some leading analysts of the economics of racism argue, as does Orley Ashenfelter, for instance, that the "extent to which the [union's] jurisdiction is composed of actual, or potential, black workers" is the main determinant of a union's "racial policy" – that is, "the larger the fraction" black, "both prior and subsequent to unionization," the "more egalitarian [the] race policy."[26] Hill, the NAACP's former labor secretary, argues that CIO unions "found it necessary at their inception, to accept black workers into membership in order to organize . . . industries . . . [with] a significant concentration of black workers." In his view, the "imperative of race" (that is, the relative racial composition of the union's membership) was "decisive" in determining the "racial practices" of CIO unions. He even goes so far as to assert that the CIO's "admission [of black workers] into union ranks was the most effective method of achieving control" over them and preventing them from becoming an antiunion force.[27]

Certainly, black workers were among the strongest proponents of racially egalitarian unionism. So it is plausible that otherwise unresponsive officials would be unlikely to ignore a large black membership, because of its

---

[26] Ashenfelter (1972, pp. 440–41; 1973, p. 94).

[27] Hill (1996, pp. 199, 201–2); cf. Olson (1970). Although Hill asserts that what made it "necessary" for CIO unions, "at their inception, to accept black workers into membership" was the "significant concentration of black workers" already employed in the places that they were organizing, none of the new AFL industrial unions (e.g., in aircraft, shipbuilding, steel, and transportation) in places with a "significant concentration of black workers" – as Hill knows but ignores in making his argument – "found it necessary, at their inception, to accept black workers."

Table 9.1. *Percentage of CIO international unions with specified aspects of interracial solidarity, by constitutional democracy and factionalism*

	Part 1. Interracial solidarity by constitutional democracy					
Constitutional democracy	Guarantee of membership equality[a]	Segregated locals "at one time or another"[b]	Committee to abolish discrimination[c]	(N)	Black officer or executive board member[d]	Index mean
Highly democratic	100	0	40	(10)	44 (9)	1.9 (9)
Moderately democratic	86	21	29	(14)	71 (7)	2.1 (7)
Oligarchic	64	55	18	(11)	43 (7)	0.9 (7)
Total	83	26	29	(35)	52 (23)	1.7 (23)
Log odds ratio	1.63*	−1.60*	0.54^z		−0.01	
Standard error	.82	.71	.50		0.50	
	Part 2. Interracial solidarity by factionalism					
Organized	100	20	50	(10)	37 (8)	1.9 (8)
Sporadic	87	37	37	(8)	57 (7)	1.6 (7)
None	40	60	0	(5)	25 (4)	0.75 (4)
Total	83	35	35	(23)[e]	42 (19)	1.5 (19)
Log odds ratio	2.63*	−0.89^y	1.23^x		0.17	
Standard error	1.23	0.60	0.72		0.61	

[a] The international's constitution had a provision guaranteeing equal eligibility for membership "regardless of race" (Summers 1946, pp. 192–207).

[b] The international had one or more segregated locals "at one time or another" (Rosen 1968, p. 204; Marshall 1965, p. 107n27; 1964, p. 186).

[c] The international established a committee to abolish discrimination in 1942 (Foner 1974, p. 257n).

[d] The international had an elected black officer or executive board member. The numbers (in parentheses) in the categories in this column differ from the numbers in the total column because the survey of black officials covered only "23 well-known internationals" (Williamson 1947, p. 1012).

[e] The total number of internationals is reduced to twenty-three here because of missing data on internal factions for the other internationals.

^{z} $p < 0.28$.

^{y} $p < 0.14$.

^{x} $p < 0.08$.

* $p < 0.05$.

potential for "making trouble" and threatening their rule – or even bolting to another, rival union more responsive to distinctive black needs. But, as Michael Goldfield suggests, "a large percentage of Black workers in a union was almost never sufficient . . . to create . . . interracial solidarity and egalitarian unionism," and, at the same time, several internationals with small black memberships displayed, as he points out, "a strong commitment to racial equality."[28]

Unfortunately, our ability to assess the independent effect of the relative size of the black membership in determining a union's commitment to interracial solidarity is highly limited by missing data (not only on this variable itself, but also on one or another of the three components of the solidarity index and on factions). Missing data reduce the set of relevant internationals to sixteen for the assessment of the independent effects of both the size of the black membership and the level of democracy, and to thirteen for the assessment of the effects of both black membership and the presence of factions. So, to facilitate analysis, we simply split the internationals into two categories on each variable: democratic versus oligarchic, factions versus no factions, and "small" black membership (10 percent or less) versus "large" (over 10 percent), and we measured the commitment to interracial solidarity by the mean score on the solidarity index – though taking these steps, as we see below, scarcely rescues the analysis from the bane of shrinking numbers.

Both overall among all internationals and in the democratic column, the relative size of the black membership barely made a difference in their measurable commitment to interracial solidarity. In the democratic column, the scores earned on the solidarity index by the internationals with a small versus a large black membership were not far apart; indeed, the ones with a small black membership scored slightly higher than those with a large black membership. But among the internationals in the oligarchic column, the difference was sharp (and consistent with what we might call the Ashenfelter/Hill hypothesis): Among the oligarchic internationals, the ratio of the solidarity score of those with a large black membership to the score of those with a small black membership was 4.5:1. The pattern is similar when we take into account both factionalism and the size of the black membership. Among the internationals with no factions, the solidarity score of

---

[28] Goldfield (1993, pp. 22, 25). Among these antiracist unions with small black memberships, for instance, were UAW Local 248 discussed in the previous chapter, which was 4.2 percent black (and well over half Jamaican) at the war's end; the NMU, 9.4 percent black (see Critchlow 1976); FE, 4.2 percent black (see Gilpin 1993); and IFLWU, 11.0 percent black (see Foner 1950). (Except for Local 248, these percentages are for December 1944, based on data in Labor Research Association 1945, p. 73, and Huberman 1946, pp. 166–80.)

Table 9.2. *Average interracial solidarity score by the size of black membership, constitutional democracy, and factionalism in CIO international unions*

Part 1. Constitutional democracy				
Relative size of black membership	Highly and moderately democratic	(N)	Oligarchic	(N)
Small (0–10%)	2.3	(6)	0.3	(3)
Large (>10%)	2.2	(5)	1.5	(2)
Total	2.3	(11)	0.8	(5)
Part 2. Presence of internal factions				
Relative size of black membership	Organized and sporadic	(N)	None	(N)
Small (0–10%)	2.3	(4)	0.3	(3)
Large (>10%)	2.0	(5)	1.0	(1)
Total	2.1	(9)	0.5	(4)

the internationals that had a large black membership was far higher than the score of those with a small black membership. But among the internationals with factions, those with a small black membership had a slightly higher score.

Although an oligarchic international leadership, or one faced by neither a durable nor even a sporadic opposition, would otherwise have been unresponsive to the will of the rank and file, a large cohesive black membership apparently was able, compared with a small one, to exert sufficient pressure on such leadership to win more egalitarian racial policies and practices. But in the democratic internationals, or where rival factions competed for leadership, not the size of the black membership but the essence of rank-and-file democracy itself enhanced interracial solidarity.

This reasoning is also consistent with our finding (contrary to Hill's reasoning) that, whether the black membership was small or large, the average solidarity score of the democratic internationals was far higher than that of the oligarchic internationals, and the pattern was the same for factionalism (see Table 9.2).

The Red and the Black

Radicalism and Interracial Solidarity

"The Communists courageously championed the Black cause," in Bert Cochran's words, ". . . when to do so was as popular or rewarding as the championship of Christianity in the time of Nero."[29] By the time of the CIO's birth, the Communists already had been championing black rights and black Americans' distinctive needs and struggles for nearly a decade. Since the enunciation in 1922 of the Comintern's new anticolonial line and, specifically, its resolution calling for self-determination of the "oppressed black nation" of the South, but especially from its early 1930s revolutionary "Third Period" on, the CP had vigorously denounced racism (and, most notably, had led the defense of – and saved from execution – the Scottsboro Nine) and engaged in an "unrelenting fight for the concrete economic needs of poor blacks."[30]

The radical TUEL and its Communist-led successor TUUL had made interracial working-class solidarity their clarion call. In opposition to the racial exclusionism of the AFL and its affiliates, the TUEL's program had stated: "The problem of the politically, and industrially disenfranchised Negroes shall occupy the serious attention of the League. The League shall demand that the Negroes be given the same social, political and industrial rights as whites, including the right to work in all trades, equal wages, admission to all trade unions, abolition of Jim-Crow [street-]cars and restaurants."[31]

---

[29] Cochran (1977, p. 225). An egregious exception to the CP's stance on behalf of racial equality came in its policy toward Japanese Americans during World War II. Not only did party officials endorse President Roosevelt's February 19, 1942, order to incarcerate in "relocation" camps, without so much as a hearing, 110,000 Japanese Americans and Japanese aliens, but they already had set an example in the way they treated their own comrades. On December 8, 1941, the day after Japanese planes bombed Pearl Harbor, Earl Browder, the party's general secretary, issued the following order: "In the name of national unity, all members of Japanese ancestry and their non-Japanese spouses shall be suspended from the CP for the duration of the war" (Pintzuk 1997, p. 72).

[30] As early as 1915, Lenin had come to the conclusion, on the basis of his studies of black sharecroppers and tenants, that blacks in the United States constituted an oppressed nation (1963). But whatever the effects of Lenin's theory and of the new Comintern line adopted under his leadership (and that of M. N. Roy, the Indian Communist theoretician and leader) in 1922, black Communists (and especially the African Blood Brotherhood, which joined the party en masse in the early 1920s) were decisive in formulating the American CP's program on the black question, including self-determination. And then, during the 1930s, "African American culture created a home for itself in Communist circles because of the growing presence of black working people. And . . . they found a way to embrace both the Communists' internationalism and their own vision of Pan-Africanism simultaneously" (Kelley 1996, pp. 110, 106–8, 121, 267n6).

[31] *Labor Herald* (July 1924, p. 156, cited in Foner 1991, p. 337).

In the early 1930s, as Communists and their radical allies built rank-and-file committees inside AFL affiliates and organized new TUUL unions, they fought for the rights of black workers, and for their inclusion at all levels. "During the strike wave of 1934," as Mark Solomon points out, "Communists targeted wage differentials based on race, fought segregation, and insisted that every vestige of union discrimination be addressed and eliminated." TUUL cadres were "unrelenting advocates of black rights" who went on to imbue the new CIO unions with their racial egalitarianism.[32]

TUUL cadres also worked hand in hand with the Communist-led Unemployed Councils in the major industrial cities, seeking to ally people of all races and ethnicities.[33] So, for instance, here is what Brown Squires, a black TUUL organizer, told a gathering of the unemployed in Chicago in January 1931:

> The working class, not by color, or not by creed, produces everything that is produced . . . ; and yet they enjoy none of it. . . . The only way by which the ruling class can keep us from food, from jobs, or even from controlling what we produce, is by using one laborer against another, one race against another.

The Communists' battle against rent evictions especially won them black support. "Evictions, evictions," TUUL's William Z. Foster said at the same gathering at which Squires spoke:

> the other day in Pittsburgh, I was present when the eviction took place – that is, when they tried to make it take place. A Negro woman, a woman with seven children, a widow – they came down to evict her from her home, because she could not pay the rent. Well, fortunately, we were able to stop it. We gathered up a few of the neighbors, one hundred or two, and they waited for this constable and this landlord. When they came to make this eviction, they gathered around this constable and this landlord, and they were damn glad to get out of there with whole skins without evicting this woman.[34]

Black participants in the unemployed movement especially "gloried in standing up to the landlords and police while singing the old spiritual 'I shall not be moved,'" as Lizabeth Cohen observes, "and in thwarting the efforts of the

[32] Solomon (1998, p. 256).   [33] Cohen (1990, p. 265).
[34] Lasswell and Blumenstock (1939, pp. 158, 160).

utility companies to turn off gas and electricity when bills went unpaid. With pride, they asserted their rights before social agencies that long intimidated them. 'It was a period of great learning,' black Communist leader William Patterson remembered."[35]

Blacks were highly prominent among the leaders of the Unemployed Councils. In Chicago, for instance, 21 percent of the leaders and 25 percent of the members of the Communist-led Unemployed Councils were black, compared with only 6 percent of the leadership and 5 percent of the membership of the socialist-led unemployed Workers' Committees. In 1932, a disproportionate 17 percent of those who voted for Foster for president of the United States lived in the Chicago Black Belt's second and third wards.[36] Black–white unity in many cities had thus been forged both in earlier Red unionism and in the Communist-led unemployed movement, and this in turn was a crucial source of interracial unity in the CIO's organizing drives.

Everywhere, but especially in the South, "Communists won the confidence of black workers," as George M. Fredrickson explains, "because they seemed to be free of racial prejudice and committed to the cause of black civil rights as well as to the expansion of industrial unionism."[37] Class-conscious radicals, mainly Communists and their allies, forged a strategy in which they tried "to show southern workers a 'different way of livin' by stimulating labor militancy and class confrontation" and creating a unique blend of southern male conceptions of "personal honor and class identity," of "individual combativeness and class struggle." They appealed to both black and white workers by stressing their common, class interests and linking "racial oppression" and "class exploitation."

In practice, of course, the success of this strategy of interracial unity "depended on a series of subtle tactical opportunities, in which the organizer had to choose the appropriate moment to raise racial concerns. . . . Seemingly intractable racial tensions could often be defused by the organizer's response."

So, for instance, "Blackie" Merrell, a former NMU organizer and officer, recalled:

> I had one white guy on a ship I was on who refused to sleep in the same quarters with a black guy after we integrated. Instead of rammin' it down his throat, I told him, now look, I'll sleep there tonight, and let you have

---

[35] Cohen (1990, p. 266).

[36] Lasswell and Blumenstock (1939, p. 280); Cohen (1990, pp. 262, 266); see also Drake and Cayton (1945, pp. 86–88, 734–740).

[37] Fredrickson (1995, p. 34). On the TUUL and Unemployed Councils in Birmingham, "the heart of southern industrialism," see Kelley (1989).

my bunk. The next night he was okay, and that was the turning point, everything straightened out then.

Or, as A. C. Burttram, a radical Steel Worker organizer in the mid-1930s in Birmingham, Alabama, explained:

We had a city ordinance here in Birmin'ham about segregated meetin's. You had to have a partition between colored an white, to within two inches of the ceilin'. You know what we told 'em? Go to hell! We're meetin' in this damn union hall, payin' rent on this son of a bitch! . . . And the white guys went along with this, because they knew it was in their own interest, plain and simple.[38]

In fact, the surprising consensus of scholars about the Communists' crucial role in organizing interracial unions and fighting for black equality contrasts sharply with the fractious scholarly debates about other aspects of their record. The Communists, says Herbert Northrup, were among "the staunchest supporters" of black unionists. Or as Jack Barbash, an ardent Reuther supporter at the time, puts it: "The Communist unions have always pursued vigorous antidiscrimination policies as a matter of political ideology and tactics."[39] David Shannon also concedes in his study of "the decline of American Communism" that "the Communists have been, in their own way, vigorous champions of the rights of minorities. . . . " "Communists," says Ray Marshall, " . . . almost always adopted equalitarian racial positions. Although many doubted the sincerity of the Communists' racial policies, there can be little question that, by emphasizing the race issue to get Negro support, the Communists forced white union leaders to pay more attention to racial matters." The Communist-led unions, according to Sumner Rosen, were "the more militant and devoted advocates of racial justice. . . . Clearly the [Communist] Party's role inside the CIO was to . . . participate effectively in organizing many Negro workers, and to single out for special attention the

---

[38] Regensburger (1987a, pp. 10, 28, 30, 134, 165; see also 1987b, 1983). On August 28, 1988, in Birmingham, Alabama, Zeitlin heard a similar story from Charlie Wilson, a former MM organizer, about how Wilson got the men to desegregate the union hall of the MM iron miners' local there in the late 1930s. On southern interracial Red unionism and Communist-led CIO unionism, see Kelley (1988; 1989; 1990); Honey (1993; 1994; 1999); and Goldfield (1994).

[39] Northrup (1944, p. 235; also see p. 131); Barbash (1948, p. 62). Barbash, remember, was the author of a famous diagnosis of "Communist penetration of unions as . . . a form of union pathology" (Barbash 1956, pp. 324–25).

problems, grievances, and ambitions of Negro workers in individual CIO unions."[40]

"Communists played very active roles in combating discrimination in both shop and union affairs. In union after union," according to Harvey Levenstein, "Communists challenged the traditional devices built into the rules of unions and work places perpetuating segregation of the races and second-class status for blacks. Their record in unions . . . was generally exemplary on this score." Michael Goldfield concludes, on the basis of his study of the secondary literature on "the racial practices of CIO unions in all parts of the country," but especially in the South, that, in general, left-led unions, "usually with integrated . . . organizers, officials, and cadre . . . were more committed in principle and in practice to racial egalitarianism than [unions led by] nonleftists."[41]

Robert Zieger similarly concludes that "the Communists and their allies . . . created and sustained the most principled biracial unions of the CIO era, unions that in some cases pioneered in promoting egalitarian workplace practices and in energizing somnolent civil rights organizations."[42] Even John Earl Haynes, author or coauthor of a number of recent works intended to illuminate the "dangerous and intolerable" activities of the Communists, whose "goal," he says, "was the destruction of American society," acknowledges that the Communists and "progressives" aligned with them were "civil rights pioneers. Communist-led CIO unions were noticeably more aggressive than others in championing equal treatment for black workers. . . . "[43]

Communists and their radical allies in the CIO were especially prominent among unionists who pressed for a permanent, constitutionally legitimated black presence in the top leadership of the internationals. As Zieger observes, "pro-Soviet unions made special efforts to recruit blacks into leadership roles and to insure African-American representation on negotiating teams, grievance committees, and other union bodies." Indeed, Irving Howe and Lewis Coser remark derisively that "Stalinists appointed themselves the special defenders of the Negro unionists. . . . And with mechanical regularity, they kept pushing Negroes into the leadership of their unions or factions, quite *regardless of whether these Negroes were competent.*"[44]

Perhaps the most important dissent from the consensus about the Communists' outstanding devotion to the struggle for black equality comes from the NAACP's Hill. He argues, based on his examination of "litigation records and

[40] Shannon (1959, p. 6); Marshall (1967b, p. 24); Rosen (1968, p. 200).
[41] Levenstein (1981, p. 332); Goldfield (1993, p. 25).
[42] Zieger (1995, pp. 373–74, 375–76, 159); also see Stevenson (1993, pp. 47, 50).
[43] Haynes (1996, pp. 198–99, 120–21).
[44] Zieger (1995, p. 159); Howe and Coser (1957, p. 380, emphasis added).

other documents," that the only unions "controlled by the Communist Party operating as CIO affiliates" that stood out as racially egalitarian – "for a brief period, mainly in the South" – were those which "were essentially all-black unions where black workers assumed leadership positions," for example, FTA. These Communist-controlled unions, he says, certainly "conducted militant struggles against the blatant racist practices of employers."[45] But, in general, he concludes:

> Industrial unions with a communist leadership and with a *predominantly white membership* were substantially *no different* in their racial practices than other labor organizations. . . . No less for communist-controlled unions . . . than for the rest of organized labor, *the imperative of race was decisive* and the prevalence of white racism overwhelmed the few scattered examples of interracial unionism.[46]

Judith Stein is less critical of Communist unionists than Hill, but she insists that "many egalitarian measures, praised in left wing unions, were standard in 'right-wing' unions," such as the efforts by the Steel Workers' international leadership to end the southern black/white differential in wages. Overall, she argues,

> [the] Communist party's role was smaller than some have argued. Insofar as the party's doctrines on "the Negro Question" encouraged *racial essentialism*, it was a positive *hindrance* to interracial unionism. National policies on race oscillating between campaigns against white chauvinism and then against black nationalism, stemmed more from party struggles than from the experiences of local unionists. The party bureaucracy often overrode the judgment of local blacks and whites.[47]

Communists and their radical allies, despite their adherence to a doctrine of class struggle, early on recognized and emphasized the specificity of black oppression, which they saw as an inherent evil to be fought and extirpated. We see no reason, however, to accept Stein's assertion that this conviction itself hindered interracial unionism. Rather (as she herself also observes) what undermined black (and other radical) support for Communist unionists, if anything, was the shifting and opportunist line (especially during the war) of

---

[45] In fact, the estimated black share of the FTA's entire membership in 1944 was only 9.2 percent (Labor Research Association 1945, p. 73). We found no regional breakdown of the racial composition of its membership.

[46] Hill (1996, pp. 201–2, emphasis added).

[47] Stein (1993, pp. 54, 62, emphasis added).

the party officialdom and their dogmatic insistence that its adherents toe that line.

Indeed, Zieger argues, to the contrary, and paradoxically, that not the Communists but the CIO's leading liberals and anti-Communist socialists (e.g., Walter Reuther) held a "class essentialist" conception of race that weakened their practical commitment to racial egalitarianism. They saw black workers as "workers first and members of a victimized minority group second." Taking a "gradualist" and "realistic" stance, liberals and anti-Communist socialists (and their allies among "right wingers") argued that fair treatment for black workers would be won through "standard collective bargaining."[48] They discouraged racial militancy in the workplace and the union hall, and followed an incremental strategy of education and moral suasion of their unions' members. In Zieger's words, "most [non-Communist] CIO unionists downplayed the race card and *subsumed concern for black workers under class appeals* that ignored or evaded confrontation with racist forces in the community and on the shop floor."[49]

The Anti-Fascist War and the "Negro Question"

Unlike the favorable consensus about the Communists' overall role in defense of black rights during the CIO era, the assessments of what they and their allies did during World War II – when their party's leaders were tireless and strident in calling for "uninterrupted production" in the "antifascist war" and denouncing strikers as traitors – are sharply divided and, typically, harshly negative.[50]

---

[48] Zieger (1995, p. 158). That racist oppression did not have to be fought independently of the class struggle was also the official line of the anti-Communist Socialist Party of America at the time. Its leaders "held steadfastly to the idea that socialism was the only way to solve the problems of blacks" (Kelley 1996, p. 106; see Foner 1977; Shannon 1955, pp. 49–52).

[49] Zieger (1995, p. 374, emphasis added); also see Stevenson (1993, p. 48).

[50] The initial setback for the Communists came on the eve of the war, in their isolation from the burgeoning March on Washington Movement in the early months of 1941. The CP condemned MOWM, in accordance with its sudden zig-zag, in the fall of 1939, from an "antifascist" line to an anti-"imperialist war" line (in response to the signing of the Nazi–Soviet nonaggression pact on August 23, 1939). They feared MOWM would encourage blacks to support "imperialist war preparations." But as MOWM grew into a black mass movement, the party shifted its position, and the *Daily Worker* began to feature news about the march, according to Philip Foner, despite the party's antiwar line in obeisance to the Hitler–Stalin Pact, weeks *before* the German surprise attack on the Soviet Union. The day before the German invasion began, that newspaper "called upon 'all fair-minded citizens' who believed in 'both peace and job equality . . . [to] throw their full weight behind the Job March to Washington in July.' Although their last-minute efforts probably helped to build

The Communists, as Julius Jacobson sums up the charge, were now "prepared to sacrifice the rights of Negroes in the interests of the war [effort]." In 1949, Roy Wilkins, then NAACP Acting Secretary, remembered "... that during the war when Negro Americans were fighting for jobs on the home front... [the Communists] abandoned the fight for Negro rights on the ground that such a campaign would 'interfere with the war effort.' As soon as Russia was attacked by Germany they dropped the Negro question... [and] sounded very much like the worst of the Negro-baiting southerners." Shannon says that "the Communists took the position that unity for the war effort demanded that racial discrimination be at least temporarily tolerated if not condoned." Wilson Record also concludes:

> For most of the war [the CP's] main activity was to stifle Negro protest and to urge black workers and soldiers to [comply]... with the white man's terms, just as it urged unions to get on with the production job, on the bosses' terms if necessary... [although] by late 1943, the Communists used such organizations as the NNC [National Negro Congress] and the SNYC [Southern Negro Youth Congress] to launch occasional protests in the military and industry.[51]

This sort of critique of the Communists' wartime history relies mainly on an examination of the pronouncements of party officials or of enunciations of the "party line" on the "Negro question" in party publications. But what Communist unionists and their allies were actually doing often differed markedly from what an examination of that "line" alone might lead one to conclude (as we have shown in our analysis of the relative prolabor content of the wartime contracts won by Communist-led internationals). As Martin Glaberman remarks correctly in his book on workers' wartime militancy: "Although the policies of the Communist Party are easy to document, [gauging] the

---

support for the march, the Communists undoubtedly lost prestige in the black community because of their earlier hostility to the MOWM and the time it took to come out in its favor" (1976, p. 278).

[51] Jacobson (1968, p. 7); Wilkins (1950); Shannon (1959, p. 6); Record (1964, pp. 120–26). Even some leading black Communists, among them Benjamin Davis, then a New York City councilman representing Harlem, also retrospectively denounced the party's wartime "errors" and "illusory conclusions" in "the field of Negro work," and charged that the party's "slogan [sic] of ending racial discrimination was in effect seriously weakened... " (quoted in Hill 1951, p. 10, from an article in the *Daily Worker*, July 22, 1945). (This "self-criticism" was a premonition of the party's self-inflicted paroxysm over "white chauvinism" among its members. See Chapter 11, esp. note 2.)

influence of the party [in the shops] is something else again." Glaberman, who was an auto union activist in Detroit at the time, observes – even though he was a fierce adversary of the Communists – that "during the war . . . [the Communists] were especially successful among black workers. Although on a national scale they attempted to restrain the militancy of the black movement, on a personal level and on the shop floor, CP members were *the most consistent and principled element in the labor movement in fighting for the rights of black workers.*"[52]

Similarly, regarding the charge that the Communists stifled black protest during the war, Bert Cochran remarks that it is "valid but [is] . . . not the whole story." Rather, he notes that the "party stake[d] out positions in different localities and organizations battling for Negro rights by varied and energetically pursued efforts. . . . Communists found favor among black activists in unions by repeatedly and forcefully advancing their demands."[53]

Despite "the [Communists'] . . . tendency to subordinate the grievances of black workers to the interests of winning the war," Philip Foner argues, "the left-wing unions had the best record in the fight against racial discrimination during World War II." Zieger's conclusion, too, is that "[a]lthough Communist-oriented unions rarely risked shop-floor confrontations [during the war] over race or anything else that might jeopardize output, they did more than other affiliates to address the distinct interests of black workers."[54]

A crude indicator of black workers' wartime support for the Communists comes, as Cochran put it, from "Communist recruitment figures . . . for whatever they are worth." Cochran notes that these figures "show no falling off of appeal [to blacks] in the war years": In the 1935–36 period, 15 to 17 percent of the total number of newly recruited party members were reported to be black; by 1943, black recruits rose to 31 percent of the total; and by 1944, to 37 percent.[55]

The influential *Negro Digest*, a popular black magazine, took a poll of its readers in late 1944 and found that some seven in ten thought the Communists

---

[52] Glaberman (1980, pp. 69, 73, emphasis added); cf. Seidman (1950).

[53] Cochran (1977, pp. 227–28). Take, for example, IFLWU, "which had an avowedly Stalinist leadership" (Zieger 1995, p. 290): The international expanded its interracial organizing throughout the war, while at the same time ardently adhering to the no-strike pledge. The union even opened an organizing "drive to the South": Its organizers in tanneries scattered across the South, in Delaware, Kentucky, Maryland, Virginia, Tennessee, and North Carolina, were both black and white, and its campaign steadfastly adhered to a commitment to "full and equal rights for all members of the union, Negro and white" (Foner 1950, pp. 622–23).

[54] Foner (1976, p. 280); Zieger (1995, p. 159).   [55] Cochran (1977, p. 228).

were still loyal to the fight for black rights: "The majority opinion was," the *Digest* noted in its December issue, "that the Communists in their all-out support of the war are supporting a cause which is synonymous with the fight for racial equality."[56] In 1945, Adam Clayton Powell, Jr., former pastor of New York City's Abyssinian Church, who had been elected to Congress from New York, declared: "There is no group in America, including the Christian Church, that practices racial brotherhood one tenth as much as the Communist Party." That same year, a prominent black Communist, Benjamin Davis, Jr., of Harlem, who had first been elected to the New York City council on the Communist ticket in 1941 and had been reelected during the war in 1943, again won reelection. In 1946, a Communist candidate for the Massachusetts legislature got one sixth of the total vote, and much of his support came from "Boston's twelfth ward, Roxbury, a generally poor neighborhood with considerable Negro and immigrant population. . . . The following year, a Communist candidate for city council from that ward received one fourth of the vote."[57]

"Operation Dixie"

Left / right differences on the question of confronting racism are illuminated by "Operation Dixie," the CIO's brief postwar Southern Organizing Campaign (SOC), which began in 1946 and faded soon after. SOC functionaries insisted that the campaign involve "no extra-curricular activities – no politics – no PAC – no FEPC, etc."[58] Banning "political agitation," as Zieger says, "was a coded way of marginalizing the [Communist] left [which] . . . had pioneered in linking industrial unionism and civil rights" in the South. The campaign – in contrast to earlier unionization drives led by "the CIO's Communists and their allies who had built small but impressive enclaves of aggressive biracial unionism in Dixie" – mainly "bypassed those industries in which large numbers of blacks toiled." SOC's head, Van Bittner, declared that they were not "mentioning the color of people." So far as the CIO was concerned, he said, there is "no Negro problem in the South."

Despite their disagreement with this strategy, and their being shunted aside, Communist unionists and their allies publicly supported the campaign. "But unionists associated with a dozen or so affiliates in which pro-Soviet leaders were prominent . . . suggested a different approach. Instead of futile assaults

---

[56] The *Negro Digest* article is quoted in Keeran (1980, p. 231).
[57] Powell (1945, p. 69); Shannon (1959, pp. 99, 100).
[58] Quoted in Zieger (1995, p. 233), from SOC minutes, April 11, 1946.

on the textile citadels, why not throw resources into areas of previous success? Why not, for example, make use of black workers' proven support for the CIO to extend organization into food processing, wood and lumber working, transport and goods handling, and tobacco working?" Men such as UE's Matles, FTA's Donald Henderson, and NMU's Joe Curran reiterated their view that "biracial unionism and ... recruitment of black workers held the key to CIO success in the South."[59]

The Political Camps and Black Rights

Now, gauging how much the Communist-led internationals differed from those in rival camps on the "black question" presents a special problem, because their influence radiated throughout the CIO and, as Rosen observes, "strengthen[ed] the rhetorical and political commitment to racial equality." That is, "competition within the CIO between Communists and non-Communists caused the latter to adopt more outspoken equalitarian positions in order to gain the allegiance of Negro workers." Even such a severe critic of the Communists as Record points out that

> it is not likely that union leaders would have given as much attention to the matter or developed the specific programs they did in the absence of prodding from Communist elements. ... [They] often made the question of Negro rights an intra-union political issue and consequently *forced non-Communist groups to take practical cognizance of it.* ... It is questionable, for example, whether the UAW–CIO would have developed its remarkably effective program for combating union and management discrimination had not the Communists served as a hair shirt.

"Often it was only the insistence of Communists and their allies," Zieger also emphasizes, "that forced CIO bodies to address such 'extraneous' matters as civil rights and civil liberties. ... Locals with vigorous Communist presence in the UAW and Packinghouse Workers [UPWA] fought for the rights of African Americans within both the union and community." In fact, long after the anti-Communist purge, the UPWA's leaders, whose exemplary record of interracial unity was exceptional, still "found themselves suspect because of their emphasis on racial justice, which some in the CIO believed smacked of Communist enthusiasms." CIO officials even withheld the organization's

---

[59] Zieger (1995, pp. 233–34, 239–40, 437–38n95). See Griffith (1988) for a history of Operation Dixie.

support from the UPWA's efforts to organize both black and white workers in the sugar- and other food-processing industries.[60]

Given the racially egalitarian impact of Communists and their allies on the policies of the UAW, UPWA, and other internationals, especially in the "shifting" camp, the measured difference between the levels of interracial solidarity in the rival camps may well be smaller than these differences were in reality.

Yet we find, despite this, that the Communist camp stood out on our measures of interracial solidarity, except for having a committee to abolish discrimination, which was more frequent in the shifting camp: 94 percent of the sixteen Communist-led internationals, 70 percent of the ten shifting internationals, and 70 percent of the ten anti-Communist internationals had a guarantee of membership equality;[61] 13, 30, and 40 percent, respectively, had one or more segregated locals;[62] and 31, 40, and 10 percent, respectively, had a committee to abolish discrimination.[63] That a higher proportion of the internationals in the shifting camp than of those in the Communist camp had a committee to abolish discrimination may, paradoxically, reflect the pressures exerted in these internationals by "a strong Communist faction contending for [their] leadership."[64] In fact, the only international in the anti-Communist camp with a committee against discrimination was the American Newspaper Guild, which had a strong Communist faction, and both the New York and the Los Angeles chapters of the guild were led by Communists. As to black representation, 64 percent of the fourteen internationals in the Communist camp and 33 percent of the nine in the shifting and anti-Communist camps combined had a black officer or executive board member.[65]

Now, using the solidarity index, the pattern is consistent with and provides further evidence in support of the historians' consensus that, "in regard to race...the Communist-influenced CIO affiliates stood in the vanguard."[66] The fourteen internationals in the Communist camp had an average solidarity score of 1.9 but the nine internationals in the shifting and anti-Communist camps combined had an average score of 1.2.

---

[60] Rosen (1968, p. 200); Marshall (1965b, p. 36); Record (1951, p. 306, emphasis added); Zieger (1995, pp. 255–56, 346–47). On the history of the UPWA, see Halpern (1991, 1997) and Halpern and Horowitz (1996).

[61] Log odds ratio (uniform association) = 0.82, $p < 0.12$; standard error = 0.53.

[62] Log odds ratio (uniform association) = -0.75, $p < 0.11$; standard error = 0.48.

[63] Log odds ratio (uniform association) = 0.49, $p < 0.30$; standard error = 0.48.

[64] Marshall (1964, p. 187n40).

[65] Log odds ratio (uniform association) = 0.62, $p < 0.14$; standard error = 0.55.

[66] Zieger (1995, p. 255).

Size of the Black Membership

Yet, as we know, some scholars suggest that the racial policies and practices of CIO internationals were determined above all by the relative concentration of black workers, or the size of the black membership. In their view, "the leadership's ideological commitments per se" mattered little, if at all.[67] So, if the "Ashenfelter/Hill hypothesis" is right, the fact that the internationals in the Communist camp stood out in their commitment to interracial solidarity is deceptive. It was a result not of their Communist leadership but, it might be surmised, rather of their typically larger black memberships. This surmise is prima facie unconvincing, because the mean size of the black membership in the three camps hardly differed: In the Communist camp, it was 11.0 percent; in the shifting camp, 9.4 percent; and in the anti-Communist camp, 9.3 percent.[68]

But what does happen when we examine the effect of the relative size of black membership? To facilitate the analysis, given the small numbers in the relevant categories, we again use the average score on the solidarity index. We find that in the two non-Communist camps, the scores are consistent with the Ashenfelter/Hill hypothesis, but not in the Communist camp: The average score of the non-Communist internationals with a large black membership was much higher than the score of those with a small black membership, or a solidarity ratio of 2.66:1 in favor of a large black membership. In the Communist camp, however, the average score of the internationals with a small black membership was actually higher than the score of those with a large black membership. We also find, looking within the size categories, that where the black membership was large, the average solidarity score of the internationals in the Communist camp was the same as that of the other camps. But where the black membership was small, the average score in the Communist camp was much higher than that in the non-Communist camps, or a solidarity ratio of 3.2:1 in favor of the Communist camp (see Table 9.3).

So, the relative size of the black membership per se does not, contrary to the claims of Ashenfelter and Hill, appear to be the primary determinant of a union's racial policies and practices. Rather, the relative size of the black membership and political consciousness (or, in Ashenfelter's phrase, "the leadership's

---

[67] Ashenfelter (1972, pp. 440–41); Hill (1996, p. 202).

[68] This anti-Communist average excludes an outlier, the virtually all-black membership of the Red Cap union, UTSE. Its estimated 1944 black membership was 77 percent. (This is probably an underestimate because it was based on the racial composition of workers in the industry.) With the Red Caps included, the mean size of the black membership in the anti-Communist camp was 22.8 percent.

Table 9.3. *Average interracial solidarity score by political camp and by the size of black membership in CIO international unions*

Size of black membership	Political camp			
	Communist	(N)	Shifting and anti-Communist	(N)
Small (0–10%)	2.4	(5)	0.7	(4)
Large (> 10%)	2.0	(5)	2.0	(2)
Total	2.2	(10)	1.2	(6)

ideological commitments per se") interacted in determining the internationals' commitment to interracial solidarity, and it was especially where the black membership was small and might otherwise not have been able to win racially egalitarian policies and practices that leadership by Communists and their allies made the difference.

A Case Study: Two Locals, One Plant

The decisiveness of the leadership's political consciousness, and thus of the struggles they led, in determining interracial solidarity, irrespective of the size of the black membership, is illustrated by the contrast between the FE and UAW locals at the International Harvester plant in Louisville, Kentucky. Recall from Chapter 6 that the plant opened in 1946 with FE as the representative of all production and maintenance workers. But when the company began production three years later in a new foundry at the same plant, it became a separate bargaining unit, represented by the UAW.

Toni Gilpin found that the two locals conducted themselves very differently on issues of black/white equality, but not because of any so-called imperative of race. The FE local had an active rank and file who participated in frequent, well-attended meetings on both workplace and community issues. Its extensive steward system protected the workers on the shop floor, and they often engaged in work stoppages and belligerently defied management to enforce their grievances. The local's militancy, as we noted in Chapter 6, provoked an official of the company to exclaim that FE's stewards were less interested in resolving grievances than engaging in "class warfare." Many of the FE local's officers, members of the bargaining committee, and shop stewards were black, and the local aggressively fought to defend black rights. The local demanded and won the abolition of the until then separate and unequal "White" and "Colored" locker rooms and washrooms, and also integrated the cafeteria. Its frequent social events, involving the workers' spouses and families, were integrated, and the local also mobilized its membership to fight for integration of transportation, parks, and hotels in Louisville. Yet only 14 percent of the local's membership was black.

In contrast, the UAW foundry workers' local in the same plant, as we discussed earlier, emphasized "stability in labor relations" rather than "class warfare." In turn, this translated in practice into accommodation with local "custom and tradition" in race relations: According to a 1953 National Planning Association study cited by Gilpin, the UAW local challenged neither the vestiges of racial job differentiation in the foundry itself nor the segregated locker rooms and washrooms to which its members were subjected. Yet one half of its members were black.[69]

Clearly, the contrasting racial strategies of these Red and anti-Red locals were determined not by any so-called racial imperative but by the differences in their leaders' political consciousness: Communist or radical in the FE, and liberal, at best, in the UAW. FE's radicalism was, however, inseparable from its rank-and-file activism and democratic political life, and both – radicalism and democracy – interacted and reinforced each other, as Gilpin's analysis reveals, in shaping the local's racial egalitarianism.

Rank-and-File Democracy, Radicalism, and Solidarity

This raises a crucial analytical problem, for, as we know, radicalism and democracy tended to coincide in the CIO's internationals: 53 percent of the nineteen internationals in the non-Communist camps combined were oligarchic, but 94 percent of the sixteen in the Communist camp were democratic. Looked at from the opposite angle, the preponderant majority of democratic internationals were in the Communist camp, whereas the opposite was true of the oligarchic internationals: 70 percent of the ten highly democratic and 57 percent of the fourteen moderately democratic internationals were in the Communist camp, but 90 percent of the eleven oligarchic internationals were in the non-Communist camps (and split evenly between them, 45 percent in each). So, in reality, and in a double sense, Communist-led unionism was democratic rank-and-file unionism.

[69] Gilpin (1988, p. 28; 1993).

Table 9.4. *Interracial solidarity score by political camp, constitutional democracy, and factionalism in CIO international unions*

	Part 1. Average index score					
			Political camp			
Constitutional democracy	Communist	(N)	Shifting and anti-Communist	(N)	Total	(N)
High and moderate	2.0	(13)	2.3	(3)	2.1	(16)
Oligarchic	2.0	(1)	0.7	(6)	0.9	(7)
Total	2.0	(14)	1.2	(9)	1.7	(23)

	Part 2. Average index score					
			Political camp			
Presence of internal factions	Communist	(N)	Shifting and anti-Communist	(N)	Total	(N)
Organized and sporadic	1.8	(10)	1.8	(5)	1.8	(15)
None	–	(0)	0.5	(4)	0.5	(4)
Total	1.8	(10)	1.2	(9)	1.5	(19)

This makes it difficult, to say the least, to assess the relative weight of the level of constitutional democracy and the political consciousness of the leadership in determining interracial solidarity. For in the Communist camp, a comparison can be made only between thirteen democratic internationals and one oligarchic international, and their scores are identical. In the non-Communist camps combined, however, the average score of the democratic internationals was much higher than the score of the six oligarchic internationals, or a solidarity ratio of 3.3:1 in favor of democracy. Now, among the democratic internationals, the average score in the Communist camp was unexpectedly somewhat lower than in the combined non-Communist camps. With only one oligarchic Communist-led international, no meaningful comparison to other oligarchic internationals is possible (but for what it is worth, its solidarity score was far higher than the average score of the non-Communist oligarchies; see Table 9.4, part 1).

Table 9.5. *Segregated locals "at one time or another" by political camp, constitutional democracy, and factionalism in CIO international unions*

Part 1. Percent with segregated locals						
	Political camp					
Constitutional democracy	Communist	(N)	Shifting and anti-Communist	(N)	Total	(N)
High	0	(7)	0	(3)	0	(10)
Moderate	13	(8)	33	(6)	21	(14)
Oligarchic	100	(1)	50	(10)	55	(11)
Total	13	(16)	37	(19)	26	(35)
Part 2. Percent with segregated locals						
	Political camp					
Presence of internal factions	Communist	(N)	Shifting and anti-Communist	(N)	Total	(N)
Organized	20	(5)	20	(5)	20	(10)
Sporadic	20	(5)	67	(3)	37	(8)
None	0	(0)	60	(5)	60	(5)
Total	20	(10)	46	(13)	35	(23)

As to the impact of contending factions, no comparison is possible between Communist-led internationals with factions and without factions, because they all had factions. In the combined non-Communist camps, the average solidarity score of the internationals with factions was much higher than that of the internationals with none, or a solidarity ratio of 3.6:1 favoring factions. This, too, lends credence to the argument that a vital, contentious political life tends to nourish a sense of community and solidarity. So, does the finding that among the internationals with factions, the average solidarity scores were identical: 1.8 in the Communist camp and in the non-Communist camps combined (see Table 9.4, part 2).

Finally, there is the question of segregated locals. Both within the Communist camp and the combined non-Communist camps, the oligarchic internationals were by far the most likely to have had segregated locals "at one time or another." As we saw earlier, of course, none of the highly democratic internationals in any camp had segregated locals. Looking at the only meaningful comparison possible to assess the effect of Communist leadership while holding the level of democracy constant, we find that among the moderately democratic internationals, the percentage with segregated locals in the non-Communist camps combined was two and a half times the percentage in the Communist camp (see Table 9.5, part 1).

With factions, the pattern (at least what there is of it that we can examine) is similar: The presence of organized versus sporadic factions made no difference in the Communist camp, but in the combined non-Communist camps, and despite the small numbers in the relevant categories, the internationals with organized factions had by far the smallest percentage with segregated locals. Now, conversely, among the internationals with organized factions, the Communist and non-Communist camps had the same percentage with segregated locals, but among those with sporadic factions (and again despite the small numbers), we find a striking difference: The percentage with segregated locals in the combined non-Communist camps was well over three times that in the Communist camp (see Table 9.5, part 2).

Conclusion

In July 1949, as the bitter attacks on the CIO's Communist left were escalating, the *Pittsburgh Courier*, a leading black newspaper, already was condemning the CIO's CRC as mere "window dressing" and charging that it had done little or nothing to overcome discrimination against black workers. In fact, the *Courier* writer declared, some CIO unions were signing contracts that "set up discriminatory job line classifications in various plants" in Pittsburgh and other cities (he probably meant, in particular, the USWA). A couple of months later, a black member of CRC, reflecting such charges, reported that "the Negro community is saying . . . [we're] being Uncle Toms for the CIO." CRC's head, Willard Townsend, "was especially concerned," in Marshall's words, "that Negroes in the South were supporting the Communist-dominated Mine, Mill and Smelter Workers, in preference to the CIO Steel Workers," which was engaged in fierce raiding of MM.[70]

The growing disenchantment with the CIO among blacks coincided in time with the arrival of what Marshall Stevenson calls "the overt anti-Communist phase of [CIO] history" from 1946 on. Open attacks on CIO Communists and their allies escalated after the defeat of Henry Wallace, whom they had supported openly, in the 1948 presidential election. "Wallace, unlike any other candidate, had barnstormed the South for racial equality during 1948" and produced the largest interracial meetings yet seen in southern cities. But by

[70] Marshall (1964, p. 17).

then the CIO's interracialism was already being openly abandoned in the South. By 1949, any antiracist union was at risk within the southern CIO, many of whose "older leaders," as Michael Honey remarks, "opposed 'communism' and antiracism as if they were interchangeable evils."[71]

At the fall 1949 CIO convention, CIO officials pushed through an amendment to the CIO constitution to enable them to purge Communists from their midst, and during 1950, as we know, they subjected its Communist-led internationals to pseudotrials, threw them out, and went on to "'cleanse' virtually all the [other] unions in which Communist influence had been significant.... And," says Rosen, "to the extent that the unions expelled had been the more militant and devoted advocates of racial justice, the cause itself lost much of its meaning and appeal."[72]

In 1955, having lost its own radical identity, the CIO returned to the bosom of its old nemesis, the AFL. Ironically, the lone prominent opponent of the CIO's self-liquidation was TWU president "Red Mike" Quill, who had been a Communist but had split with the party in 1948 because of its support for Wallace's presidential campaign. Quill denounced the merger agreement as a "surrender" to the "'three R's' of the AFL – racism, racketeering, and raiding." He was certainly right about the CIO's capitulation to the AFL's first "R": For "after the merger . . . ," as Hill says, "the CIO's enlightened racial policies were, in many cases, replaced by the traditional racial practices of the major AFL affiliates."[73]

---

[71] So, for instance, when two white unionists "demanded desegregation of the CIO union hall at a meeting of the Memphis CIO's Industrial Union Council in 1947, the Council expelled them both for 'Communist' agitation" (Honey 1999, pp. 235, 181–82). Under the left leadership of the Memphis local of the International Furniture Workers, the growth of employment of black women in the Memphis furniture industry had been much greater than elsewhere in that industry (Cornfield 1989, p. 211). Such antiracist southern locals were raided by other CIO internationals under the cover of the Taft–Hartley Act and anti-Communism (see, e.g., Lembcke and Tattam 1984).

[72] Rosen (1968, pp. 199–200); also see Cornfield (1991).

[73] Zieger (1995, pp. 366, 370); Lichtenstein (1995, p. 323); Hill (1973, p. 121); on Quill's relationship to the CP, see note 25, page 11, above.

10

CONCLUSION: AN AMERICAN
TRAGEDY

Communists and their radical allies in the CIO won responsibility and trust in America's industrial unions not by "infiltration" or "colonization" but by an insurgent political strategy: fighting for the cause of industrial unionism and organizing the unorganized for years before the CIO's birth, leading workers' "secessions from below" out of the AFL and into the CIO once it was under way, organizing workers wherever they could and on their own rather than under the tutelage of a CIO organizing committee, and forging coalitions with other cadres of organizers and uniting their forces through amalgamation.

These same insurgent practices, paradoxically, though not in exactly the same way, by producing political variety and organizational diversity, also tended to vitalize the union's inner life and increase the likelihood both that opposition factions would emerge in an international union and that it would be democratic. But even if we take account of the specific insurgent political practices involved in organizing them, the Communist-led international unions continue to stand out as highly democratic. Whether or not earlier Red unionism had taken hold in their industry, whether they seceded from the AFL from below or from above, and whether they were organized independently or under the aegis of a CIO organizing committee, the Communist-led international unions in each of these categories were more likely than their rivals to be highly democratic and far less likely to be oligarchic.

For Communists brought with them into the new unions their own radical, homegrown ideas of "rank-and-file power," forged in earlier Red organizing, coupled with their memories of repression at the hands of AFL "misleaders of labor" — all of which committed them to constitutional forms that limited the concentration of executive power and guaranteed freedom of political association. Their transcendent conception of the mission of unionism and a stubborn willingness to confront all sorts of public issues, other than the matters supposed to be negotiable with employers through collective bargaining, continually regenerated controversy and kindled conflicts in the unions they led, and this, in turn, provoked organized opposition to them – often instigated by "outside groups" – and nourished a vibrant democratic political life in the Communist-led unions.

In turn, both Communist leadership and rank-and-file democracy tended to create and sustain a sense of common identity among the membership and transform the union into a close-knit working-class political community. This unifying class capacity proved to be a far more effective counterforce to capital's power than businesslike conduct and bureaucratically imposed directives and discipline. The contracts won by the locals both of democratic and Communist-led unions, as we have shown in detail, effectively denied management the "right" to exercise unilateral authority over production and – by holding ready the strike weapon and enforcing a self-reliant, shop-floor– based grievance procedure – held employers maximally accountable to the workers under their dominion.

Throughout the CIO era, and consistent with the political consciousness of their international leadership, the contracts won by locals of internationals in the Communist camp were far more likely to be prolabor than those won by the unions in the "shifting" and anti-Communist camps. In fact, during every period of that era, most of the contracts won by locals of Communist-led internationals were prolabor on almost every one of the crucial provisions: denial of management "rights," retention of the right to strike during the contract, and an uncomplicated and timely grievance procedure, with few steps. This was so even during World War II, when the CP itself had a political line of "class collaboration" aimed at obtaining "uninterrupted production" in the "antifascist war," and even in the late postwar period, when the "Communist-dominated" unions – and their entire leadership – came under relentless siege on all sides, by their erstwhile CIO brothers, by congressional committees, and by federal agencies.

Similarly, the contracts won by locals of the stable highly democratic international unions were consistently the most likely to be prolabor, as compared with their moderately democratic and oligarchic counterparts; in fact, the preponderant majority of them were prolabor on each of the six provisions examined. In sum, both Communist leadership and union democracy – when controlling for the effects of the other – independently increased the chances of winning prolabor contracts. The characteristic "political regime of production" incarnated in these prolabor contracts – or the regime defining, regulating, and enforcing capital's subordination of labor within the immediate labor process – was, in a word, not "hegemonic" but "counterhegemonic." For in "the constant war of capital upon the working and living standards of labor," as the *FE News* declared, it tended to alter the existing balance of class power in the workers' favor.[1]

Radicalism and democracy were also decisive for the defense and advance of women's interests. The Communist-led UE stood out as a champion of what is now termed "comparable worth" long before others recognized this as a crucial objective in the struggle for women's equality. Overall, democratic unions and Communist-led internationals elevated more women to top leadership positions than their oligarchic and non-Communist counterparts; they also passed more union resolutions and supported more public initiatives favoring women's rights. Most important, the democratic and Communist-led internationals were far more likely to win provisions in their local contracts requiring equal pay for equal work.

On the cardinal question of combating racism, both radicalism and democracy also made a significant difference. Our findings are consistent with and support the historical assessment that although "Communists in CIO unions... thought true equality could come only under communism," as Harvey Levenstein observes, "in practice they fought much more than any other predominantly white group to bring it to American industry."[2] Generally, the internationals in the Communist camp displayed far more interracial solidarity in practice than their rivals. On measures such as equality of access to union membership (and refusal to allow segregated locals), equality of representation in the highest leadership councils, and establishment of "special equalitarian racial machinery" to combat racism, the Communist-led unions generally stood out.

So too did the democratic internationals. Overall, as measured by our solidarity index (combining the measures of membership equality, black representation, and "equalitarian racial machinery"), they were in the forefront. Crucially, whether the black membership was small or large, the democratic internationals and those with factions had a far higher level of interracial solidarity than the oligarchic internationals and those with no factions.

The political consciousness of the leadership and the relative size of the black membership interacted in determining the internationals' commitment to interracial solidarity. Especially where the black membership was small and might otherwise not have been able to win racially egalitarian policies and practices, leadership by Communists and their radical allies was decisive in enhancing interracial solidarity.

Now, as we know, the CIO's "Big 3" – UE, UAW, and USWA – simultaneously represented and formed the core of the CIO's rival political camps

---

[1] *FE News* (May 22, 1946), the newspaper of the Red-led FE, as quoted in Gilpin (1988).
[2] Levenstein (1981, p. 332).

and, each in its own way, exemplified and incarnated the varying levels of democracy and factionalism. Over the entire CIO era, the pattern of prolabor provisions in the national agreements won by each of the "Big 3" with its industry's major employer and in the supplementary agreements won by its locals paralleled the larger pattern characterizing its political camp, level of democracy, and factionalism. UE's national and local agreements – even during both wartime's "uninterrupted production" and the late postwar period, when UE was besieged by agencies of the state and incessant raiding by union rivals – were by far the most consistently prolabor. The UAW was next, and the USWA was a distant third.

The efforts and achievements of the "Big 3" were similar with regard to gender egalitarianism. The UE energetically fought for comparable worth and other policies in support of women's rights, and made important gains in its plants. The UAW made more modest gains for women in the auto plants. And the USWA seems to have been uninterested at best in promoting women's rights.

As to racial egalitarianism, none of the international leaders of the "Big 3" seem to have made the fight for black equality within the industry or union a major national priority, although the UAW and especially UE, both had fairly consistent records of public political support for the FEPC, civil rights legislation, and other integrationist political measures. In UE's case, the international leadership's relentless battles with employers to assure women's rights apparently limited their struggle for black equality. Some UE locals and districts stood out, however, in fighting for black / white equality, and these were, on the available historical evidence solidly Communist-led, particularly the New York–New Jersey and the St. Louis districts. In contrast, the Philco local in Philadelphia, which the NAACP singled out as having a long record of racial discrimination, was the main base of the UE's right-wing opposition. UAW Ford Local 600 at the Ford Rouge plant, the UAW's most powerful Red bastion, had an unparalleled record of black/white solidarity; and the racial egalitarianism of the Red-led Local 248 at the Allis–Chalmers plant in Milwaukee was also exceptional.

The Fate of "the Late, Great CIO"[3]

For an ephemeral historical moment half a century ago when Communists and their radical allies stood at the helm of so many of America's industrial unions, the workers under their leadership measured "social actuality" against "historical possibility" and found it wanting, and thus carried out a "practical–critical"

---

[3] Zieger (1995, p. 333).

rejection of actually existing capitalism.[4] But with the dawn of the Cold War, they were increasingly isolated within the CIO, as they refused to conform to its officials' newly minted and inexorably imposed political orthodoxy – of endorsement of the Truman Doctrine, the Marshall Plan, the Atlantic Pact, and support for Truman's presidential candidacy.[5] The unions they led were subjected to escalating raiding of their membership by CIO rivals, in a strange campaign that actually "disorganized the organized." The raiding – the "pure and simple cannibalism," as Matles put it – became unrestrained during the 1948 campaign and especially in the wake of Truman's upset victory over Republican Thomas Dewey and the dismal showing of Progressive Henry Wallace, despite CIO head Philip Murray's assurances to UE that he would do everything possible to put a halt to the raids, chiefly by the UAW.[6]

In mid-1949, *Fortune* could confidently inform its readers that "expulsions at the C.I.O.'s [November] . . . convention [were] a foregone conclusion."[7] UE leaders made a last-ditch attempt, when the convention was about to open, to get Murray to arrange a no-raiding agreement between UE and UAW, modeled after the UAW–IAM agreement. Albert Fitzgerald, UE's president, told reporters that he hoped the CIO would "agree with us and stop raiding this union and stop financing the secessionists in the UE. . . . " Murray's reply to the UE delegation, as he tossed their proposed agreement on the desk, was, "There is only one issue, and that's Communism." Asked by newsmen if this meant that the UE would be leaving the CIO, Fitzgerald answered, "That's up to the CIO."[8]

---

[4] Marx (1973a, p. 13).

[5] The then vice-president Truman had, of course, succeeded to the presidency in April 1945 upon FDR's death. His Truman Doctrine, enunciated before Congress in February 1947, claimed the right and duty of global intervention by the United States to "support free peoples who are resisting subjugation by armed minorities or by outside pressures," and it was initiated in practice that spring and summer by U.S. military backing of the ancien régime in Greece's civil war, and then by the establishment of the Marshall Plan to reconstruct capitalism in Western Europe (Shannon 1959, pp. 27–29; Caute 1978, pp. 29–31, 35–38).

[6] Matles and Higgins (1974, p. 193).   [7] "Labor Violence – New Style," p. 151.

[8] Morris (1949a, p. 10; 1949c, p. 3). Weeks earlier, *Business Week* had reported that "U.E. tempers are high over national C.I.O. refusal to take a firm stand against United Auto Workers' raids in U.E. plants. . . . A protest to the executive board of C.I.O. two weeks ago brought no definite action. [U.E.] Board members tabled charges against U.A.W. and other right-wing unions until a special board meeting in October. . . . U.E. convention delegates heard reports of raiding losses [and] . . . there was noticeable floor sentiment that 'if we're going to be raided by C.I.O. unions, we might as well be on our own. Let's get the hell out.' U.E. leaders didn't take it as a mandate, but the sentiment got on the record" ("U.E. Keeps Left," p. 114).

The CIO convention, over the beleaguered objections of the delegates from the other Communist-led internationals, then passed a resolution authorizing the executive board by a two-thirds' majority to refuse to seat anyone at the convention who belonged to the CP or consistently agreed with its "program or purposes," and also shouted through a companion resolution giving the board the right to expel any international that adhered to the party line. They then "expelled" UE – whose delegation did not attend the convention – and, with it, FE, which five days before the convention had merged with UE, defying the CIO's instruction to merge with UAW.

Reading from the six-page indictment of the UE – which charged it with opposition to the Marshall Plan, the Atlantic Pact, and the CIO's political endorsements – Harry Bridges said:

> I don't find a single charge that says that the UE has not done a good job for its members. Not a single economic charge is leveled. So now we have reached the point where a trade union is expelled because it disagrees with the CIO on political matters. ... My union did not support the Marshall Plan . . . [or] the Atlantic Pact, either, so will you expel us too?

"Yes!" shouted out an answering chorus of delegates; and, over the next eight months, in a succession of pseudotrials, the CIO then proceeded to throw out nine more "Communist-dominated" internationals – precisely because they "wouldn't," as United Public Workers (UPW) president Abram Flaxer declared, "go down the line."[9] For certainly, as our analysis has shown, consistent with the weight of historical evidence, it was not because the unions led by Communists and their allies were not good unions. Even an opponent of theirs as enduring and vehement as David Saposs, who celebrated the expulsions, conceded:

> The evidence and arguments of the CIO that the Communist-dominated unions failed fully to pursue pure trade-union procedures are rather tenuous. ... ILWU, Fur, and UE had leadership as competent as the most successful unions. Moreover, purely from a trade-union point of view,

---

[9] Morris (1949d, p. 3); Zieger (1995, p. 286); Levenstein (1981, p. 291). The last to be drummed out, on August 29, 1950, was the longshoremen and warehousemen (ILWU). Earlier, ILWU officers had made an offer to the CIO executive board to hold a referendum among ILWU members on CIO policies; if a majority of them voted to conform, "the [ILWU's] officers would then conform or resign." But the CIO's executive board rejected ILWU's offer out of hand ("Coast Dockers, 2 More Unions Ousted by CIO," p. 3; "Blast CIO's Expulsion of Coast Dockers," p. 8).

they were as successful organizationally – as revealed by their membership – as any of the superlatively successful unions, and their record
in securing wages and better working conditions for their members
through collective bargaining is at least as favorable as that of any of
the outstanding unions. Undoubtedly, their achievements in the trade-
union field enable them to hold the loyalty of their members, the great
majority of whom were not Communists.[10]

From the outset of the CIO's assaults on Communist unionists, "CIO functionaries collaborated closely with the government's anti-Communist organs."
A special staff member of Murray's USWA and CIO general counsel Arthur
Goldberg (who was later to become a supreme court justice) consulted regularly with the FBI and kept Army intelligence well informed of the CIO's
anti-Communist campaign. James Carey, CIO secretary-treasurer and head of
the newly chartered IUE, "actively worked with the FBI and with congressional zealots to defeat his enemies in the UE. Both Carey and UAW president
Reuther, though publicly deploring the practices of HUAC, used the information and especially the publicity generated by the committee's hearings to
undermine their rivals."[11]

During HUAC's hearings on Communism in the UAW in early 1952,
Reuther's alliance with HUAC was so blatant that *Business Week* (March 2,
1952) headlined its story, "A New 'Ally' for Reuther" and gloated that Reuther
and the committee that he had once denounced as "witch-hunters" were
now "working together like a well-rehearsed vaudeville team." During three
months of hearings, between February and April 1952, HUAC subpoenaed
twenty-three officers of Local 600, several of them black, to testify about their
political beliefs and associations. As was standard practice in these sorts of proceedings, the star attraction was a defector, the editor of the local's newspaper,
Ford Facts. He told HUAC that he had merely been a messenger boy for a group
of Local 600's Communists, who really controlled *Ford Facts*. Reuther seized
the moment, as we know, to put the local under an administratorship, charging it with violating the UAW's prohibition against Communists holding
office.[12]

He resorted to the administratorship to strip Local 600 of its elected Communist officers (expelling nine Communist shop committeemen and the local's

[10] Saposs (1959, pp. 184–85).   [11] Zieger (1995, p. 292).
[12] Levenstein (1981, pp. 316–17). Reuther wrote to HUAC during its hearings to request an
opportunity to testify. The committee turned him down, pleading a "tight schedule" (John
S. Wood to Walter Reuther, March 11, 1952, Wayne State University Archives, Walter
P. Reuther collection, box 249, folder 249–24).

PAC director and taking over *Ford Facts*) for the same reason that the CIO's crusaders against Communist domination had to resort to the expulsions of eleven Communist-led internationals: The "rank-and-file uprisings" that they expected and did all they could to engender never came. They could not "dislodge" the Communists from power. In four other internationals in the Communist camp (maritime (NMU), transport (TWU), the Furniture Workers, and the Shoe Workers), the Communists were "dislodged" only when their presidents, and some other top officers, taking care to continue to identify themselves as men of the left, reneged in time to prevent their union's expulsion; they denounced and turned against their erstwhile Communist comrades and succeeded in ousting them from office.[13]

"Whole unions, whether international, regional, or local, escaped from Communist domination," as Saposs points out, "only if some of the key leaders discarded their Communist connections . . . [but] where the outstanding leader staunchly adhered to his Communist affiliation, as [Harry] Bridges did [in the ILWU], the opposition remained weak and control was retained by the Communists," making "expulsion or peremptory action . . . the only course."[14]

What difference it would have made over the coming decades to the objectives, strategy, and practices of organized workers and what they won or lost in their "constant war" with capital if the Communist-led unions had cohered and endured as a significant force in organized labor is the critical historical question posed by their expulsion and subsequent fate. The evidence of what did happen, with the Communists driven out, is suggestive of what could have happened.

At the CIO's first postpurge convention in November 1950, Murray celebrated the defeat of the Communist "plot" to "take over" the CIO and predicted that, "[b]y removing the obstructionists, we have gained effectiveness and militance." In fact, his prediction was wrong on both counts. For in casting out the Communist-led unions and purging the rest, the CIO deprived itself, as we now know, of the elements that were most dynamic, egalitarian, democratic, class-conscious, and advanced on issues of women rights and interracial solidarity.[15]

The organization of the CIO had signaled the rebirth of a radical ethos and democratic temper in organized labor, but by the time the shrunken and purified CIO merged again with the AFL in 1955, little of either remained.[16]

---

[13] Prickett (1975, p. 441). For some reason, perhaps its minuscule size, IB, even though its leaders failed to renege, was overlooked and not expelled.

[14] Saposs (1959, pp. 111, 199, 110).   [15] Zieger (1995, pp. 292, 374).

[16] The CIO, said *Fortune* in July 1949 – anticipating the expulsions – was already "in effect, only four unions: the steelworkers, the auto workers, the textile workers, and the men's clothing workers. And in terms of carrying the largest burdens, C.I.O. may be seen essentially as two

In the wake of the expulsions, many others who dissented from CIO policies – including anti-Communist radicals – soon were also "frozen out of union politics, and often hounded out of the labor movement because of their alleged 'subversiveness.'"[17] So from the moment of its conception, the AFL–CIO was – and would continue to be during the second half of the century – "the most conservative and ideologically acquiescent [central labor organization] among capitalist democracies."[18] In the years to come, the remnants of the CIO, having abdicated their birthright, were to participate in forging a new "labor–management" compact that reestablished the unchallenged hegemony of capital in America.

CIO organizing stagnated and overall membership actually declined during the years of the intensifying assault on the Communist camp. AFL, the CIO's once-lethargic nemesis, steadily outstripped it; in 1950, after the CIO had thrown out some million workers in the Communist-led internationals, the AFL legitimately claimed twice the membership of the truncated CIO. "The CIO and its affiliates expended millions of dollars in attempting to raid the memberships of such pro-Soviet organizations as the UE, the Mine, Mill, and the FE. These actions," as Robert Zieger says mildly, "did nothing to advance the cause of the industrial working class, and invited employers' counterattacks."[19]

"The bloodletting had serious consequences . . . ," as Bert Cochran puts it, for "once the Communist issue was disposed of the CIO began to lose cohesiveness." Indeed, the cannibalism apparently was addictive: In the fall of 1951, the CIO's remaining unions now turned upon themselves in a raiding war, pitting the UAW, the oil workers (OWIU), the Utility Workers, the IUE, and the Gas, Coke and Chemical Workers (GCC) against each other – which threatened to consume what remained of the CIO.[20] Workers took note and turned away. In 1952, for the first time, the CIO lost more NLRB representation elections than it won. The CIO's own research department confessed at the end of 1953 that "no significant industry or service which was not organized before 1945–46 has been organized since then."[21] The geographical spread of the CIO also shrank, to the extent that by 1954 over half of the CIO's members

unions – steel and auto, which together make up nearly 40 per cent of the dues-paying C.I.O. membership" ("Labor Violence – New Style," p. 152).

[17] Zieger (1986, pp. 131–32).   [18] Caute (1978, p. 352); Zieger (1986, pp. 131–32).

[19] Zieger (1995, p. 376). IUE alone got $100,000 a month from the CIO from the day it was set up in November 1949 until June 1950; by the end of September 1950, the CIO had given it a total of $805,000. Murray's Steelworkers threw in another $200,000 (Emspak 1972, p. 342).

[20] Steuben (1951, p. 20, citing the *New York Times*, August 27, 1951).

[21] Zieger (1995, pp. 343, 344); Cochran (1977, p. 312).

were concentrated in only four states – Michigan, Ohio, New York, and Pennsylvania – and only 14 percent worked in the South and Southwest. At the final CIO convention on the eve of the formal AFL–CIO merger, Furniture Workers president Morris Pizer, who five years earlier had turned against and succeeded in "dislodging" his Communist allies from power, lamented: "Organizing the unorganized was number 1 [in the early CIO], and it has become no. 6, 7 or 10." He was seconded by the right-wing vice-president of the Textile Workers, William Pollack, who said: "There has been little or no growth in the unions in the past eight years."[22] Thus began the downward slide over the decades to come of the unionized share of the labor force. CIO leaders and affiliates were not even able to complete the organization of the CIO's own heartland. In the central industrial core, nearly a third of the workers were still nonunion when the CIO dissolved itself in 1955. (In the vast chemical and petroleum industries, in particular, the CIO had little representation among their 750,000 workers, 80 percent of whom were then still unorganized.) In an ironic twist, the AFL had more workers organized by then on an industrial basis than the CIO.[23]

After the expulsions, the CIO also all but ignored white-collar workers, among whom the CIO's Communist-led unions – for example, the UPW and the Office and Professional Workers (UOPW) – had built important enclaves. The CIO's failure even to try to organize low-wage "service" and other workers outside the industrial core also meant, in effect, the abandonment of black workers, who were heavily concentrated in the most exploited jobs in the "tertiary sector."

In reality, with their Reds driven out, black representation in the highest councils of CIO internationals was drastically reduced, and the CIO's executive board itself turned lily-white. Early in 1950, in the midst of the ongoing expulsions, a columnist for the *Washington Afro-American* declared: "This new CIO policy ... calls for conformity with America's traditional policy of segregation and Jim Crowism."[24] Few of the CIO's officials or affiliates still "regarded the concerns of black workers as central.... Since the pro-Soviet unions had highlighted civil rights," as Zieger puts it, "ardent racial progressivism might suggest pro-Communist sympathies.... When it came to racial matters

[22] Zieger (1995, p. 339); Morris (1955, p. 32).
[23] Zieger (1995, pp. 359, 305); "The Merger: Summing It Up," p. 20. But let it not be said that the new AFL–CIO, with the CIO safely tucked back under its wing, now intended to put a priority on organizing. "We will not organize," said AFL president George Meany, "just for the sake of organizing" (Simon 1956, p. 52, citing *U.S. News* and *World Report,* February 25, 1955).
[24] Foner (1974, p. 292).

within the CIO, the response of the white-led federation and its affiliates was modest . . . [or] dilatory and often insincere."

Even the head of the CIO's predominantly black Red Cap union (UTSE), Willard Townsend, "a dutiful CIO loyalist" and anti-Communist, was moved to exclaim in 1955 that "one thing . . . is certain – they [the Communists] did keep the civil rights question alive." Townsend's heretical outburst was an all-too-belated recognition, as Zieger puts it, of the "admirable, and on the whole sincerely compiled, record of Communist-oriented affiliates . . . [and of] the often courageous and principled actions of many pro-Soviet individuals on racial matters." This, says Zieger, makes "the strongest case for repudiating the anti-Communist purge."[25]

Embarked on a new strategy of collaboration with capital, aptly dubbed "the politics of productivity," CIO leaders "had little to say about the internal life of the plants in which their members toiled."[26] The internationals remaining in the truncated CIO were increasingly more likely to cede to management the unilateral "right" to shape the social organization of labor within the plant and, decisively, remained silent on the question of the very continued existence of the plant itself. In fact, from 1947 to 1954 alone, during the very years of the CIO's self-immolation in the flames of anti-Communism, "capital mobility" substantially transformed America's "economic geography."

Capital mobility – and with it, plant relocation – was, in reality, a weapon wielded by the biggest employers in their continuing battles with organized workers. Reuther's abdication to Ford on the issue of "decentralization" – his tragic refusal to join with Local 600's "Stalinist" leaders in their battle to halt what they called Ford's "Operation Runaway" – was emblematic of the inaction of the CIO and its affiliates in the face of the pseudotechnical "locational decisions" by means of which employers reshuffled their plants and shifted employment into the union-free and "right-to-work" hinterland of the country (and, simultaneously and increasingly, abroad). The CIO's liberals and right-wingers offered no resistance – How could they have, given their newfound ideological zeal for "free enterprise"? This abrupt geographical dispersal of industry was, alas, premonitory of the great wave of "plant closings," from the

---

[25] Zieger (1995, pp. 346, 348, 375–76). Remember, this is coming from someone who *approves* of the CIO's "anti-Communist purge." As Zieger asks rhetorically, even if racism had been the primary issue facing the CIO, "how long could a CIO tainted with the practical and moral incubus of Communist association have remained an effective force?" (1995, p. 376).

[26] Maier (1987); Zieger (1995, p. 325).

mid-1970s through the 1980s, that was to roll over the unprepared unions and crush so many of their members' communities.[27]

To entice employers into staying put and just saying "no" to *Business Week*'s rhetorical question, "Should you move your plant?," the postpurge CIO internationals tried to mollify them by containing workers' militancy. The URW's leadership, for example, when faced with a rapid shift of tire-making into new, nonunion factories, sought to curb the rank-and-file activism of its "breedapart" tire builders and recalcitrant pitmen in its Akron strongholds.[28] Already by the spring of 1953, *Fortune* could report that "[n]o-strike clauses now prevailed in 89 per cent of all union contracts," and an outright, unconditional ban on strikes, which appeared in 39 percent, was most frequent in utilities, paper, oil, and maritime – industries whose workers were represented by CIO internationals.[29]

Confrontation with management at the point of production by a phalanx of aggrieved workers and their shop steward, as the way to resolve immediate grievances and reinforce a modicum of workers' control, became something of a lost art. Instead, most CIO contracts by the mid-1950s enmeshed shop stewards and "committeemen," each responsible for hundreds of workers taking care only of contractually defined "grievable issues," in a routinized and calculable "workplace rule of law," in David Brody's phrase; this simultaneously both protected workers from arbitrary and capricious authority and undermined their self-reliance. Most CIO contracts now stipulated a system of "dispute resolution" involving a multilevel series of steps in which shop stewards or committeemen increasingly found themselves on the sidelines. With most contracts now capped by "resort to arbitration by a neutral party," in a system that relied heavily on precedents, union heads "were reluctant to trust even individual grievances, which might have broad implications, to mere rank-and-file representatives." The cynical remark of the president of a UAW local in the early 1950s said it all: "You may as well forget that we have any stewards. They're a joke."[30]

The range of direct action "permissible" under the contract shrank as the unions became more deeply enmeshed in a system of centralized and virtually compulsory arbitration, buttressing managerial authority. Rulings

---

[27] Rosswurm (1992, p. 15); "Should You Move Your Plant?"; "Industry Shifts Its Plants"; Reid (1951); Sobel (1954); Fulton (1955); Zeitlin (1981, 1982a, 1982b, 1983, 1984, 1985).

[28] "Should You Move Your Plant?"; Zieger (1995, p. 324).

[29] Prickett (1975, p. 419); "Labor Notes."

[30] Brody (1981, esp. pp. 176ff.); Zieger (1995, pp. 324–26; the local president's quote, as cited by Zieger, is from Sayles and Strauss (1953, p. 34).

by arbitrators and the courts simultaneously reaffirmed the so-called rights of management to run its business and "assigned to union leaders the related role of discouraging irrational militancy and assuring order and discipline in the workplace," thus strengthening their hand vis-à-vis workers' shop-floor power – and estranging them even more from the class they claimed to represent.[31]

A UAW chief shop steward at Chrysler explained in 1954:

> In the old days . . . [the steward] was the Union, he was the Contract. Everything he did was decisive in the plant. Now he is a Philadelphia lawyer. It's embarrassing. Time and again Management does things that I know it has a right to do under the Umpire system, but the men don't know it. If I explain to them that the Company has that right under four or five rulings made previously, they get sore at me. They will say, "You don't represent us; you represent the Company." As a result – in our setup, and I'm sure it's true elsewhere – the Stewards . . . tend to fake on this stuff. They write grievances when they know they shouldn't [and] . . . instead of being real leaders, tend to become more and more political fakers. . . . [32]

In the course of establishing their new "class accord" with capital, the CIO's leaders and remnant unions had bound themselves – some unwittingly, others intentionally – inside a legal / administrative straitjacket from which they and their successors could not escape.

"The Great Purge of American Working Life"

The question remains, why did all but a few of the expelled Communist-led internationals apparently so quickly disintegrate and disappear?[33] The answer, so it seems, is obvious: "[T]he anti-Communist political repression of the late 1940s and 1950s," with the state as both its executor and guarantor, argues Ellen Schrecker, "devastated the labor left. . . . Once anti-Communism became

---

[31] Zieger (1995, pp. 326, 324); Lichtenstein (1985).   [32] Widick (1954, p. 506).

[33] By the spring of 1955, only four of them were still "operating as separate organizations": UE, the mine, mill, and smelter workers (MM), the longshoremen and warehousemen, (ILWU), and the American Communications Association (ACA) ("What Reds Are Up to in Unions," p. 107). The IFLWU had just concluded a merger agreement, back in February, with the AFL's Amalgamated Meat Cutters and Butcher Workmen. Yet until then, all raids against Fur and Leather had been successfully defeated (Steuben 1954, p. 17). (On this merger, following the CP line of "returning to the mainstream" of labor, see Chapter 11.)

official policy, the left-wing unions, the most influential organizations within the Communist movement, were doomed."[34] "Doomed" or not, that is the question. Certainly they were badly injured if not crippled by the "sweeping internal purification of the ranks of labor" that was formally initiated by the 1947 Taft–Hartley Act and willingly executed by the CIO and the AFL.[35]

The CIO's Communists and their allies were only the most conspicuous targets of "the great purge of American working life" begun under Truman in 1946, completed under Eisenhower, and carried out – alongside the radical self-cleansings done by the CIO and AFL – by agencies of the state (aided and abetted by the omnipresent Cold War liberalism that emerged as the dominant ethos in the press and the world of learning) on several closely connected political fronts: by the federal government (the industrial-personnel security program, the port-security program, the Loyalty Review Board and over 200 loyalty security boards for various government agencies, the Attorney General's List (1947–55),[36] the Coast Guard, Army intelligence, the FBI, the Immigration and Naturalization Service, the Internal Security Division of the Justice Department, the Subversive Activities Control Board (SACB)); by Congress (the Alien and Sedition Act (1940), Labor–Management Relations Act (1947), the Internal Security Act (1950, which among other things authorized concentration camps for the internment of Communists in the event of a "national emergency"), the Port Security Act (1950), the Witness Immunity Act (1954), the Communist Control Act (1954), and the rampaging

---

[34] Schrecker (1992, pp. 139, 157).

[35] By 1954, some fifty-nine out of one hundred AFL affiliates had amended their constitutions to bar Communists from holding office, and forty barred them even from membership. "Nor were such provisions mere window dressing; expulsions were numerous and almost always upheld by the courts" (Caute 1978, p. 353). Among the pockets of Communist influence within AFL affiliates, most notoriously, were some in Hollywood's talent guilds – whose purge HUAC facilitated by interrogating the likes of Lucille Ball and Ginger Rogers under the kleig lights. The Screen Writers Guild, the Screen Directors Guild, the Screen Actors Guild (where Ronald Reagan played the lead), especially, and even the Stage Hands Union (or IATSE, the International Alliance of Theatrical Stage Employees and Motion Picture Machine Operators) all "joined vigorously in the housecleaning," not to mention the less headline-grabbing Hotel and Restaurant Workers Union (Saposs 1959, pp. 15–115; Navasky 1980).

[36] The Attorney General's list, first compiled in November 1947, pursuant to Truman's loyalty order (starting with 78 organizations and growing by 1955 to include some 276 "organizations, groups, and movements" allegedly of "significance in connection with National Security," all listed in Ginger and Christiano 1987, pp. 250–57) was used from the outset, in David Caute's words (1978, p. 169), "to intimidate and morally outlaw the left, to pillory and ostracize critics of the Truman administration, and to deter potential critics."

"investigations" by HUAC, the House Committee on Education and Labor (Fred Hartley), the Senate Labor and Public Welfare Committee (Hubert Horatio Humphrey), and the Senate Governmental Operations Committee (Joe McCarthy), and a host of others of the same ilk); by the nation's judiciary, which shredded the constitution (especially the supine Supreme Court, under Chief Justice Fred Vinson, which became, from 1949 through 1954 – until the amazing advent of Earl Warren as Chief Justice – "a compliant instrument of administrative persecution and Congressional inquisition"); and, not to be outdone, by city and state "antisubversion" laws and specialized agencies (in 1949 alone, fifteen states passed such laws; by the end of 1952, about half the states barred "subversives" from elective office, and thirty-two from any public employment; seventeen states explicitly excluded "Communists" from the ballot). Much of this and much else – in collusion with employers, the U.S. Chamber of Commerce, the National Association of Manufacturers (NAM), and the National Industrial Conference Board – was done to "isolate and exclude [leftists] from the company of patriotic Americans."[37]

The Taft–Hartley Act fell heaviest on Communist unionists and their suspect radical allies, exposing their unions to NLRB decertification and raiding by rivals if they failed to sign a non-Communist affidavit.[38] By August 1948, a year after the act went into effect, 81,000 union officers, including officials of eighty-nine AFL affiliates and thirty of the CIO's, already had sworn and signed an affidavit, and the act's penetration of union ranks deepened over the next nine years. By July 1957, some 250 international unions were in compliance (involving affidavits sworn and signed by some 2,750 unionists) and about 21,500 locals (involving affidavits by another 193,500). "These figures reveal the vast scale," as David Caute observes, "on which conformity was imposed – at shop floor level nearly 200,000 trade-union leaders had formally sworn that they did not belong to the CP or believe in its doctrines."[39]

---

[37] Caute (1979, pp. 353, 50, 144, 32, 71, 74, 339, 75).

[38] "The bill [for the Taft–Hartley Act] was written," explained a Democratic congressman who voted against it, "sentence by sentence, paragraph by paragraph, page by page, by the National Association of Manufacturers." NAM's board was dominated by sixty of the country's largest corporations, among the nearly 17,000 companies on its roster. Or, as Senator Robert A. Taft himself conceded: "The bill . . . covers about three-quarters of the matters pressed upon us very strenuously by the employers" (Ginger and Christiano 1987, p. 243). The 1959 Landrum–Griffin Act repealed the non-Communist affidavit provision, but in section 504 made it illegal for a Communist (or anyone who was an ex-Communist less than five years) to be a union official (Schrecker 1992, p. 155).

[39] Levenstein (1981, p. 218); Caute (1979, p. 356). Only two major unions still stubbornly held out: the UMW and the ITU.

When they signed, many unionists who were suspected of still being party members or sympathizers were brought to trial by the government on perjury charges, which the Justice Department wielded as instruments to bludgeon and try to smash the ousted unions and frighten or demoralize their members into seceding and joining a "clean" union. So, for instance, Hugh Bryson, president of the militant, interracial Marine Cooks and Stewards (MCS), was tried, convicted, and sent to prison for perjury for falsely filing an affidavit. Ben Gold, president of the International Fur and Leather Workers Union (IFLWU), resigned from the CP, of which he had long been an open member, and signed the affidavit; he was indicted by the Eisenhower Justice Department and convicted of perjury anyway, but managed to avoid prison in an exhausting series of appeals.

The same was done to Maurice Travis, secretary-treasurer of MM, which was unyielding in trying to fulfill its constitution's commitment to the "emancipation of the working class." Travis publicly resigned from the CP in 1948, and then signed the affidavit. But he was intrepid or foolish enough to say, in a talk with his union's members, that being in the party "has always meant to me . . . that I could be a better trade unionist," and that he would "continue to fight" for the same goals. Travis was also convicted of perjury, on the government's second try, fined $8,000, a sum far more than his annual officer's salary, and sentenced to eight years' imprisonment. To get around the problem of insufficient or tainted evidence against individuals, Eisenhower's Justice Department revivified the doctrine of "conspiracy" so it could bring charges against a group of union officers, and in 1956 indicted fourteen other MM officers for allegedly "conspiring to file false affidavits," eleven of whom were brought to trial in 1959, and nine of whom were convicted of perjury and imprisoned.[40]

Even without the Taft–Hartley prosecutions, HUAC and a host of other congressional committees holding hearings on "Communist infiltration" of the unions simultaneously exacerbated the climate of hysteria and took the lead in harassing unionists and punishing them with "contempt" citations if

---

[40] Caute (1979, pp. 357–58); Kampelman (1957, p. 268). Schrecker says that sixteen MM officers, rather than fourteen, as Caute and Kampelman say, were prosecuted for conspiracy. MM fought the case for nearly a decade, until the Supreme Court overturned the conspiracy conviction (1992, pp. 152–53). Max Perlow, secretary-treasurer of the Furniture Workers, who had never kept his long-standing membership in the party a secret from his union's members, was the first of the top Communist unionists – a month before Travis – to resign from the party and sign the affidavit, while professing his continued adherence to "Marxism." Others who did roughly the same, and were subsequently tried and convicted of perjury, were Donald Henderson, president of FTA, in 1948; Anthony Valentino of the Packinghouse Workers, in 1952; and Melvin Hupman of the UE, in 1954 (Kampelman 1957, pp. 185, 261–64).

they refused to go along with the committees' unconstitutional investigations of their political opinions and associations or remanding them for prosecution by federal authorities on charges of "perjury" if they denied being Communists.

"Wherever capital was in dispute with organized labor, the Committee [HUAC] was ready," as Caute says, "to invoke the specter of Communism on behalf of capital." Typical was the pattern of attacks on UE by HUAC, in a sustained barrage from 1949 through 1956. The committee would schedule hearings when an NLRB election, often initiated by the employer, was being held: to choose, depending on the local involved, between UE and IUE, UE and IAM, UE and IBEW, UE and UAW, UE and the Teamsters. Local officers would be subpoenaed. If they pleaded the Fifth Amendment or the First, the employer suspended them and gave them a chance to recant, and if they did not, fired them, while HUAC cited them for contempt – often one contempt citation per every refusal to answer a question. (When HUAC reeled off a list of unionists to UE's Julius Emspak at a hearing in December 1949, demanding that he identify each one, he refused, and the committee held him in contempt on sixty-eight counts, one for every name he wouldn't name. A federal grand jury indicted him a year later on every count, and the Justice Department tried to have him punished on each count by both a $1,000 fine and a year in prison.)[41] "The often reckless denunciations by anti-Communists and FBI infiltrators," as Cochran sums it up, "provided newspapers with a Roman festival to inflame the community and intimidate UE activists in the plants."[42]

"What happened to [UAW's] Harold Christoffel could well serve – and was intended to serve – as an example to any other union leader tempted to adhere to the Marxist principles he had absorbed in the thirties." Removed by Walter Reuther from his post in Local 248, at the Allis–Chalmers plant in Milwaukee, Christoffel was subpoenaed in March 1947 by the House Education and Labor Committee, headed by Fred Hartley (coauthor of the Taft–Hartley Act). Christoffel denied that he was a Communist, a grand jury

---

[41] On July 1950, HUAC cited James Matles and six other UE officers and members for contempt on several counts, and they, too, were indicted by a federal grand jury and prosecuted by the Justice Department. All were acquitted in trials in February 1951, except Emspak, who was found guilty and sentenced to a term of four to twelve months in prison and a $500 fine. The conviction rested on the technicality that when he refused to testify, he had not directly cited the first or fifth amendments, but had simply said: "This is an attempt to harass the union, its leadership and its members. . . . I don't think this Committee has a right to go into any question of my beliefs or my associations" (Filippelli and McColloch 1995, pp. 132–33, 143, 152–53, 159, 166; Cahn 1950; Goodman 1969, pp. 283–85).

[42] Cochran (1977, p. 293).

indicted him for perjury, and in March 1948 he was convicted. When his case was thrown out by the Supreme Court on a technicality, he was tried again.[43]

The government relied heavily, in his second trial, on the hearsay testimony of ex-Communist Louis Budenz about Christoffel's past, including his sensational charge that Christoffel had called a prewar strike, in 1941, on the party's orders to "sabotage national defense." Another witness called to testify on Christoffel's party membership was Hugh Swafford, a former labor reporter for the Hearst-owned *Milwaukee Sentinel.* An "investigator" of "subversive activities," he had written a series of articles in 1946 (appearing in fifty-nine consecutive issues during a major, eleven-month Local 248 strike) on Communist domination of the local, and knew enough about Christoffel's activities to tell the Court what he had for breakfast every morning. Now conscience-stricken, Swafford testified that Budenz had told him that he knew that the workers's grievances would have driven them to strike in 1941 even if Christoffel had tried to stop them. Swafford also insisted, in response to the prosecutor's question, that he had found "no evidence" at all that Christoffel was a member of the CP. Christoffel was convicted of perjury anyway and sentenced to two to six years in prison. On appeal, his sentence was reduced in May 1953 to sixteen months.[44]

The full weight of virtually every agency of the federal government pressed relentlessly upon the Communist unionists and their allies, from the top officers of the expelled internationals to their loyal adherents at all levels of district and local union leadership. The FBI not only harassed and sought to intimidate left unionists directly, but also to isolate them and suborn informing on them, by sternly if politely inquiring of their associates, neighbors, friends, relatives, corner grocer and druggist, children's school principal and teachers, as well as their clergy and fellow parishioners if they happened to know with whom they were consorting. The Eisenhower appointees on the NLRB turned over the names of any unionists whom they suspected of not having truly repented to the Justice Department to investigate for perjuriously signing a non-Communist affidavit. The Internal Revenue Service gave special attention to their tax returns and often hauled them in to justify every deduction. The Immigration and Naturalization Service scrutinized the decades-old entry papers of foreign-born unionists and subjected many of them, including (successfully) IFLWU's Irving Potash and TWU's John Santo and (unsuccessfully) ILWU's Harry Bridges and UE's James Matles, to years of harassment and trials, in an effort to deport them.

---

[43] Caute (1979, pp. 358–59).   [44] Ibid.; Handler (1951).

The Communist Control Act of 1954 (which was passed unanimously by the Senate and with only two nays by the House and had been inspired in part by liberal Hubert Horatio Humphrey's bill to make membership in the CP a crime), for the first time in American history, gave a board of political appointees the authority to judge and outlaw an opposition political party and any other organizations deemed "Communist-infiltrated." It now placed all labor unions under the surveillance of the Attorney General and the SACB. Now the government, besides going after individual union leaders, could target the unions themselves, as organizations, and impose drastic disabilities on any the Attorney General, with the assent of the SACB, designated as "Communist-infiltrated." Convicted unions would be denied access to the NLRB, lose their eligibility to complain about unfair labor practices, and be stripped of the right to act as a "representative or bargaining agent" for its members. The union's contracts also could be invalidated if 20 percent of the workers petitioned NLRB for an election to determine a new bargaining agent.

Among the first unions against whom "the government brandished," as a *New York Times* story said, "[this] . . . new weapon against a new adversary . . . in its warfare on subversion," were MM in July 1955 and UE in December. In response, "the superlatively combative . . . UE," as Saposs puts it, "immediately took the case to the courts," claiming the act was invalid and demanding an injunction against the Attorney General and SACB. The U.S. Court of Appeals dismissed UE's suit the next year. UE continued to fight back in the courts for four more years, until on April 10, 1959, the Justice Department dropped its prosecution, conceding that its "evidence" against UE was tainted. It was not until 1966, after over a decade of litigation, that MM won its own case.[45]

So by the early to mid-1950s, many if not most of the leading Communist unionists were "involved almost full-time in staying out of prison. Their lives had become an endless bout of court cases," detracting them from union affairs, ruining their health, demoralizing and disrupting their families.[46]

The Defense Department, the Munitions Board, and the Atomic Energy Commission also warned employers with government contracts from dealing with their unions.[47] The Navy's Shipyard Loyalty Board and the Coast Guard,

---

[45] Saposs (1959, pp. 251–52; see also p. 251, citing the *New York Times*, July 29, 1955, whose reporter, in Saposs's words, "waxed eloquent" in reporting the new policy); Caute (1979, p. 358); Schrecker (1992, p. 155); Kampelman (1957, p. 268).

[46] Levenstein (1981, p. 314). UE's William Sentner and Julius Emspak both died of heart attack at an early age (Filippelli and McColloch 1995, p. 172).

[47] Caute (1979, passim).

under the Port Security Program, "screened" tens of thousands of men (800,000 by 1958) who worked in the maritime industry, on both coasts, in the shipyards, on the docks, and aboard ship, including cooks and stewards, to ferret out the radicals in their midst, and hauled in thousands of unionists to ask them such pertinent questions as,

"Which newspapers do you read?"
"What bookclub do you belong to?"
"How many books do you buy?"
"Would you say your wife has liberal political viewpoints?"
"Did you ever go to the [insert name here] theater?"
"Has your boy been going to Sunday School?"
"Does your wife go to Church regularly?"

By 1956, some 3,783 maritime workers – most in the San Francisco Bay area, the bastion of the ILWU – had been denied clearance, and most lost their jobs, for giving the wrong answers.[48]

Simultaneously, under the federal Industrial Personnel Security Program (established in November 1946 by Truman's executive order and perpetuated by another order by Eisenhower in 1953), some 2.3 million federal civil service employees, 3 million employees in military departments (including civilians), and some 4.5 million Americans in private employment, including tool-and-die makers, cooks and dishwashers, plumbers, technicians, and engineers, in about 21,000 different facilities, were undergoing "clearance" by some 200 agency loyalty boards, during the period 1947 to 1956 alone, to determine their "loyalty" and decide whether they could have access to confidential, secret, or top secret information.[49]

Another 2 million men and women in state and municipal employment were covered by local and regional loyalty security programs imitative of the federal one. Finally, at a conservative estimate, another 1.5 million men and women in private employment were subjected to private company security programs and checks, through special departments or private detective agencies (staffed mainly by ex-FBI agents) sifting information about "what workers read, joined, and thought." The real aim of such private "loyalty security" programs, as the National Industrial Conference Board indiscreetly said in a document sent to employers, was to "help you rid your plant of agitators who create labor unrest."

[48] Brown and Fassett (1953); Caute (1979, pp. 392–93, 396); Schrecker (1992, p. 145).
[49] The industries most affected were those with contracts with the Atomic Energy Commission and the Defense Department and maritime workers covered by the Port Security Program.

All told, at any given moment in the 1950s, *"one out of every five working people* had to take an oath or receive clearance as a condition of employment." Given the normally high turnover in employment, the actual number of Americans affected at one time or another must have been far higher.[50]

Meanwhile, the CP's leaders themselves were fighting a desperate struggle to avoid imprisonment under the Alien and Sedition Act (Smith Act).[51] Between July 28, 1948, and the end of 1954 – from the first indictment of twelve members of the national board of the CP for *"conspiracy* to *advocate"* overthrow of the government through subsequent indictments of other, middle-echelon leaders – the federal government put ninety-six party leaders on trial, of whom only three were acquitted, five had their cases severed for poor health – among them the Party's "helmsman" William Z. Foster – and one died during trial.[52]

During these years of unrelenting repression, "the opportunities for an actual, living, active Communist," in David Shannon's sardonic but precise summation, "were limited indeed. Forces and conditions outside the party, in the real world – what Communists call the 'objective situation' – put the American

---

[50] Caute (1979, pp. 268–69, 272, 274, 364, 370–71, 369, 278, 270, emphasis added). For a comprehensive study of "loyalty-security" employment tests during this period, see Brown (1958).

[51] Not without irony, in 1944 the CP leadership (among whom were many now on trial themselves) had endorsed the indictment, trial, and conviction under the selfsame Smith Act of eighteen Trotskyists (members of the SWP) active in Minnesota's labor movement. And Minnesota's CIO, under Communist leadership, went "on record condemning the disruptive and seditious activities of the group and ... their vicious attacks against the CIO and ... opposing any aid or comfort to those serving terms in the federal penitentiary ... " (Kampelman 1959, p. 114).

[52] Shannon (1959, p. 189); Caute (1979, pp. 187–93). *Fortune* reported in 1957 that 108 "top leaders" had been convicted under the Smith Act. "Most of these either did not serve their sentences, or served brief ones, or won their cases on appeal" (Starobin 1975, p. 241n2). Despite Foster's heart condition, and severance from the trial, he played a critical role in shaping the party's defense in the Smith Act trials. Convinced that war and fascism were imminent and that a fair trial was impossible, he stubbornly insisted that the defense should deemphasize First Amendment rights and turn instead on a justification of Communist doctrine. He wrote exhaustive doctrinal analyses, which were circulated among the defendants. In effect, he made it easier for civil libertarians – who were not exactly flocking to assist – to remain aloof from the Communists' defense (Johanningsmeier 1994, pp. 325–26). When the California Communists chose to defend themselves on First Amendment grounds, and as individuals rather than mere members of a monolithic party, they were roundly criticized. "As far as Foster was concerned," writes Dorothy Healey, then a leading California Red, "this was evidence ... of our misguided faith in 'bourgeois legalism' ... " (1993, p. 143).

Communists on the defensive. The Communists had to be more concerned with their party's survival than with its advancement. . . . "[53]

Yet the repression per se, as damaging as it was politically, and as much as it inflicted personal suffering on so many thousands of Communists and their families (and many more thousands of others with no connections to the party who were political casualties of those years), was not what determined the party's political isolation and reduced it by the late 1950s to a moribund sect. Nor was it government and public repression, in combination with anti-Communist union "raiding," that fragmented and cut down the eleven expelled Red-led international unions to but four survivors by the spring of 1955 and determined the disappearance of an independent left presence in American labor.[54] Rather, it was the party leadership's assessment of the "objective situation" and their consequent political incapacity in the face of it – as they navigated erratically in the immediate postwar decade between their own imagined Scylla of "right-wing opportunism" and Charybdis of "left sectarianism" – that determined both.[55]

This is not to deny the real, dangerous political reefs that suddenly lay ahead of them, as the Cold War dawned. Truman and liberal Democrats in Congress capitulated without a whimper to the Republicans' frenzied and unyielding assaults on the remnants of the New Deal, and, to try to

---

[53] Shannon (1959, p. 190).

[54] That repression determined the party's demise is an all but untestable argument so long as its own "imbecilities" at the time are attributed, as does Joseph Starobin (not without tongue in cheek), to repression: "the Party's propensity to imbecilities," he says, "was accentuated by increasing governmental and public repression of the Party . . . " (1975, p. 196).

[55] After the wartime meeting of the Allied leaders at Teheran, the CP's "prime strategy became," as *Fortune* reported, "an over-all war and postwar fusion of the interests of labor and capital in existing American capitalism" ("Hammer and Tongs: The New C.P. Line," p. 105). The Communists, Earl Browder argued, "must help to remove from the American ruling class the fear of a socialist revolution in the United States in the post-war period" (Isserman 1982, pp. 186, 188–89). In mid-1945, the party made an abrupt about-face to resume the "struggle of class against class" and also rediscovered "capitalist crisis" and "American imperialism." That Communists would find abhorrent the abandonment of "socialist revolution" and even of "class struggle" itself was, of course, both legitimate and understandable – or how could they have continued to consider themselves Communists? But *how* they discovered their "errors" (in response to an authoritative signal from abroad, in the form of an article by leading French Communist Jacques Duclos) and *what* they did to "correct" these errors (a drive for self-absolution through the excommunication of Browder, the leader they had followed without a hint of dissent over the previous two decades) revealed the party's historical exhaustion and, soon enough, irrelevance.

repel Republican cries of "20 years of treason" and Democratic "coddling of Communists," they launched a war against the left, as we know, marked formally by the initiation of the loyalty program in late 1946, in which they "codified the association of dissent with disloyalty."[56]

Truman, having vetoed the Taft–Hartley Act, sat on his hands afterward and, even after his political resurrection at the hands of labor, made no effort to repeal it.[57] While pushing a massive program to reestablish capitalism in Germany and Western Europe and inaugurating the era of U.S. global intervention in the defense of colonialism, Truman and his Democrats actively sought to remove left-wing critics from the company of patriotic Americans.[58] In this "objective situation," any principled left party with a mass following would have been hard put to devise and implement an effective strategy to protect its own flanks, preserve an alliance with at least some left liberals and "progressives," and enhance the unity and political strength of the organized working class. Any party that was "the main expression of native, working class radicalism in the United States"[59] and committed to international working-class solidarity (as well as to support for anticolonial movements) would have had a hard time meeting these objectives.

In the event, from mid-1945 through 1956, the CP's leaders would pursue a self-contradictory, incoherent, and ultimately disastrous political "strategy" that met none of these objectives – in part if not in the main because their party was the expression not only of American radicalism, but also of a self-imposed, corrupted form of internationalism whose authoritative leadership was located in the Soviet regime.[60] First, they suddenly reversed their cautious line of backing the "Roosevelt–Wallace coalition" against Truman within the Democratic Party in an effort to win the presidential nomination for Wallace and decided instead to go for broke and push a third party ticket which, especially after Wallace's crushing loss, precipitated the shattering of

---

[56] Caute (1979, p. 28). Although his advisors had been urging the step for months, it was following the Republican congressional election victory in November 1946 that Truman issued his first of a succession of executive orders initiating the government's loyalty program (Caute 1979, p. 268).

[57] In the 1952 election, Adlai Stevenson, an emblematic liberal Democrat, openly favored the Taft–Hartley Act and endorsed the Smith Act prosecutions.

[58] Caute (1979, p. 32).

[59] Laslett (1981, p. 115). Or in Theodore Draper's more damning terms, "the Communists could still be agents of the Soviet Union, whether or not they were the main expression of native, working-class radicalism" (1985b, p. 49).

[60] They were crippled, too, by their party's "democratic centralism," which in reality concentrated the power of decision in a bare handful of "helmsmen" (its five-man "secretariat") and excluded genuine political debate about the party's objectives and strategy.

the center–left alliance in the CIO and the ensuing anti-Communist cleansing. Then, with the ink barely dry on the CIO's expulsions, they instructed "Left and progressive unionists" to "return to the mainstream" of labor and, thereby, and to the extent that these unionists were foolish enough to act accordingly, were responsible for the final dismemberment and burial of most of the expelled Communist-led internationals.

The Progressive Party

The CP's leaders were sharply divided and riven with doubts about building a third party, especially one whose candidate, though he stood for "peace," rather than the gestating Cold War, advocated, as did Wallace, "progressive capitalism" (which was perilously akin to the "Browderist" heresy). As of the autumn of 1947, they had been backing the efforts of the "Wallace–Pepper forces" to reform the Democratic Party and win the Democratic Party's 1948 presidential nomination.[61] Echoing this, Harry Bridges declared at a 1947 Labor Day rally that the ILWU would "support the progressive forces *in the Democratic Party* led by Henry Wallace and other Roosevelt New Deal Democrats."[62]

Communist Party officials were still emphasizing at the time that "mass struggle," as Eugene Dennis, the party's general secretary, put it, must not be confused with "adventurous, desperate, and sectarian actions," which would split the CIO. Rather, Dennis argued, a victory would be possible if "independent and third party forces" supported "a coalition candidate, . . . *running as a Democrat.* To put it realistically," he said, " . . . this is the *only* way for the third-party and pro-Roosevelt forces to ensure the defeat of the G.O.P. candidate in 1948." They were still opposing any initiative for a third party unless it was, in the words of leading Communist John Gates, "broadly based" and was favored, in addition to the CIO's Communist-led unions, by "substantial

---

[61] Pepper was Senator Claude Pepper, Democrat, of Florida. In 1950, he was to lose the Democratic primary to his opponent, who accused him of being a Communist sympathizer. In later years, after Pepper made a political comeback and was elected and reelected to serve many terms in the House, he used to tell audiences that what really did him in back in 1950 was not the Red-baiting but his opponent's accusation that he (Pepper) "practiced conjugal love," which apparently just enough of Florida's voters did not know meant "married love."

[62] *Daily People's World*, September 3, 1947; Starobin (1975, p. 167). Bridges added that "the evils of the two-party system cannot be tolerated for the rest of our lives," but, as Levenstein notes, it seemed that these evils were "tolerable at least through the next general election" (Levenstein 1981, p. 223, emphasis added).

sections of the labor movement," including the UAW and ACW.[63] Foster, the CP's venerable chairman, was privately even more skeptical about the idea of a third party. In a conversation with comrades in California in September 1947, he said (according to an FBI bug planted in his hotel room) that "the Communist Party must not make the mistake it made twenty years ago regarding the Third Party movement ... or history will repeat itself and the

[63] Starobin (1975, pp. 159–62, citing the August 1947 issue of the party's theoretical organ, *Political Affairs*); Shannon (1959, p. 153). Articles in *Political Affairs* and *New Masses* in September 1947 also stressed, respectively, "that the Communists alone, and even with them the Left supporters in the labor and people's movement will not and cannot organize a third party," and "without the active participation of a substantial section of the trade union movement and without the support of a large number of Democratic voters, no serious new party can be formed" (Starobin 1972, p. 288n10). That a "substantial section" of organized labor might actively support a third-party ticket was still not out of the question at that time. At the 1944 Democratic Party convention, center and right-wing CIO leaders, including Philip Murray, Sidney Hillman, Emil Rieve, and Walter Reuther, had fought, but failed, to get Wallace renominated as the vice presidential candidate. In early 1946, third-party talk was already rife in labor circles. Walter Reuther, newly elected UAW president, declared on March 27, 1946, that "all liberal elements should work toward a realignment to draw together the best elements of both parties into a third party, but he doubted, he said, that this could be done in time for the 1948 campaign. Even the anti-Communist Textile Workers declared that the union would "not close the door" to "independent political action through the medium of a third party.... if and when the full powers of labor and all other liberal elements in our nation can be mobilized behind it." David Dubinsky, head of the AFL's ILGWU, disgusted by Truman's abandonment of the New Deal, told reporters that "only an independent labor party is the solution." Then, in late 1946, when Truman asked Congress for emergency powers to break the railway workers' strike and draft strikers if necessary, as well as subject labor leaders who persisted with the strike to fines and imprisonment, A. F. Whitney, president of the conservative Railway Brotherhood, pledged the union's entire treasury to defeat Truman in the next presidential election. The repressive law "comes from Wall Street," he angrily shouted at hearings before the House Labor Committee in February 1947. But by the time Wallace formally declared his candidacy on December 29, 1947, the winds had shifted: Whitney quit the Progressive Citizens of America and endorsed Truman; AFL president William Green said the third party was a mistake; Reuther called Wallace a "lost soul"; and Sidney Hillman's ACW pulled out of New York's American Labor Party – shortly followed, on January 22, 1948, by the CIO executive board's resolution – with eleven voting "nay" – to condemn the new third party and Wallace's candidacy. "Philip Murray [then] wrote to 387 industrial union councils, 34 regional directors and 100 lesser CIO officials, to advise them that they 'should be governed' by national CIO policy on the Marshall Plan and the New Party. In the *New York Times* ... the veteran labor editor, Louis Stark, correctly predicted that a disciplinary purge of any who refused to go along was planned. Undoubtedly, Stark had direct information from within the CIO's highest echelons" (MacDougall 1965, vol. 1, pp. 42–44; vol. 2, pp. 318–19; Starobin 1972, pp. 109–11).

Communist Party will be no further ahead twenty years from now." A third party could not be a success, he stressed, "unless the CIO could be convinced to support it wholeheartedly." He also implied that Communist unionists should be focusing on simpler, prosaic goals: "Send wages higher – get the money."[64]

The next month, according to later newspaper reports, high-ranking party officials met with several leading left unionists in New York City soon after the CIO's Boston Convention ended. They had a long discussion focusing on two issues: how to get the unions to join in opposing Congress's passage of legislation authorizing the Marshall Plan (or European Recovery Program) and, critically, "how to get the C.I.O. to reverse its convention stand and to accept *the idea of dumping Mr. Truman.*" No mention at all was made of a third party.[65]

---

[64] Johanningsmeier (1994, pp. 318–19; the middle quotation on the CIO is Johanningsmeier's paraphrase of Foster's recorded statement). Foster was referring to the withdrawal of the Communists from the "La Follette movement of 1924" led by Senator Robert ("Fighting Bob") La Follette and his "Progressive Independent Party," which was a genuine new third party of farmers and workers that won 17 percent of the votes cast. As he said in an article published in 1952, withdrawal from this movement was "a political error" that largely "divorced the Communists from their center group allies . . . . The Left–Center split . . . was one of the basic reasons why the [Samuel] Gompers bureaucrats could ride so roughshod over the Left Wing at the A.F. of L. convention, as they did, a few months later" (Foster 1952b, pp. 30–31). Had Foster changed "Gompers" to "Murray" and "A.F. of L." to "CIO," it would have aptly described the 1948 CIO convention held after the Wallace electoral debacle. Such was Foster's veiled "self-criticism" of his own and the party's third-party misadventure.

[65] News stories about this meeting in mid-October 1947 appeared within days of each other over half a year later, in May 1948, in the *Washington Post*, the *New York Post*, and the *Chicago Daily News*; the stories are cited and quoted extensively in McDougall (1965, I, pp. 251–63). Shannon (1959, p. 137) asserts, contrary to these stories, which report that no discussion of a third party took place at this meeting, that the party's leaders at that meeting explained "the new line on the third ticket . . . to them." He relies for this claim on the May 17, 1950, testimony by TWU president Michael Quill (who had broken with the party in April 1948) at the CIO hearings on the expulsion of the ILWU. Shannon quotes extensively (filling over two pages) both from Quill's testimony about that meeting and from Harry Bridges's so-called cross-examining of Quill about his testimony; for Quill said, too, that Bridges had participated with him in other, previous meetings between high party officials and CIO unionists, as well as in that crucial meeting, which was held, as Quill says, "in the afternoon of Saturday October 18th [1947,] and the God damned thing dragged out until late at night." Shannon writes that the exchange was "real drama, Quill insisting in his Irish brogue about the veracity of his testimony, and Bridges curiously never directly denying it, playing innocent and trying to get Quill to contradict himself" (Shannon 1959, p. 138). But Shannon curiously never quotes or even mentions a previous passage from the

Even some two months after Wallace's radio talk on December 29, 1947, saying he would run for the presidency on a third-party ticket, the Communist leadership's doubts and inner strife over whether or not to support him, and the dangers this would pose to splitting the CIO, were still on display. At the CP's national committee meeting in February 1948, Foster condemned Murray and other CIO leaders as "labor-imperialists" who had "abdicated the working-class leadership," and the party's labor secretary, John Williamson, hinted openly at their readiness to break up labor "unity":

> We Communists have always supported the idea of a unified trade union movement because it is in the general interests of the workers. However, different conditions dictate different approaches. . . . It is *impossible to think in terms of trade union unity* on the basis of support of Wall Street's imperialist program and *two-party system*.

Dennis, however, again warned against "any sectarian tendency to convert the political struggle within the trade unions in behalf of Wallace and the new people's party into a movement to split or withdraw from the established trade union centers."[66]

In fact, Dennis – who had been polemicizing against that "sectarian tendency" for a year – already had yielded to it himself and become its authoritative

Quill/Bridges exchange (two pages earlier in the CIO transcript), in which Bridges shows that Quill's memory of another such meeting after the CIO convention a year earlier, was a bit faulty:

> BRIDGES: Was it your impression that all the people at the meeting were Communists?
> QUILL: Yes.
> BRIDGES: Including yourself?
> QUILL: That's right. . . .
> BRIDGES: You couldn't be mistaken of the place of the convention? It couldn't have been Detroit or some other place?
> QUILL: No, it so happens, Harry, that the convention was really at Atlantic City.
> BRIDGES: And you couldn't be mistaken?
> QUILL: No.
> BRIDGES: Don't you know that I didn't attend the Atlantic City convention? We had a strike on the Pacific Coast at that time and all during the convention I was on the Pacific Coast every single day and we have official records to prove that. . . . Any other meetings prior to that time of that nature that I attended and you attended?
> QUILL: Not that I remember (CIO 1950, p. 64; Prickett 1975, p. 402).

[66] Shannon (1959, pp. 155–56, citing the February and March 1948 issues of *Political Affairs*).

advocate inside the CP around mid-November 1947.[67] Then, according to later newspaper reports, a meeting took place on December 15 between CP officials and CIO unionists, at which Dennis and the party's New York State chairman Robert Thompson, Foster's protégé (and member of the party's ruling "secretariat") told the unionists that the decision had been made to create a third party; he instructed them to support Wallace's soon-to-be-announced Progressive Party candidacy and to bend every effort, despite the unfavorable and explosive prospects of doing so, to win the CIO leadership's endorsement.

"By all accounts, the announcement was greeted with consternation and resentment." TWU's "Red Mike" Quill reportedly asked Thompson who had made the decision and was told "the Central Committee" had done so. Quill shouted, "To hell with you and your central committee." The party's central committee, he said, could not tell him or his union what to do, and he warned that supporting Wallace and building a third party would split the CIO. Tell that, he said, to that "crack-pot, Foster." Thompson, unmoved, replied that the decision had to be pressed "even if it splits the C.I.O. right down the middle."[68]

The mystery is why the party's top leadership suddenly reversed their line and plunged forward in mid-December 1947 with a policy that they knew would, if their unionist adherents went along, split the CIO. Was it simply a rational but erroneous assessment of the temper of the electorate?[69] Or was it, once again, what they perceived as a signal from abroad that made them reverse course and court almost certain disaster?

---

[67] Starobin (1975, p. 172); Johanningsmeier (1994, p. 319).

[68] Johanningsmeier (1994, p. 319); *Washington Post*, May 2, 1948; McDougall (1965, I, pp. 251–63); Starobin (1975, pp. 175–76). Quill went along with the party line on the Progressive Party for a while, and even joined the Labor Committee for Wallace and tried to convince CIO leaders to support him, at a CIO executive board meeting some weeks later, in January 1948; but he finally broke with the party publicly in April 1948 (Starobin 1972, p. 293n36).

[69] Progressive and open Communist candidates received impressively high numbers of votes on November 4 in various state and local elections in Chicago, New York, and California (Shannon 1959, p. 148; Starobin 1975, pp. 169–79). Was this what convinced party leaders that Wallace would be a viable candidate and that, even if he lost, his campaign would serve to establish the Progressive Party as that long sought after "third party," a mass party of the left? If so, they certainly would not have been alone in making this calculation; at the time and for months afterward, and even late in the campaign, many were the pundits who expected Wallace to make heavy inroads into the electorate. "During the campaign there were wild rumors about suppressed polls, most of them ascribed to Roper, which showed that the Progressive party was going to get anywhere between 11 million and 18 million votes. (Walter Winchell, who settled for 15 million, reported this 'fact' in all seriousness.) On election day, of course, the earth caved in under the Progressives...." ("Where Are the Radicals?," p. 115).

In early October 1947, there came an announcement of the establishment of a new Communist Information Bureau – the so-called Cominform – consisting of six eastern European Communist parties plus the parties of France and Italy. The Cominform manifesto called on Communists everywhere to oppose the Marshall Plan, "as only a European branch of the general world plan of political expansion being realized by the United States." Andrei Zhdanov, then second only to Stalin in the Soviet party, declared that "[a] special task devolves upon the fraternal Communist parties of France, Italy, England and other countries." Zhdanov also advised his fellow Communists not to underestimate the capacity of the working class for struggle against imperialism and urged the formation of "united fronts from below" in Western Europe. No mention was made of the American party. A *Daily Worker* editorial on October 7, in the same issue reporting the Cominform's establishment, merely welcomed this "overseas resistance to the same crowd which is rooking [every American]...and his family and trying to wreck his unions and democratic liberties." Crucially, the editorial said nothing about a third party, but again called "urgently [for]...a strong anti-monopoly, anti-war coalition based on the Roosevelt–Wallace line."[70]

But Foster, whom the FBI had just overheard in September expressing skepticism about and implied opposition to launching a third party, was soon openly hinting at his own (and with him, the party's) coming zig-zag. On October 20, in a speech at a public meeting hailing the formation of the Cominform, Foster called on the American left to "cut loose from the leading strings of the Democratic and Republican parties, and launch a great mass, anti-monopoly, progressive peace party of its own."[71] Despite Stalin's still conciliatory line and an authoritative rebuke of Foster back in March 1947 by French Communist Jacques Duclos for his pessimism and stress on the menace of U.S. imperialism, he had continued warning all along of the imperialist "war danger." Now he thought himself to be vindicated and would later point to this with pride.[72]

The logic of the Cominform's call for united fronts from below, if applied in the United States, cut away the ground under the insistence by party leaders (including Foster until then) that the backing of "substantial sections of the

---

[70] Shannon (1959, pp. 136–37); Starobin (1975, p. 171); Johanningsmeier (1994, p. 320).

[71] Shannon (1959, p. 140, citing the *Daily Worker*, October 22, 1947).

[72] At the party's National Convention in August 1948, Foster would say: "The formation of the Information Bureau affirmed the correctness of our line, especially on the all-important question of the role of American imperialism and the danger of war and fascism connected with it" (Starobin 1975, p. 171).

labor movement" was a precondition for the formation of a viable third party. The Cominform resolutions and Zhdanov's remarks were now apparently taken by them as a signal to end their hesitation – indeed, as Foster was to say later, they had been plagued until then by "a rather complacent attitude" – about going for a third party and splitting the center–left alliance in the CIO.[73]

Now, responding to an imagined prod from abroad, and armed with a dusted-off 1920s' concept of a "united front from below," given new gleam by the Cominform, the CP's officials repudiated, as Dennis put it, "the erroneous views of certain [!] party leaders and district organizations, as well as *many of our trade union cadres* who, up till the announcement of Wallace's candidacy, expressed doubts as to the advisability of an independent Presidential ticket and confused the maneuverings and treacherous position of most of Labor's top officials with the position being taken by the rank and file."[74]

As the ruinous consequences of their repudiation of "many" if not most of their own unionists was becoming apparent within the CIO, and Wallace's star seemed to be fading as the election approached, they drew the wagons around themselves.[75] Their line, said Foster in September 1948, was "fundamentally correct." But it was being undermined, he complained, by "weaknesses and mistakes . . . of a Right-opportunist character" in applying it.[76] Soon enough their wild lurch to the "left" ended in a debacle for the

---

[73] Ibid.; Johanningsmeier (1994, p. 320). Yet it should be noted that six weeks *before* the Cominform's appearance, the left in California already had formed the new Independent Progressive Party (IPP), aiming to get on the ballot in the 1948 elections. Hugh Bryson, president of MCS, and close to Harry Bridges, played a major role in IPP's formation. Healey, then a leading Communist in California, rejects Starobin's argument that the Cominform's formation "was the deciding factor in the Party's decision to go ahead with the Progressive Party campaign. There were all too many occasions on which we shaped our approach to domestic politics in response to some Soviet diplomatic declaration or policy, but *this was not one of them*" (Healey and Isserman 1993, p. 109, emphasis added).

[74] Starobin (1975, p. 179, citing *Political Affairs*, March 1948).

[75] As Shannon notes, "if foreign Communists had deliberately tried, they could not have done much more than they did to hurt the Wallace campaign. In Late February came the Communist coup in Czechoslovakia. In June, the Russians began their blockade of West Berlin, and the United States air force retaliated with the airlift. In late June and early July, the Soviets and the Cominform excommunicated Yugoslavia's Tito" (1959, pp. 178–79).

[76] Yet while warning against "right opportunism," Foster again painted their own candidate, on whom they had gambled so much, as a sort of right winger himself. Unlike Wallace, he said, "we Marxist-Leninists [do not] believe that the badly crippled world capitalist system can be saved and transformed into 'progressive capitalism'" (Shannon 1959, p. 177;

party and the swift elimination of the Communist bastions in the CIO. With this, the most significant achievement of the Communists, the building of a combative, class-conscious industrial union movement, was all but destroyed.

Johanningsmeier 1994, p. 321, both citing the same September 1948 issue of *Political Affairs*).

11

EPILOGUE: THE "THIRD LABOR FEDERATION" THAT NEVER WAS

"If we but knew where we stand and whither we are tending," declared the CP's new general secretary, Eugene Dennis, in February 1946 – in a phrase borrowed from an address by Abraham Lincoln – "we should then know what to do and how to do it." Dennis and his comrades, he insisted, knew where they stood and whither history was tending, what was to be done, and how. But as it turned out, they were wrong on all counts.[1] To understand how it happened, we have to return now to the immediate postwar years and follow them through to the mid-1950s.

From roughly 1947 through 1953, the CP was torn internally by its own hunts for heresy ("right-wing opportunism," "ultraleftism," "Trotskyism," "Titoism," and, especially, "a whole series of manifestations of white chauvinism within various Party organizations and even within the ranks of leading committees of the Party"). The Communists held their own political "trials" and purged longtime comrades who now were deemed "unreliable elements" and, at the least, excoriated others – among them, leading CIO unionists – for engaging in one or another alleged "wrongful tendency" or "objective deviation."[2]

Gripped by an apocalyptic mood heightened by the passage of the Internal Security Act (McCarran Act) in late 1950 and then by the Supreme Court decision, on June 4, 1951, upholding the Smith Act convictions and sentences of eleven top party officials – which, said Dennis, was "the five minutes to midnight" bell – the party's leaders made the fateful decision to go "underground."

---

[1] Starobin (1975, p. 108). The phrase is from Lincoln's "House Divided" speech.

[2] Henderson (1952, p. 30). "Thousands of people were caught up in [the white chauvinism] campaign," which lasted roughly from 1949 through 1953, "not only in the Party itself, but within . . . some of the Left unions as well. In Los Angeles alone," recalls Healey, "we must have expelled two hundred people on charges of white chauvinism, usually on the most trivial of pretexts. People would be expelled for serving coffee in a chipped coffee cup to a Black or serving watermelon at the end of dinner" (Healey and Isserman 1993, p. 126).

The party remained open, with many spokespersons staying at their posts, but a select number of its highest and second-echelon leaders and "several thousand cadres" were ordered into hiding, under assumed identities and separated from their workmates, friends, and family (often husband and wife saw each other only furtively, if at all) – where, scattered and isolated from each other, without direction, they were in effect paralyzed politically. This amounted, over the next half a decade or so, to a de facto dissolution of the party.[3]

So from 1950 on, precisely at a moment when the fate of the expelled Communist-led unions was at stake, the party leadership, indeed, the party itself, barely existed. What there was of an intact leadership, both above-ground and "underground," as well as most of the national board members who were now dispersed in federal penitentiaries across the country, gave incoherent, inconsistent, self-contradictory "advice" to "left and progressive" unionists.[4]

---

[3] Preparations for the "underground" were under way by the spring of 1951, according to Starobin (1975, pp. 198–205, 219–23); Johanningsmeier (1994, p. 329). The experience of Ethel Shapiro-Bertolini, a rank-and-file Communist unionist in the AFL's ILGWU, is emblematic: "I found out after I went into the underground that it was a disastrous mistake. I lost contact with everybody that I had built up a relationship with after sweating it out in these shops and taking abuse I wouldn't ordinarily take from the bosses. Since going to work in Los Angeles I had built up a list of 200 names. . . . When I went underground, I had to destroy the list. There was no one else to turn it over to. All those contacts lost. . . . The basic link between the [party] and the masses of the people was removed and buried for four or five years. And the FBI had me in their net from the very beginning" (Healey 1993, p. 124). As "friendly witnesses" who were until that moment deemed party members in good standing began to sprout before HUAC and other committees, revealing that the FBI had fully infiltrated it at all levels, the party's watchword became "on guard against enemy infiltration." This intensified an inner-party atmosphere deadening to debate let alone dissent. "The eyes and ears of all comrades and Party leaders should at all times be kept wide open for the least signs of enemy penetration. Every suspicion and every doubt should be pursued and resolved" (Larson 1952, p. 27).

[4] The legendary Foster, the party's chairman throughout these years, was spared a Smith Act trial because of his age and ill health and – unlike Eugene Dennis, party general secretary, and other top leaders – never saw a day in prison. Despite his illness, he remained, according to his biographer, mentally sharp and alert and was undoubtedly – both because of his incomparable, youthful experience of mass labor leadership as well as his personal triumph over "Browderism" – the man to whom all in the party leadership deferred (Johanningsmeier 1994, p. 340). Aside from Foster, the others in the party's controlling triumvirate during these years, when they were not in prison, were Dennis, general secretary; Robert Thompson, chairman of the New York Party – "an intransigent Fosterite," in Healey's words – and John Williamson, labor secretary. (Gus Hall was acting general secretary in 1950 while Dennis was serving a year's sentence for "contempt of Congress.") The National Committee was the largest leadership body, presided over by the National Executive Committee, usually

The CIO had barely finished expelling the unions they led when the party abruptly instructed them to strive for "labor unity," eschew "dual unionism," and "return to labor's mainstream." Party cadres in the unions were instructed in early 1951 to build a "united front from below," push for "independent political action" and for the formation of a "labor party," while still mobilizing support for the moribund Progressive Party, and, above all, to make working for "peace" – which, in practice, meant unwavering support for Soviet foreign policy – their preeminent, self-defining, political task. The party's leadership deprecated and all but relegated the "progressive-led unions" to the margins and declared that they were no longer its "primary base." Rather, party officials now extolled the "right-led unions," both in the CIO and the AFL, and their "15 million trade unionists" as the "main direction" and "concentration point" of the party's activities.[5] This line was the party's ultimate political contortion on labor's stage. For it put an end to the remote but real historical possibility that the expelled unions would endure as the core of a unified and resilient if compact base of the left within the organized working class.

In the face of the intensifying assaults on the CIO's Communist-led internationals from late 1947 on, they displayed little of their reputed nationwide "discipline" and even less of a common strategy – except, perhaps, as *Business Week* reported in the waning days of the 1948 election season, a "strategy so far [which] has been to make whatever sacrifices that might be necessary to stay in the C.I.O." But when, in October 1948, "left-wing locals" in New York City pulled out of the right-wing Retail, Wholesale and Department Store Union (RWDSU) – which had ordered officers of the locals to sign non-Communist affidavits – this was seen by various pundits and capitalist spokesmen as implying a major change of Communist strategy. The bolt by RWDSU's left-wing locals (District 65) was, they said, the opening gambit in a Communist strategy of offense – secession from the CIO and self-organization of a new left-led "third labor federation." Left-wing "secessionists *denied*," said *Business Week* doubtfully, "that their move was intended as a test of the ability of leftist leaders to take unions out of the C.I.O."[6]

Communist Party leaders and spokesmen were at pains to decry the predictions being "flung around" about "'secession' and formation of a 'third labor movement.'" The CIO's "rightwingers," wrote the *Daily Worker*'s labor

referred to as the National Board – which was "ostensibly the Party's top policy-setting body (in truth, real policy was generally determined by the Political Bureau or Secretariat)." Healey (1993, pp. 176, 123, 157); Shannon (1959, pp. 72–73).

[5] CPUSA (1951, pp. 12–15); Williamson (1951b, p. 67); and the relevant citations below.

[6] "C.I.O. Begins Careful Crackdown," p. 104, emphasis added.

columnist at the end of August 1949, were making these predictions ". . . to cover up, or to justify, their own announced plans to expel left-led unions at the next CIO convention." That same week, the party's labor secretary went so far as to issue a warning to Communist unionists "to combat all tendencies of narrowing down trade union work to the members of Left–Progressive-led unions."[7]

On the eve of the CIO convention, *Business Week* reported that "pre-convention hopes of a left-wing defeat in the U.E. didn't pan out. The anti-Communist forces . . . failed to take control by a wide margin." And this meant, averred the magazine, that the "C.I.O. will have to make up its mind what it wants to do about its party-line affiliates. The decision may mean a third labor federation in America. . . . That prospect . . . gives employers the jitters."[8] The next week, *Business Week's* anxiety about that prospect – that "cutting pro-Communist unions out of the C.I.O. . . . may mean a third union federation in America" – was expressed in even more portentous language:

> Another 1935? – Another labor split is looming. And in broad out-line, at least, the situation bears some resemblance to fateful 1935 when the C.I.O. was born. Now, as then, the labor front is disturbed and strife-ridden. Now, as then, millions of wage and salary earners remain to be recruited by zealous, resourceful organizers. Now, as then, a "radical" group of unions is at cross-purposes with the reigning labor hierarchs. And now – as in 1935 – management faces the prospect of trouble: new jurisdictional feuds, competitive and frenzied organizing, interunion rivalry for greater employer concessions. . . .

What especially was making employers nervous, apparently, was the giant shadow now being cast again by John L. Lewis. "Job for Lewis?," asked *Business Week*. "There's talk of a federation headed by John L. Lewis. It would include his United Mine Workers and District 50, along with orphaned C.I.O. left-wing unions and any independents that could be lured in. Lewis still hates Communists, as such. . . . But he has grudging admiration for their industrial union work."[9]

When UE and FE merged days before the CIO convention, *Fortune* commented that this " . . . move would allow financial resources to move more freely

---

[7] Morris (1949e); Williamson (1949b, p. 4).

[8] "U.E. Leftists Win – But for How Long?," p. 95.

[9] "Will C.I.O. Split Apart?," p. 107. Remember that Lewis had taken the UMW back out of the AFL again in the fall of 1947 because AFL officials would not squarely refuse compliance with Taft–Hartley's non-Communist affidavit.

through the party life-lines and might be the first step in the 'third labor federation.'" Then, when UE refused to pay its per capita taxes, withdrew its delegates from the convention, and effectively made its exit from the CIO, *Newsweek*'s most salient observation was that "the UE has long been rumored to be the prospective nucleus of a new 'progressive' labor federation – haven for all unions with Communist sympathies." The CIO executive board itself flatly charged, once the expulsions were under way, that the UE/FE merger and walkout had been "the first step in the long range plans of the Communist Party to establish a Communist-dominated labor federation in America."[10]

Although "secession" as a "first step" in a strategy aimed at conserving their forces within an independent left labor federation would have been sensible for the Communist-led internationals – who were facing certain expulsion anyway – the CIO's charge was, as we see below, unfounded.[11] The party line was precisely the opposite. As the fateful 1949 CIO convention was nearing, CP leaders, as if in denial that they themselves – with their third-party gamble – had set the split in motion, were instructing left and progressive unionists, in no uncertain terms, "to fight against a split in the CIO" and to do their utmost to carry out "a policy of collaborating with the workers in all trade unions, especially those under right leadership." This, said the party, was "to be achieved by a united front from below, regardless of trade union affiliation."[12]

In tune with this line, three months before the fateful CIO convention, a conference on "democracy and autonomy in the CIO" held in New York City on August 30, attended by 1,550 officers, executive board members, and shop stewards of locals of "progressive-led" internationals as well as from locals in other camps, warned that "the entire future of the CIO [is] at stake." The conference delegates resolved "to fight to remain within the CIO and to exert all our influence to return the CIO to its founding principles of democracy and autonomy." The *Daily Worker*'s labor columnist commented that "all those attending [the meeting] saw the conspiracy behind the widely

---

[10] Starobin (1975, pp. 202–3); cf. also Saposs (1959, p. 208); *Newsweek* (November 14, 1949, pp. 23–25, as cited in Peevey 1961, p. 28); "Civil War in C.I.O.," p. 206; Fitch (1949, p. 645).

[11] George Morris, the *Daily Worker*'s labor columnist, wrote about UE's walkout: "Told point blank that they will be raided," and aid and comfort given to their enemies within the UE, "...the UE's leaders left the convention and the union's board voted not to pay any more per capita" (1949a, p. 10). This was an exculpatory remark on UE's behalf that Morris would not repeat; the party's leadership soon was openly condemning UE's secession (see below).

[12] Williamson (1949b, p. 4); Lawson (1949, p. 8).

spread newspaper publicity that the conference was called to 'form a third labor movement.'"[13]

That such adamant Communist denials of any intention to encourage formation of a left-led third labor federation were greeted with skepticism by CIO "right-wingers" and employers is understandable, given the CP's propensity to make quick zig-zags and sudden reversals of its line. But, as we see below, to this particular strategic line (though often expressed in muddled, hazy, and ambiguous tactical formulae), the party's leaders adhered unswervingly, to the bitter end.

UE's exodus from the CIO was, in fact, exactly contrary to the party's line, "which at that time," in the words of former leading Communist Joseph Starobin, "was to engage in the most effective possible rearguard action."[14] The other Communist-led internationals all attended the CIO convention and continued to affirm their right and desire to remain in the CIO. Yet despite months of warning signs preceding the convention, their leaders seemed unprepared, if not in disarray, and "unable to agree on a common stance in the face of the inevitable onslaught. . . . The absence of coordination was manifest." Yet their disorder at the convention and later actions and denials did not "torpedo all that crap," as Harry Bridges told reporters, "about us forming a bloc and the organization of a third labor movement."[15]

As the CIO's expulsions were unrolling, various conferences on "autonomy and democracy" and "mutual aid and cooperation" among the unions that "left the CIO or were expelled or about to be expelled" (as they were described in the *Daily Worker*) sprouted up across the country; as a result, "all that crap" became a virtual refrain in the press. From the autumn of 1949 through the end of 1950, as *Business Week* (December 9, 1950) reported in a story headed ominously, "Leftist Labor Alliance," "Left-wing unionists were getting together on local levels" in New York, Philadelphia, Chicago, San Francisco, Los Angeles, and other highly unionized towns from Butte to Birmingham to Newark. "Their goal: 'to revitalize and resurrect the militant traditions of the American labor movement.'"[16]

How, exactly, the "left-wing unionists" were going to bring about this revitalization and resurrection, however, remained, at best, obscure. For they abjured any form of practical unification among themselves. Although they

---

[13] "Unionists Call N.Y. Parley on Autonomy"; Morris (1949b, p. 2).

[14] Williamson (1949b, p. 4); Starobin (1975, pp. 202–3). UE's leaders "were later criticized for this [exodus] by the labor secretary of the Communist Party" (Saposs 1959, p. 208), and the breach of Matles and Emspak with the party, as we see below, was soon irreparable.

[15] Levenstein (1981, p. 281, 301–2).   [16] "Leftist Labor Alliance," p. 92.

consistently resolved, in a variant of the same phrase, "to unite labor unions in common action regardless of affiliation to defend the basic interests of labor," they also declared, almost in the same breath, that the local labor alliance they were setting up would "*not* function as a third federation or dual organization of labor."[17]

This muddled CP line was reiterated with rigidity and often asperity. A major CP resolution on May Day, 1950, declared: "... under the present conditions of the acute peril of war and fascism, [we] call for promoting the struggle for the unification of the working class" and "effecting *united labor action from below* for the day-to-day needs of the masses." Yet the party also urged Communist unionists, in the May Day message of its "helmsman," William Z. Foster, to "actively participate in [developing] .. all possible joint action pacts among the unions. *Especially among the expelled unions must we build a strong bond of cooperation.*"

Party labor secretary John Williamson made sure to insist that "the issue today is not the organization of a new, a third Federation of Labor," but the party's union line seemed, for a moment, to still be flexible. He said that it was "necessary that *the Left forces in the trade unions be ideologically united and that there be maximum unity of action*," and he urged "the unions under attack . . . to coordinate their activities and find the most effective form of cooperation for their mutual protection and extension of their influence. . . ."[18]

But, significantly, he went on to emphasize that " . . . our vanguard Party [cannot] be subordinated to the Left trade-union leaders. . . . There is only one Party that unites all members, whether they be rank-and-filers or trade union leaders, and all Communists are subject to the same policies, discipline and organizational structure." For the last two years, he disclosed, "the trade-union department" had been in "continuous ideological struggle with comrades in

---

[17] Among the left labor conferences and local labor alliances held during 1950, at roughly the same time in late November, were the Los Angeles "Committee for United Labor Action," sponsored by thirteen local unions; the "Chicago Committee for Labor Unity," cochaired by Grant Oakes of the farm equipment workers (FE) and Ray Dennis of the mine, mill, and smelter workers (MM) and attended by some seventy delegates; and the "United Labor Conference for Mutual Aid," chaired by Aaron Schneider of the office workers (UOPW), attended by 300 delegates from twenty local unions in New York City ("Urge Parley of Unions Expelled by CIO," p. 4; "Labor Hi-Lites" (August); "National Labor Parley Call"; "20 New York Local Unions." (In addition, with the Korean War under way, left-sponsored "labor conferences on peace" were also being held and interunion "political action committees" were being set up in these and other cities) (see, e.g., Stone 1950).

[18] CPUSA (1950, pp. 7–8); Foster (1950, p. 9); Williamson (1950a, pp. 96, 97). Emphasis added.

leading trade-union positions, combating pressures, expressions and practices of Right opportunism . . . and of a general under-estimation of the role, practices, and discipline of the Party itself."[19]

What's more, to make the point eminently clear, he issued the bizarre warning to Communist unionists to beware of committing the twin sins of "Right opportunism" and "'Left' sectarianism." The first "expressed itself in *voluntarily withdrawing . . . from reactionary-controlled labor federations,*" the second, in "*looking for premature and narrow Left Centers of the trade unions.*"[20] If the first was an obvious, if veiled, condemnation of UE's (and FE's) leaders, the implication was that they were guilty also of the second sin.

The party demanded that "the main progressive-led Internationals . . . [engage in] united action in the same industry or allied industries with the members of other Right-led unions."[21] At the party's national committee plenum that September, within days of the last of the CIO's expulsions, Williamson again obtusely complained that

[a]lmost nowhere is there a real organized fight for united labor action by those unions where the Left is in the leadership, a situation which leads to isolation from the masses of the rank-and-file in the Right-led trade unions.[22]

In the face of such recalcitrance, Williamson declared: "The single biggest job today is to learn to rely upon the mass of our Party members in the trade

---

[19] Williamson (1951b, p. 72).   [20] Williamson (1950a, pp. 96–98, emphasis added).

[21] A couple of weeks after the May Day resolution and speeches, when a special convention of the Communist-led UOPW instructed its officers to arrange mutual aid pacts with other expelled unions and called for "united labor action" among "all unions," the *New York Times* staff persisted in their disbelief, anyway. The story was headed, "Office Union Takes Step Toward Formation of Possible New Leftist Labor Federation," and this was also the story's lead, although over halfway through the story came the statement, "All the leftist unions have denied that they had any intention of forming a new federation of their own. James H. Durkin of New York, president of the office union, told reporters the resolution was not aimed at inducing other workers to leave their unions." Cf. also "Merger: DWU, FTA, UOPWA" (emphasis added), whose report on the subsequent merger of the Office Workers with the Distributive Workers and Food and Tobacco Workers stressed Durkin's assurance "that *the merger was in no sense a 'third labor federation'*"; the only aim of the merger, Durkin said, was to "contribute to the unity of all workers so necessary at this time when anti-labor employers are using the war situation to try to slash workers' living standards and take away their right to organize, strike and defend their working conditions."

[22] Williamson (1950c, p. 57).

unions and *not just on a few leaders*."[23] He then got down to cases. Over much of the past year, he said, the party's labor department had to give "more systematic attention and leadership . . . to the work in the electrical industry than at any other time in our Party history." He said that "decisive forces in the top leadership" of UE were "resisting an approach of real united action of U.E. and I.U.E.," and he condemned their "blind factionalism."[24]

In the course of "carrying through a struggle for Party consciousness and main reliance upon the Communists in the shops and local unions," he disclosed, " . . . *we correctly parted company with some trade-union leaders who had previously been associated with us*"! And in an intimation of worse things to come, he went so far as to threaten a possible Communist uprising against the "top leadership" of the biggest and most powerful Red-led union: "We must yet battle through and *defeat all opposition* to considering work among members of the I.U.E. of equal and necessary importance as activity among workers in U.E."[25]

What were Communist unionists to make of this crazy-quilt "line"? The party wanted them at one and the same time to be building a "united front from below" with the members of the "right-led" unions – while the Communist-led unions were still engaged in fierce defensive battles against these same unions' raids of their own members – but also to be "building a strong bond of cooperation" among the expelled unions, yet while also making sure that this "strong

---

[23] Ibid. (emphasis added). A couple of weeks later MM announced a new "unity program": Its officers were to take "whatever further steps are necessary to develop a program of mutual aid and cooperation among the unions which have been expelled from CIO, as well as any other affiliated or unaffiliated unions willing to join in such a program." But, once again, in conformity with the party line, MM's officers felt compelled to stress, reported the *Daily Worker* ("Mine Mill Union Votes," p. 4), "that there is no intention to form a third labor federation in the United States."

[24] Williamson (1950c, p. 43). IUE, remember, was the anti-Communist union set up by the CIO in UE's jurisdiction, with the collusion of GE's and Westinghouse's managements; under Taft–Hartley, employers could now petition for an NLRB election, without which IUE, this new memberless union, could not have gotten on an NLRB ballot. GM did the same, also petitioning for an NLRB election to decide who should bargain for its 27,000 UE members (Peevey 1961, p. 29, citing *Business Week*, January 7, 1950, p. 65).

[25] Williamson (1950c, pp. 42, 43, 52–53, emphasis added). Bert Cochran, relying on the memory of former *Daily Worker* editor John Gates, puts the "climax" of the rupture between UE's leaders and the party in early 1951. According to him, James Matles, "in a stormy session with the Party's bureau members," told them that he no longer had any confidence in their leadership (1977, p. 294); also see Levenstein (1981, p. 308). But Williamson's public disclosure at its September 1950 plenum that the CP already had broken with UE indicates that at least one, much earlier, "stormy session" had occurred.

bond" in no way tended to grow into "a new, third federation" or "dual organization" of labor, let alone threatening the party's "vanguard role" and suzerainty.
No wonder it was taking "a continuous ideological struggle" and snapping
of the party's disciplinary whip against "all Communists" to keep them "in
line."

Then, in mid-November 1950, the event whose contemplation had been
giving employers "the jitters" seemed, finally, about to happen. The *New York
Times* reported:

> A group of leaders of left-wing labor union[s] has called a conference
> for Nov. 28 in Washington, leading to speculation that a new national
> federation of labor is in the making. Heading the list of sponsors is Harry
> Bridges, president of the International Longshoremen's and Warehouse-
> men's Union, a likely leader of such a federation.[26]

But again, the *Times* staff seems to have been reading tea leaves rather than
the Communist press, which had been reiterating ad nauseum the party's
adamantine opposition to the formation of anything resembling an independent left labor front. At most, as Williamson advised readers of *The {Sunday}
Worker*, the upcoming November 28 conference should "serve as the gadfly
that can lead to unified labor action by all workers, Negro and white, and
all trade unions locally and again nationally."[27] And not a word of the conference call itself by officers of eight "independent progressive unions" (not
including UE's James Matles and Julius Emspak, who were conspicuous by
their absence), said anything even intimating otherwise.[28] Rather, in the face
of the "all out political attack on the rights of labor," the call declared that
labor "desperately needs united action" to defeat these attacks and repeal the
Taft–Hartley Act and other repressive legislation and "re-enact the Wagner
Act."

---

[26] "Left-Wing Unions of Nation to Meet."   [27] Williamson (1950b, p. 8, emphasis added).
[28] The other sponsors, in addition to Bridges, were Maurice Travis, secretary treasurer of the
mine, mill, and smelter workers (MM); Ben Gold, president of the fur and leather workers
(IFLWU); Hugh Bryson, president of the marine cooks and stewards (MCS); Arthur Osman,
president of the distributive workers (DPOW); Joseph Selly, president of the telegraphers and
radio operators (ACA); Ernest deMaio, president of UE District 11; James McLeish, president
of UE District 4; Grant Oakes, former farm equipment (FE) president and now secretary
treasurer, UE District 11; and Abram Flaxer, president of the public workers (UPW). The
expelled eleven were now down to eight, as the result of mergers among them: FE with UE,
MCS and the Fishermen both with ILWU, and the UOPW and FTA with district 65 to form
the new Distributive, Processing and Office Workers ("8 Unions Call 'Repeal Taft–Hartley'").

Epilogue: A "Third Labor Federation"

At the National Conference, 872 delegates from "two dozen unions in 18 states" who had expectantly "streamed into Washington, D.C.," to answer the call for "united action" heard Harry Bridges (who was, again, out on bail) tell them: "We're here primarily to protect ourselves, to pool our resources to resist the attacks on labor, to fight back with everything we've got, and with others who join us." But what they would not do, Bridges said, was to try to "form a third federation. We're not setting up any formal *or even informal* apparatus here. We must continue to work for *labor unity at the bottom*, and there are many ways to go about it." The only glimmer that they might do anything more to "pool their resources to fight back" came when Bridges off-handedly remarked that his union intended to ask other participating unions to send their executive boards to a meeting sometime soon, to convene "to *develop at a higher level* a joint program of action."[29]

That was enough for *Business Week* to report a week later that "[s]eed of a third labor federation was sowed in Washington last week by eight unions that had been ousted from CIO for Communist-line activities." Although other leaders besides Bridges "stressed the same theme of 'no third labor federation now,'" *Business Week* knew that

the idea of a new federation was in the backs of most minds.... [T]he extreme leftists clearly left the way open for a federation later. They want a further alliance in the future with "some trade unions outside of this group who ... adhere to the principles of trade unionism." Bridges amplified this statement later, in a bid for support from "other independent trade unions" – including John L. Lewis' strong, anti-Communist United Mine Workers.[30]

But *Business Week* and the jittery employers the magazine represented need not have worried, for at the CP's convention, in January 1951, the main resolution pronounced:

We must face the fact that the overwhelming bulk of the organized workers are in the A.F. of L., C.I.O. and independent Right-led unions.

[29] Rubin (1950, emphasis added). The delegates gave "standing applause" to David Livingston, head of district 65 of the Distributive, Processing and Office Workers, when he declared that "there was no question about the loyalty of the delegates. 'They have shown their loyalty to all that established and made this nation,' he said" (Fiske 1950, p. 9).

[30] "Leftist Labor Alliance"; in January 1951, *Fortune*, too, noted that although they "decided once again not to set up a third labor federation ... it was obvious that the shattered Stalinists are working slowly toward a greater degree of cooperation" ("End of the Road").

307

It is this which must determine the main direction of all of the Party's work, and especially its trade-union and industrial concentration policy. *The Party rejects the point of view that work in the present Progressive-led unions represents the primary base for progressive militant activity and influence in the working class.* . . . Unless such tendencies are met head on and *completely wiped out*, they can only lead to the complete isolation of the Party from the main and most decisive sections of the American working class, and, *in the name of Left-sounding phrases*, to the surrender of the majority of workers to the tender mercies of the labor misleaders.

"Such tendencies" must have been proliferating if not ubiquitous already among Communist unionists if the party leadership found it necessary to threaten – in the argot of the Mob – *wiping them out*. Already in the autumn of 1949, in a comment symptomatic of the inner rift emerging between the party and many of its unionists, the party's labor secretary had to lecture them on the essentials of "Marxism-Leninism":

In the course of fulfilling our vanguard role . . . we must teach the trade unionists that the trade union movement by itself cannot eliminate capitalist exploitation. This can be accomplished only by the working class, under the leadership of the Communist Party.[31]

What, then, was propelling the party leadership along this self-destructive path – and, along the way, to maligning "the main progressive-led Internationals" and even "parting company" with the leadership of UE, for not doing their bidding? Why especially did the party's spokesmen go so far as to persist in condemning as *"enemies of the Left"* anyone who posed "the problem of the establishment of a 'third labor movement'"?[32]

The commitment by the party's leadership to building a "united front from below" was a throwback to another era, when the fledgling Communist but already great labor organizer Foster, in 1921, had fought against the party leadership's push to build "revolutionary unions" and had argued instead for "boring from within" the existing AFL unions to take power from the "misleaders of labor."[33] Now, three decades later, party leaders became willing captives to Foster's – and the party's own – distant, transmogrified heroic past.

To legitimate their opposition to a "third labor movement," they reached back, as did the party's labor secretary in March 1951, to Foster's "struggle

---

[31] Williamson (1949b, p. 4, emphasis added).   [32] Morris (1951, p. 78, emphasis added).
[33] In fact, as we know, the TUUL unions left a crucial legacy to CIO organizers.

against . . . 'the fatal policy of dual unionism' . . . [which] left the masses of trade-union members at the mercy of the reactionary leaders." To guide the party's work now, its cadres were to make a "consistent effort to adhere to [Foster's] . . . slogan of 1922, *'Keep the militants in the organized labor movement.'*"[34] Another party leader reached even further back to the "Left-wing and socialist militants . . . who took the path of dual unionism [in 1905], forming the I.W.W. [and thus] . . . turned over the bulk of the organized workers to the tender mercies of the labor bureaucrats." But soon, in 1912, "Comrade Foster, seeing the error of this ultra-'Left' policy . . . , fought for *a policy of tireless and methodical work within the official labor movement.*"[35]

Thus, the party's leadership, with the legendary Foster now at the helm, were absurdly misapplying his once-upon-a-time organizing strategy to the current, entirely incomparable situation. And certainly the CIO's officials and the leaders of its affiliates were the real practicing dual unionists. They were the ones who, on ideological grounds, had raided and expelled existing unions with a million or so members and set up rival, that is, "dual," unions in their fields (e.g., IUE, the Insurance Workers, and the Government and Civic Employees).[36]

Foster actually believed, as he had told a comrade in 1946, that *"the biggest mistake he had ever made* was agreeing in the 1920s [with the Comintern's advice] to have the Trade Union Education[al] League, which tried to work within the AFL, transformed into the Trade Union Unity League, *our none-too-successful attempt to create an independent revolutionary federation of unions."*[37] The exquisite irony is that had Foster and his comrades listened this time to that same authoritative advice from abroad, they would not have taken their damaging course, and gone against the views of most of their own unionists. In late 1947, in a conversation in Moscow, the *Daily Worker's* editor was advised by Solomon Lozovsky (former head of the Red International of Labor Unions (RILU)) that, "[i]n trade union tactics, it is not the job of a labor leader to cooperate with the more radical political leaders but *it is the job of the radical political leaders to cooperate with the labor leaders."*[38]

---

[34] Williamson (1951a, pp. 24–29, emphasis added).

[35] Williamson (1951a, p. 29); Swift (1953c, p. 31; 1952b, p. 31). "Swift" was Gil Green, a top party leader, then in hiding in the "underground" (Starobin 1972, p. 300n17).

[36] Of course, the CP leadership seemed to have forgotten that the CIO itself was born as a dual labor federation when AFL officials expelled the affiliates that belonged to the founding Committee for Industrial Organization.

[37] Foster made that confession to Healey (Healey and Isserman 1993, p. 159, emphasis added).

[38] (Starobin 1975, p. 287n8, emphasis added). Lozovsky was then one of the few still-not-executed old Bolsheviks. As the head of RILU from its founding until its dissolution in 1937, he had been the young Communist Foster's guide during the TUEL and TUUL years.

The Inner Rift

The party officialdom's polemics against some of its own leading unionists, whom they accused of "anti-Marxist, opportunistic concepts on questions of the relationship of the Party to Union in Left circles" – including "Right-deviationism," "opportunist capitulation to reaction," "renegacy," "Titoism," "'Left' sectarianism," and "'Left' syndicalism" – provide only a glimmer of the inner debate raging between them.[39] But that this inner rift between party officials and some leading Communist unionists was deep and wide, and becoming unbridgeable, cannot be doubted.

How many leading Red unionists fell in the various deviationist and opportunist categories, singly or in any combination thereof, and to what extent their views on "the relationship of the Party to Union" formed a coherent postexpulsion strategy, is impossible – given the paucity of available information – to say. No historians of labor and Communism have yet investigated this deep split between leading Communist unionists and the party leadership, and few have even alluded to the issue of a postexpulsion "third labor federation."[40] Yet news of the split's existence has long been around. In 1972,

---

Foster's memory of his "biggest mistake" was extraordinarily faulty, for in 1926, in the first strike initiated and conducted by the TUEL, among the 15,000 wool and silk workers in and around Passaic, New Jersey Foster had imposed "labor unity" on the Communist unionists leading the strike; in response to the AFL's United Textile Workers' charge that the TUEL was engaged in "dual unionism," Foster ordered the withdrawal of the Communists from the strike's leadership and turned conduct of the strike over to the UTW, on condition that they would incorporate the strikers as members. UTW sought an accommodation with employers and, basically, sabotaged the strike. Foster's surrender of the strike and the strikers, and the incipient union being formed there, was, he himself acknowledged later, a "serious error" and a "wrong policy mistake of affiliating the Passaic strikers to the AFL, even at the expense of eliminating the Communist leadership." In fact, as Foster admitted in 1937, "For this whole course of action we were later severely criticized by the R.I.L.U." – whose head was, of course, none other than Lozovsky (Foner 1994, p. 162; Foster 1937, p. 202). In 1949, Lozovsky was arrested "for 'plotting against Stalin'; he was executed in 1952 for conspiring 'to tear the Crimea away from the USSR' and create a Jewish state as a bulwark of American imperialism on Soviet territory." In 1956, he was "rehabilitated" by Khrushchev, who expressed "particular regret" about Lozovsky's murder by Stalin (Johanningsmeier 1994, p. 179).

[39] Kendrick (1952, p. 51). "Kendrick" was New York party chairman Thompson's "underground" nom de guerre (Starobin 1972, p. 300n14).

[40] Harvey Levenstein is one of these few who at least mention, but then drop without following it up, the issue of a "third federation of labor." He writes: "For some months after the purges, there was desultory talk of forming a new left-wing labor federation, but the outbreak of the

---

Starobin insisted that already by 1950–51 *"most* influentials," as he calls the CIO's top Communist union leaders, "had little but contempt for the Party's emissaries and did not hesitate to show it."[41]

What is evident, from reading the party's polemics, is that plenty of top "left and progressive" unionists, including "decisive forces in the top leadership of UE," although they still adhered to "the general principles" of the party, refused to subordinate themselves to it or be bound any longer by "the same policies, discipline, and organizational structure" as "all Communists." Most crucial, they rejected the party's line that, because most union members by far belonged to "right-led unions," this "fact" should now "determine the main direction" of the work of Communist unionists.

Rather, they had no doubt that the "primary base for progressive militant activity and influence in the working class" had to be their own unions. They certainly did not have to be taught by the party's labor secretary that unions alone could not eliminate capitalist exploitation, but only "at best ease the grip of exploitation."[42] To ease that grip, after all, had been and continued to be their primary, practical objective as union men and women. Whether or not, in their heart of hearts, they believed in the radical syndicalist proposition that unions are "the critical site for revolutionary activity," all our evidence shows that, in practice, they were, in fact, "left syndicalists."[43] For what distinguished

Korean War, which made the leftist unions even larger targets for government persecution, undermined the idea of creating an organization with that high a profile." As we have seen, a lot more than "desultory talk" about this issue was going on long after the purges. And we found no evidence in the polemics around it to support Levenstein's claim that it was "the outbreak of the Korean war" that "undermined the idea" (1981, p. 308). David Saposs repeats the CIO's charge that "[i]t was evidently UE's intention to prepare the way for the Communist-dominated unions to withdraw voluntarily, with a view to founding a separate trade-union national center." Saposs then says, "For a brief period, they [the Communists] toyed with the idea of founding a third federation. [Michael] Quill, who was part of the inner circle of Communist-dominated unions, charged that . . . 'in the month of January, 1947, Bill Foster told me that the National Board of the Communist Party had decided to form a third Federation of Labor. . . .' The plan for a third national trade union center failed to materialize" (1959, pp. 208–9). David Shannon also reports Quill's claim, but he puts the date "in early 1948" when Foster is supposed to have told Quill that he favored formation of "a Third Federation of Labor . . . carved out of A.F. of L. and the C.I.O." (1959, p. 156). Either Foster was even more of a "crack-pot" than Quill thought or Quill got it all wrong or, more likely, made it up, for the documentary evidence, as we have seen, is that Foster was the immovable rock in the way of any left "tendencies" toward "dual unionism," let alone a "third labor federation."

[41] Starobin (1975, pp. 202–3, emphasis added).   [42] Williamson (1951a, p. 26).
[43] Healey (1994, p. 133).

their own brand of unionism from their rivals' – within the tactical limits imposed on all unionists by "collective bargaining" – was precisely a strategy of struggle designed to undermine the sway of capital within the sphere of production and thus to "ease the grip of exploitation."

But they understood, as Williamson and other party leaders did not, that the precondition for continuing that struggle was the survival and consolidation of their own expelled unions. Defending and consolidating their collective base – by establishing a single "coordinating center" that would unite the expelled internationals and all the "Left-wing rank-and-file groups in the Right-led unions" and enable them to pool resources, provide mutual assistance, and maximize their collective strength – was the left's paramount task at that historical moment. In a word, a "third labor federation" was the sine qua non of an enduring, organized radical presence in the working class.[44]

The tantalizing but unanswerable question, then, is, what would have happened if "most influentials" in the highest councils of the expelled internationals had not only shown "contempt for the Party's emissaries," but had taken the initiative and organized a left federation of labor? This was, it seems, finally in the offing in late 1951. On October 9, the *New York Daily Mirror* sensationally featured a story under the headline, "Left Unions Parley," in which they "revealed" that a conference (which had not been announced to the press) of the heads of eight independent unions expelled from the CIO was taking place at the Hotel New Yorker.

For the first time since the expulsions, so far as is known, the presidents and other top officers of all of the expelled internationals were meeting together – including, significantly, Albert Fitzgerald, UE's non-Communist president, and also, despite the party's having "parted company" with them, James Matles and Julius Emspak. Perhaps even more startling was that Arthur Osman, president of the Distributive, Processing and Office Workers (DPOW) and David Livingston, head of DPOW's core District 65, were also at the conference.[45] The participation of these four men in the conference had a double-edged significance. First, back in June, *Fortune* had reported that DPOW was

---

[44] Williamson (1950a, p. 98; 1950c, pp. 43, 53, 55–56; 1951b, pp. 67, 72; 1951a, p. 31); CPUSA (1951, pp. 12–16); Kendrick [Thompson] (1952, p. 52); Swift [Green] (1953a [Feb], p. 27; 1953c, p. 39).

[45] The rest of the eleven conferees, besides Fitzgerald, Matles, Emspak, Osman, and Livingston – all presidents of their respective international – were John Clark, MM; Harry Bridges, ILWU; Ben Gold, IFLWU; Abraham Flaxer, UPW; Joseph Selly, ACA; and Hugh Bryson, MCS (Barry 1951, p. 15).

"stepping off the party line."[46] So these leading left union officers who had "parted company" with the party had now come together "for the purpose of exchanging ideas and information on questions of mutual concern to [them] and the entire labor movement." Second, these same men already had taken the initiative, contrary to the party's "advice" at the time, to secede from "right-led" organizations. Remember, back in October 1948 it was the bolt of "District 65" in New York City from RWDSU to join in establishing DPOW that first provoked *Business Week*'s anxieties about the coming of a "third labor federation." And, of course, it was UE's exodus from the CIO that had been seen by observers and CIO officials as "the first step in the long range plans of the Communist Party to establish a Communist-dominated labor federation in America."

What's more, the conference was held at a time when John L. Lewis was again making waves in union waters, renewing the possibility that he and UMW and the expelled internationals would create organizational linkages. Starobin, who was still a prominent Communist journalist at this time, says unequivocally that after their expulsion, "many [left-wing union] leaders ... continue[d] seeking the will-o-the-wisp of a 'third labor federation,' *together with Lewis*. ... "[47] Lewis had called repeatedly during 1950 for new forms of labor unity, for "mutual aid pacts" and "pooling of resources" between his UMW and the CIO, but had been stoutly rebuffed by Philip Murray. A *New York Times* editorial saw Lewis's efforts as "a bid for leadership of all unions." When the UMW *Journal* called in the spring of 1950 for more "militant labor leadership," the *New York Times* saw this as a sign that Lewis was "seeking the disaffection of workers from their current leadership." When initial informal "unity" talks began between AFL and

---

[46] "The Thin Red Line," p. 72. Communists were in District 65's top leadership from its birth on, and the district "was always closely associated with the Left and Communist forces" in New York City (Kendrick and Golden 1953, p. 27; "Merger: DWU, FTA, UOPWA").

[47] Starobin (1975, p. 291n24). But the "evidence" Starobin purports to substantiate this claim, unfortunately, actually contradicts it. He says: "See the left wing monthly, *March of Labor*, in the early fifties," but cites no specific article or issue of this magazine. Our close reading of every item in every issue of it published between June 1949 and September 1956 (thanks to the courtesy of the Southern California Library for Social Studies and Research in Los Angeles) found nothing to sustain his claim that *March of Labor*, edited by veteran Communist John Steuben, was a voice on behalf of a "third federation of labor." To the contrary, it was unwaveringly an exponent of the party's "united front from below" as the road to "labor unity." Starobin was a party insider during these years, and one whose ties to it were quickly loosening and who apparently already shared the "contempt" of "most influentials" for the "Party's emissaries." So he must have been privy to the real goings-on, even though his memory of the role of *March of Labor* was incorrect.

CIO representatives, Lewis declared that there could be no "unity" without inclusion of the UMW.[48]

To top all this off, in March 1951, out at the Rouge, Carl Stellato, until then a Reuther champion, barely was reelected president of Local 600 – by 429 votes out of 33,000 cast, over the progressive candidate, Joe Hogan. All five union leaders who Reuther had put on "trial" four months earlier for their "subservience to the Communist Party" were reelected by overwhelming, record-breaking votes; in the seventeen building units comprising the local, progressives won the leadership of seven, with a membership of 28,600, as opposed to Stellato's supporters, who won only six units, with a membership of 22,500. At the UAW convention a few weeks later, 55 percent of Local 600's delegates were now "anti-Reuther."[49] Stellato then quickly switched into the local's "anti-Reuther" camp and made an alliance with the recalcitrant Reds long in Local 600's leadership. To make sure Reuther got the message, when the local's tenth anniversary celebration was held that June, Lewis – not Reuther nor any other UAW International officer – was the featured speaker. Stellato then declared that the local stood squarely behind Lewis's "effort to unite labor" and called on Reuther to "stop driving a wedge" into labor.

All this alarmed Reuther so much that he charged that Lewis's address at the local's celebration was a signal that certain Ford local leaders were planning to cut the local out of the UAW. And that was when Reuther imposed the administratorship on the local – in what he declared was an "emergency action" to "save" the UAW from "antiunion" forces.[50]

News of this potential secession drive, allegedly being encouraged by none other than John L. Lewis, under whose wing so many of the left's labor leaders had come to power, arrived about the same time that the DPOW leadership was "stepping off the party line" and in the wake of the party leadership's "parting company" with UE's leaders. The party leadership now also received a rude blow when, on June 4, the Supreme Court upheld the sentences of the eleven "Foley Square" defendants, the party's entire first-level leadership, who were ordered to begin serving their sentences on July 4.[51] Then within a few months came the unpublicized get-together, in private, of the eleven top officers of the expelled internationals. All this, in combination, must have appeared ominous to what remained of an intact party leadership.

What was said at the October 9 conference of the eleven top officers of the expelled internationals, we do not know. Nothing more is available about

---

[48] *New York Times*, March 8, 1950, p. 24; March 10, p. 24; March 12, IV, p. 7; March 19, p. 66.

[49] Lock (1951, p. 9).   [50] Swift (1952a, p. 38).

[51] Starobin (1975, p. 220). Thompson, Green, Henry Winston, and Gus Hall then jumped bail and promptly went "underground."

that conference in the public record (although verbatim transcripts of it and of these men's private conversations in their hotel rooms recorded via FBI bugs are probably secreted, long forgotten, in some bureau filing cabinet), and it has not even been mentioned, to our knowledge, by any historian. But aficionados of Sherlock Holmes will no doubt immediately recognize the deep significance of another "curious incident" at the conference, namely, Harry Bridges's statement to the press afterward: He gave none.

That was the curious incident. To be more precise, neither he nor any of the other men attending the conference this time said anything at all like, it was a lot of "crap about us forming a bloc and the organization of a third labor movement." Yet, as we know, at the National Conference in Washington, D.C., and at all of the local left unionist conferences held the previous year, as well as when MM set out to form "mutual assistance pacts" with AFL unions whose members worked in or around the copper mines and smelters, and DPOW was formed out of three Communist-led unions, someone always was sure to issue a denial that the conferees intended establishing a "third labor federation."[52]

That this October 9 conference was portentous and a momentarily visible sighting of the deep inner schism between the party and its leading unionists, and that formation of a "third labor federation" (or its equivalent) was in the offing, can be inferred also from the party's big guns rolled out to shoot down an "ultra-'left' tendency" or "point of view" that "for some period of time has grown up . . . [and] *at this particular moment {is} the main danger in the ranks of our Party,"* as Gil Green, one of the party's top eleven leaders convicted under the Smith Act, wrote from the "underground." Included in his bill of particulars about the dangerous growth of "'left' sectarianism," not incidentally, was what he called the "preposterous" charge that Local 600 leaders intended to take the local out of the UAW.[53]

Green wrote repeatedly during 1952 and 1953 to combat the "point of view" that the left should fight the right "head on . . . by establishing its own independent Left-led [trade union] organization."[54] He even declared that

> . . . *Left-led organizations can become obstacles to reaching the masses.* This will be so if and where they are seen as the *main* mediums for our work. Or,

---

[52] Walter Barry, reporting on the conference for *March of Labor*, sort of made up his own denial, by saying that, "confusing propaganda . . . that this conference would launch a 'left' third Federation of Labor" was "dished out" by "anti-labor sheets" and by "Big Business and its political and 'union' associates." But Barry was not able to get any of the eleven men who attended the conference to agree or supply a quote that this was "propaganda" or "crap" (1951, p. 15).

[53] Swift (1953a, p. 33).   [54] Swift (1952a, p. 31; 1953a, pp. 27, 33, emphasis added).

if their needs are counterposed to the main task of working within, and influencing the larger mass organizations. . . . [55]

But rather than again denouncing "dual unionism," Green pleaded instead that establishing a left federation would be a suicidal move:

> . . . a base which becomes completely surrounded and hemmed in by the enemy will not long remain a base. For the very concept of a base is that it be a strong point *from* which and not merely *in* which to operate. . . . it would be a mistake to ignore the mass intimidation and terror which exists today. Every organization established by the Left is branded as "subversive" by the real subversives.[56]

The paradox however, is that if the expelled internationals had established their own independent left labor federation, CP officials would undoubtedly have denounced the federation's leaders and thereby endowed them and their new federation with the blessings of political legitimacy. So, as an especially telling example, when, in 1952, DPOW's top leaders (Osman, Livingston, and Kenneth Sherbell) openly did step off the party line and assume what they called a "third camp" position critical of both the party and the right wing, they were subjected to a vituperative barrage for their "renegacy" by Thompson, writing from the "underground."[57]

In any event, the "third labor federation" never materialized. Why, alas, is a question that must await others' research to try to answer, although the answer is probably all too simple: Most of the eleven, in the end, could not bring themselves to break with the party with which they had been associated since their youth nor especially to oppose the will of that once exemplary labor movement pioneer, William Z. Foster.

---

[55] Swift (1953a, p. 28, emphasis added, except "main" is emphasized in original).

[56] Ibid.

[57] Shannon (1959, p. 260). "They seek," Thompson and his coauthor wrote, "to cloak each move to the Right . . . with radical-sounding phrases of third force demagogy." DPOW's leadership, "many of them Party members of long standing," were now revealed for what they were – a "petty-bourgeois" and "corrupted group of trade union officials" who own "homes in Long Island, deep freezers, cars, etc." In addition, "an important factor" in their corruption was "the influence of Zionism and Jewish bourgeois nationalism"; their participation in "Jewish charities, aid to Israel, etc., brought union leaders and [Jewish dry-goods] employers together." And if this was not enough, these "renegades" were also guilty of "white chauvinist attitudes, the most advanced expression of their ideological and political degeneration" (Thompson and Golden 1953, pp. 27, 33, 37).

Epilogue: A "Third Labor Federation"

Some two and a half years after the Hotel New Yorker conference, on April 30, 1954, Lewis; Dave Beck, president of the Teamsters; and David J. McDonald, president of the USWA (who had succeeded Murray as USWA president after his death) announced a pact for joint union action, bearing "many of the characteristic earmarks of Lewis' leadership." The pact, Foster wrote, "may have far reaching effects upon the future of the whole labor movement." Among its main announced aims were (1) to compel government action to end unemployment, (2) to repeal the Taft–Hartley Act, and (3) to secure remedial labor legislation at the federal and local levels. Foster's response to the new pact was to caution that it

can be constructive only if it is a strong force for labor unity. One thing that *must be guarded against*, however, is *any tendency toward the establishment of a new labor federation*. Reaction would hail such a development.... and *any attempt to establish one could only prove disastrous* by inflicting a bitter organizational struggle upon the labor movement. It would be especially disastrous to try to disintegrate the C.I.O.[58]

If even John L. Lewis and the other heads of three of the country's most powerful industrial unions, representing over 3 million workers, had to be warned by Foster that their actions could be "disastrous" and a "step backward" for the labor movement, what unbearable pressures must have been brought to bear upon those eleven leaders of the expelled Red-led internationals? And what must have been the burden of history they felt?

What Might Have Been

Had they not succumbed but actually realized their quest to establish a left federation, then the eight still vital expelled internationals would have endured as a cohesive, resilient, and growing left presence in America's working class.

Suggestive of the difference a left federation would have made is the simple fact that, even on their own, UE, MM, ILWU, IFLWU, and the American Communications Association (ACA) were able to resist and survive in the teeth of

---

[58] Foster also added that the potential of the pact "will depend very much, if not decisively, upon the attitude taken towards it by the Left and progressive forces ... [and their] clear sightedness, militant spirit, and tireless energy.... The move for joint action ... should be developed so as to include all labor organizations [and] ... care should be exercised to prevent the movement from being misdirected into an attack against either the C.I.O. or A.F. of L., or towards *the formation of a new labor federation. This* would be *a major step backwards*" (Foster 1954, pp. 4, 7, emphasis added).

raids and government attacks; none of them was beset by serious "rank-and-file uprisings." In fact, anti-Communism proved to have only the weakest appeal to rank-and-file unionists. "Time and again, at the very crest of the 1950s' wave of anti-Communist hysteria," as Harvey Levenstein observes, "a sizable majority proved itself virtually immune to the appeals of anticommunism."[59] Or, as George Lipsitz puts it:

> In truth, [workers'] loyalty to union leaders or activists associated with past struggles constituted an endorsement of previous militancy and affirmation of that militancy as part of working-class identity. Coupled with an enduring faith in direct action, rank-and-file defense of Communist leaders represented a clear ideology, although it did not involve a choice between abstractions of capitalism or communism. . . . Even in the face of concentrated repression, workers chose to advance their class interests.[60]

In 1955, *Business Week* took the measure of UE, MM, IFLWU, and ACA and reported that, in NLRB representation elections over the previous half-decade, they

> . . . have undoubtedly done as well as, or better than, many AFL and CIO unions. . . . And the leftists' victories and setbacks have come from aggressive actions, in which they sought to add members, as well as from defensive actions, in which they were trying to protect their membership ranks.[61]

---

[59] Levenstein (1981, p. 326). In 1957, Max Kampelman, in a tone of frustration, wrote: "The power of nationalism and patriotism is great. . . . Yet many thousands of American citizens have supported Communists as their union leaders, and even today continue to vote for those leaders in secret elections under Government supervision in the face of a barrage of hostile editorial comment, speeches, and Congressional investigations which expose their leaders as Communists" (1957, p. 251).

David Saposs, too, found it necessary to note and try to explain the "glaring instances" when union men and women "failed to respond to appeals, even in elections by secret ballot conducted by the NLRB. The rank and file in Communist-dominated unions have been slow to respond [to attempts] . . . to weaken or destroy the organization which has brought favorable results and served its members faithfully. . . . As Communism became discredited in this country, it became possible to appeal to the rank and file on that issue. . . . But loyalty to the organization and to the leaders who had demonstrated their ability to get tangible results was difficult to overcome" (1959, pp. 219–20).

[60] Lipsitz (1994, pp. 200–201).   [61] "How Leftist Unions Are Fairing."

ILWU was impregnable to raiding – though sniped at by the Teamsters and Seafarers – and so, too, was IFLWU. Indeed, both internationals expanded in the wake of their expulsion. IFLWU won the affiliation of the country's biggest tannery plant in 1951, and won six out of ten NLRB elections from 1950 to 1955.[62] In 1957, despite the Port-Security Program, ILWU succeeded in organizing the Port of New Orleans, its first foothold in an Atlantic or Gulf port. The Fishermen (their "industry" already dying) and MCS, as noted earlier, merged with the ILWU. The UPW, decimated by the Loyalty and Security Program's purification of unionized federal employees and their officers, folded on the mainland but, under the ILWU's umbrella, "proved to be an effective ally in dominating the union situation" in Hawaii. The small ACA held on tenaciously to its core membership among telegraphers and marine radio operators. It continued "operating with considerable success" and to service, among others, the international communications of "various branches of the armed forces and other government departments," despite repeated subjection to congressional hearings and federal loyalty investigations and raiding attempts by the AFL–CIO's Commercial Telegraphers Union.[63] DPOW withstood the storm but then, having effected its "renegacy" and with no haven to be found in a left labor federation, returned to the CIO in 1954.[64]

MM – "one of the most radical, colorful, and violent unions ever to operate on American soil," as *Business Week* called it – was subjected to constant raiding during the immediate postwar years by USWA and UAW. But MM won the vast majority of contested elections throughout its wide-ranging membership – from the copper mines and smelter plants of Montana to the "brass valley" of Connecticut (though in 1948 it had lost its large die-casting locals in plants around Cleveland and Detroit to UAW raids). In the first ten months after its expulsion, MM won thirty-eight of forty-seven NLRB elections, and by the autumn of 1951, at the time of the conference at the Hotel New Yorker, MM was still, as *Business Week* put it, "strong, tough, and dangerous."[65] Indeed, MM went on that year to call the first simultaneous industry-wide strike in the mining and smelting industry's history and, though beset by Taft–Hartley injunctions, won a settlement that "elated" its leaders and enhanced the loyalty of its members.[66]

In Butte in 1954, at a time when "anti-Communist feeling was probably at its highest pitch in the country," *Fortune* reported, "the Steelworkers had made the proved party-line affiliations of the old Mine, Mill and Smelter Workers a prime issue," and the local leaders "had defected and joined" them.

---

[62] "Labor Hi-Lites" (July and August); "How Leftist Unions Are Fairing."
[63] Saposs (1959, pp. 263–65).   [64] O'Brien (1968, p. 193).
[65] "Red Metal Union Riding High," p. 34.   [66] Dix (1967); Jensen (1954); Keitel (1974).

But the battered Mine-Mill defeated the powerful USWA. What happened? Why did a rank and file, which is basically non-Communist, decisively support a Communist-line leadership? . . . Butte Local No. 1 has had a turbulent radical tradition. The residue of class-consciousness . . . made the Butte miners deaf to the charge of Red. For Mine, Mill, the victory was crucial. . . . Its smashing victory gives it a firm grip on the key Montana locals.[67]

During the half-decade after its expulsion, MM staved off most raids on its membership; as the president of the new AFL–CIO's Metal Trades department (in which the USWA was a stalwart) conceded in 1956, MM "has the vast majority of employees in the industry." MM also retained most of its members in allied fields and was still dominant in the copper fabrication region of the Connecticut River's "Brass Valley" and other plants in New York. Where MM lost units, it was mainly in the new and peripheral uranium mining and processing industry.[68]

Through the early 1960s, MM was still "showing surprising muscle in getting workers to rally to its corner" in its battle against USWA raiding. Although the betting was that, "with its low treasury and alleged Communist dominated hierarchy," *Business Week* noted, MM "would be routed at locations where the Steelworkers were trying to move in," it continued to win in its heartland.[69] But in 1966, MM, still unbowed, chose to merge with USWA, for, though it fought off the raiders and created practical unity with the multitude of craft unions operating in the industry, it was not able alone to stem the decline of hard rock mining in America.

MM had resisted raids by the right wing and survived, and, unlike UE, IFLWU, and the UPW, had also evaded disaster at the hands of the party's foremost leaders, who in 1952 first called from the "underground" for "a return of the left wing to the mainstream of American labor." And as the moves toward merger of the AFL and CIO gained momentum, the party's call became ever more insistent.[70]

Soon, anyone who was really listening could hear it. In March 1955, *U.S. News & World Report* informed its readers that

[w]ord is out from the Communist Party that it is time for [the CIO's expelled] . . . unions to shed their independence and join forces with labor groups affiliated with the AFL. . . . As AFL and CIO leaders see it, these

---

[67] "How the Commies Won'" p. 36.   [68] Saposs (1959, pp. 259, 261).
[69] "USW Set Back by 'Weak' Mine-Mill," p. 150; also see O'Brien (1968, pp. 198–200).
[70] Starobin (1975, p. 203).

moves mean that the Communist Party is ready to take a desperate gamble . . . [and] sacrifice what's left of the "left wing" union strength in order to plant some agents in the new organization to be formed by the AFL and CIO. Communist official publications are making it clear that followers of the party should use their influence to swing these unions, known in Communist jargon as "progressives," into the AFL-CIO merger. The party line seems to be: Find a way to join some AFL union, at any cost.[71]

The broad-based and deeply rooted Communist leadership of IFLWU answered the call, although every sign indicated that it could have continued as a vital, independent union. Its leaders negotiated a merger with the AFL Amalgamated Meat Cutters and Butcher Workmen on onerous terms. In February 1955, IFLWU's 75,000 members, after an overwhelming recommendation in favor of it by the delegates at a special convention, voted to proceed with the merger with the Meat Cutters (who made no secret of their intention to "decommunize" the IFLWU). In fact, the merger agreement stipulated that every officer and staff member would have to execute a non-Communist affidavit yearly, and Ben Gold and Irving Potash, the two highest officers, and both lifelong party members, were to fall on their swords and hold no office in the new merged union.[72]

This was not enough for AFL officials, so, in response to their prompting, the Meat Cutters board reneged on the merger agreement and "initiated a cleansing program" of their "autonomous" "Fur & Leather Department," especially in "the strategic New Jersey–New York area"; expelled eleven officers there, and more in Canada; and then placed the department in trusteeship. By October, barely eight months after the merger agreement, the Meat Cutters were able to announce "that 'more than 100 Communists' had been removed from its fur & leather division" and its locals in New York City, Los Angeles, Chicago, and Canada."[73]

One would have thought that the experience of their comrades in IFLWU would have lessened the merger ardor among Communists in union leadership elsewhere. But, no; UE, too, was to suffer grievous wounds inflicted by its own erstwhile comrades responding to party orders. In mid-1953, UE still had contracts covering 250,000 workers.[74] That year, the major Schenectady local, led by Leo Jandreau and his wife, Ruth Young, UE's highest woman leader – both of whom were long associated with the party – defected to the IUE. Then

---

[71] "What Reds Are Up to in Unions," p. 107.
[72] Letz (1955); Saposs (1959, p. 257); Cochran (1977, p. 331).
[73] Saposs (1959, pp. 256–60).   [74] "The New C.P. Line."

in 1955, much as the party's labor secretary had threatened five years earlier, came a Communist uprising against them. Four UE district presidents and thirty staff members and local union business agents announced that the UE was "finished," proclaimed it time to find a "haven" in the "mainstream," and, cheered on by the *Daily Worker's* labor columnist, prevailed on their members to secede from the UE.[75]

They dispersed in a rout, making their own deals, all promised jobs in their new havens, and going over into four internationals: a few locals to IUE, others to the AFL's electric "brotherhood" (IBEW), a dozen locals to the UAW, and over forty-five locals to the AFL's machinists (IAM). By the time the carnage ended, about 50,000 of UE's members had been carved out by the defectors.[76] But, as in IFLWU, their own deals quickly went sour. IAM put the defectors on trial, invoked its constitution's anti-Communist clause, and by June 1957, had dropped ten of them from the staff and thrown out seventeen new ex-UE "membership applicants" altogether. Much the same happened to the other UE defectors in their so-called havens.[77] Thus it came to pass, as Hal Simon, the New York party's union specialist had already scathingly pronounced months

---

[75] "A few weeks ago," said a delegate to the UE's 1956 convention, "I picked up a *Daily Worker*, a newspaper which I had read religiously for twenty years, and . . . one of my favorite [columnists] . . . says he does not blame the members of the UE for leaving this organization" (Prickett 1975, p. 367, citing UE's *Proceedings of the Twenty-First Convention*).

[76] In November 1955, district 8's core of a dozen ex-FE International Harvester locals, to which the UE had given shelter from Reuther's UAW back in 1949, now bolted and took its 17,000 members into, yes, the UAW ("On the Merger Front"). Then in the spring of 1956 the entire district 4, the most solidly under control of party loyalists, led by James McLeish, went over to the IUE; a few weeks later, district 3 defected to the IAM, followed in August by the solidly Communist district 7 under John Gojack (Filippelli and McColloch 1995, pp. 157–59; "Breakup of the U.E."; "UE Loses a Key District"; Matles and Higgins 1974, p. 231; Saposs 1959, p. 266). UE lost ten locals claiming 4,000 members who shifted to IAM in Detroit in late 1956. UE's former district 9 in Michigan and Indiana shifted almost intact to IAM. These defections left UE "with a last-ditch garrison force of approximately ninety thousand" (Matles and Higgins 1974, pp. 230–31; cf. also "In Labor").

[77] Saposs (1959, pp. 266–67). The party expelled its members who stayed loyal to UE after 1955 (Emspak 2000b). Locals of the Public workers in New York City had sought their own haven in the Teamsters, but when a rival union identified a couple of former UPW business agents as Communists, the Teamsters' Dave Beck said he would set up an independent citizens committee to hold hearings to find out whether they were still pro-Communist. Nothing came of it. The official explanation was the refusal of the FBI and other government agencies to make their files available to the committee. But, reported the *New York Times,* "observers familiar with the Teamsters' operations suggested than an outside inquiry might have turned up embarrassing links between higher-ups in the union and prominent city officials" (Saposs 1959, p. 265).

earlier, that "[t]he Left has no organized forum, no spokesman, nor any voice in the labor movement."[78]

What historical timing! Had these disciplined Communist unionists not abided by the party leadership's instructions, had they even hesitated but a few months, what a difference it might have made. For on the evening of April 28, 1956, at the first open meeting of a plenum of the CP's national committee in five years, Khrushchev's "secret speech" to the Soviet party's Twentieth Congress three months earlier was now read out loud, word for word to the assembled Communist officials.[79]

Khrushchev's revelations about Stalin's reign of terror was a blow from which the American CP would never recover. For, as David Shannon puts it,

> Everything that capitalist critics had ever said about Stalin was now repeated by Khruschev – and more. The Communists were jarred most severely. Many had joined the party because they sincerely saw communism as freedom, justice, and brotherhood; now they saw that Stalin's Russia was the negation of all these values. And for the party heretic, those who were struggling with Foster for a more liberal party, there was a particularly terrible realization. As *Daily Worker* columnist Howard Fast put it to a meeting of the paper's staff, "I wonder if there is any comrade here who can say now, out of what we know and have seen, that if our own party leaders had the power of execution, he or she would be alive today." They were alive because their party did not have the power. To realize failure is a bitter experience; to realize that it is better to have failed is worse.[80]

In early 1956, the party had conducted a membership registration. Despite all that they had endured during the past half decade of the Great Fear, and despite the inner purges with which the party had been tearing itself

---

[78] Thompson, Simon's boss in the New York party, was still heaping praise on Foster, and thus himself, for what they had done. *Political Affairs* again quoted him in March 1956 as condemning "dual unionism" as an "American brand of 'Left' sectarianism." "[T]he elimination of this disease from Party theory and tactics," declared Thompson, was one of "Comrade Foster's first contributions" (Thompson 1956). The contrast between Simon's realistic lament and Thompson's self-praise suggests how sharp was the debate raging out of public view during the past few years among the party's leaders – and where most unionists stood. Simon had resigned in 1946 from "an important post in the *UE* as a Washington representative (he had also been a member of the War Labor Board [!]), to become New York state trade union expert for the Communist Party" (Starobin 1975, p. 277n7).

[79] Healey (1993, p. 152).   [80] Shannon (1959, p. 293).

apart, over 20,000 men and women were still members. By the summer of 1957, the national committee estimated the total membership had fallen to about 10,000. In late winter of 1957–58, the party again registered its members; this was its first accurate count in over two years. The party was now down to slightly under 3,000 members. In just over two years in the wake of Khrushchev's disclosures, the membership of the party had dropped over 85 percent.[81]

Had UE's Communists not yet carved out their locals and districts, had the leaders of IFLWU still held on to their union's independence and not "returned to the mainstream," their exodus from the party would have freed their unions of the Soviet incubus, and a left labor federation established by the eight expelled internationals certainly would have endured.

For already by UE's 1958 convention, Matles and Emspak could report that not one plant had been lost to any other union in the preceding year, and four former UE shops had rejoined the UE. Early the next year, UE won four more NLRB elections.[82] James B. Carey, IUE president, then went before the stockholders meeting of GE (ten days after UE announced the return of the four locals) "and made what anyone must call a plea for aid." Carey told GE stockholders: "There is a real and present danger that the Communists can control the work force at GE and in view of the types of work performed by GE, I urge the management of the company to look into this matter with concern."[83]

By then, UE was "no longer on the defensive; instead it [was] now actively campaigning to expand its membership." In 1960, *Business Week* lamented that UE had gained 28,000 new members and won 69 percent of the NLRB elections in which its bargaining rights were contested.[84] Meanwhile, IUE was floundering under Carey's leadership, and that year lost a major strike to GE, called by Carey despite the opposition of four of IUE's most important locals (including Jandreau's). IUE could not close down even one GE plant. The *New York Times* reported that this was the "worst setback any union has received in a nationwide strike since World War II." In fact, preceding the strike, Matles had offered UE's support to IUE against GE, but Carey, unbending still, refused the offer.[85]

---

[81] Ibid., p. 360.
[82] Peevey (1961, p. 31, citing *UE Report of General Officers*. 23d Annual Convention, New York, September 1–5, 1958; *UE News*, April 13, 1959).
[83] Peevey (1961, p. 32, citing the *Wall Street Journal*, April 23, 1959, p. 22).
[84] Peevey (1961, p. 33, citing *Business Week*, April 2, 1960, pp. 70–72).
[85] Peevey (1961, p. 52).

As combative and innovative as ever, still "leftwing in orientation and . . . perhaps the most vocal of all such labor bodies on so-called 'progressive' views and goals," UE was now again putting forth a bargaining program that was giving "employers some anxious moments," as *Business Week* reported in September 1961. Notable was its demand that "companies installing new automatic machinery should be required by law to give [a union] full information on the new machinery and on the consequences of its installation." For instance, UE said, unions should be furnished information on the number of people likely to be displaced; total labor costs under the new operation as compared with the old; and the rate of production and unit costs of the new apparatus as compared with the old. Further, UE said, employers "should be required by law to bargain collectively on all questions of jobs and earnings" that arise from the installation of new machinery.[86]

By 1963, IUE had suffered repeated setbacks and was being torn by internal dissension over Carey's leadership. He was replaced as president in 1965 by the unanimous vote of IUE's executive board. Reuther's UAW was already trying to take over IUE. UE then offered an immediate merger with IUE to stave off the UAW's takeover attempt, but the offer was promptly rejected, with a little bit of Red-baiting thrown in, by IUE's new president.

Over the next years, under Matles's and Fitzgerald's leadership (Emspak had died of a heart attack in 1962), UE won back shops that it had lost earlier and won major organizing victories in new plants in the East and Midwest and on the West Coast, and was now able to reconstitute its old districts there. By 1966, UE represented 165,000 workers.[87] A labor historian, writing at the time, commented that UE "seems to have made something of a comeback while the IUE has been floundering."[88]

Nor did UE's renewed growth during the late 1960s come by trimming its radicalism. *UE News* consistently criticized the bloated Cold War military budget and was heavily involved in the civil rights movement and in the growing opposition to the U.S. war in Vietnam. Some of UE's old enemies were swept up in these movements and turned around. Even the now Monsignor Charles Owen Rice declared, in an article in the *Pittsburgh Catholic* in 1966, that UE, against whose leadership he had fought as a young ACTU priest so vehemently in the past, had been a victim of "McCarthyism." All the AFL–CIO unions representing GE workers should face "the enemy as a unit," he wrote, and they would be "even stronger if they were to accept the UE as an ally."

---

[86] "UE's New Goals," p. 78.   [87] Matles and Higgins (1974, p. 259).
[88] O'Brien (1968, p. 209).

Shortly after the article appeared, Monsignor Rice telephoned Albert Fitzgerald, who was attending UE's convention in Pittsburgh.

Rice: "Fitzie, you are surprised to hear from me. I read the news that your convention is in town and I'm calling to wish you well."

Fitzgerald: "Your good wishes are coming twenty years too late."

Rice: "Even twenty years is not too long for a man to change his mind."

Later, at the UE convention, Fitzgerald told the delegates that Father Rice regretted "all the losses that you have taken for the last twenty years." "I forgive him," said Fitzgerald, "and I suppose you do, too."[89]

In 1969, IUE agreed to UE's call for a common bargaining stance against GE, and ten craft unions representing other GE workers also joined the pact. At Matles's initiative, the UAW – which Walter Reuther had just taken out of the AFL–CIO in opposition to its conservatism and stasis – and the Teamsters committed their unions to support of the unity pact against GE. A nationwide strike, solidly supported by most GE production workers, began on October 29, and UAW donated $200,000 to UE's strike fund. GE, unprepared for the newfound solidarity among its many competing unions, agreed to a settlement much superior to its original offer. The *New York Times* called it an "unmistakable departure from the take it or leave it spirit of past bargaining."[90]

Before and during the strike, the boards of UE, IUE, and the UAW met to coordinate moves. After twenty years, union leaders "long estranged" from each other, as the *New York Times* reported, now met again for the first time, in solidarity. What did Matles and Reuther say to each other when they met again for the first time since Reuther, in 1949, had denounced UE as a "cancer" on the CIO? "No one on either side," according to Matles, "said a single word about the past. All of us acted as if we had seen each other a few days before." Matles opened the meeting, saying only: "Guys, we want to talk about how best we can pull ourselves together to handle the bastards this time around."[91]

Conclusion

Over the coming decades, wherever former Communist influence lingered on, this continued to make a difference in the success rate of union organizing. So, for example, a UE that was but a shadow of its former self in size and

[89] Matles and Higgins (1974, pp. 258–59).
[90] Filippelli and McColloch (1995, pp. 167–74).   [91] Matles and Higgins (1974, p. 261).

significance nonetheless continued to have a far higher rate of success than the IUE in organizing new members (and winning NLRB union recognition elections). The ILWU also did better than its East Coast conservative (and gangster-ridden) rival, the ILA.[92]

These are but intimations of what might have been, of how much more of an impact would have been made on America's working class had these and other left-led unions been united over the years in a combative and cohesive "third labor federation." It would have served, at the least, as a gadfly on the left, as an exemplar of innovative prolabor programs, of interracial solidarity, of the push for women's employment equality, of dissent from the U.S. government's intervention–both covert and overt–to buttress ancien régimes from Iran to VietNam to Chile, and as a spur in the side of an indolent and declining AFL–CIO. At best, that left federation would have become a pole of attraction for dissidents and rebels everywhere in labor's ranks, for local unions discontent with their stagnant internationals, and even for other internationals, such as the distributive workers (DPOW) and transport workers (TWU) (whose "Red Mike" Quill continued to earn his sobriquet long after he had distanced himself from the Party).[93] Instead, the "third labor federation" – whose specter alone had haunted employers – never was. American labor thus suffered a tragic loss from which it has yet to recover.

---

[92] During 1972–84, the UE outpaced the IUE, 60 percent versus 43 percent; ILWU outpaced the ILA, 60 percent versus 52 percent. These results are supported by a cross-sectional regression model controlling for a number of relevant variables. When the union is the UE, it increases the likelihood of success by as much as 13 percent, and when it is the ILWU, by as much as 9.4 percent. During these same years (1972–84), where the UE and IUE have competed head-on for the workers' allegiance, that is, in jurisdictions where they both already had sizable bases, UE "almost always" has won (97 percent) (Goldfield 1987, pp. 216, 298).

[93] And consider what Reuther and his UAW might have done, after bolting from the AFL–CIO and tasting the wine of renewed solidarity with James Matles – if his jet plane had not slammed into a stand of trees several month later, on May 7, 1970, killing him and everyone else aboard.

REFERENCES

Books, Articles, Dissertations, and Other Sources

Aaron, Benjamin, and Michael I. Komaroff. 1949. "Statutory Regulation of Internal Union Affairs – II." *Illinois Law Review* 44 (December): 631–74.

Allen, V. L. 1954. *Power in Trade Unions*. London: Longmans, Green.

Allen–Bradley Company. 1965. *The Allen–Bradley Story*. Milwaukee: Allen–Bradley Company.

Alsop, Joseph, and Stewart Alsop. 1947a. "Will the CIO Shake the Communists Loose?" Part One. *Saturday Evening Post* (February 22): 15–16, 105–6, 108.

Alsop, Joseph, and Stewart Alsop. 1947b. "Will the CIO Shake the Communists Loose?" Part Two. *Saturday Evening Post* (March 1): 26–27, 117–18.

American Civil Liberties Union (ACLU). 1948. "A Bill of Rights for Union Members." Pp. 191–92 in *Unions, Management and the Public*, eds. E. W. Bakke and C. Kerr. New York: Harcourt, Brace.

American Civil Liberties Union. 1952. "Democracy in Labor Unions: A Report and Statement of Policy." New York: American Civil Liberties Union. (This was drafted by Clyde Summers and adopted by the ACLU Committee on Civil Rights in Labor Relations.)

Aminzade, Ronald. 1981. *Class, Politics, and Early Industrial Capitalism*. Binghamton, N.Y.: SUNY Press.

Anderson, John. 1978. "A Comparative Analysis of Local Union Democracy" *Industrial Relations* 17, no. 3 (October): 278–95.

Anderson, Karen Tucker. 1982. "Last Hired, First Fired: Black Women Workers during World War II." *Journal of American History* 69 (June): 82–97.

Anderson, Perry. 1967. "The Limits and Possibilities of Trade Union Action." Pp. 263–80 in *The Incompatibles: Trade Union Militancy and the Consensus*, eds. Robin Blackburn and Alexander Cockburn. Harmondsworth, Middlesex, England: Penguin.

Anderson, Perry. 1990. Letter to the authors (March 6).

References

"Anti-Communists in High at Ford." 1950. *Fortune* (October): 48, 50.

Aronowitz, Stanley. 1973. *False Promises: The Shaping of American Working Class Consciousness.* New York: McGraw Hill.

Ashenfelter, Orley. 1972. "Racial Discrimination and Trade Unionism." *Journal of Political Economy* 80 (May/June): 435–65.

Ashenfelter, Orley. 1973. "Discrimination and Trade Unions." Pp. 88–112 in *Discrimination in Labor Markets*, eds. Orley Ashenfelter and Albert Rees. Princeton, N.J.: Princeton University Press.

Association of Catholic Trade Unionists. ca. 1944. "Election of General Council Delegates at Ford Local 600." Walter P. Reuther Archives, Wayne State University. ACTU Collection, box 24, folder Local 600 1939–45.

Averill, David. 1950. "Decentralization of the Ford Motor Company and the Union's Position in Relation to It" (ca. July). Publicity Department, Ford Local 600, UAW-CIO. Wayne State University. Archives of Labor History and Urban Affairs.

Averitt, Robert. 1968. *The Dual Economy: The Dynamics of American Industry Structure.* New York: Norton.

Avery, Andrew. 1946. "The Communist Fifth Column." *Chicago Journal of Commerce* (June 25).

Axle Unit Right Wing Caucus. N.d. (probably 1946). "Camouflage" and "Unite for Progress." Walter P. Reuther Archives, Wayne State University, Andrew Ignasiak Collection, folder 196.

Backman, Jules. 1962. *The Economics of the Electric Machinery Industry.* New York: NYU Press.

Baker, Bob. 1990. "Reformers Taking Aim at Entrenched Teamsters." *Los Angeles Times* (November 1): A1, A30–31.

Bakke, E. Wright. 1946. *Mutual Survival: The Goal of Unions and Management.* New York: Archon.

Baldwin, Roger N. 1946. "Union Administration and Civil Liberties." *Annals of the American Academy of Political and Social Science* 248 (November): 54–61.

Barbash, Jack. 1943. "Ideology and the Unions." *American Economic Review* 33 (December): 868–76.

Barbash, Jack. 1948. *Labor Unions in Action.* New York: Harper and Bros.

Barbash, Jack. 1956. *The Practice of Unionism.* New York: Harper.

Barrett, James R. 1999. *William Z. Foster and the Tragedy of American Radicalism.* Urbana and Chicago: University of Illinois Press.

Barry, Walter. 1951. "Regrouping for Victory." *March of Labor* (December): 15, 27.

Bell, Daniel. 1952. *Marxian Socialism in the United States.* Princeton, N.J.: Princeton University Press.

Bell, Daniel. 1960. "Union Growth and Structural Cycles." Pp. 89–93 in *Labor and Trade Unionism*, eds. W. Galenson and S. M. Lipset. New York: Wiley.

Bell, Daniel. 1961. *The End of Ideology: On the Exhaustion of Political Ideas in the Fifties*. New York: Collier.

Beloff, Max, ed. 1987. *The Federalist, or, The New Constitution, by Alexander Hamilton, James Madison, and John Jay*. New York: Basil Blackwell.

Bernstein, Irving. 1971. *Turbulent Years: A History of the American Worker 1933–1941*. Boston: Houghton Mifflin.

"Blast CIO's Expulsion of Coast Dockers." 1950. *Daily Worker* (September 1): 8.

Bonosky, Philip. 1953. *Brother Bill McKie: Building the Union at Ford's*. New York: International Publishers.

Boris, Eileen. 1998. "'You Wouldn't Want One of 'em Dancing with Your Wife': Racialized Bodies on the Job in World War II." *American Quarterly* 50 (March): 77–108.

Boulding, Kenneth. 1953. *The Organizational Revolution*. New York: Harper.

"Box Score on Communist Influence in U.S. Labor." 1952. *Fortune* (June): 51.

Boyer, Richard O., and Herbert M. Morais. 1955. *Labor's Untold Story*. New York: Cameron Associates.

Brady, Robert Alexander. 1943. *Business as a System of Power*. New York: Columbia University Press.

"Break up of the U.E." 1955. *Fortune* (June): 61.

Brecher, Jeremy. 1990. Letter to the authors (January 8).

Brighton Labour Process Group. 1977. "The Capitalist Labour Process." *Capital and Class* 1 (Spring): 3–26.

Brochier, Hubert. 1957. "An Analysis of Union Models as Illustrated by French Enterprise." Pp. 136–47 in *The Theory of Wage Determination, Proceedings of a Conference Held by the International Economic Association*, ed. John T. Dunlop. London: Macmillan and New York: St. Martin's Press.

Brody, David. 1975. "The New Deal and World War II." Pp. 267–309 in *The New Deal: The National Level*, vol. 1, eds. J. Braeman, R. Bremner, and D. Bremner. Columbus: University of Ohio Press.

Brody, David. 1981. *Workers in Industrial America: Essays on the 20th Century Struggle*. New York: Oxford.

Brody, David. 1991. "Labor's Crisis in Historical Perspective." Pp. 277–311 in *The State of the Unions*, eds. George Strauss, Daniel Gallagher and Jack Fiorito. Madison, Wis.: Industrial Relations Research Association.

Brooks, George W. 1957. "Reflections on the Changing Character of American Labor Unions." Pp. 33–43 in *Proceedings of the Ninth Annual Meeting of Industrial Relations Research Association, December 28–29, 1956*, ed. L. Reed Tripp.

Brown, Leo. 1947. *Union Policies in the Leather Industry*. Cambridge, Mass.: Harvard University Press.

Brown, Ralph S., Jr. 1958. *Loyalty and Security: Employment Tests in the United States*. New Haven: Yale University Press.

Brown, Ralph S., Jr., and John D. Fasset. 1953. "Security Tests for Maritime Workers: Due Process under the Port Security Program." *Yale Law Journal* 62: 1163–208.

Brueggemann, John, and Terry Boswell. 1998. "Realizing Solidarity: Sources of Interracial Unionism during the Great Depression." *Work and Occupations* 25: 436–482.

Buffa, Dudley. 1984. *Union Power and American Democracy*. Ann Arbor: University of Michigan Press.

Burawoy, Michael. 1979. *Manufacturing Consent: Changes in the Labor Process under Monopoly Capitalism*. Chicago and London: University of Chicago Press.

Burawoy, Michael. 1981. "Terrains of Contest: Factory and State Under Capitalism." *Socialist Review* 11: 83–124.

Burawoy, Michael. 1983. "Between the Labor Process and the State: The Changing Face of Factory Regimes under Advanced Capitalism." *American Sociological Review* 8: 587–605.

Burawoy, Michael. 1985. *The Politics of Production: Factory Regimes under Capitalism and Socialism*. New York and London: Verso.

Cahn, Bill. 1950. "Un-American Committee Steps Up Union-Busting Program with Indictment of UE Leaders." *March of Labor* (December): 9.

California Institute of Technology. N.d. Union Contract Index Manual. Pasadena: California Institute of Technology.

Campbell, D'Ann. 1984. *Women at War with America*. Cambridge, Mass.: Harvard University Press.

Cantor, Milton, ed. 1969. *Black Labor in America*. Westport, Conn.: Negro Universities Press.

Carlyle, Thomas. [1837] 1906. *The French Revolution*, 2 vols. Introduction by Hilaire Belloc. London: J.M. Dent and Sons; New York: E.P. Dutton and Co.

Carr, Edward Hallett. 1961. *What Is History?* New York: Vintage.

Casey, William J. 1946. "Communism and Your Labor Relations." *Forbes* 58 (August 1): 14–15, 31.

Caute, David. 1979. *The Great Fear: The Anti-Communist Purge under Truman and Eisenhower*. New York: Simon and Schuster.

Cayton, Horace R., and George S. Mitchell. 1939. *The Negro Worker and the New Unions*. Chapel Hill: University of North Carolina Press.

Chamberlain, Neil W. 1948. *The Union Challenge to Management Control*. New York: Harper and Bros.

Chamberlain, Neil W., ed. 1958. *Sourcebook on Labor*. New York: McGraw-Hill.

Cherny, Robert W. 1998. "Harry Bridges and the Communist Party: New Evidence, Old Questions; Old Evidence, New Questions." Paper delivered at the annual meeting of the Organization of American Historians, April 4.

"C.I.O. Begins Careful Crackdown on Left Wing." 1948. *Business Week* (October 23): 103–4.

"CIO Victory." 1954. *New Republic* (March 29): 4.

"Civil War in C.I.O." 1949. *Fortune* (November): 204, 206.

Clarke, Tom. 1978. "The Raison d'Etre of Trade Unionism." Pp. 7–23 in *Trade Unions under Capitalism*, eds. Tom Clarke and Laurie Clements. Hassocks, Sussex, England: Harvester.

Clegg, Hugh Armstrong. 1979. *The Changing System of Industrial Relations in Great Britain*. Oxford: Blackwell.

"Coast Dockers, 2 More Unions Ousted by CIO." 1950. *Daily Worker* (August 30): 3.

Cochran, Bert. 1977. *Labor and Communism: The Conflict That Shaped American Unions*. Princeton: Princeton University Press.

Cohen, Lizabeth. 1990. *Making a New Deal: Industrial Workers in Chicago, 1919–1939*. Cambridge, Eng., and New York: Cambridge University Press.

Collins, Orvis, Melville Dalton, and Donald Roy. 1945. "Restriction of Output and Social Cleavage in Industry." *Applied Anthropology* 4 (Winter): 1–14.

Communist Party of the United States (CPUSA). 1950. "On the International Day of Labor." *Political Affairs* (May): 1–8.

Communist Party of the United States (CPUSA). 1951. "Working-Class and People's Unity for Peace! Main Resolution of the 15th National Convention, C.P.U.S.A." *Political Affairs* (January): 1–37.

Congress of Industrial Organizations (CIO). 1936. *Union News Service* (June 15).

Congress of Industrial Organizations (CIO). 1938. Daily Proceedings of the First Constitutional Convention. Pittsburgh, Pa.: Congress of Industrial Organizations.

Congress of Industrial Organizations (CIO). 1942. *The CIO and the Negro Worker: Together for Victory*. Washington, D.C.: CIO.

Congress of Industrial Organizations (CIO). California CIO Council. 1943. Proceedings of the 6th Annual Convention, October 21–24, 1943. Fresno: California CIO Council.

Congress of Industrial Organizations (CIO). Committee to Abolish Racial Discrimination (CARD). 1943. *Working and Fighting Together: Regardless of Race, Creed, or National Origins*. Washington, D.C.: CIO.

Congress of Industrial Organizations (CIO). 1944. Proceedings of the 7th Annual Convention, August 31-September 3, 1944. Los Angeles: California CIO Council.

Congress of Industrial Organizations (CIO). 1945. "Jobs for All." Proceedings of the 8th Annual Convention, December 5–9, 1945. San Francisco: California CIO Council.

Congress of Industrial Organizations (CIO). ca. 1949. *The CIO: What It Is and What It Does*. Washington, D.C.: CIO.

Congress of Industrial Organizations (CIO). 1950. *Hearings Before the Committee to Investigate Charges Against International Longshoremen's and Warehousemen's Union*. (May 17). Microfilm: University of California, Berkeley.

Conn, Harry. 1952. "Communist-led Unions and US Security." *New Republic* (February 18): 16–17.

"The C.P.'s Last Base." 1949. *Fortune* (March): 175–77.

Conot, Robert. 1974. *American Odyssey*. New York: William Morrow.

Cook, Alice. 1963. *Union Democracy: Practice and Ideal*. Ithaca: Cornell University Press.

Cornfield, Daniel. 1989. *Becoming a Mighty Voice: Conflict and Change in the United Furniture Workers of America*. New York: Russell Sage Foundation.

Cornfield, Daniel. 1991. "The US Labor Movement: Its Development and Impact on Social Inequality and Policies." *Annual Review of Sociology* 17: 27–49.

Craig, John, and Edward Gross. 1970. "The Forum Theory of Organizational Democracy." *American Sociological Review* 35, no. 1 (February): 19–33.

Cranefield, Harold A. 1951. UAW–CIO "Inter-Office Communication" to Walter P. Reuther. (November 8). Wayne State University, Archives of Labor History and Urban Affairs, Walter P. Reuther Collection, box 249, folder 249–23.

Critchlow, Donald T. 1976. "Communist Unions and Racism." *Labor History* 17 (Spring): 230–44.

"Current Labor Statistics: Earnings and Hours." 1950. *Monthly Labor Review* 70 (May): 572–86.

"Current Labor Statistics: Employment Data." 1993. *Monthly Labor Review* 116 (July): 84.

Dahl, Robert A. 1956. *A Preface to Democratic Theory*. Chicago: University of Chicago Press.

Dahl, Robert. 1971. *Polyarchy: Participation and Opposition*. New Haven: Yale University Press.

Dahrendorf, Ralf. 1959. *Class and Class Conflict in Industrial Society*. Stanford, Calif.: Stanford University Press.

Dalfiume, Richard M. 1969. "The 'Forgotten Years' of the Negro Revolution." Pp. 298–316 in *The Negro in Depression and War*, ed. Bernard Sternsher. Chicago: Quadrangle.

Daugherty, Carrol R. 1938. *Labor Problems in American Industry*. New York: Houghton Mifflin.

David, Henry. 1951. "One Hundred Years of Labor in Politics " Pp. 90–112 in J. B. S. Hardman and Maurice Neufeld, eds., *The House of Labor*. New York: Prentice-Hall.

Davis, Horace B. 1953. "Receivership in American Unions." *Quarterly Journal of Economics* 67 (May): 231–52.

Davis, Mike. 1980. "The Barren Marriage of American Labour and the Democratic Party." *New Left Review* (November-December): 43–84.

Deaux, Kay, and Joseph Ullman. 1983. *Women of Steel: Female Blue-Collar Workers in the Basic Steel Industry*. New York: Praeger.

"Declaration of Independence." [1776] 1994. Pp. 453–54 in *The World Almanac and Book of Facts*, 1995 (from the text of the original printed by John Dunlap). Mahwah, N. J.: Funk and Wagnalls.

Derber, Milton. 1945. "Electrical Products." Pp. 682–805 in *How Collective Bargaining Works*, ed. Harry Millis with Natalie Pannes. New York: Twentieth Century Fund.

Dickerson, Dennis C. 1986. *Out of the Crucible: Black Steelworkers in Western Pennsylvania*. Albany: SUNY Press.

Dix, Edward Keith. 1967. "A Study of Collective Bargaining in the Nonferrous Metal Industry." Ph.D. dissertation, University of Maryland.

Drake, St. Clair, and Horace Cayton. 1945. *Black Metropolis*. New York: Harcourt, Brace.

Draper, Theodore. 1957. *The Roots of American Communism*. New York: Viking.

Draper, Theodore. 1960. *American Communism and Soviet Russia*. New York: Viking.

Draper, Theodore. 1972. "The Communists and the Miners." *Dissent* (Spring): 371–92.

Draper, Theodore. 1985a. "American Communism Revisited." *New York Review of Books* 32 (May 9): 32–37.

Draper, Theodore. 1985b. "Communism Re-Revisited." *New York Review of Books* 32 (September 26): 60.

Draper, Theodore. 1985c. "The Popular Front Revisited." *New York Review of Books* 32 (May 30): 44–50.

Draper, Theodore. 1985d. "Revisiting American Communism: An Exchange." *New York Review of Books* 32 (August 15): 40–44.

Drucker, Peter Ferdinand. 1950. *The New Society: The Anatomy of the Industrial Order*. New York: Harper.

Drucker, Peter. 1982. "Are Unions Becoming Irrelevant?" *Wall Street Journal* (September 22).

Dubin, Robert. 1954a. "Collective Bargaining and American Capitalism." Pp. 270–79 in *Industrial Conflict,* eds. Arthur Kornhauser, Robert Dubin, and Arthur M. Ross. New York: McGraw-Hill.

Dubin, Robert. 1954b. "Constructive Aspects of Industrial Conflict." Pp. 37–47 in *Industrial Conflict*, eds. Arthur Kornhauser, Robert Dubin, and Arthur M. Ross. New York: McGraw-Hill.

Dubin, Robert. 1958. *Working Union-Management Relations: The Sociology of Industrial Relations.* Englewood Cliffs, N.J.: Prentice Hall.

Dubois, W. E. B. 1948. "Race Relations in the United States, 1917–1947." *Phylon* 9 (Third Quarter): 234–47.

Dubovsky, Melvin. 1988. *We Shall Be All: A History of the Industrial Workers of the World*, 2nd ed. Urbana: University of Illinois Press.

Duverger, Maurice. 1959. *Political Parties: Their Organization and Activity in the Modern State.* London: Methuen.

Edelstein, J. David. 1967. "An Organizational Theory of Union Democracy." *American Sociological Review* 32 (February): 19–31.

Edelstein, J. David, and Malcolm Warner. 1976. *Comparative Union Democracy.* New York: John Wiley and Sons.

"8 Unions Call 'Repeal Taft–Hartley and Mc Carran' Conference." 1950. *March of Labor* (November): 5.

Eldersveld, Samuel. 1964. *Political Parties: A Behavioral Analysis.* Chicago: Rand McNally.

"Election of General Council Delegates at Ford Local 600." N.d. Wayne State Archives of Urban and Labor Affairs, ACTU Collection, box 24, folder Local 600 1939–45.

Emspak, Frank. 1968. "The Association of Catholic Trade Unionists and the United Automobile Workers." M.A. Thesis, University of Wisconsin.

Emspak, Frank. 1972. "The Breakup of the Congress of Industrial Organizations (CIO)." Ph.D. dissertation, University of Wisconsin.

Emspak, Frank. 1984. "The Breakup of the CIO." *Political Power and Social Theory* 4: 101–39.

Emspak, Frank. 2000a. Email and telephone consultation with Zeitlin (April 26).

Emspak, Frank. 2000b. Email consultation with Zeitlin (May 10).

"End of the Road," "The C.I.O.'s New Line-Up." 1951. *Fortune* (January): 44, 48, 50.

Engels, Frederick. [1891] 1973. "Introduction to 'The Civil War in France.'" Pp. 178–89 in Karl Marx and Frederick Engels: *Selected Works in Three Volumes*, vol. 2. Moscow: Progress.

Engels, Frederick. [1893] 1959. "Letter to Friedrich A. Sorge," London, December 2, 1893. P. 458 in *Marx and Engels: Basic Writings on Politics and Philosophy*, ed. Lewis Feuer. Garden City, N.Y.: Anchor.

Epstein, Albert, and Nathaniel Goldfinger. 1950. "Communist Tactics in American Unions." *Labor and Nation* 6 (Fall): 36–43.

Fairlie, Robert W., and William A. Sundstrom. 1996. "The Racial Unemployment Gap in Long-Run Perspective." Unpublished draft (September), kindly provided by the authors.

Fantasia, Rick. 1988. *Cultures of Solidarity: Consciousness, Action, and Contemporary American Workers*. Berkeley and Los Angeles: University of California Press.

FEPC. 1945. *First Report, Fair Employment Practice Committee, July 1943–December 1944*. Washington, D.C.: FEPC.

Feurer, Rosemary. 1992. "William Sentner, the UE, and Civic Unionism in St. Louis." Pp. 95–117 in *The CIO's Left-Led Unions*, ed. Steve Rosswurm. New Brunswick, N.J.: Rutgers University Press.

Filippelli, Ronald. 1970. "The United Electrical, Radio and Machine Workers, 1933–1949." Ph.D. dissertation, Pennsylvania State University.

Filippelli, Ronald L. 1984. "UE: An Uncertain Legacy." *Political Power and Social Theory* 4: 217–52.

Filippelli, Ronald L., and Mark D. McColloch. 1995. *Cold War in the Working Class: The Rise and Decline of the United Electrical Workers*. Albany: SUNY Press.

Fink, Gary, ed. 1977. *Labor Unions*. Westport, Conn.: Greenwood Press.

Fiske, Mel. 1950. "Labor Parley in Capital Maps United Petition Drive." *Daily Worker* (November 29): 2, 9.

Fitch, John A. 1949. "The CIO and Its Communists." *The Survey* (December): 642–47.

Flanders, Allan. 1968. "Collective Bargaining: A Theoretical Analysis." *British Journal of Industrial Relations* 6 (March): 1–26.

Foner, Philip. 1950. *The Fur and Leather Workers Union*. Newark, N.J.: Nordan Press.

Foner, Philip. 1965. *History of the Labor Movement in the United States: The Industrial Workers of the World, 1905–1917*, vol. 4. New York: International.

Foner, Philip. 1976. *Organized Labor and the Black Worker 1619–1973*. New York: International.

Foner, Philip. 1977. *American Socialism and Black Americans: From the Age of Jackson to World War II*. Westport, Conn.: Greenwood.

Foner, Philip. 1980. *Women and the American Labor Movement*. New York: Free Press.

Foner, Philip. 1991. *The History of the Labor Movement in the United States*, Vol. 9: *The T.U.E.L. to the End of the Gompers Era*. New York: International.

Foner, Philip. 1994. *History of the Labor Movement in the United States*, vol. 10: *The T.U.E.L. 1925–1929*. New York: International.

Fonow, Mary Margaret. August 2000. Personal correspondence with Stepan-Norris.

Fonow, Mary Margaret. (Forthcoming). *Forging a Feminism in Steel*. Minneapolis: University of Minnesota Press.

Ford Industrial Archives. 1946. Executive Communication. Motor Assembly Move.

Ford Industrial Archives. 1949. Executive Communication. Bethlehem Steel Location Study.

Ford Local 600 By-Laws Committee. 1942. "Proposed By-Laws of Ford Local #600." Walter P. Reuther Archives, Wayne State University, ACTU box 24, Local 600 – General.

Form, William H. 1976. *Blue-Collar Stratification: Autoworkers in Four Countries*. Princeton, N.J.: Princeton University Press.

Form, William H. 1985. *Divided We Stand: Working-Class Stratification in America*. Urbana and Chicago: University of Illinois Press.

Fortune editors (with Russell W. Davenport). 1951. *U.S.A.: The Permanent Revolution*. New York: Prentice-Hall.

Foster, James C. 1975. *The Union Politic: The CIO's Political Action Committee*. Columbia: University of Missouri.

Foster, William Z. 1920. *The Great Steel Strike and Its Lessons*. New York: B. W. Huebsch.

Foster, William Z. 1927. *Misleaders of Labor*. Chicago, Ill.: Trade Union Educational League.

Foster, William Z. 1937. *From Bryan to Stalin*. New York: International.

Foster, William Z. 1942. "Trade Unions in the War Emergency." *The Communist* 21 (January): 57–70.

Foster, William Z. [1936] 1947a. "Labor and Politics." Pp. 136–43 in *American Trade Unionism: Selected Writings*, ed. William Z. Foster. New York: International.

Foster, William Z. [1937] 1947b. "Organizational Problems of Industrial Unionism." Pp. 244–60 in *American Trade Unionism: Selected Writings*, ed. William Z. Foster. New York: International.

Foster, William Z. 1950. "Keynote Message of Greetings to the Plenum [of the Communist Party National Committee]." *Political Affairs* (May): 9–13.

Foster, William Z. 1952a. *American Trade Unionism: Principles and Organization, Tactics and Strategy: Selected Writings*. New York: International.

Foster, William Z. 1952b. "The Communists and the La Follette Movement of 1924."*Political Affairs* (February): 21–31.

Foster, William Z. 1952c. "Peace – Today's Central Issue." *Political Affairs* (September): 1–5.

Foster, William Z. 1954. "The Lewis–Beck–McDonald Trade Union Pact." *Political Affairs* (June): 4–10.

Fox, Alan. 1966. *Industrial Sociology and Industrial Relations: An Assessment . . . {for} the Royal Commission.* Series: Great Britain, Royal Commission on Trade Unions and Employers' Associations, research papers, 3. London: H.M.S.O.

Fredrickson, George M. 1995. "Red, Black, and White." *New York Review of Books* (June 8): 33–35, 38–39.

Freedman, David A. 1991. "Statistical Models and Shoe Leather." *Sociological Methodology* 21: 291–313.

Freedman, David A. 1999. "From Association to Causation: some Remarks on the History of Statistics." Technical Report No. 21. Statistics Department, University of California, Berkeley.

Freeman, Bill. 1982. *1005: Political Life in a Union Local.* Toronto, Canada: James Lorimer and Company.

Freeman, Joshua B. 1989. *In Transit: The Transport Workers Union in New York City, 1933–1966.* New York and Oxford: Oxford University Press.

Friedman, Robert. 1952. "The Attitudes of West Coast Maritime Unions in Seattle Toward Negroes in the Maritime Industry." M.A. thesis, State College of Washington.

Friedman, Samuel. 1982. *Teamster Rank and File: Power, Bureaucracy and Rebellion at Work in a Union.* New York: Columbia University Press.

Fulton, Maurice. 1955. "Plant Relocation – 1965." *Harvard Business Review* 33: 40–50.

Gabin, Nancy. 1990. *Feminism in the Labor Movement: Women and the United Auto Workers, 1935–1975.* Ithaca and London: Cornell University Press.

Galenson, Walter. 1940. *Rival Unionism in the United States.* New York: American Council on Public Affairs.

Galenson, Walter. 1960. *The CIO Challenge to the AFL: A History of the American Labor Movement 1935–1941.* Cambridge, Mass.: Harvard University Press.

Galenson, Walter, 1974. "Communists and Trade Union Democracy." *Industrial Relations* 3 (October): 228–36.

Galenson, Walter, and Seymour Martin Lipset. 1960. "Democracy and Bureaucracy in Trade Union Government." Pp. 203–5 in *Labor and Trade Unionism,* eds. W. Galenson and S. M. Lipset. New York and London, England: Wiley.

Gates, Albert. 1944. "What Happened at the U.E. Meeting." *The New International* {The Workers Party} 10: 316–18.

Gates, John. 1951. "Sharpen the Fight Against Browderism, Titoism, Trotskyism." *Political Affairs* (February): 79–87.

Geiger, Theodor Julius. 1949. *Die Klassengesellschaft im Schmelztiegel*. Koeln: G. Kiepenheuer.

"General Council Allocation of Delegates." 1947. Wayne State Archives of Urban and Labor Affairs, ACTU box 24, Local 600 – Conference.

General Electric. 1938–50. "Agreement between General Electric Company and United Electrical, Radio and Machine Workers of America."

General Motors Corporation. 1937–50. "Agreement between General Motors Corporation and the UAW–CIO."

Giddens, Anthony. 1973. *The Class Structure of the Advanced Societies*. New York: Barnes and Noble.

Giddens, Anthony. 1982. "Class Structuration and Class Consciousness." Pp. 157–74 in *Classes, Power and Conflict: Classical and Contemporary Debates*, eds. A. Giddens and D. Held. Berkeley and Los Angeles: University of California Press.

Gilpin, Toni. 1988. "The FE–UAW Conflict: The Ideological Content of Collective Bargaining in Postwar America." Paper presented at the North American Labor History Conference, Wayne State University, Detroit.

Gilpin, Toni. 1993. "Left by Themselves: A History of the United Farm Equipment and Metal Workers Unions." Ph.D. dissertation, Yale University.

Ginger, Ann Fagan, and David Christiano. 1987. "Big Business and Government Unleash Taft–Hartley." Pp. 243–46 in *The Cold War Against Labor: An Anthology*, vol. 1, eds. Ann Fagan Ginger and David Christiano. Berkeley, Calif.: Meikeljohn Civil Liberties Institute.

Ginger, Ann Fagan, and David Christiano. 1987. "Marie Richardson Harris." P. 391 in *The Cold War Against Labor: An Anthology*, vol. 1, eds. Ann Fagan Ginger and David Christiano. Berkeley, Calif.: Meikeljohn Civil Liberties Institute.

Glaberman, Martin. 1980. *Wartime Strikes: The Struggle Against the No-Strike Pledge in the UAW during World War II*. Detroit, Mich.: Bewick Editions.

Glazer, Nathan. 1961. *The Social Basis of American Communism*. New York: Harcourt, Brace and World.

Glenn, Norval D. 1963. "Some Changes in the Relative Status of American Nonwhite, 1940 to 1960." *Phylon* (Second Quarter): 109–22.

Gold, Ben. 1987. "President Murray's Report" (excerpted from Gold's 1984 *Memoir*). Pp. 297–303 in *The Cold War Against Labor*, eds. Ann Fagan Ginger and David Christiano. Berkeley, Calif.: Meikeljohn Civil Liberties Institute.

Goldberg, Arthur. 1964. *AFL-CIO United*. New York: McGraw-Hill.

References

Goldfield, Michael. 1993. "Race and the CIO: The Possibilities for Racial Egalitarianism during the 1930s and 1940s." *International Labor and Working-Class History* 44 (Fall): 1–32.

Goldfield, Michael. 1994. "The Failure of Operation Dixie: A Critical Turning Point in American Political Development." Pp. 166–89 in *Race, Class, and Community in Southern Labor History*, eds. Gary M. Fink and Merle E. Reed. Tuscaloosa and London: University of Alabama Press.

Goldfield, Michael. 1995. "Was There a Golden Age of the CIO? Race, Solidarity and Union Growth during the 1930s and 1940s." Pp. 80–110 in *Trade Union Politics*, eds. Glenn Perusek and Kent Worcester. Atlantic Highlands, N. J.: Humanities Press.

Goldfield, Michael. 1997. *The Color of Politics*. New York: New Press.

Goldstein, Robert J. 1978. *Political Repression in Modern America from 1870 to the Present*. Boston: G. K. Hall.

Goldthorpe, John H. 1969. *The Affluent Worker in the Class Structure*. London: Cambridge University Press.

Goldthorpe, John H., David Lockwood, Frank Bechhofer, and Jennifer Platt. 1968. *The Affluent Worker: Political Attitudes and Behavior*. London: Cambridge University Press.

Goode, Bill. 1994. *Infighting in the UAW: The 1946 Election and the Ascendancy of Walter Reuther*. Greenwood Press.

Goodman, Ernest. 1951. "Civil Action to Enjoin Ford from Violating Contract of September 14, 1950," draft copy (October 31), box 249, folder 23. WSUA.

Goodman, Walter. 1969. *The Committee: The Extraordinary Career of the House Committee on Un-American Activities*. London: Secker and Warburg.

Goodrich, Carter. 1920. *The Frontier of Control: A Study in British Workshop Politics*. New York: Harcourt, Brace and Howe.

Gouldner, Alvin W. 1947. "Attitudes of 'Progressive' Trade Union Leaders." *American Journal of Sociology* 52: 389–92.

Gouldner, Alvin W. 1955. "Metaphysical Pathos and the Theory of Bureaucracy." *American Political Science Review* 49 (June): 496–507.

Gramsci, Antonio. [1929–35] 1971. *Selections from the Prison Notebooks*. Edited and translated by Q. Hoare and G. N. Smith. New York: International Publishers.

Green, James R. 1980. *The World of the Worker*. New York: Hill and Wang.

Griffin, Larry J., Michael E. Wallace, and Beth A. Rubin. 1986. "Capitalist Resistance to the Organization of Labor before the New Deal: Why? How? Success?" *American Sociological Review* 51: 147–67.

Griffith, Barbara. 1988. *The Crisis of American Labor: Operation Dixie and the Defeat of the CIO*. Philadelphia: Temple University Press.

Grob, Gerald N. 1960. "Organized Labor and the Negro Worker, 1865–1900." *Labor History* 1, no. 2 (Spring): 164–76.

Gurda, Jon. 1992. *The Bradley Legacy*. Milwaukee, Wis.: The Lynde and Harvey Bradley Foundation.

Gutman, Herbert. 1968. "The Negro and the United Mine Workers of America." Pp. 49–127 in *The Negro and the American Labor Movement*, ed. Julius Jacobson. New York: Anchor.

Halaby, Charles N. 1986. "Worker Attachment and Workplace Authority." *American Sociological Review* 51: 634–49.

Halpern, Eric Bryan. 1989. "'Black and White Unite and Fight': Race and Labor in Meatpacking, 1904–48." Ph.D. dissertation, University of Pennsylvania.

Halpern, Martin. 1988. *UAW Politics in the Cold War Era*. Albany: SUNY Press.

Halpern, Rick [Eric Bryan]. 1991. "Interracial Unionism in the Southwest: Fort Worth Packinghouse Workers, 1937–1954." Pp. 158–82 in *Organized Labor in the Twentieth-Century South*, ed. Robert H. Zieger. Knoxville: University of Tennessee Press.

Halpern, Rick. 1997. *Down on the Killing Floor: Black and White Workers in Chicago's Packinghouses, 1904–54*. Urbana and Chicago: University of Illinois Press.

Halpern, Rick, and Roger Horowitz. 1996. *Meatpackers: An Oral History of Black Packinghouse Workers and the Struggle for Racial and Economic Equality*. New York: Twayne.

Hamilton, Richard F. 1967. *Affluence and the French Worker in the Fourth Republic*. Princeton: Princeton University Press.

"Hammer and Tongs: The New C.P. Line." 1946. *Fortune* (June): 105–7.

Handler, Esther. 1951. "Frameup: Taft–Hartley Style." *March of Labor* (December): 19–20, 28.

Harbison, Frederick H. 1954. "Collective Bargaining and American Capitalism." Pp. 270–79 in *Industrial Conflict*, eds. Arthur Kornhauser, Robert Dubin, and Arthur M. Ross. New York: McGraw-Hill.

Harris, Donald J. 1978. "Capitalist Exploitation and Black Labor: Some Conceptual Issues." *Review of Black Political Economy* 8 (Winter): 133–51.

Harris, Howell J. 1982. *The Right to Manage*. Madison: University of Wisconsin Press.

Hastings, Frederick C. 1953. "Basing the Party in the Shops." *Political Affairs* (May): 16–29.

Haynes, John Earl. 1996. *Red Scare or Red Menace? American Communism and Anticommunism in the Cold War Era*. Chicago: Ivan R. Dee.

Haynes, John Earl, Harvey Klehr, and Kyrill M. Anderson. 1998. *The Soviet World of American Communism*. New Haven and London: Yale University Press.

Haynes, John Earl, Harvey Klehr, and Fridrikh Igorevich Firsov. 1995. *The Secret World of American Communism*. New Haven and London: Yale University Press.

Healey, Dorothy. 1981/82. Interview with Zeitlin. Los Angeles, California. (April 10, 1981, and July 8, 1982).

Healey, Dorothy Ray. 1994. "Pages from a Worker's Life." *The Nation* (July 25/August 1): 132–34.

Healey, Dorothy Ray, and Maurice Isserman. 1993. *California Red: A Life in the American Communist Party*. Urbana and Chicago: University of Illinois Press.

Henderson, Samuel T. 1952. "White Chauvinism and Negro Bourgeois Nationalism." *Political Affairs* (December): 28–40.

Herberg, Will. 1943. "Bureaucracy and Democracy in Labor Unions." *Antioch Review* 3 (Fall): 405–17.

Herding, Richard. 1978. "Job Control and Union Structure." Pp. 260–87 in *Trade Unions under Capitalism*, eds. Tom Clarke and Laurie Clements. Sussex: Harvester.

Hill, Herbert. 1951. *The Communist Party – Enemy of Negro Equality*. Reprint, as a pamphlet, of an article in the June-July 1951 issue of *The Crisis*, official organ of the NAACP. New York: NAACP.

Hill, Herbert. 1952. "Memorandum to Mr. [Walter] White from Herbert Hill. Re: Philadelphia Plant – Philco Corporation." Manuscript Division, Library of Congress.

Hill, Herbert. 1968a. "The Racial Practices of Organized Labor." Pp. 286–357 in *The Negro and the American Labor Movement*, ed. Julius Jacobson. New York: Anchor.

Hill, Herbert. 1968b. "Testimony of Herbert Hill, National Labor Director, National Association for the Advancement of Colored People, Before the Ad Hoc Committee Hearings on Federal Contract Compliance, House of Representatives." Washington, D.C. (December 5). Copy kindly provided by Hill to Zeitlin.

Hill, Herbert. 1973. "Comment." Pp. 113–23 in *Discrimination in Labor Markets*, eds. Orley Ashenfelter and Albert Rees. Princeton, N.J.: Princeton University Press.

Hill, Herbert. 1985. *Black Labor and the American Legal System*. Madison: University of Wisconsin Press.

Hill, Herbert. 1988. "Mythmaking as Labor History: Herbert Gutman and the United Mine Workers of America." *International Journal of Politics, Culture and Society* 2 (Winter): 132–200.

Hill, Herbert. 1996. "The Problem of Race in American Labor History." *Reviews in American History* 24 (June): 189–208.

Hill, Herbert. 1998. "Lichtenstein's Fictions: Meany, Reuther and the 1964 Civil Rights Act." *New Politics* 7 (Summer): 82–107.

Hill, Herbert. 1999a. Letter to Zeitlin (February 12).

Hill, Herbert. 1999b. Letter to Zeitlin (August 20).

Hill, Herbert. 2000. Telephone conversation with Zeitlin (January 25).

Hill, Lee, and Charles Hook. 1945. *Management at the Bargaining Table*. New York: McGraw-Hill.

Hill, Richard Child. 1974. "Unionization and Racial Income Inequality in the Metropolis." *American Sociological Review* 39 (August): 507–22.

Holmes, John Jay. 1946. "The CIO and the Negro Worker in the Baltimore Area: A Study of Five CIO Unions." M.A. thesis, Howard University.

Honey, Michael K. 1993. *Southern Labor and Black Civil Rights: Organizing Memphis Workers*. Urbana and Chicago: University of Illinois Press.

Honey, Michael K. 1994. "Black Workers Remember: Industrial Unionism in the Era of Jim Crow." Pp. 121–37 in *Race, Class, and Community in Southern Labor History*, eds. Gary M. Fink and Merle E. Reed. Tuscaloosa and London: University of Alabama Press.

Honey, Michael K. 1999. *Black Workers Remember: An Oral History of Segregation, Unionism, and the Freedom Struggle*. Berkeley and Los Angeles: University of California Press.

Hook, Sidney. 1953. *Heresy, Yes – Conspiracy, No*. New York: John Day.

"How Leftist Unions Are Fairing." 1955. *Business Week* (April 30): 61.

"How the Commies Won." 1954. *Fortune* (July): 36.

Howe, Irving, and Lewis Coser. 1957. *The American Communist Party: A Critical History (1919–1957)*. Beacon Hill, Mass.: Beacon.

Howe, Irving, and B. J. Widick. 1949. *The U.A.W. and Walter Reuther*. New York: Random House.

Huberman, Leo. 1946. *The Truth about Unions*. New York: Reynal and Hitchcock.

Huntley, Horace. 1977. "Iron Ore Miners and Mine, Mill in Alabama: 1933–1952." Ph.D. dissertation, University of Pittsburgh.

Huntley, Horace. 1990. "The Red Scare and Black Workers in Alabama: The International Union of Mine, Mill and Smelter Workers, 1945–1953." Pp. 129–45 in *Labor Divided: Race and Ethnicity in United States Labor Struggles, 1835–1960*, eds. Robert Asher and Charles Stephenson. Albany: SUNY Press.

Hutchins, Grace. 1952. *Women Who Work*. Labor Research Association. New York: International Publishers.

Hyman, Richard. 1974. "Workers' Control and Revolutionary Theory." Pp. 241–78 in *The Socialist Register*, 1974, eds. R. Miliband and J. Saville. London, England: Merlin.

Hyman, Richard. 1985. "Class Struggle and the Trade Union Movement." Pp. 99–123 in *A Socialist Anatomy of Britain*, eds. David Coates, Gordon Johnston, and Ray Bush. Cambridge: Polity.

Ignasiak, Andrew Collection. Walter P. Reuther Archives, Wayne State University. ACTU Collection, Box 24.

"In Labor." 1956. *Business Week* (September 15): 179.

"Industry Shifts Its Plants." 1951. *Business Week* (September 8): 22–24.

"The Inflationary Push on Pay for Union Brass." 1980. *Business Week* (May 12): 86–89.

Isserman, Maurice. 1982. *Which Side Were You On? The American Communist Party during the Second World War*. Middletown, Conn.: Wesleyan University Press.

"The I.U.E.'s Live Wires." 1950. *Fortune* (June): 47–50.

Jacobs, Paul. 1963. *The State of the Unions*. New York: Atheneum.

Jacobson, Julius. 1968. "Union Conservatism: A Barrier to Racial Equality." Pp. 1–26 in *The Negro and the American Labor Movement*, ed. Julius Jacobson. New York: Anchor.

Jacoby, Sanford. 1981. "Union–Management Cooperation: An Historical Perspective." Working Paper Series, no. 32 (April). Los Angeles: UCLA Institute of Industrial Relations.

James, Larry. 1984. *Power in a Trade Union*. New York: Cambridge University Press.

Jensen, Vernon. 1954. *Nonferrous Metals Industry Unionism 1934–1954: A Study of Leadership Controversy*. Ithaca: New York State School of Industrial and Labor Relations.

Johanningsmeier, Edward P. 1994. *Forging American Communism*. Princeton, N.J.: Princeton University Press.

Kampelman, Max M. 1957. *The Communist Party vs. the CIO*. New York: Prager. Reprint, New York: Arno and the *New York Times*, 1971.

Karsh, Bernard, and Phillips L. Garman. 1961. "The Impact of the Political Left." Pp. 77–119 in *Labor and the New Deal*, eds. Milton Derber and Edwin Young. Madison: University of Wisconsin Press.

Keeran, Roger. 1980a. *The Communist Party and the Auto Workers Union*. Bloomington: Indiana University Press.

Keeran, Roger. 1980b. "Labor and Communism: An Exchange." *Industrial Relations* 19 (Spring): 136–39.

Keitel, Robert S. 1974. "The Merger of the International Union of Mine, Mill and Smelter Workers into the United Steelworkers of America." *Labor History* 15: 36–43.

Kelley, Robin D. G. 1988. "'Comrades, Praise Gawd for Lenin and Them!' Ideology and Culture among Black Communists in Alabama, 1930–1935." *Science and Society* 52 (Spring): 59–82.

Kelley, Robin D. G. 1989. "A New War in Dixie: Communists and the Unemployed in Birmingham, Alabama, 1930–1933." *Labor History* 30 (Summer): 367–84.

Kelley, Robin D. G. 1990. *Hammer and Hoe: Alabama Communists during the Great Depression.* Chapel Hill: University of North Carolina Press.

Kelley, Robin D. G. 1996. *Race Rebels: Culture, Politics and the Black Working Class.* New York: Free Press.

Kempton, Murray. 1955. *Part of Our Time.* New York: Simon and Schuster.

Kendrick, Alex H. 1952. "The Party and the Trade Unions in the Post War Period." *Political Affairs* (December): 41–56.

Kendrick, Alex H., and Jerome Golden 1953. "Lessons of the Struggle Against Opportunism in District 5." *Political Affairs* (June): 26–37.

Kersten, Andrew E. 1999a. Telephone conversation with Zeitlin (October 19).

Kersten, Andrew E. 1999b. "Jobs and Justice: Detroit, Fair Employment, and Federal Activism during the Second World War." *Michigan Historical Review* 25 (Spring): 76–101.

Kersten, Andrew E. 1999c. Letter to Zeitlin (October 20).

Kersten, Andrew E. 1999d. "Stretching the Social Pattern: The President's Fair Employment Practice Committee and St. Louis." *Missouri Historical Review* 93 (January): 149–64.

Kersten, Andrew E. 2000. Untitled book manuscript, Chapter 8: "Stretching the Social Pattern: The FEPC and St. Louis" (a revision of 1999a).

Kessler-Harris, Alice. 1975. "Where Are the Organized Women Workers." *Feminist Studies* 3 (Fall): 92–105.

Killian, Lewis M. 1952. "The Effects of Southern White Workers on Race Relations in Northern Plants." *American Sociological Review* 17: 327–31.

Kimeldorf, Howard. 1988. *Reds or Rackets?* Berkeley and Los Angeles: University of California Press.

Kimeldorf, Howard. 1998. "Radical Possibilities: The Rise and Fall of Wobbly Unionism on the Philadelphia Docks." Pp. 97–130 in *Waterfront Workers: New Perspectives on Race and Class*, ed. Calvin Winslow. Urbana and Chicago: University of Illinois Press.

Kimeldorf, Howard. 1999. *Battling for American Labor: Wobblies, Craft Workers, and the Making of the Union Movement*. Berkeley and Los Angeles: University of California Press.

Kingery, Helen. 1951. "Sex for Sale." *March of Labor* (April): 24–25.

Klare, Karl E. 1977/78. "Judicial Deradicalization of the Wagner Act and the Origins of Modern Legal Consciousness, 1937–1941." *Minnesota Law Review* 62: 265–339.

Klehr, Harvey. 1984. *The Heyday of American Communism*. New York: Basic.

Kornhauser, Arthur, Robert Dubin, and Arthur M. Ross. 1954. "Alternative Roads Ahead." Pp. 501–18 in *Industrial Conflict*, eds. Arthur Kornhauser, Robert Dubin, and Arthur Ross. New York: McGraw-Hill.

Kornhauser, William. 1950. "Labor Unions and Race Relations: A Study of Union Tactics." M.A. thesis, University of Chicago.

Korstad, Robert, and Nelson Lichtenstein. 1988. "Opportunities Found and Lost: Labor, Radicals and the Early Civil Rights Movement." *Journal of American History* 75 (December): 786–811.

Kovner, Joseph. 1948. "The Legal Protection of Civil Liberties within Unions." *Wisconsin Law Review* (January): 18–27.

Kovner, Joseph. 1952. "Union Democracy." Pp. 83–88 in *Interpreting the Labor Movement*, eds. George Brooks, Milton Derber, David McCabe, and Philip Taft. Industrial Relations Research Association, University of Illinois.

Kutler, Stanley L. 1982. *The American Inquisition: Justice and Injustice in the Cold War*. New York: Hill and Wang.

"Labor Hi-Lites." 1950. *March of Labor* (October): 28.

"Labor Hi-Lites." 1951. *March of Labor* (July): 28; (August): 29.

"Labor Notes." 1953. *Fortune* (March): 84.

"The Labor Priests." 1949. *Fortune* (January): 150–52.

Labor Research Association. 1945. *Labor Fact Book No. 7*. New York: International Publishers.

Labor Research Association. 1947. *Labor Fact Book 8*. New York: International Publishers.

Labor Research Association. 1953. *Labor Fact Book 11*. New York: International Publishers.

"Labor Violence – New Style." 1949. *Fortune* (March): 175–77.

Larrowe, Charles P. 1977. *Harry Bridges: The Rise and Fall of Radical Labor in the U.S.*, 2nd ed. Westport, Conn.: Lawrence Hill.

Larson, Elmer. 1952. "On Guard Against Enemy Infiltration." *Political Affairs* (October): 18–36.

Laslett, John H. M. 1981. "Giving Superman a Human Face: American Communism and the Automobile Workers in the 1930s." *Reviews in American History* 9: 112–17.

Lasswell, Harold D. and Dorothy Blumenstock. 1939. *World Revolutionary Propaganda: A Chicago Study.* Reprint, Freeport, N.Y.: Books for Libraries Press, 1970.

Latouche, John, and Earl Robinson. 1939. *Ballad for Americans* (Paul Robeson, soloist). RCA Victor.

Lawson, Elizabeth. 1949. "How the CIO Views the Crisis." *Daily Worker* (August 18): 6, 8.

Leab, Daniel J. 1967. "'United We Eat': The Creation and Organization of the Unemployed Councils in 1930." *Labor History* 8 (Fall): 300–315.

Lee, Alfred McClung, and Norman D. Humphrey. 1943. *Race Riot.* New York: Dryden.

"Leftist Labor Alliance." 1950. *Business Week* (December 9): 92.

"Left-Wing Unions of Nation to Meet." 1950. *New York Times* (November 14): 20.

Leiserson, William M. 1959. *American Trade Union Democracy.* New York: Columbia University Press.

Lembcke, Jerry. 1984. "Uneven Development, Class Formation and Industrial Unionism in the Wood Products Industry." *Political Power and Social Theory* 4: 183–215.

Lembcke, Jerry, and William M. Tattam. 1984. *One Union in Wood.* British Columbia and New York: Harbour and International.

Lenin, Vladimir. 1963. "New Data on the Laws Governing the Development of Capitalism in Agriculture." Pp. 13–102 in Lenin, *Collected Works*, vol. 22. London: Lawrence and Wishart.

Lens, Sid. 1947. "Meaning of the Grievance Procedure." *Harvard Business Review* 27: 713–22.

Lens, Sid. 1949. *Left, Right and Center: Conflicting Forces in American Labor.* Hinsdale, Ill.: Henry Regnery.

Lens, Sid. 1961. *The Crisis of American Labor.* New York: A. S. Barnes.

Lester, Richard. 1958. *As Unions Mature.* Princeton: Princeton University Press.

Letz, Esther. 1955. "Two Unions Merge." *March of Labor* (February): 15–17.

Levenstein, Harvey A. 1981. *Communism, Anticommunism, and the CIO.* Westport, Conn.: Greenwood.

Levinson, Edward. 1956. *Labor on March.* New York: University Books.

Lewis, H.G. 1963. *Unionism and Relative Wages in the United States: An Empirical Study.* Chicago and London: University of Chicago Press.

Lichtenstein, Alex. 1997. "'Scientific Unionism' and the 'Negro Question': Communists and the Transport Workers Union in Miami, 1944–1949." Pp. 58–85 in *Southern Labor in Transition, 1940–1995*, ed. Robert H. Zieger. Knoxville: University of Tennessee Press.

Lichtenstein, Nelson N. 1974. "Industrial Unionism under the No-Strike Pledge: A Study of the CIO during the Second World War." Ph.D. dissertation, University of California at Berkeley.

Lichtenstein, Nelson N. 1980. "The Communist Experience in American Trade Unions." *Industrial Relations* 19 (Spring): 119–30.

Lichtenstein, Nelson N. 1982. *Labor's War at Home: The CIO in World War II.* Cambridge, Eng., and New York: Cambridge University Press.

Lichtenstein, Nelson. 1985. "UAW Bargaining Strategy and Shop-Floor Conflict: 1946–1970." *Industrial Relations* 24 (Fall): 360–69.

Lichtenstein, Nelson. 1991. "The Unions' Retreat in the Postwar Era." Pp. 525–39 in *Major Problems in the History of American Workers: Documents and Essays*, eds. Eileen Boris and Nelson Lichtenstein. Lexington, Mass.: D. C. Heath.

Lichtenstein, Nelson N. 1995. *The Most Dangerous Man in Detroit: Walter Reuther and the Fate of American Labor.* New York: Basic Books.

Lipset, Seymour Martin. 1960. "The Political Process in Trade Unions." Pp. 357–402 in *Political Man: The Social Bases of Politics.* New York: Doubleday.

Lipset, Seymour Martin. 1963. *The First New Nation.* New York: Basic.

Lipset, Seymour M., Martin A. Trow, and James S. Coleman. 1962. *Union Democracy.* Garden City, N.Y.: Doubleday Anchor.

Lipsitz, George. 1994. *Rainbow at Midnight: Labor and Culture in the 1940s.* Urbana and Chicago: University of Illinois Press.

Local Union No. 600, United Automobile, Aircraft and Agricultural Implement Workers of America, UAW–CIO et al. v. Ford Motor Company. 1953. Federal Supplement, 113 F. Supp. 834 (June 5): 834–45. Minneapolis: West Publishing.

Lock, Ed. 1951. "Ford Vote Rocks Reuther." *March of Labor* (April): 9–10.

Losche, Peter. 1975. *Industriegewerkschaften im Organisierten Kapitalismus; Der CIO in der Roosevelt-Ara.* Opladen, West Germany: Westdeutscher Verlag.

Love, Richard. 1994. "In Defiance of Custom and Tradition: Black Tobacco Workers and Labor Unions in Richmond, Virginia, 1937–1941." *Labor History* 35 (Winter): 25–47.

Lozovsky, A. [Solomon Abramovich]. 1935. *Marx and the Trade Unions.* New York: International.

McAdam, Doug. 1982. *Political Process and the Development of Black Insurgency, 1930–1970.* Chicago: University of Chicago Press.

"McClellan Committee Hearings – 1957." 1958. The Bureau of National Affairs, Inc.

McColloch, Mark [D.] 1988. "The Ideological Dimension of Shop-Floor Unionism." Paper presented at the North American Labor History Conference, Detroit.

McColloch, Mark [D.] 1992. "The Shop-Floor Dimension of Union Rivalry: The Case of Westinghouse in the 1950s." Pp. 183–99 in *The CIO's Left-Led Unions*, ed. Steve Rosswurm. New Brunswick, N.J.: Rutgers University Press.

McConnell, Grant. 1958. "Factionalism and Union Democracy." *Labor Law Journal* 9 (September): 635–40.

McDonald, Dwight. 1944. "Comment." *Politics* 6 (November): 294.

MacDougall, Curtis. 1965. *Gideon's Army*, 3 vols. New York: Marzani and Munsell.

McMahon, Edward J. 1969. "Vital Interests of Employer and Union." Pp. 266–67 in *Dealing with a Union*, ed. LeRoy Marceau. New York: American Management Association.

McWilliams, Brian. 1999. "President's Report: Return of the Cold War." *The {ILWU} Dispatcher* (April): 1.

Magaline, A. D. 1975. *Lutte de classes et devalorisation de capital*. Paris: Maspero.

Magrath, C. Peter. 1959. "Democracy in Overalls: The Futile Quest for Union Democracy." *Industrial and Labor Relations Review* 12: 503–25.

Maher, John. 1961. "Wage Patterns in the United States, 1946–1957." *Industrial and Labor Relations Review* 15, no. 1: 3–20.

Maier, Charles S. 1987. "The Politics of Productivity: Foundations of American Economic Policy after World War II." Pp. 121–52 in *In Search of Stability: Explorations in Historical Political Economy*, ed. C. S. Maier. New York and Cambridge, Eng.: Cambridge University Press.

Mann, Eric. 1987. "Taking on General Motors: A Case Study of the UAW Campaign to Keep GM Van Nuys Open." UCLA Institute of Industrial Relations.

Mann, Michael. 1973. *Consciousness and Action among the Western Working Class*. London and Basingstoke, England: Macmillan.

Mannheim, Karl. 1956a. *Essays in the Sociology of Culture*. London: Routledge and Kegan Paul.

Mannheim, Karl. 1956b. *Man and Society in an Age of Reconstruction*. New York: Harcourt Brace.

Marshall, Ray. 1964. "Unions and the Negro Community." *Industrial and Labor Relations Review* 22 (January): 179–202.

Marshall, Ray. 1965a. *The Negro and Organized Labor*. New York: John Wiley and Sons.

Marshall, Ray. 1965b. "Union Racial Practices." Pp. 167–86 in *The Negro and Employment Opportunity: Problems and Practices*, eds. Herbert R. Northrup and Richard L. Rowan. Ann Arbor: University of Michigan Press.

Marshall, Ray. 1967a. *Labor in the South*. Cambridge, Mass.: Harvard University Press.

Marshall, Ray. 1967b. *The Negro Worker*. New York: Random House.

Marshall, Ray. 1968. "The Negro in Southern Unions." Pp. 128–54 in *The Negro and the American Labor Movement*, ed. Julius Jacobson. New York: Anchor.

Marshall, T. H. 1965. *Class, Citizenship, and Social Development*. Garden City, N.Y.: Anchor.

Martin, Roderick. 1968. "Union Democracy: An Explanatory Framework." *Sociology* 2: 205–20.

Martin, Roderick. 1971. "Edelstein, Warner, and Cook on 'Union Democracy.'" *Sociology* 5: 242–44.

Marx, Karl. [1844] n.d. *Economic and Philosophic Manuscripts of 1844*, edited and translated by M. Milligan. Moscow: Foreign Languages Publishing House.

Marx, Karl. [1845] 1973a. "Theses on Feurbach." Pp. 13–15 in *Karl Marx and Frederick Engels: Selected Works in 3 volumes*, vol. 1. Moscow: Progress.

Marx, Karl.[1847] 1976. "The Poverty of Philosophy." Pp. 105–212 in *Karl Marx and Frederick Engels: Collected Works,* vol. 6. New York: International Publishers.

Marx, Karl. [1852] 1963. *The Eighteenth Brumaire of Louis Bonaparte*. New York: International.

Marx, Karl. [1865] 1973b. "Wages, Price and Profit" (elsewhere entitled, "Value, Price, and Profit"). Pp. 31–76 in *Karl Marx and Frederick Engels: Selected Works in 3 Volumes*, vol. 2. Moscow: Progress.

Marx, Karl. [1867] 1906. *Capital*. New York: Modern Library.

Marx, Karl. [1871] 1973c. "The Civil War in France." Pp. 202–44 in *Karl Marx and Frederick Engels: Selected Works in Three Volumes*, vol. 2. Moscow: Progress.

Marx, Karl. [1871] 1973d. "Letter to L. Kugelmann" (April 17, 1871). Pp. 421–22 in *Karl Marx and Frederick Engels: Selected Works in Three Volumes,* vol. 2. Moscow: Progress.

Matles, James, and James Higgins. 1974. *Them and Us: Struggles of a Rank-and-File Union*. Englewood Cliffs, N.J.: Prentice-Hall.

Meehl, Paul E. 1978. "Theoretical Risks and Tabular Asterisks." *Journal of Consulting and Clinical Psychology* 46: 806–34.

Meier, August, and Elliott Rudwick. 1979. *Black Detroit and the Rise of the UAW*. Oxford and New York: Oxford University Press.

Meier, August, and Elliott Rudwick. 1982. "Communist Unions and the Black Community: The Case of the Transport Workers Union, 1934–1944." *Labor History* 23 (Spring): 163–97.

"Merger: DWU, FTA, UOPWA Combine." 1950. *March of Labor* (October): 12–13.

"The Merger: Summing it up." 1956. *March of Labor* (January): 19–20.

Merton, Robert K. 1987. "Three Fragments from a Sociologist's Notebooks: Establishing the Phenomenon, Specified Ignorance, and Strategic Research Materials." *Annual Review of Sociology* 13: 1–28.

Meyer, Stephen. 1992. *"Stalin over Wisconsin": The Making and Unmaking of Militant Unionism, 1900–1950.* New Brunswick: Rutgers University Press.

Michels, Robert. [1915] 1949. *Political Parties.* Glencoe, Ill.: Free Press.

Milkman, Ruth. 1987. *Gender at Work.* Urbana and Chicago: University of Illinois Press.

Milkman, Ruth. 1991. "How Women Were Purged from the War Plants." Pp. 486–95 in *Major Problems in the History of American Workers*, eds. Eileen Boris and Nelson Lichtenstein. Lexington, Mass.: Heath.

Mill, John Stuart. 1963. *Essays on Politics and Culture*, ed. G. Himmelfarb. Garden City, N.Y.: Doubleday Anchor.

Mills, C. Wright. 1948. *The New Men of Power: America's Labor Leaders.* Reprint, New York: Augustus M. Kelley, 1971.

Mills, Herb, and David Wellman. 1987. "Contractually Sanctioned Job Action and Workers Control: The Case of San Francisco Longshoremen." *Labor History* 28: 167–95.

Mine, Mill and Smelter Workers (MM). 1947. "Constitution of the International Union of Mine, Mill and Smelter Workers Affiliated with the C.I.O." N.P.: MM. U.S. Department of Labor Library.

"Mine Mill Union Votes Program on Labor Unity." 1950. *Daily Worker* (September 18): 3–4.

Mitchell, George Sinclair. 1936. "The Negro in Southern Trade Unionism." *Southern Economic Journal* 2 (January): 27–38.

Montgomery, David. 1979. *Workers' Control in America: Essay on the 20th Century Struggle.* London: Cambridge University Press.

Montgomery, David. 1989. "Class, Capitalism, and Contentment." *Labor History* 30 (Winter): 125–37.

Moore, Barrington, Jr. 1945. "The Communist Party of the USA: An Analysis of a Social Movement."*American Political Science Review* 34: 31–41.

Moore, Barrington, Jr. 1966. *Social Origins of Dictatorship and Democracy.* Boston: Beacon.

Moore, David. 1994. Telephone conversation with Stepan-Norris.

Morris, Aldon. 1984. *The Origins of the Civil Rights Movement: Black Communities Organizing for Change.* New York: Free Press.

Morris, George. 1949a. "After the CIO Purge – What Next." *The {Sunday} Worker* (November 6): 6, 10.

Morris, George. 1949b. "Autonomy Conference." *The {Sunday} Worker* (September 4): 2, 23.

Morris, George. 1949c. "CIO Rightwing Bars Unions from Picking Own Choice on the Board." *Daily Worker* (November 2): 3, 6.

Morris, George. 1949d. "CIO Right Wing Ousts UE." *Daily Worker* (November 3): 3, 11.

Morris, George. 1949e. "World of Labor: Treading the Path of the Old AFL Bureaucracy." *Daily Worker* (August 30): 6.

Morris, George. 1955. "What the C.I.O. and A.F. of L. Conventions Show." *Political Affairs* (January): 69–79.

Morris, George. 1955. "The AFL–CIO Merger." *Political Affairs* (March): 30–40.

Muste, A. J. 1928. "Army and Town Meeting." Pp. 187–92 in *Unions, Management and the Public*, eds. E. W. Bakke and Clark Kerr. New York: Harcourt, Brace, 1948.

Myrdal, Gunnar. 1944. *An American Dilemma*. New York: Harper.

Naison, Mark. 1985. "Communism from the Top Down." *Radical History Review* 32: 97–101.

National Association for the Advancement of Colored People (NAACP). 1988. *Papers of the NAACP* (Part 13). *NAACP and Labor, 1940–1955. Series B: Cooperation with Organized Labor, 1940–1955, various reels*, eds. John H. Bracey, Jr., and August Meier. New York: NAACP.

"National Labor Parley Call." 1950. *The Worker* (November 20): 7–8.

Navasky, Victor. 1980. *Naming Names*. New York: Viking Press.

Nelson, Bruce. 1998. "The 'Lords of the Docks' Reconsidered: Race Relations among West Coast Longshoremen, 1933–61." Pp. 155–92 in *Waterfront Workers: New Perspectives on Race and Class*, ed. Calvin Winslow. Urbana and Chicago: University of Illinois Press.

Neumann, Franz. 1944. *Behemoth*. New York: Harper and Row.

Neumann, Franz. 1957. "The Concept of Political Freedom." Pp. 160–200 in *The Democratic and Authoritarian State: Essays in Political and Legal Theory*, ed. H. Marcuse. New York: Free Press.

"The New C.P. Line." 1953. *Fortune* (June): 80.

Nissen, Bruce, ed. 1990. *U.S. Labor Relations, 1949–1989: Accommodation and Conflict*. New York: Garland.

Noland, E. William, and E. Wight Bakke. 1949. *Workers Wanted: A Study of Employee Hiring Policies, Preferences, and Practices*. New York: Harper and Row.

Northrup, Herbert R. 1943. "Organized Labor and Negro Workers." *Journal of Political Economy* 51 (June): 206–21.

Northrup, Herbert R. 1944. *Organized Labor and the Negro*. New York: Harper and Brothers.

Northrup, Herbert R. 1961. "Management's 'New Look' in Labor Relations." *Industrial Relations* 1, no. 1 (October): 20–22.

Nyden, Linda. 1977. "Black Miners in Western Pennsylvania, 1923–1931: The NMU and the UMW." *Science and Society* 41 (Spring): 69–101.

Nyden, Philip. 1985. "Democratizing Organizations: A Case Study of a Union Reform Movement." *American Journal of Sociology* 90: 1179–203.

O'Brien, F. S. 1968. "The 'Communist-Dominated' Unions in the United States since 1950." *Labor History* 9: 184–209.

Offe, Claus, and Helmut Wiesenthal. 1980. "Two Logics of Collective Action: Theoretical Notes on Social Class and Organizational Form." *Political Power and Social Theory* 1: 67–115.

"Office Union Takes Step Toward Formation of Possible New Leftist Labor Federation," 1950. *New York Times* (May 17): 25.

Olson, James S. 1970. "Race, Class, and Progress: Black Leadership and Industrial Unionism, 1936–1945." Pp. 153–64 in *Black Labor in America*, ed. Milton Cantor. Westport, Conn.: Negro Universities Press.

Omi, Michael, and Howard Winant. 1986. *Racial Formation in the United States: From the 1960s to the 1980s*. New York: Routledge and Kegan Paul.

"On the Merger Front." 1955. *March of Labor* (May): 18.

Oshinsky, David. 1974. "Labor's Cold War: The CIO and the Communists." Pp. 117–51 and 310–15 in *The Specter: Original Essays on the Cold War and the Origins of McCarthyism*, eds. R. Griffith and A. Theoharis. New York: Franklin Watts.

Ozanne, Robert. 1954. "The Effect of Communist Leadership on American Trade Unions." Ph.D. dissertation, University of Wisconsin.

Ozanne, Robert. 1967. *A Century of Labor–Management Relations at McCormick and International Harvester*. Madison: University of Wisconsin Press.

Ozanne, Robert. 1984. *The Labor Movement in Wisconsin: A History*. Madison: State Historical Society of Wisconsin.

Palladino, Grace. 1991. *Dreams of Dignity, Workers of Vision: A History of the International Brotherhood of Electrical Workers*. Washington, D.C.: IBEW.

Paschell, William. 1958. "Structure and Membership of the Labor Movement." Pp. 53–69 in *Sourcebook on Labor*, ed. Neil W. Chamberlain. New York: McGraw-Hill.

Pateman, Carole. 1970. *Participation and Democratic Theory*. Cambridge, Eng.: Cambridge University Press.

Pearlin, Leonard, and Henry Richards. 1960. "Equity: A Study of Union Democracy." Pp. 265–81 in *Labor and Trade Unionism*, eds. Walter Galenson and S. M. Lipset. New York and London: Wiley.

Peevey, Michael Robert. 1961. "The Effect of Rival Unionism on Wages in the Bakery and Electrical Industries." M.A. Thesis, University of California, Berkeley.

Pelling, Henry. 1960. *American Labor*. Chicago: University of Chicago Press.

Perlman, Selig. 1928. *A Theory of the Labor Movement*. New York: Macmillan. Reprint, New York: Augustus M. Kelley, 1949.

Peterson, Florence. 1944. *Handbook of Labor Unions*. Washington, D.C.: American Council of Public Affairs.

Pinsky, Paul. 1948. *The International Fishermen and Allied Workers of America, Local 33*. [San Francisco]: International Fishermen and Allied Workers of America.

Pintzuk, Edward C. 1997. *Reds, Racial Justice, and Civil Liberties: Michigan Communists during the Cold War*. Minneapolis: MEP Publications, University of Minnesota.

Pitzele, Merlyn S. 1947. "Can American Labor Defeat the Communists?" *Atlantic Monthly* 179 (March): 27–32.

Piven, Frances Fox, and Richard A. Cloward. 1977. *Poor People's Movements: Why They Succeed, How They Fail*. New York: Vintage.

Polenberg, Richard. 1972. *War and Society: The United States, 1941–1945*. Philadelphia, Pa.: Lippincott.

Political pamphlets. Walter P. Reuther Archives, Wayne State University, Walter P. Reuther Collection, box 249–18, Local 600, 1947–52.

Poulantzas, Nicos. 1973. *Political Power and Social Classes*. London, England: New Left Books and Sheed.

Powell, Adam Clayton, Jr. [1945] 1973. *Marching Blacks*. New York: Dial Press.

Preis, Art. 1972. *Labor's Giant Step: Twenty Years of the CIO*. New York: Pathfinder.

Prickett, James Robert. 1975. "Communists and the Communist Issue in the American Labor Movement, 1920–1950." Ph.D. dissertation, University of California at Los Angeles.

Przeworski, Adam. 1977. "Proletariat into a Class: The Process of Class Formation . . . " *Politics and Society* 7: 343–401.

Przeworski, Adam. 1980. "Material Bases of Consent." *Political Power and Social Theory* 1: 21–66.

Quam-Wickham, Nancy. 1992. "Who Controls the Hiring Hall? The Struggle for Job Control in the ILWU." Pp. 47–67 in *The CIO's Left-Led Unions*, ed. Steve Rosswurm. New Brunswick, N. J.: Rutgers University Press.

Record, Wilson. 1951. *The Negro and the Communist Party*. Chapel Hill: University of North Carolina Press.

Record, Wilson. 1964. *Race and Radicalism*. Ithaca, N.Y.: Cornell University Press.

"Red Metal Union Riding High." 1951. *Business Week* (August 25): 34–35.

"Red Strip." 1954. *Fortune* (December): 66, 70.

"Reds on the Run." 1954. *Fortune* (December): 70.

Reed, Merle E. 1973. "The FEPC, the Black Worker, and the Southern Shipyards." *South Atlantic Quarterly* 74 (Autumn): 446–67.

Reed, Merle E. 1991. *Seedtime for the Modern Civil Rights Movement: The President's Committee on Fair Employment Practice, 1941–1946.* Baton Rouge: Louisiana State University Press.

Regensburger, William E. 1983. "The Emergence of Industrial Unionism in the South, 1930–1945: The Case of Coal and Metal Miners." Pp. 65–127 in *How Mighty a Force? Studies of Workers' Consciousness and Organization in the United States*, ed. Maurice Zeitlin. Los Angeles: Institute of Industrial Relations, UCLA.

Regensburger, William E. 1987a. "Ground into Our Blood: The Origins of Working-Class Consciousness and Organization in Durably Unionized Southern Industries, 1930–1946." Ph.D. dissertation, UCLA.

Regensburger, William E. 1987b. "Worker Insurgency and Southern Working-Class Combativeness: Miners, Sailors, and the Emergence of Industrial Unionism in the South." Pp. 71–159 in *Insurgent Workers: Studies in the Origins of Industrial Unionism*, ed. Maurice Zeitlin. Los Angeles: Institute of Industrial Relations, UCLA.

Reich, Michael. 1981. *Racial Inequality: A Political Economic Analysis.* Princeton: Princeton University Press.

Reid, Ira De A. 1930. *Negro Membership in American Labor Unions.* New York: National Urban League.

Reid, Paul M. 1951. *Industrial Decentralization: Detroit Region, 1940–1950.* Detroit: Detroit Metropolitan Area Regional Planning Commission.

Research Institute of America. 1946. *The Communists in Labor Relations Today: Special Report.* New York: Research Institute of America.

Reynolds, Lloyd. 1951. *The Structure of Labor Markets.* New York: Harper and Bros.

Rice, Monsignor Charles Owen. 1967/68. "Oral History Interview." (October 18, 1967, and April 5, 1968). Pennsylvania State University.

Rice, Monsignor Charles Owen. 1977. "The Tragic Purge of 1948." Paper delivered at the fourth Southwest Labor History Conference, March 4–5, 1977, Tempe, Arizona.

Richardson, Thomas. 1987. "United Public Workers: A Real Union Organizes." Pp. 174–81 in *The Cold War Against Labor*, eds. Ann Fagan Ginger and David Christiano. Berkeley, Calif.: Meiklejohn Civil Liberties Institute.

Rosen, Sumner M. 1968. "The CIO Era, 1935–55." Pp. 188–208 in *The Negro and the American Labor Movement*, ed. Julius Jacobson. New York: Anchor.

Rosenzweig, Roy. 1976. "Organizing the Unemployed: The Early Years of the Great Depression, 1929–1933." *Radical America* 10, no. 4 (July/August): 37–62.

Ross, Arthur M. 1967. "The Negro in the American Economy." Pp. 3–48 in *Employment, Race, and Poverty*, eds. Arthur M. Ross and Herbert Hill. New York: Harcourt, Brace and World.

Rosswurm, Steven. 1990. "Communism and the CIO: An Assessment." Conference Paper (March 9–10). Madison: State Historical Society of Wisconsin.

Rosswurm, Steven, ed. 1992. *The CIO's Left-Led Unions*. New Brunswick, N.J.: Rutgers University Press.

Rosswurm, Steven, ed. 1992. "Preface." Pp. ix–xvi in *The CIO's Left-Led Unions*. New Brunswick, N. J.: Rutgers University Press.

Roy, Donald. 1952. "Restriction of Output in a Piecework Machine Shop." Ph.D. dissertation, University of Chicago.

Rubin, Beth A., Larry J. Griffin, and Michael E. Wallace. 1983. "'Provided Only That Their Voice Was Strong': Insurgency and Organization of American Labor from NRA to Taft–Hartley." *Work and Occupations* 10: 325–47.

Rubin, Naomi. 1050. "Counter-offensive." *March of Labor* (December): 12–13.

Rueschemeyer, Dietrich, Evelyn Huber Stephens, and John D. Stephens. 1992. *Capitalist Development and Democracy*. Chicago: University of Chicago Press.

Ruiz, Viki. 1998. *From Out of the Shadows*. New York and Oxford: Oxford University Press.

Saperstein, Lou. 1977. "Ford Is Organized II." *Political Affairs* 56, no. 5: 23–30.

Saposs, David J. 1926. *Left-Wing Unionism*. New York: International.

Saposs, David J. 1959. *Communism in American Unions*. New York: McGraw Hill. Reprint, 1976, Westport, Conn.: Greenwood Press.

"Save Our Union." N.d. (probably 1946). Axle Unit Progressive Caucus, Walter P. Reuther Archives, Wayne State University, ACTU Collection, box 24, folder: Local 600 – Contract 1946.

Sayles, Leonard R., and George Strauss. 1953. *The Local Union: Its Place in the Industrial Plant*. New York: Harper and Bros.

Schatz, Ronald W. 1977. "American Electrical Workers: Work, Struggles, Aspirations, 1930–1950." Ph.D. dissertation, University of Pittsburgh.

Schatz, Ronald W. 1983. *The Electrical Workers: A History of Labor at General Electric and Westinghouse 1923–1960*. Urbana: University of Illinois Press.

Scheyer, David. 1935. "Peace Comes to the Fur Market," *The Nation*, August 14.

Schlesinger, Arthur M., Jr. 1957. *The Crisis of the Old Order*. Boston: Houghton Mifflin.

Schumpeter, Joseph. 1942. *Capitalism, Socialism and Democracy*. New York: Harper and Brothers.

Schwartz, Harvey. 1980. "Harry Bridges and the Scholars: Looking at History's Verdict." *California History* 59: 66–79.

Sealander, Judith. 1982. "Feminist Against Feminist: The First Phase of the Equal Rights Amendment Debate: 1923–1963." *South Atlantic Quarterly* 81 (Spring): 147–61.

Seaton, Douglas. 1981. *Catholics and Radicals*. London and Toronto: Associated University Presses.

Seidman, Joel. 1953a. *American Labor from Defense to Reconversion*. Chicago: University of Chicago Press.

Seidman, Joel. 1953b. "Democracy in Labor Unions." *Journal of Political Economy* 61 (April): 221–32.

Seidman, Joel. 1950. "Labor Policy of the Communist Party during World War II." *Industrial and Labor Relations Review* 4: 55–69.

Selekman, Benjamin M. 1949. "Varieties of Labor Relations." *Harvard Business Review* 27 (March): 175–99.

Seligman, Daniel. 1949. "UE: The Biggest Communist Union." *American Mercury* 69 (July): 35–45.

Selznick, Philip. 1943. "An Approach to a Theory of Bureaucracy." *American Sociological Review* 8 (February): 47–54.

Selznick, Philip. 1949. *TVA and the Grass Roots*. Berkeley: University of California Press.

Selznick, Philip. 1952. *The Organizational Weapon: A Study of Bolshevik Strategy and Tactics*. Santa Monica, Calif.: Rand Corporation. Reprint, with a new preface, Glencoe, Ill.: Free Press, 1960.

Selznick, Philip. 1960. "Preface." In *The Organizational Weapon: A Study of Bolshevik Strategy and Tactics*. Santa Monica, Calif.: The Rand Corporation. Reprint, Glencoe, Ill.: Free Press, 1960.

Selznick, Philip. 1969. *Law, Society, and Industrial Justice*. New York: Russell Sage.

Shannon, David A. 1955. *The Socialist Party of America*. New York: Macmillan.

Shannon, David A. 1959. *The Decline of American Communism: A History of the Communist Party of the United States since 1945*. Chatham, N.J.: Chatham Bookseller (Fund for the Republic).

Shister, Joseph. 1945. "Trade-Union Government: A Formal Analysis." *Quarterly Journal of Economics* 60 (November): 78–112.

"Should You Move Your Plant?" 1949, *Business Week* (September 17): 70–72.

Simon, Hal. 1956. "The Labor Merger." *Political Affairs* (January): 51–65

Skocpol, Theda. 1980. "Political Response to Capitalist Crisis: Neo-Marxist Theories of the State and the Case of the New Deal." *Politics and Society* 10: 155–201.

Slichter, Sumner H. 1941. *Union Policies and Industrial Management.* Washington, D.C.: Brookings.

Slichter, Sumner H. 1951. "The Taft–Hartley Act." Pp. 456–76 in *Readings in Labor Economics and Industrial Relations,* ed. Joseph Shister. Chicago, Ill.: Lippincott.

Sobel, Irvin. 1954. "Collective Bargaining and Decentralization in the Rubber-Tire Industry." *Journal of Political Economy* 62: 12–25.

Soffer, Benson. 1959. "On Union Rivalries and the Minimum Differentiation of Wage Patterns." *Review of Economics and Statistics* 41 (February): 53–60.

Solomon, Mark. 1998. *The Cry Was Unity: Communist and African Americans, 1917–36.* Jackson: University Press of Mississippi.

"Sonotone's Crossed Wires." 1955. *Fortune* (June): 62, 66.

Sorensen, Aage B. 1998. "Theoretical Mechanisms and the Empirical Study of Social Processes." Pp. 238–66 in *Social Mechanisms: An Analytical Approach to Social Theory,* eds. Peter Hedstrom and Richard Swedberg. Cambridge, Eng., and New York: Cambridge University Press.

Spero, Sterling D., and Abram L. Harris. 1931. *The Black Worker.* New York: Columbia University Press.

Stark, David. 1980. "Class Struggle and the Transformation of the Labor Process: A Relational Approach." *Theory and Society* 9: 89–130.

Starobin, Joseph R. 1975. *American Communism in Crisis, 1943–1957.* Berkeley and Los Angeles: University of California Press.

Stein, Judith. 1991a. "Race and Class Consciousness Revisited." *Reviews in American History* 19 (December): 551–60.

Stein, Judith. 1991b. Southern Workers in National Unions: Birmingham Steelworkers, 1935–1951." Pp. 223–49 in *Organized Labor in the Twentieth Century South,* ed. by Robert H. Zieger. Knoxville: University of Tennessee Press.

Stein, Judith. 1993. "The Ins and Outs of the CIO." *International Labor and Working-Class History* 44 (Fall): 53–63.

Stepan-Norris, Judith. 1988. "Left Out: The Consequences of the Rise and Fall of Communist Union Leaders in the CIO." Ph.D. dissertation, University of California, Los Angeles.

Stepan-Norris, Judith. 1997a. "The Integration of Workplace and Community Relations at the Ford Rouge Plant, 1930s–1940s." *Political Power and Social Theory* 11: 3–44.

Stepan-Norris, Judith. 1997b. "The Making of Union Democracy." *Social Forces* 76: 475–510.

Stepan-Norris, Judith. 1998. "Strangers to Their Own Class?" *Sociological Inquiry* 68: 329–53.

Stepan-Norris, Judith, and Maurice Zeitlin. 1989. "'Who Gets the Bird?' or, How the Communists Won Power and Trust in America's Unions." *American Sociological Review* 54: 503–23.

Stepan-Norris, Judith, and Maurice Zeitlin. 1991a. "Insurgency, Radicalism, and Democracy in America's Industrial Unions." Working Paper Series, no. 215. Institute of Industrial Relations, University of California, Los Angeles.

Stepan-Norris, Judith, and Maurice Zeitlin. 1991b. "'Red' Unions and 'Bourgeois' Contracts?" *American Journal of Sociology* 96: 1151–200.

Stepan-Norris, Judith, and Maurice Zeitlin. 1995. "Union Democracy, Radical Leadership, and the Hegemony of Capital." *American Sociological Review* 60 (December): 829–50.

Stepan-Norris, Judith, and Maurice Zeitlin. 1996a. "Insurgency, Radicalism, and Democracy in America's Industrial Unions." *Social Forces* 75: 1–32.

Stepan-Norris, Judith, and Maurice Zeitlin. 1996b. *Talking Union*. Urbana: University of Illinois Press.

Stephens, Evelyn Huber, and John Stephens. 1982. "The Labor Movement, Political Power and Workers' Participation in Western Europe." *Political Power and Social Theory* 3: 215–49.

Stephens, John. 1989. "Democratic Transition and Breakdown in Western Europe, 1870–1939." *American Journal of Sociology* 34 (5): 1019–77.

Steuben, John. 1951. "Split Up on Top." *March of Labor* (October): 19–20.

Steuben, John. 1954. "Labor Unity." *March of Labor* (December): 16–17.

Stevens, Max. 1994. "Employer Resistance and Union Leadership: The Political Effects of Management Strategies during the CIO Era." M.A. paper, University of California, Los Angeles.

Stevenson, Marshall F., Jr. 1993. "Beyond Theoretical Models: The Limited Possibilities of Racial Egalitarianism." *International Labor and Working-Class History* 44 (Fall): 45–52.

"Stocks Sweeten Pay at the Top." 1980. *Business Week* (May 12): 56–57.

Stolberg, Benjamin. 1938. *The Story of the CIO*. New York: Viking Press.

Stolberg, Benjamin. 1939. "Communist Wreckers in American Labor." *Saturday Evening Post* (September 2): 5–4, 32, 34, 36.

Stone, Martha. 1950. "Unity on Issues: Key to Victory." *The {Sunday} Worker* (New Jersey edition, December 3): 8.

Strauss, George. 1960. "Control by the Membership in a Building Trades Union." Pp. 282–94 in *Labor and Trade Unionism*, eds. Walter Galenson and S. M. Lipset. New York and London, Eng.: Wiley.

Strauss, George. 1991. "Union Democracy." Pp. 201–36 in *The State and the Unions*, eds. George Strauss, Daniel Gallagher, and Jack Fiorito. Madison, Wis.: Industrial Relations Research Association.

Sugrue, Thomas. 1996. "Segmented Work, Race-Conscious Workers: Structure, Agency and Division in the CIO Era." *International Review of Social History* 41: 389–406.

Summers, Clyde. 1946. "Admissions Policies of Labor Unions." *Quarterly Journal of Economics* 61: 66–107.

Summers, Clyde. 1950. "Disciplinary Powers of Unions." *Industrial and Labor Relations Review* 3 (July): 483–513.

Summers, Clyde. 1951. "Union Powers and Workers' Rights." *Michigan Law Review* 49: 805–38.

Summers, Clyde. 1955. "The Political Liberties of Labor Union Members: A Comment." *Texas Law Review* 33 (May): 603–19.

Summers, Clyde. 1984. "Democracy in a One-Party State: Perspectives from Landrum-Griffin." *Maryland Law Review* 43, no. 1: 93–118.

Swafford, Michael. 1980. "Three Parametric Techniques for Contingency Table Analysis: A Nontechnical Commentary." *American Sociological Review* 45: 664–90.

Sward, Keith. 1948. *The Legend of Henry Ford.* New York: Rinehart.

Swift, John. 1952a. "The Ford Local Union Election." *Political Affairs* (November): 18–35. (Although "swift" was the *nom de guerre* of Gil Green, *this* Swift was someone else, given the article's content.)

Swift, John. 1952b. "Some Problems of Work in Right-Led Unions." *Political Affairs* (April): 30–41.

Swift, John. 1952c. "Some Problems of Work in Right-Led Unions, II." *Political Affairs* (May): 30–40.

Swift, John. 1953a. "The Left and the Struggle for Labor Unity, I." *Political Affairs* (July): 33–42.

Swift, John. 1953b. "The Left and the Struggle for Labor Unity, II." *Political Affairs* (August): 37–50.

Swift, John. 1953c. "The Struggle for a Mass Policy." *Political Affairs* (February): 16–34.

Taft, Philip. 1944. "Opposition to Union Officers in Elections" *Quarterly Journal of Economics*, 58, no. 2 (February): 246–64.

Taft, Philip. 1946. "Understanding Union Administration." *Harvard Business Review* 24 (Winter): 345–57.

Taft, Philip. 1948. "The Constitutional Power of the Chief Officer in American Labor Unions." *Quarterly Journal of Economics* 62: 459–71.

Taft, Philip. 1953. "Communism in American Trade Unions." *Industrial Relations Research Proceedings* (December 28–30): 23.

Taft, Philip. 1957. *The AFL in the Time of Gompers.* New York: Harper.

Taft, Philip. 1962. *The Structure and Government of Trade Unions.* Cambridge, Mass.: Harvard University Press.

Taft, Philip. 1964. *Organized Labor in American History*. New York and London: Harper and Row.

Taft, Philip, and Philip Ross. 1969. "American Labor Violence: Its Causes, Character, and Outcome." Pp. 270–376 in *Violence in America: Historical and Comparative Perspectives*, eds. Hugh D. Graham and Ted R. Gurr. Washington, D.C.: U.S. Government Printing Office.

Tannenbaum, Arnold. 1965. "Unions." Pp. 710–63 in *Handbook of Organizations*, ed. James March. Chicago: Rand McNally.

Tannenbaum, Arnold, and Robert Kahn. 1958. *Participation in Union Locals*. Evanston, Ill., and White Plains, N.Y.: Row, Peterson.

"Ten Who Deliver." 1946. *Fortune* (November): 146–51.

Therborn, Goran. 1877. "The Rule of Capital and the Rise of Democracy." *New Left Review*, no. 103: 3–141.

"The Thin Red Line." 1951. *Fortune* (June): 72, 74, 76.

Thompson, Robert. 1950. "Two Paths for American Labor." *Political Affairs* (March): 7–17.

Thompson, Robert. 1951. "Comrade Foster's New Book – A Great Marxist Work."" *Political Affairs* (February): 88–105.

Thompson, Robert. 1956. "Into the Mainstream . . ." *Political Affairs* (March): 32.

Tilly, Charles. 1986. *The Contentious French*. Cambridge, Eng.: Belknap.

Tomlins, Christopher L. 1985. *The State and the Unions: Labor Relations, Law, and the Organized Labor Movement in America, 1880–1960*. Cambridge, Eng., and New York: Cambridge University Press.

"The Treaty of Detroit." 1950. *Fortune* (July): 53–55.

Trotter, Joe William. 1985. *Black Milwaukee: The Making of an Industrial Proletariat, 1915–1945*. Urbana: University of Illinois Press.

Troy, Leo. 1956. *Membership of American Trade Unions by State, Territory and Canada, 1939 and 1953*. New York: National Bureau of Economic Research (mimeographed).

Troy, Leo. 1957. *Distribution of Union Membership among the States: 1939 and 1953*. New York: National Bureau of Economic Research.

Troy, Leo. 1965. *Trade Union Membership, 1897–1962*. New York: Columbia University Press.

TUUL. 1930. *The Trade Union Unity League: Its Program, Structure, Methods and History*. New York: TUUL.

"The 20 Highest-Paid Chief Executives." 1990. *Business Week* (May 7): 57.

"20 New York Local Unions Adopt Militant Mutual Aid Program at Conference." 1950. *Daily Worker* (November 20): 5.

"U.E. Keeps Left." 1948. *Business Week* (September 11): 112, 114, 116.

"U.E. Leftists Win – But for How Long?" 1949. *Business Week* (October 1): 94–96.

"UE Loses a Key District as Locals Shift to IAM." 1956. *Business Week* (June 16): 173.

"UE's New Goals." 1961. *Business Week* (September 30): 78.

"Unionists Call N.Y. Parley on Automy in CIO." 1949. *Daily Worker* (August 18): 2.

United Automobile Workers of America (UAW). 1947. "Constitution of the International Union United Automobile, Aircraft and Agricultural Implement Workers of America (UAW-CIO)," adopted in Atlantic City, New Jersey, November. U.S. Department of Labor Library.

United Electrical, Radio and Machine Workers of America (UE). 1936. *Constitution of the United Electrical, Radio and Machine Workers of America.* New York: UE. U.S. Department of Labor Library.

United Electrical, Radio and Machine Workers of America (UE). 1946. 10th Convention Proceedings. New York, September.

United Electrical, Radio and Machine Workers of America (UE). 1948. *Constitution of the United Electrical, Radio and Machine Workers of America.* New York: UE. U.S. Department of Labor Library.

United Farm Equipment and Metal Workers of America (FE). 1949. *Constitution and By-Laws of the United Farm Equipment and Metal Workers of America.* Chicago: FE. U.S. Department of Labor Library.

United States Bureau of the Census. 1953. *U.S. Census of Population: 1950.* Report P-C1 (reprint of vol. 2, pt. I). Washington, D.C.: Government Printing Office.

United States Chamber of Commerce. 1947. "Communists Within the Labor Movement." Washington, D.C.: Chamber of Commerce.

United States Congress. 1948. House Committee on Education and Labor. *Investigation of Communist Infiltration of UERMWA.* 80th Cong., 2nd sess. Washington, D.C.: U.S. Government Printing Office.

United States Congress. 1952a. House Committee on Labor and Public Welfare. *Hearing on Communist Domination of Unions.* 82nd Cong., 2nd sess. Washington, D.C.: U.S. Government Printing Office.

United States Congress. 1952b. House Committee on Un-American Activities. *Communism in the Detroit Area.* 82nd Cong., 2nd Sess. Washington, D.C.: U.S. Government Printing Office.

United States Congress. 1954. House Committee on Un-American Activities. *Investigation of Communist Activities in the State of Michigan*, Part Two (Detroit – Labor). 83d Cong., 2nd sess. Washington, D.C.: U.S. Government Printing Office.

United States Congress. 1937. Senate Committee on Education and Labor. *Violations of Free Speech and Rights of Labor.* Parts 1–3. Washington, D.C.: U.S. Government Printing Office.

United States Congress. 1937–38. Senate Committee on Education and Labor. *Violations of Free Speech and Rights of Labor.* Preliminary Report No. 46 (Parts 1–4). Washington, D.C.: U.S. Government Printing Office.

United States Department of Justice. N.d. Federal Bureau of Investigation, John Gallo FBI File 100–138889 (quoting the *Daily Worker*, November 18 and 19, 1943, and quoting the *Pittsburgh Courier*, Detroit edition, September 30, 1944).

United States Department of Labor. 1946. "Summary Reports." Pp. 56–57 in The President's National Labor–Management Conference, November 5–30, 1945. Washington, D.C.: U.S. Department of Labor.

United States Department of Labor. 1968. "Report and Recommendations of Panel for Office of Federal Contract Compliance [OFCC] in Matter of Allen–Bradley Company (Official Text)." OFCC Docket No. 101–68. *Daily Labor Report* no. 251 (December 26): E1–E9. Washington, D.C.: Bureau of National Affairs.

United States Steel Company (formerly Carnegie–Illinois Steel Corporation). "Agreement Between Carnegie–Illinois Steel Corporation and the United Steelworkers of America [,] CIO. Pittsburgh, Pennsylvania."

United Steelworkers of America (USWA). 1945. "USA–CIO Executive Board Unanimously Approves Industrial 'Peace Charter.'" *Steel Labor* (July): 4.

United Steelworkers of America (USWA). 1948. *Constitution of the United Steel Workers of America.* Boston: USWA.

"Urge Parley of Unions Expelled by CIO." 1950. *Daily Worker* (August 4): 4.

"The U.S. Labor Movement." 1951. *Fortune* (February): 91–93, 161.

"USW Set Back by 'Weak' Mine-Mill." 1962. *Business Week* (September 8): 22–24.

Valentine, Cynthia. 1978. "Internal Democracy: Does It Help or Hinder the Movement for Industrial Democracy?" *Insurgent Sociologist* 8 (Fall): 40–51.

Vedder, Richard K., and Lowell Gallaway. 1992. "Racial Differences in Unemployment in the United States, 1890–1990." *Journal of Economic History* 52 (September): 696–702.

"Wage Earner Editorial." 1952. *The Wage Earner* 12 (January): 1–2.

Walker, Thomas J. E. 1982. "The International Workers Order: A Unique Fraternal Body." Ph.D. dissertation, University of Chicago.

Wallis, John J. 1989. "Employment in the Great Depression: New Data and Hypotheses." *Explorations in Economic History* 26 (January): 45–72.

War Labor Board. 1944. "The War Labor Board Orders Equal Pay for Equal Work, 1944." Pp. 465–66 in *Major Problems in the History of American Workers*, eds. Eileen Boris and Nelson Lichtenstein. Lexington, Mass.: Heath.

Weaver, Robert C. 1939. *The Urban Negro Worker in the United States, 1925–1936*, 2 vols. Washington, D.C.: U.S. Department of the Interior, Office of the Advisor on Negro Affairs.

Weaver, Robert C. 1946. *Negro Labor: A National Problem*. New York: Harcourt, Brace.

Weber, Max. 1946. *From Max Weber: Essays in Sociology*, translated and edited by H. H. Gerth and C. W. Mills. New York: Oxford University Press.

Weber, Max. 1949. *Max Weber on the Methodology of the Social Sciences*, translated and edited by E. A. Shils and H. A. Finch. Glencoe, Ill.: The Free Press.

Weber, Max. [1925] 1956. *Wirtschaft und Gesellschaft. Grundriss der verstehende Soziologie*, edited by J. Winkelmann. Tubinger, West Germany: J. C. B. Mohr (Paul Siebeck).

Weber, Max. 1961. *General Economic History*, translated by F. H. Knight. New York: Collier.

Weber, Max. 1968. *Economy and Society*, edited by C. Wittich and G. Roth. New York: Bedminster.

Weber, Max. 1968. "Types of Class Struggle." Pp. 930–32 in *Economy and Society*, eds. G. Roth and C. Wittich. New York: Bedminster.

Weber, Max. 1988. *The Agrarian Sociology of Ancient Civilizations*, translated by R. I. Franks. London, Eng., and New York: NLB, Verso.

Wecksler, A. N. 1949. "What the Unions Are Doing About Communism." *Mill and Factory* (November): 95–99.

Weinstein, James. 1975. *Ambiguous Legacy: The Left in American Politics*. New York and London: New Viewpoints.

Weisberg, Jacob. 1999. "Cold War Without End." *New York Times Magazine* (November 28): 117–23, 155–58.

Wellman, David. 1995. *The Union Makes Us Strong*. Cambridge, Eng., and New York: Cambridge University Press.

Wesley, Charles H. 1927. *Negro Labor in the United States*. New York: Vanguard Press.

"What Reds Are Up to in Unions." 1955. *U.S. News and World Report* (March 4): 107–9.

"Where are the Radicals?" 1952. *Fortune* (October): 115, 250, 252.

Widick, B. J. 1954. "A Shop Steward on the Frustrations of the Contract System." Pp. 505–6 in *Major Problems in the History of American Workers: Documents and Essays*, eds. Eileen Boris and Nelson Lichtenstein. Lexington, Mass.: D.C. Heath.

Wilkins, Roy. 1950. "A Reply to the CRC [Civil Rights Congress]" (November 22, 1949), as reprinted in *Memo from Roy Wilkins to NAACP Branches on "The Communists vs. the NAACP's Civil Rights Fight."*

"Will C.I.O. Split Apart?" 1949. *Business Week* (October 15): 106–8.

Williams, J. S. 1954. "The Political Liberties of Labor Union Members." *Texas Law Review* 32: 826–38.

Williamson, John. 1947. "The Trade Unions and the Negro Workers." *Political Affairs* (November): 1007–1017.

Williamson, John. 1949a. "Defend and Extend the Rights of Negro Workers." *Political Affairs* (June): 28–37.

Williamson, John. 1949b. "What CP Worked for in Trade Unions." *The Worker Magazine* (September 4): sec. 2, pp. 4, 10.

Williamson, John. 1950a. "Lessons of Recent Strikes and United Labor Action." *Political Affairs* (May): 83–100 ["Report to the Plenum on the Situation in the Trade Union Movement and the Party's Tasks"].

Williamson, John. 1950b. "The Significance of the Nat'l Labor Conference." *The {Sunday} Worker* (November 20): 7–8.

Williamson, John. 1950c. "Trade-Union Tasks in the Struggle for Peace, Jobs, and Negro Rights." *Political Affairs* (November): 37–59.

Williamson, John. 1951a. "An American Labor Leader Without Peer." *Political Affairs* (March): 22–35.

Williamson, John. 1951b. "The Main Direction of the Party's Trade-Union Work." *Political Affairs* (February): 54–73.

Wilson, Valerie. 1993. "CIO Unions and Gender, 1944–1946: Did Politics Matter?" M.A. paper, UCLA Department of Sociology.

Winn, Fran. 1943. "Labor Tackles the Race Question." *Antioch Review* 3 (Fall): 341–60.

Winship, Christopher, and Robert Mare. 1983. "Structural Equations and Path Analysis for Discrete Data." *American Journal of Sociology* 89: 54–110.

Winston, Henry. 1946. "Party Tasks among the Negro People." *Political Affairs* (April): 349–61.

Wolters, Raymond. 1970. *Negroes and the Great Depression: The Problem of Economic Recovery.* Westport, Conn.: Greenwood.

Wynn, Neil. 1976. *The Afro-American and the Second World War.* New York: Holmes and Meier; London: Elek.

"A Yaleman and a Communist." 1943. *Fortune* (November): 147–48, 212, 214, 216, 218, 221.

Young, Harris. 1951. "1952 and Labor's Political Change." *Political Affairs* (December): 53–62.

Yousler, James. 1956. *Labor's Wage Policies in the Twentieth Century.* New York: Twayne.

Zeitlin, Jonathan. 1985. "Shop Floor Bargaining and the State: A Contradictory Relationship." Pp. 1–45 in *Shop Floor Bargaining and the State: Historical and Comparative Perspectives*, eds. Steven Tolliday and Jonathan Zeitlin. Cambridge, Eng.: Cambridge University Press.

Zeitlin, Maurice. 1967. *Revolutionary Politics and the Cuban Working Class*. Princeton: Princeton University Press.

Zeitlin, Maurice. 1981. "How We Got Here, and How to Get Out." *Voice of the Cement, Lime, Gypsum and Allied Workers* 44, no. 1 (January): 14–19.

Zeitlin, Maurice. 1982a. "Democratic Investment." *Democracy* 2 (April): 69–79.

Zeitlin, Maurice. 1982b. "Shooting Down the Flight of Capital." *Los Angeles Times* (July 9): Op-ed page (Part II: 7).

Zeitlin, Maurice. 1983. "The American Crisis: An Analysis and Modest Proposal." Pp. 118–37 in *The Future of American Democracy*, ed. Mark E. Kann. Philadelphia, Pa.: Temple University Press.

Zeitlin, Maurice. 1984a. *The Civil Wars in Chile (or the bourgeois revolutions that never were)*. Princeton, N.J.: Princeton University Press.

Zeitlin, Maurice. 1984b. "High Wages Are Not Industry's Trouble." *Los Angeles Times* (October 8): Op-ed page (Part II: 5).

Zeitlin, Maurice. 1985. "The Growing Assault Against Unions." *Los Angeles Times* (January 24): Op-ed page (Part II: 5).

Zeitlin, Maurice. 1989. *The Large Corporation and Contemporary Classes*. New Brunswick, N.J.: Rutgers University Press.

Zeitlin, Maurice, and Howard Kimeldorf. 1983. "How Mighty a Force? The Internal Differentiation and Relative Organization of the American Working Class." Pp. 1–64 in *How Mighty a Force? Studies of Workers' Consciousness and Organization in the United States*, ed. M. Zeitlin. Los Angeles: Institute of Industrial Relations, University of California.

Zeitlin, Maurice, and Howard Kimeldorf, eds. 1984. *Political Power and Social Theory* 4 (a special issue on U.S. organized labor, 1930–50).

Zeitlin, Maurice, and L. Frank Weyher. 1997. "'Black and White, Unite and Fight': Interracial Solidarity in Organized Labor and Interracial Economic Inequality," American Sociological Association Annual Meeting, Toronto, Ontario, Canada, August 9, 1997.

Zeitlin, Maurice, and L. Frank Weyher. 1998. "'Black and White, Unite and Fight': Interracial Working-Class Solidarity and Interracial Inequality in America." Los Angeles: Institute of Industrial Relations. University of California. Working Paper Series No. 98–08.

Zeitlin, Maurice, and L. Frank Weyher. 2001. "'Black and White, Unite and Fight': Interracial Working-Class Solidarity and Racial Employment Equality." *American Journal of Sociology* 107 (September): 430–67.

Zieger, Robert H. 1980. "Reply to Prof. Lichtenstein." *Industrial Relations* 19 (Spring): 131–35.

Zieger, Robert H. 1984. "The Popular Front Rides Again." *Political Power and Social Theory* 4: 297–302.

Zieger, Robert H. 1986. *American Workers, American Unions, 1920–1985.* Baltimore, Md.: Johns Hopkins University Press.

Zieger, Robert H. 1995. *The CIO, 1935–1955.* Chapel Hill: University of North Carolina Press.

Zieger, Robert H., ed. 1991. *Organized Labor in the Twentieth Century South.* Knoxville: University of Tennessee Press.

Zetterberg, Hans L. 1965. *On Theory and Verification in Sociology.* New York: Bedminster.

Interviews

Oral history interviews by Judith Stepan-Norris (in Detroit, Michigan, unless otherwise noted).

Paul Boatin, September 1983.

Walter Dorosh, January 1984, Dearborn, Michigan.

Henry McCusker, September 1983.

Art McPhaul, September 1983.

John Mando, August 1984.

David Moore, January 1984.

John Orr, September 1983.

Kenneth Roche, January, 1984, Dearborn, Michigan.

Horace Sheffield, October 1986, telephone interview.

Shelton Tappes, September 1983, interview by Stepan-Norris and Zeitlin.

Saul Wellman, December 1985, telephone interview; April 1986, Van Nuys, Calif.

AUTHOR INDEX

SUBJECT INDEX

Addes, George, 7

African American workers, *see* black workers

Amalgamated Clothing Workers of America (ACW), 15, 44 fn. 45, 237 fn. 12, 290; gender equality in, 199, 200

American Civil Liberties Union (ACLU), 60, 83

American Communications Association (ACA), 317–18, 319

American Federation of Labor (AFL), 5–6, 32, 39–41, 50, 51, 55, 56, 68, 70, 76, 79, 80, 197 fn. 26, 236 fn. 10, 266, 274, 279, 299, 320–1; exclusion of blacks, 232–3, 236 fn. 10; merger with CIO, 265; policies on Communists, 5–6, 279 fn. 35; racial equality in, 236; suspension of CIO unions, 2; union democracy in, 55–6; WWII policies, 152

American Newspaper Guild (ANG), 67, 258

anticapitalist tendencies in unions, 129; *see also* hegemony; political regime of production

anti-Communism, 1–2, 84, 276; and collective bargaining, 141–3; and factionalism, 82–94; and gender equality, 198–9; and racial equality, 257–60; and union democracy, 82–94; *see also* Communist-led unions, repression of; red baiting

Architects, Engineers, Chemists and Technicians (AECT), 40

Association of Catholic Trade Unionists (ACTU), 15 fn. 34, 45, 69–70, 85, 101, 102, 110, 113, 228, 325; and closeness of elections, 114; and UAW Local 600, 109–11, 119

Auto Workers Union (AWU), 25, 99

automobile workers, *see* black workers; Congress of Industrial Organizations, Big 3; Ford Motor

Company; United Automobile Workers; women workers

black workers, 102, 212–65; at Ford, 102, 108; in auto industry, 212; CIO union policies toward, 212–65; in electrical, 212; in steel, 213; numbers in unions, 243–6; *see also* racial equality

Boatin, Paul, 112

Bridges, Harry, 7–8, 17, 40, 148 fn. 76, 155, 271, 273, 283, 289, 291 fn. 65, 302, 307, 315

Brophy, John, 5

Browder, Earl, 12 fn. 25, 146, 154

Bryson, Hugh, 281, 295 fn. 73, 306 fn. 28

Bureau of Investigation, 24 fn. 2

Carey, James, 81, 182, 272, 324, 325

Christoffel, Harold, 16 fnn. 35 and 36, 229, 282–3

Civil Rights Committee (CRC), 239, 264

class struggle, 20, 145; intra, 20, 32, 68–9; in production, 126–30

collective bargaining, 126–88; contract term, 139; employment contract, 133–4; grievance procedure, 140, 277–8; management prerogatives, 133–6, 139; and political leadership, 141–58, 166–87; prolabor index, 141; right to strike, 139; trade off, 140; and union democracy, 161–4, 165, 166–9, 170 table 6.3

Committee for Industrial Organization, 2, 39, 233

Committee to Abolish Racial Discrimination (CARD), 239

Communist-led unions, CIO, 1, 3 fn. 11, 4, 5, 16, 17, 19 table 1.1, 22, 26–9, 38, 40, 43, 46, 48 table 2.1, 141, 142, 144, 147–8, 149, 152,